'REBELLIOUS AND CONTRARY'

The Glasgow Dockers, c. 1853 to 1932

SCOTTISH HISTORICAL REVIEW

MONOGRAPHS SERIES

No. 10

# 'REBELLIOUS AND CONTRARY'

## The Glasgow Dockers, *c.* 1853 to 1932

WILLIAM KENEFICK

TUCKWELL PRESS

First published in Great Britain in 2000 by
Tuckwell Press
The Mill House
Phantassie
East Linton
East Lothian EH40 3DG
Scotland

Copyright © William Kenefick, 2000

ISBN 1 86232 180 9

*British Library Cataloguing in Publication Data*

A catalogue record for this book is available
on request from the British Library

The right of William Kenefick to be identified as the author of this work has been
asserted by him in accordance with the Copyright, Design and Patent Act 1988

Typeset by Hewer Text Limited, Edinburgh
Printed and bound by The Cromwell Press, Trowbridge

To my wife
Pauline,
daughters
Susan and Alison
and
my parents
William and Agnes

# Contents

# Illustrations

Plate 1 is reproduced by courtesy of Alex M. Thomas, East Kilbride. The remaining plates are reproduced by courtesy of the People's Palace, Glasgow Museums.

# List of Maps and Figures

# List of Tables

# Abbreviations

| | |
|---|---|
| BofT | Board of Trade |
| CNT | Clyde Navigation Trust |
| DWRGLU | Dock, Wharf, Riverside and General Labourers Union |
| GCA | Glasgow City Archives |
| GHLU | Glasgow Harbour Labourers Union (the 'Old Society') |
| *IRSH* | *International Review of Social History* |
| NJC | National Joint Council |
| NTWF | National Transport Workers Federation |
| NUDL | National Union of Dock Labourers |
| NSFU | National Seamen's (or Sailors') and Firemen's Union (Formerly NASFU, 1887 to 1894) |
| *SLHS* | Scottish Labour History Society |
| SRO | Scottish Records Office |
| STGWU | Scottish Transport and General Workers Union |
| SUDL | Scottish Union of Dock Labourers |
| STUC | Scottish Trades Union Congress |
| TGWU | Transport and General Workers Union |
| TUC | Trades Union Congress |

# Acknowledgements

My interest in docks and dockers started to take shape when contemplating a research topic for an Honours year dissertation in History at the University of Strathclyde in 1990. The result was a local case history on Ardrossan Harbour which laid the foundations for what was to become a doctoral thesis on the Clydeside and Glasgow dock labour force the following year. The thesis was completed in 1995 and since then several chapters and articles, and one small book, have been published drawing on the research materials gathered for this study. Rebellious and Contrary *completes the research and publication process.*

Much has happened over that time and along the way many friends and colleagues have offered their help, assistance and advice. As my doctoral advisor of studies at the University of Strathclyde, Dr Arthur McIvor deserves special thanks. We had our problems and difficulties but he successfully guided me through these and is now a dear friend and colleague. I would also like to acknowledge the co-advisory role of Dr Gordon Jackson. His advice and direction in maritime matters was invaluable. I would also like to thank Professor Hamish Fraser for convincing me to take the dockers study further, Professor Tom Devine who oversaw the successful application and award of the John Anderson Postgraduate Scholarship, and both Dr Simon Adams and Professor Jim McMillan, who, as subsequent Heads of Department, continued to provide much appreciated support and guidance.

The role of the Carnegie Trust for the Universities of Scotland throughout this period was invaluable. Without their financial assistance it would have proved extremely difficult to conclude the doctoral research in the time available. Indeed, they have continued to provide financial assistance since then for new research initiatives.

From September 1994 I have been employed as a lecturer in History at the University of Dundee. During this period I have received a great deal of support from various colleagues, not least Dr Mark Cornwall and Dr Chris Storrs, but particularly Professor Chris Whatley. He can be a hard man to please, but his guidance and direction over the last years has been most appreciated. I would also like to thank Jennifer Tait, University Archives, for her help with the draft manuscript of this book and most importantly our two departmental secretaries, Helen Carmichael and Sara Reid, but chiefly Sara for her careful and patient proof reading and occasional stylistic suggestions.

Others have given their time and assistance over the years, not least Tom O'Connor, ex-docker and one of the last trade union officials of the Scottish Transport and General Workers' Union. Audrey Canning, of the Willie Gallacher Memorial Library, was always willing to help, as were the staff of the Mitchell Library and the People's Palace photographic Archive at the Burrell. And I happily acknowledge the role of my long time friend Jean Gillies. She not only encouraged me to follow an academic career, but has been a constant source of wisdom and kindness ever since. I would also like to thank Noel Whiteside for her helpfulness since first grappling with my thesis, and David and Susanna Forsyth, and Neil Rafeek, for their continued friendship and good spirit.

Finally, I would like to thank the Kenefick Clan for their love and support, particularly my daughters Susan and Alison, my mother and father Agnes and William, and especially my dear wife Pauline. She has made a positive and important contribution to my personal development over the years, and I thank her for her patience and support and her continued friendship and love. My family have been a constant source of strength and inspiration and if I have achieved anything that is good it is as a result of the love and support they freely give.

# Glasgow Docks and Dockers in the Nineteenth and early Twentieth Centuries

Despite Clydeside's overwhelming importance in terms of Scottish trade and the central function of Glasgow as Scotland's premier port, remarkably little has been written about the city's waterside. Still less is known about the labour force which handled the goods that passed through the Clydeside ports.[1] What has been written in relation to port development and dock life generally refers to England. Writers such as David Wilson, John Lovell and Eric Taplin, reflect on certain aspects of dock life in Scotland, but these amount to little more than passing references and occasional footnotes.[2] The present study fills this historiographical gap by considering the nature of the port transport industry on Clydeside, the central importance of the port of Glasgow in particular, and the dock labour force that serviced the port transport industry in this area.

Given that Glasgow was Scotland's premier port and a leading British port from the second half of the nineteenth century onward, it is important that the Scottish dimension of dock life is more fully explored and clearly defined as an area of academic interest in its own right. This does not mean that the port of Glasgow need be studied in isolation. What is needed is a comparative historical approach. This study will, therefore, compare and contrast the experience of dock life and dock work at Glasgow with what we know of other ports. By studying the historiography of other British docks we add to our understanding of Glasgow, and by studying the port of Glasgow we also add to the current historiography of the British docks.

There are other valid reasons for studying the port transport industry in the Scottish context. As argued by Bill Knox and Conan Fischer, historical concern thus far has tended to concentrate on the 'organisations and interests of the skilled, male, Protestant worker', which has acted to downgrade the role of the unskilled, female or non-Protestant worker, in shaping labour's historical development in Scotland. In short, there has been a general lack of interest shown in the position of the unskilled worker in Scottish historiography and such omissions, argue Knox and Fischer, 'have distorted the historical record'.[3] The evidence from Glasgow

---

[1] G. Jackson, *The History and Archaeology of Ports* (Tadworth, 1983), see preface.

[2] D. Wilson, *The Dockers: The Impact of Industrial Change* (1972); John Lovell, *Stevedores and Dockers* (1969); E. Taplin, *The Dockers' Union: A Study of the National Union of Dock Labourers, 1889–1922* (Leicester, 1986).

[3] B. Knox and C. Fischer, 'Shedding the Blinkers: German and Scottish Labour Historiography from c.1960 to Present', *Scottish Labour History Society* (*SLHS*), 26, 1991.

suggests that the dockers were overwhelmingly Irish and most probably Catholic, and their work was generally regarded as unskilled. Seen in this context, a study of the Glasgow dockers would help set this particular record straight.

A major problem associated with any enquiry into dock life and work, however, is the lack of documentary material related to it (not discounting the dearth of secondary published works). Trade union records for bodies of unskilled workers are virtually non-existent and what survives tells us little about the day-to-day concerns of the ordinary docker. Other sources have often proved more fruitful, particularly the records of Glasgow Trades Council, STUC and TUC minutes and reports. In the area of social science survey and government enquiry, published in the volumes of British Parliamentary Papers, a far richer vein has been uncovered. These sources are particularly useful in helping to construct an image of the docker – what he did and how he functioned – but such reports often related to dock life outside Scotland. One exception was the Transport Workers Court of Inquiry (Shaw Inquiry), which reported in 1920. The Shaw Inquiry heard and collected a considerable body of evidence on dock work and conditions, and this provides a valuable record of how the port transport industry operated and functioned at the Glasgow docks. In addition, there were numerous reports in the press, most notably the *Glasgow Herald, Forward* and the *Daily Record*. The *Glasgow Herald* in particular proved an invaluable source of information and considered many facets of port life in Glasgow, including regular reports and articles on the continued improvements to the River Clyde, the expansion of Glasgow docks, Glasgow's increasing prosperity and importance as a port, the pivotal role of the Clyde Navigation Trust and extensive commentaries on labour relations at the port. When this evidence is considered closely, and placed alongside what is known of other ports, a clearer picture of life along the Glasgow waterfront begins to take shape.

Changing developments in the labour process, and the manner in which this factor impacted on the port transport industry, is another under-researched area of study. This type of historical inquiry is most often viewed from the perspective of the 'craft' sector of British industry and is seldom applied in any meaningful sense to the port transport industry. The sheer pace of change and the growth in trade in the port transport industry largely came about because of the widespread application of steam power. From the 1870s onward, steamships began to replace sailing ships in ever greater numbers and modern construction methods made it possible to build bigger and faster ships. These technical breakthroughs in shipping led to the development of more regular lines of trade than was ever possible under sail and wind power. The demands of the steam age in turn precipitated the spread and penetration of mechanical appliances (mostly hydraulic and steam, and latterly electric, powered equipment) as shipowners worked furiously to realise the quickest possible turn-round times in discharging and loading the cargo they handled. With so much invested in the modern steam vessel, the employers needed to recoup capital outlay as quickly as possible and procure the highest potential return on this investment to offset ongoing costs. In short, a vessel and its crew did not earn their keep while they were tied-up in port. Initially, these changes led to a growth in employment and a further augmentation in the diversity of goods handled. This resulted in the development of a multifunctional dock labour force, where expertise lay in the handling of specific goods, or where groups of dockers became associated with the handling of specific types of cargo such as the bulk trade in coal and iron ore, or grain. Many dockers, therefore, developed a strong attachment to the customs, traditions and workplace practices that were associated with these goods, which in turn helped create many sectional barriers between dockers across much of the port transport industry.

Despite the potential for division, the dock labour force grew significantly from the late 1870s onward. This phase of rapid growth was a major factor behind the development of port-wide dock unionism at Glasgow during the period of the 'New Unionism' in the late 1880s. Census statistics for the period show an almost threefold increase in the dock labour force in the Clydeside area between 1861 and 1891. Indeed, by 1891, around 44% of the total Scottish dock labour force were largely to be found living and working along a 2 mile stretch of the Clyde waterfront, centred within the heart of the city of Glasgow. The rapid increase in the number of new recruits had been a relatively recent phenomenon, however, and there seems little doubt that it was a cause of considerable friction between the new arrivals and an older, well-established group of dock workers at Glasgow. This older group of the dock labour force were shipworkers, and were considered skilled stowers of cargo. They were chiefly engaged to work on sailing vessels and were the most regularly employed section of the dock labour force at Glasgow. They were also members of the Glasgow Harbour Labourers' Union (GHLU), which was one of the first dock trade unions of its type to be formed in Britain in the mid-nineteenth century. Like other early dock unions, the GHLU functioned along the same lines as the artisan trade unions of the period. The GHLU's formation in 1853 marked the roots of the early artisanal phase of dock unionism at Glasgow.

By contrast, the newest section of the dock labour force were predominantly quayworkers, or top-side ship workers, chiefly employed by steamship owners, and generally regarded as unskilled. They were almost all employed on a casual basis and were predominantly Catholic-Irish in composition. Largely excluded by the GHLU, the quayworkers were not represented by any trade union at Glasgow until the late 1880s. There seems little doubt that the new recruits were seen as a danger to the shipworkers, posing a threat to the privileged position they held at Glasgow. The new workers invoked the spectre of a division of labour at a time when uncertainty was already running high due to the changes brought about by the impact of steam. Perhaps it is for these reasons the GHLU became exclusive and sectional in outlook, and this explains why they rejected the National Union of Dock Labourers (NUDL), the first national union of general dock workers in Britain, after its formation in Glasgow in the late 1880s. It will become clear that despite such difficulties the Glasgow dockers were to play a crucial rôle in the development of dock unionism not only in Scotland but also in Britain.

The results of this investigation will be presented in three main sections. Part One will consider major and significant factors which affected the life and work of dockers in the wider national context and through a comparative analysis place

Clydeside and Glasgow in an industry-wide perspective. Chapter 1 will outline political and sociological investigation of the port transport industry and the current state of historical enquiry in this area. The chapter will illustrate the main differences between Clydeside and other dockland areas, through an analysis of the current literature and the investigations of historians such as John Lovell on the port of London and Eric Taplin's accounts of emergent dock trade unionism at Liverpool. One of the principal issues of this part of the study will be to explain why the Glasgow dockers cultivated a particular type of trade unionism peculiar to that area. The main factors contributing to this development will be discussed at length in later chapters, but are introduced in Chapter 1 in order to clearly identify the key events which lay behind the evolution of dock trade unionism between 1853 and 1932. The process begins with the emergence of early dock trade unionism at Glasgow in 1853, the growth of general dock trade unionism in the late 1880s, and the amalgamation of the GHLU and the NUDL in 1899 (an event which united the dock labour force at a time when division was rife at many other ports). It is also important to highlight other meaningful episodes such as the circumstances that led to the Glasgow dockers leaving the ranks of the NUDL *en masse* in 1910, and why those same dockers flocked to join the ranks of the new Scottish Union of Dock Labourers (SUDL) after its formation in 1911. Explaining such incidents help us to understand events that were to unfold later. Why were the Glasgow dockers so uncertain and suspicious of the SUDL proposals to join the Transport and General Workers' Union (TGWU) in 1922, for example, and why did such anxieties endure even after the SUDL was officially 'closed down' in January 1923? It will become clear that the Glasgow dockers were unhappy about the manner in which the whole amalgamation issue was handled in the first instance and that this explains why the relationship between Glasgow and the London executive of the TGWU was so problematic throughout the 1920s and the early 1930s. Distrust and disagreement intensified over the issue of trade union democracy. The Glasgow dockers wanted to elect their own branch officials, for example, but the TGWU executive more or less wished to select branch officers as they saw fit – and another point of conflict came with the TGWU proposals to decasualise dock work in the 1920s. Relations finally deteriorated to such an extent that in January 1932 the Glasgow dockers seceded from the TGWU to form their own independent Scottish union.

Clearly, the question of trade union democracy was one factor dear to the hearts of the Glasgow dockers, but this was inextricably bound-up with the question of decasualisation. The casual system of employment was one that the vast majority were willing to defend and the one common factor which united many different groups of dock workers across the country. So enduring was the dockers attachment to casualism that it was only finally abolished in the late 1960s. It was the durability of casualism and the host of 'peculiar practices' that emerged from its operation that encouraged many social and parliamentary surveys of the industry (the documentary remnants of which are of fundamental importance to the modern historian in this field). Casualism was to become a way of life for the dockers, to which they developed a strong attachment. Nowhere was this more so than in Glasgow. The Glasgow dockers engaged in a determined struggle to fight against proposals to decasualise the industry, even when these carried the support of the large and influential TGWU and the personal backing of Ernest Bevin (the TGWUs powerful and autocratic leader). The whole issue was to seriously affect relations between London and Glasgow during the interwar period. It is important, therefore, to consider the development of the casual system and its impact on the port transport system as a whole. The significance of Chapter 2 will be found in the explanation of how the casual system of employment came into being, the manner in which it operated, and how the dockers became so deeply attached to it.

The growth of trade and the main factors which helped promote change within the port of Glasgow and its economic hinterland, will be examined in Chapter 3. By 1914 Glasgow was rightly proud of its status as Second City of the British Empire. The roots of this achievement lay in the period of rapid expansion that took place between 1870 and 1914 and was linked to the ascendancy of steam over sail. Glasgow expanded in terms of trade and, as both tonnage and the value of trade soared, there was also a significant increase in the dock labour force. This chapter will illustrate that dockers from different ports, or even within a given port, could and did generate traditions that were intimately linked with local conditions and developments. The main aim here is to highlight the factors that were to prove the most important in relation to the dock community at Glasgow, and assess how the impact of these localised conditions helped shape the workplace experience.

Chapter 4 will consider the commercial operation of the port. The intention is to illustrate how the complexities and peculiarities of port life created such a degree of diversity and occupational variation. There was a great range of cargo handled at Glasgow. There were also a great number of employers operating within the port. As a rule, they only engaged men who had a practical working knowledge of the goods they were contracted to handle. This chapter will help to generate a profile of the employment structure at Glasgow, while also considering complicating factors such as product specialisation and the question of skill, and how this created a potential for division along the Glasgow waterfront. It will also be shown that wider society tended to view dock work as unskilled, and assumed that all dockers were more or less the same. This chapter will illustrate, however, that dock work was never that simple, and that the generic term 'docker' is a somewhat inappropriate title used mainly as a convenience. This chapter brings Part One to a conclusion.

Chapters 5 to 7 comprise Part Two of this study. These chapters are principally concerned with the investigation of more discrete factors specific and appropriate to the port of Glasgow. The effects of the growing number of workers entering the dock industry, particularly between 1871 and 1891, is the main focus of Chapter 5. It will be stressed that official figures suggest a very rapid increase in numbers during the period in question, but it will also be shown that official figures significantly underestimate the actual numbers entering dock work at this time. This will reveal that in the 1890s, for example, the numbers working at the port of Glasgow were double official estimates. It will be argued that the increase in the numbers of those engaged in dock work and their density within a relatively tight geographical area hastened and aided the formation of general trade unionism among the dockers during the late 1880s. It will also be shown that the Irish, and to a lesser extent the Scottish Highlanders, were of considerable importance in this process, and that both these culturally distinctive groups were an integral part of the waterfront community at Glasgow (indeed, it will be shown that their involvement with the dock labour force at Glasgow dated back to the late 1830s). A statistical evaluation of the 1891 Census Enumerators' returns suggests that about 65% of the total dock labour force at Glasgow were Irish-born workers, and that around 15% were born in the Scottish Highlands. The evidence presented in this chapter will clearly illustrate that this racial and cultural composition was quite unique and played a crucial role in the events leading to the formation of the NUDL at Glasgow in 1889.

Chapter 6 will examine the attitudes of the dock workers at Glasgow to mechanisation. It will be suggested that the introduction of mechanisation hardened the dockers' attachment to traditional and customary workplace practices and that in time these were used to form a defence against the further spread of mechanisation from the late nineteenth century onwards. It will be shown that mechanisation affected the trade in bulk cargo, such as coal, iron ore, or grain, and that the effects of labour displacement were more keenly felt in these areas of commercial activity than any other. It will be shown too that mechanisation led to speed-up and work intensification and that these factors affected most sections of the dock labour force. It will also be argued that work intensification was one factor which contributed to growing levels of industrial militancy from the time of New Unionism onwards. The docker was, to a certain extent, a product of his environment, and while it was not one of his own making he had become accustomed to it and would fight to preserve it. It was in the defence of these interests that the dockers gained a deserved reputation for militant and direct industrial action.

The question of occupational health and safety is the focus of Chapter 7. There are, however, many problems associated with this topic – not least the lack of quantitative evidence regarding the accident rate along the British waterfront as a whole. In part this is due to the problems of extending health and safety legislation to cover the port transport industry, the uncertainty associated with interpreting the law as it related to dock work, and the considerable problems involved in collecting and analysing accident and injury data. It will also be shown, however, that dockers themselves were reluctant, or even afraid, to report accidents. First, the non-reporting of accidents may be linked to the belief that if a docker was good at his job he would not get injured. Accidents would, therefore, not be reported in such instances because this would have undermined a docker's credibility within the industry. Secondly, the fear of victimisation by the employers and hiring foremen may have persuaded many dockers not to report accidents. These occurrences were part and parcel of port life, an integral part of dock culture, and as such need to be closely analysed and explained in greater detail. Given the problems associated with this area of investigation and research, this chapter will be largely speculative in its account of occupational health and safety on the docks. The analysis will nevertheless provide an informed insight into docklands culture and notions of masculinity.

Part Three takes up the issues raised in the preceding chapters and illustrates how such factors influenced the development of trade unionism on Clydeside between 1853 and 1932. Chapter 8 returns to dock unionism at Glasgow and the formation of the GHLU (also referred to as the 'Old Society'). As noted earlier, the GHLU was essentially an 'artisanal' trade union, composed mainly of shipworkers, whose members were considered the most skilled of the Glasgow dock labour force. This chapter will briefly consider the role of the GHLU at Glasgow and investigate the relationship of its members with other groups of workers at the port. The chapter will close by reflecting on the relationship between the old and the new dock unions (explained from the standpoint of the GHLU) and attempt to analyse the reasons for the particularly bitter sectional conflict that was to develop between the GHLU and the NUDL during the early 1890s.

The next chapter begins by considering the same period, but from the viewpoint of the NUDL. The NUDL was being formed and already in conflict with the employers at Glasgow some six months before the Great London Dock Strike of August 1889, and it was in Glasgow that the first cohesive and general organisation of dock workers in Britain was formed. This was done with considerable help from the Glasgow Trades Council (of central importance in the Scottish context) and the National Amalgamated Seamen's and Firemen's Union (NASFU). Indeed, the link with the NASFU was particularly strong during the period of New Unionism up until 1894 when NASFU went bankrupt. This close relationship was maintained, however, after the old Seamen's Union was reformed as the National Seamen's (or Sailor's) and Firemen's Union (NSFU) from then through to the labour unrest of 1910–14. Chapter 9, therefore, considers the formation of the NUDL and the role of the Irish (and to a lesser degree the Scottish Highlanders) in this development. Meetings were held to promote the campaign for a new dock union in the very waterfront districts where the Irish had settled in large numbers. At these meetings numerous references were made to the issue of Irish Home Rule and Land Reform. Indeed, the subject of Land Reform provided a political issue which created unity among the Irish and the Scottish Highlanders. It may come as no surprise to discover that the men who were to become the leaders of the NUDL were closely identified and associated with the Irish Home Rule and Land Reform campaign in Scotland, and were Irish by birth. This chapter also considers the conflict with the GHLU, but from the distinctly different viewpoint of the NUDL.

Given the obvious problems that existed between the GHLU and NUDL in the early 1890s, it may seem strange to discover that the GHLU was to become absorbed into the NUDL in 1899. This development is all the more remarkable not only because it occurred after a prolonged and bitter sectional conflict which took place at Glasgow over the decade before, but it also coincided with a determined employers' counter-attack, which, for a time, seriously threatened the very survival of dock trade unionism at the port. Moreover, there was also a significant trade depression during this period and trade union membership fell sharply as a result. But dock trade unionism at Glasgow emerged from these troubles intact, even if somewhat battered and bruised by the process. Thus, before the passing of the nineteenth century, the Glasgow dockers were united within one port-wide trade union and at that point the NUDL's position at the port seemed secure. The twentieth century heralded fresh problems, not least the severe downturn in trade and the economic depressions experienced between 1903–5 and 1907–9. In one sense this spelled disaster for the NUDL, and severely weakened the financial base of the union at Glasgow. Membership levels fell further and by 1910 the union had virtually disintegrated. But poor economic conditions were not the only reason for the collapse of the NUDL at Glasgow. There are other contributing factors to consider. The deteriorating relationship between Glasgow and the Liverpool executive of the NUDL was of major importance. It will be shown that James Sexton, the leader of the NUDL, blatantly disregarded the wishes of the Glasgow dockers and that the autocratic nature of the union's executive was in part responsible for the dockers' growing disenchantment with the NUDL by 1910 (a theme that would re-emerge later to confound relations between the TGWU in London and the dockers of Glasgow). By December 1910, therefore, the Glasgow dockers left the ranks of the NUDL *en masse*. Within six short months, however, they had reasserted their commitment to trade unionism at Glasgow by joining the newly formed SUDL in even greater numbers than ever before. The Glasgow dockers did not have a problem with organised trade unionism, but they did care deeply about the democratic process, executive accountability and the manner in which organised trade unionism operated.

Chapter 10 charts the rise of the SUDL, the virtual renaissance of dock unionism on Clydeside from 1911, and in particular the period of industrial discontent that immediately followed the formation of Glasgow's new dock union. Membership levels rose considerably during 1911, and this was largely due to the SUDL's role in orchestrating a series of successful small-scale disputes, which resulted in the dockers gaining considerable improvements in wages and working conditions. The events of 1911 engendered a growing sense of solidarity among the Clydeside dock labour force and prepared the way for the general strike which began at Glasgow and spread throughout Clydeside during the early months of 1912. This strike was particularly hard-fought and brought the port to a standstill. For a time, the dockers openly challenged the managerial prerogatives of the port employers and were determined to push through their collective demands. The employers had stubbornly held out against any interference in their rights to manage their industry since the days of the New Unionism. But because of the dockers actions in the strikes of 1911, they reluctantly accepted the principle of joint-collective bargaining, and gave way to the dockers demands to enlarge 'gang sizes'. During the general strike the following year, however, the employers sought to over turn their decision to increase gang sizes. They were determined not to concede any more ground to the dockers, and to illustrate this declared a lock-out. Some employers felt they were being held to ransom and were being denied the right to manage their own affairs, and they blamed the unacceptable demands of the SUDL and the entrenched position of the dockers on the twin-effects of socialism and syndicalism on the one hand, and the disintegration caused by the Trades Dispute Act, 1906, on the other. Explaining the strike of 1912 is somewhat more complex than the version of events offered by the employers, however. But there is little doubt that in the aftermath of the 1912 strike, industrial relations along the Clydeside waterfront were to change significantly – evident in a growing commitment to joint-collective bargaining on the part of both the employers and the dockers.

It is clear that the events of this period mark a distinct break with the past, and that this episode was responsible for the wholesale penetration of dock unionism throughout Glasgow and Clydeside as well as several other locations around Scotland. Dock unionism was never to pale into insignificance after the labour unrest of 1910–14 as it did after the initial shock-wave of unrest subsided in the wake of New Unionism in the early 1890s. This chapter seeks to define the impact of the period of the labour unrest at Glasgow in the longer-term and reflect on the political and industrial implications of the dockers' actions in the light of later events which were to become associated with Red Clydeside. Moreover, in the aftermath of the strikes of 1911–12, this chapter will also examine the degree of involvement of the organised dock labour force within the broader Clydeside labour movement from 1911 onward.

The final chapter offers a survey of the main events taking place at Glasgow docks over the period 1914–32. It considers the impact of the First World War on the lives of the dockers, the post-war position of the dockers and the setting up of the Shaw Inquiry, the SUDL's ill-fated sympathy strike on behalf of the miners in April 1921, and the financial collapse of the SUDL in 1922. This chapter will examine the Glasgow dockers' reluctance to join the TGWU before 1922, the cause and consequence of growing disagreements between Glasgow and the London headquarters of the TGWU during the 1920s, and Glasgow's battle to free itself from the 'tyranny' of English trade unionism by seceding from the TGWU in 1932 to form their own rival and independent Scottish Transport and General Workers Union.

Despite the Glasgow dockers' contribution to the development of dock trade unionism in both Scotland and Britain, their role is rarely acknowledged in the literature on the history of industrial relations along the British waterfront. Moreover, as Knox and Fischer suggest, few publications to date chart the important role played by the unskilled and largely non-Protestant section of the working class in shaping labour's historical development in Scotland. This study of the Glasgow dockers makes a major contribution in all these areas. It also provides the first significant and authoritative historical account of life and work along the Glasgow waterfront in the nineteenth and twentieth centuries.

# Part One

# CHAPTER ONE

# Docks, Dockers and Dock Unionism: Sources and Historiography, *c.*1853 to 1932

One objective of this study is to plug the current gap in the literature relating specifically to the Scottish experience within the port transport industry. What follows, therefore, is a brief historiographical analysis of relevant material. These include early sociological surveys, official government commissions and enquiries, modern social science investigations, together with recent historical studies of the dock industry and its labour force. The one common denominator which runs through the great bulk of the literature is the structure of employment, symbolically enshrined in the system of casualism. It is this factor, above all else, that is argued to have been the biggest single problem of the port transport industry since the middle of the nineteenth century until well into the second half of the twentieth century. It is also recognised in many studies that this system was intrinsically suited to the needs of an industry based on the irregular and often chaotic nature of supply and demand as it operated within the capitalist enterprise system, and was thus the reason for the equally irregular system of employment that prevailed within the industry.

To the modern observer it is the durability of the casual system of employment that is both intriguing and problematic, as too are the many waterside traditions and industrial strategies devised to safeguard this system. As a result many of the later studies are more concerned with the labour and industrial question, and with the protective labour organisations which emerged from within the industry, rather than with any social critique of the system of casualism itself, or with any perspective on the historical development of the system. The latter was very much the case with earlier investigators, and the decades before and after 1900 saw numerous studies conclude that the main problem with the industry was that it did not conform with accepted socio-economic standards. If it can be argued, however, that the port transport industry mirrored closely the peaks and troughs of general economic activity, and was victim to irregularity in demand, it can equally be argued that the extent of political intervention needed to regulate this industry before 1914 would have been no more imaginable at that point than the idea of centralised state control, or regulation, of the capitalist economy. Calls to decasualise the industry, therefore, to force it to change – either voluntarily or through the legislative framework – were summarily dismissed by both politician and civil servant alike, as well as by a majority of employers and by the great mass of the workforce itself.

This is not to suggest that the labour force unquestioningly accepted the degradation that often accompanied the casual system. In time they constructed their own protective organisations to eliminate its worst excesses, particularly during the period of New Unionism in the late 1880s and early 1890s. But the antagonisms that were to emerge in industrial terms were very much rooted in both the individual and collective experience of the past. The evidence of this study clearly illustrates that the docker came to possess a highly developed sense of his own history. To the docker, past injustices and occasional victories, in both the local and national arena, became moulded into an organisational and community consciousness, and this was to account for the high levels of industrial dispute experienced along the waterfront. As the Shaw Inquiry of 1920 was to note:

> The men's memory has not to go far back to recall conditions of labour which . . . made their minds revolt against the employer that recognised such conditions, and even against a society which permitted them.[1]

The dockers were, therefore, generally mistrustful of society. The gains that this occupational community had made over the years were achieved through the trials and tribulations of the dockers themselves.

### Sociological and Political Inquiry

One of the first surveys of dock life, *London Labour and the London Poor*, written by Henry Mayhew around the mid-nineteenth century, shows considerable awareness of the problems confronting the ordinary docker. His observations were considered to be both 'remarkable in quality and scope', with Mayhew described as an 'early pioneer of sociological investigation'.[2] His observations of London's waterside constitute a very small proportion of his study, but nevertheless an important one. When these are compared to later observations, it can be seen that little had changed within the industry in almost forty years.

For Mayhew, the docks were a 'forest of ships' masts and tall chimneys vomiting black smoke. The air pungent with the smells of tobacco, the fumes of rum and the fragrance of coffee and spices, contrasted with the stench of hides and huge bins of horns. Nearly everywhere, he noted, 'you meet stacks of cork, yellow bins of sulphur or lead coloured copper ore'.[3] This is a vivid and evocative description of the richness and diversity of a port handling general merchandise, but he was also concerned with the dockers who handled these goods. He stressed the irregular nature of waterside work and described the

---

[1] *Inquiry into the Wages and Conditions of Employment of Dock and Waterside Labour: Report and Evidence*, i, (*Parliamentary Papers* (hereafter *PP*), 1920, xxiv, Cmd 936) and *Inquiry into the Wages and Conditions of Employment of Dock and Waterside Labour: Appendices, Documents, and Index*, ii (*PP*, xxiv, Cmd 937). (Hereafter referred to as Shaw Inquiry, i, and Shaw Inquiry, ii.)

[2] P. Quennell (ed.), *Mayhew's London: Being a Selection from 'London Labour and the London Poor'* (n.d.), Introduction, p. 18.

[3] Mayhew, cited in Quennell, Ibid., pp. 548–54.

docker as 'mere brute force . . . as unskilled as the power of the hurricane. Mere muscle is all that is needed'.[4] He describes the 'call-on', the method by which the docker was engaged, and the all encompassing power and influence of the hiring foreman:

> and so begins the scuffling and scrambling forth of hands high in the air, to catch the eye of him whose voice may give them work . . . Indeed, it is a sight to sadden the most callous, to see thousands of men struggling for only one days hire; the scuffle being made the fiercer by the knowledge that hundreds . . . must be left to idle the day out of want. To look at the faces of that hungry crowd is to see a sight that must be remembered.[5]

Mayhew concluded that to the superficial observer, to the untrained eye, the docks were the very focus of metropolitan wealth, both 'boundless and amazing', but so too was the excess of poverty that surrounded them. 'Many have come to see the riches', noted Mayhew, 'but few the poverty, abounding in absolute masses round the far famed port of London.'[6]

This theme is perhaps Mayhew's most enduring legacy, one that was seized and expanded upon in later surveys. By the 1890s, and the publication of Charles Booth's *Life and Labour of the People of London* – some forty years on – the system of employment had changed little. Men were still engaged through the degrading 'call-on'. The dock labourer as described by Mayhew in the 1840s, however, was not typical of the dock worker of the later nineteenth century. He was not one of the army of 20,000 souls depicted by Mayhew, comprising 'out of work bakers, soldiers and sailors, broken down gentlemen, servants and thieves, or anyone who wanted a loaf and was willing to work for it', but one who had become identified with dock employment and sought no other work beyond the confines of a particular dock or wharf. It is true that much of the docker's work still depended on 'brute force', but the docker had also acquired certain specialist functions in the intervening period. This made him something more than 'unskilled muscle'. But the degree of irregularity in employment and the poverty closely associated with it were still major problems for the industry.

The level of poverty and irregularity connected with dock work was often considered to be the problem of the docker himself. From the time of Charles Booth's survey onward the docker was often seen as a perpetuator of his own casualism, rather than its victim. To Beatrice Potter, a contributor to Booth's investigation, the docker had many positive features, but the undertone of her commentary also intimates a degree of disapproval. She noted that 'they shared all with one another, and as a class they were quixotically generous':

> It is this virtue and courage with which they face privation which lend a charm to life among them. On the other hand, however much they may have their

---

[4] Ibid., pp. 547–8.
[5] Ibid., p. 550.
[6] Ibid., p. 554.

own peculiar attractiveness, from the social point of view, economically they are worthless; and morally worthless, for they drag others who live among them down to their level.[7]

Through such surveys the 'evils' of underemployment came to be exposed, but they also tended to show the docker, within specific social contexts, as an almost sub-human species. The dockers' communities were seen as something quite distinctive and distant and the docker himself equally distinct and distant – sufficiently so to become viewed as one who was not a fully functioning citizen, and, therefore, someone who did not contribute positively within the wider socio-economic environment.[8] It may be argued strongly, given the opinions of such eminent social commentators, that it is little wonder that the docker felt threatened by the attentions of outsiders, and remained distant from wider society.[9]

During the war the government had been forced to intervene in the running of the economy and its influence was keenly felt in the dock industry when it came under the administration of the Military Service Act, 1916. The Board of Trade were given the responsibility to form joint committees of employers and workers, known as Port Labour Committees, in 32 of the larger ports in Britain. As the Standing Advisory Committee for the Port Transport Industry was to report (in a *Memorandum* dated December 1936):

The position of the Port Transport Industry in the economic structure of the country was more fully recognised during the war and it became necessary to obtain the co-operation of the representatives of the port employers and the workers.[10]

There was as great a desire to maintain this co-operation after the war, hence the relative ease with which the Shaw Inquiry was set up to discuss the port transport industry in 1920. Likewise, in 1924 the government set up the MacLean Committee to consider the problems of the industry (at a time of widespread industrial unrest)

[7] C. Booth (ed.), *Life and Labour of the People of London* (Second Series, 1903); see report by Beatrice Potter (iv), p. 32. Potter argued there were many out and out casuals, not permanent and not fundamentally members of the 'professional dock labour force', with the result that the casual 'by misfortune tends to become the casual by inclination'. 'Communism is a necessity in their lives and the stern reality of ever-pressing starvation', argued Potter, 'draws all together'. ('Communism' in this instance is not defining a 'political philosophy', rather it is offered as a metaphor for the collective social outlook of the dock labour force.)

[8] See Quennell, *Mayhew's London*, pp. 547–54; Booth, *Life and Labour*, and reference to Booth survey in T. S. Simey (ed.), *The Dock Worker: An Analysis of Conditions of Employment in the Port of Manchester* (Liverpool 1956); see also *in Report of Royal Commission on the Port of London, Minutes of Evidence*, 1901 (*PP*, 1902, xliii, Cd 1151); *Report of Royal Commission on the Poor Law and Relief of Distress* (*PP*, 1909, xxxvii, Cd 4499); S. and B. Webb (eds.), *The Public Organisation of the Labour Market: Being Part of the Minority Reports of the Poor Law Commission* (1909); and F. Keeling, 'Towards the Solution of the Casual Labour Problem', *Economic Journal*, March, 1913.

[9] W. Kenefick, ' "Quixotically Generous . . . Economically Worthless": Two views of the dockers and the dockland community in Britain in the 19th and early 20th centuries', *The Historian*, 56, Winter 1997, pp.

[10] PRO, LAB 101/18, Standing Advisory Committee for the Port Transport Industry, *Memorandum on the History of Registration Schemes for Dock Workers* (hereafter *Port Transport Memorandum*), Dec. 1936, section ii, para. 11, p. 4.

and reconvened this committee again in the 1930s.[11] Throughout this period as a whole, however, the emphasis was on finding a method by which the dock labour force could be more regularly employed, and pivoted around the issue of the registration of dockers, and to promote a scheme of registration similar to that set up in Liverpool in 1912.

There were other inquiries. E. C. P. Lascelles and S. S. Bullock in 1924, *Dock Labour and Decasualisation* (1924), and John Hilton's *Are Trade Unions Obstructive: An impartial Enquiry* (1935),[12] and sometime earlier, William Beveridge's *Unemployment: A Problem for Industry* (1909 – revised and republished in 1930), in which Beveridge argued, among other things, that the problems of the dock industry in London was that it had not changed significantly over the preceeding twenty years. He did note improvements in wages and conditions, which stemmed principally from the advances made from the time of the London dock strike in 1889. He suggested too that the industry at that time attracted a 'slightly higher class' of men than hitherto, and that the memory of the 'historic movement' had given 'some measure of respect to the once despised calling of the docker'.[13] But irregularity in employment – underemployment – was still the major problem.

In *The Problem of the Unemployed* (1906), John A. Hobson noted that before 1914, out of London's estimated total of 22,000 dockers, the average daily average requirement was only 7,006. This in effect meant that only about one third of the labour force were ever needed on a daily basis, and that two-thirds were regularly unemployed.[14] Casualism, thus, created an overstocked labour market. The only way this problem could be solved was by the strict regulation of the industry, the decasualisation of the workforce and the registration of all *bona fide* dockers. Under such a scheme only registered dockers would be able to work on the docks, and once registered they would expect more regular employment. In this way overall numbers operating around a given port could be controlled and, in time, casualism would become a thing of the past. However, Frederick Keeling noted, in 'Towards the Solution of the Casual Labour Problem' (1913), an important vital detail that many had simply overlooked, or disregarded, in previous investigations: the system would be impossible to overhaul without the voluntary consent of those involved. Without that consent state would be forced to intervene.

It is true that some time earlier Beveridge, and Beatrice Potter before him, argued that some form of intervention would be needed if the casual system was to be eradicated for good. Keeling argued the case for intervention along economic lines, however, and he showed great sympathy for the docker. He closely analysed the role of the port employers and argued that since they were determined to preserve the system of casualism then the same employers should shoulder the

[11] The theme of unfulfilled citizenship was one that concerned the Shaw Inquiry in particular, but it had been alluded to and touched on before in previous investigations into the dock industry (see note 8 above).
[12] See E. C. P. Lascelles and S. S. Bullock, *Dock Labour and Decasualisation* (1924), and J. Hilton (et al.), *Are Trade Unions Obstructive: An Impartial Enquiry* (1935).
[13] W. H. Beveridge, *Unemployment: A Problem of Industry* (1930 edn.), p. 92.
[14] J. A. Hobson, *The Problem of the Unemployed* (1906), pp. 27–8.

responsibility for the social problems that resulted from its operation. In essence, he was arguing for the maintenance of the casual dock labour force, which he pointedly summed up in the phrase 'they also serve who only stand and wait'.

The subject of the maintenance of the dock labour force, when not employed, had never been fundamentally addressed before and this introduced a new variable into the whole decasualisation debate. But Keeling also knew that the docker would not quickly give up his commitment to casualism, and commit himself to registration and regularity of work, unless those displaced by such an overhaul were taken into consideration. Clearly, the main difference between Keeling and others was that he considered the point of view of the labour force, and demonstrated a greater understanding of the industry than many who had gone before. The findings of the Shaw Court of inquiry into the Transport Industry in 1920 more or less followed the same line of logic as Keeling's original proposal, when for the first time dock work and conditions were thoroughly explored in an investigation centred entirely on the dock industry. The Shaw Inquiry stressed that the docker would have to be intimately involved in any discussion intended to bring about change in the casual system of employment. Without the dockers' consent and agreement, however, decasualisation would be difficult, if not impossible, to bring about (the very point stressed by Keeling in 1913).

In *Report on Dock Labour and the Relief of Distress* (1908), Gerald Walsh investigated the ports of Bristol, London, Liverpool and Glasgow. This report helps us to better understand the general structure of the dock labour force across Britain before 1914, but he also offers us a greater insight into the operation of the casual system at Glasgow. He noted, for example, the parallel operation of a 'preference structure' (a system which gave a minority of dockers greater regularity in employment), that there was a 'three-tier' occupational hierarchy (dockers were designated 'A', 'B' and 'C' men), and that this system was very similar to that in operation at London. Booth had also briefly described a type of occupational hierarchy operating in the London context, but until Walsh's report, however, it was far from clear whether this preference system operated elsewhere in the country.[15]

With particular reference to Glasgow, Walsh noted that the 'A' group of workers were non-union and generally worked for the larger steam-shipping lines. The 'B' men, on the other hand, were unionised and concentrated their efforts with the smaller stevedore employer (who worked the smaller vessels involved in the coastal trade). The group 'C' men were the so-called 'out and out' casuals, who would supplement the 'B' class group when necessary. As will be shown in a later chapter, however, there are many problems associated with Walsh's categorisation, but he does indicate the type of docker who would tend towards unionisation and that the degree of irregularity in employment varied significantly between given groups of dockers. If some dockers tended to work more regularly than others, this might help account for their defence of the system of casualism. Conversely, those who

---

[15] PRO, LAB 101/18, *Port Transport Memorandum*; it was reported that London had operated a four-tier structure in the 1890s, but they had found this unworkable. Therafter they pomoted the 'three-ticketing' system: A – regular casuals, B – first preference casuals, and C – all other casuals, section i, para. 7, p 2.

knew no other work, and worked less regularly, found themselves trapped within a system from which they feared the consequences of escape.

John Hilton considered more fully the question of mechanisation from both the viewpoint of the employers and the dock labour force. The employers for many years had argued that a full programme of mechanical implantation had been halted by the dock unions and this held back the modernisation of the port transport system. The trade unions, on the other hand, doggedly defended their position on further mechanisation from the viewpoint that it was a major cause of labour displacement and unemployment within the industry. Hilton also stressed the tenacity of dockers in defending gains made in the past, noting not only their attachment to custom and practice, and to the casual system, but the manner in which their defence of these traditions had become incorporated in their trade union strategy (a major theme of this study).

*Historical Study of the Port Transport Industry*

There are, without doubt, some major problems associated with research into trade unionism in Scotland, not least in relation to those unions generally considered to represent 'unskilled' workers. This may explain why no history of dock workers in Scotland has been attempted. Records of early Scottish trade unions are so fragmentary that any in-depth analysis of certain groups of workers is difficult if not impossible. To W. H. Marwick, writing in the mid 1930s, the reasons were simple:

> Scottish trade unionism has never found its Webbs, and it may be that the opportunity has passed. Many old minute books and other records have perished, few if any odd copies survive of such 'Labour' periodicals as the *Liberator* and the *Sentinel*, references in ordinary periodicals are slight, often uninformed, and uninformative. Most of the existing bodies are of recent origins, and are merely branches of an English body.[16]

Marwick was writing shortly after the Glasgow dockers had decisively rejected the notion of being 'a mere branch of an English body' to become the separate and independent STGWU. Despite the evidence presented in the following chapters, however, suggesting that the breakaway formed part of an historical continuum that stretched back to the period of the New Unionism in Glasgow in the late 1880s, the STGWU were without doubt of recent origins, and previous records of earlier Scottish unions had been more or less lost to posterity. Indeed, the few references that are made to early general Scottish unions, contained in the few documentary remnants that do remain, can, ironically, be attributed to the Webbs and the collections they left behind. The Glasgow Harbour Labourers' Union is one such example. However, there are other sources which can be exploited, such as newspapers and Parliamentary papers, as well as a few scattered remnants outwith

---

[16] W. H. Marwick, 'Early Trade Unionism in Scotland', *Economic History Review*, v, 2, Apr. 1935, p. 87.

the Webb collection, as noted in Ian MacDougall's catalogue of *Labour Records in Scotland*, which helps widen the field of investigation.[17]

The Webbs are, without doubt, very important to the development of labour history in Britain. But they are also important from the standpoint of the historical methodology that they largely determined, and which many historians thereafter adopted and built upon. Eric Hobsbawm, *Worlds of Labour* (1984), suggested that modern labour historians to some extent 'stood on the shoulders of the Webbs', which attested to their 'erudite and impeccable scholarship'.[18] Jonathan Zeitlin notes that the Webbs are also very closely associated with the 'institutional approach' to labour history; the study of the 'formal institutions of the labouring classes, rather than informal social groups'.[19] The Webbs themselves argued that the study of the 'manners and traditions of the governed may relieve and enliven history, but if it were to be history at all, it must follow the course of continuous organisation'.[20] Zeitlin, writing in the late 1980s, uses the Webbs in this instance to advance his own theories on labour history and the need to construct 'an alternative conception of labour history as the history of industrial relations, understood broadly as the changing relationships between workers, trade unions, employers and the state'.[21]

This alternative would seem to be a reasonable and imaginative way of researching labour history. But it should not exclude an approach which considers the workplace and the community experience, which is very much the intention of the first part of this study. If the latter were not to be considered, this would preclude the working experience of the great majority of dockers up to the period of the New Unionism of the late 1880s and early 1890s. Moreover, because there are so few original 'institutional' documents in existence, or that what remains is of a relatively poor quality, an 'institutional' history of the dockers in Scotland before 1914 would never have been a viable topic for academic research.[22]

The difficulty is even greater when considering Clydeside dock labour, given its ethnic, racial and cultural antecedents, and the role of the Irish in particular. For example, Joseph Melling has suggested that even by the early 1890s, 'the descendants of Irish immigrants were not only confined to unskilled areas of work, but . . . they, like their fathers, had no history of trade unionism before then'.[23] As we shall see, Melling is clearly wrong at least in relation to the dock labour force on Clydeside, but perhaps even in the wider context too. As noted by W. P. Ryan in the *Irish Labour Movement* (1920), 'the Irish had a long tradition of combination' not least in rural

[17] I. MacDougall, *Labour Records in Scotland* (Edinburgh, 1978).
[18] E. Hobsbawm, 'Labour History and Ideology', *Worlds of Labour* (1984), pp. 1–2.
[19] J. Zeitlin, 'From Labour History to the History of Industrial Relations', *Economic History Review*, xl, 2, May 1987, p. 159.
[20] S. and B. Webb, *History of Trade Unionism* (1920 edn.), pp. viii–ix.
[21] Zeitlin, *From Labour History*, p. 159.
[22] W. Kenefick, 'An Historiographical and Comparative Survey of Dock Labour c.1889–1920 and the Neglect of the Port of Glasgow', *The Journal of Scottish Labour History Society*, 31, 1996, pp. 51–71.
[23] J. Melling, 'Scottish Industrialists and the Changing Character of Class Relations in the Clyde Region c.1880–1918', in T. Dickson (ed.), *Capital and Class in Scotland* (1982), p. 92.

areas and this was often replicated in the industrial sphere.[24] This is also shown in the work of John Lovell, *Stevedores and Dockers* (1969), where he notes the central role of the Catholic Irish at London docks in relation to the early development of dock unionism there from around the mid-nineteenth century.[25] (A theme developed further in a later article on the 'Irish and the London Docker', 1977.[26])

From the evidence presented in Chapter 5, it will be shown that the NUDL, formed in Glasgow in February, 1889, was overwhelmingly composed of Catholic Irish – as well as Scottish Highlanders (some of whom were Catholic), who formed the next significant group of workers within the Clydeside dock labour force.[27] Indeed, as Martin Mitchell has cogently argued in his recent publication, in which he takes a position contrary to that of Melling, the Irish had a long history of trade union and political combination in Scotland. This was seen in Irish involvement in the weavers' and cotton spinners' unions, and the Radical and Chartist Movements, during the first half of the century.[28] While it may be argued that these Irish were in fact in skilled trades, perhaps dominated by Protestants, Mitchell has shown that a great many were Catholic and thus their involvement in the British and Scottish labour movement was not simply a relatively new phenomenon. It dated further back than the New Unionist period.[29] As argued by G. D. H. Cole and Raymond Postgate, the role of the Irish in the British labour movement can at the very least be traced back to the early part of the nineteenth century.[30] As Mitchell has shown, the same is true of the Scottish labour movement.

There is a great deal of recent literature concerning the role of the Irish and it is not principally the concern of this study to survey these sources. Given that the Irish figure so prominently in this study, however, it is essential that a sense of Irish involvement within the labour movement generally is more clearly defined in order to place the Irish within this broader historical perspective.[31] As Eric Hobsbawm

---

[24] W. P. Ryan, *The Irish Labour Movement: From the Twenties to Our Own Day* (New York, 1920), p. 44. Reference to the Ralahine Agricultural Co-Operative and Manufacturing Association, constituted *c*.1831. Although essentially a rural based organisation, it did nevertheless bring both the rural and the manufacturing sectors together in one organisation. The Ralahine experiment was closely associated with the ideas of Robert Owen and William Thompson, the latter an Irish landlord and it was an attempt to create a co-operative farming scheme, which allowed for improvements in land use and the use of mechanical implements – using the first reaping machine in Ireland. It was seen as a success. Thompson died in 1833 (Robert Owen having viewed and approving the scheme), but those who took over wound up the co-operative and cleared the labourers off the land, pp. 36–50.

[25] J. Lovell, *Stevedores and Dockers* (1969), pp. 57–8.

[26] J. Lovell, 'The Irish and the London Dockers', in *Society for the Study of Labour History* (hereafter *SSLH*), 35, 1977, pp. 16–18.

[27] N. Longmate, *Milestones in Working Class History* (1975), p. 101.

[28] M. Mitchell, *The Irish in the West of Scotland 1797–1848: Trade Unions, Strikes and Political Movements* (1998), see Introduction.

[29] Which A. E. Musson, among others, suggests dates back to the 1870s in any case, see *British Trade Unions, 1800–1875* (1972), pp. 64–5.

[30] G. D. H. Cole and R. Postgate, *The Common People 1746–1946* (1961), pp. 229–248.

[31] R. Swift, *The Irish in Britain* (1990), pp. 11–14; see also W. Kenefick, 'Irish Dockers and Trade Unionism on Clydeside', *Irish Studies Review*, 19, 1997, pp. 22–29; and W. Kenefick, 'A Struggle for Recognition and Independence: The Growth and development of Dock Unionism at the Port of Glasgow', in Sam Davies (et al.), *Dock Workers: International Explorations in Comparative Labour History, 1790–1970*, Part I (Ashworth, 2000).

and other historians note, to many of the English and Scottish middle classes, the Irish were thought to be 'dirty, feckless and undesirable semi-alien subjects'. More recently, as David Woods notes, the Irish were viewed as a violent race of wife-beaters with an inherent resentment of British authority, which was mainly manifested against the police.[32] Reports on the extent of the Irish immigration into Scotland between 1861 and 1881, noted in the Scottish Census, for example, underpin Hobsbawm and Woods' position, in that various reports compared the Irish to a poison reeking havoc to the body of any society they descended on.[33] This type of description was not simply confined to the Irish-born, but also second-generation Irish, particularly in the Scottish context, who were likewise considered 'semi-alien subjects'. This is clearly articulated in a letter sent to the *North British Daily Mail* in March 1893. Referring to the second generation Irish playing football for the Scottish national team, and signed 'Covenanter', the writer accused the Scottish Football Association of:

> misrepresenting Scotland by allowing Irish, or Celtic players, in a Scotland representative team. With all due deference to the Celtic men's ability, I hold an accident of birth don't make them Scotchmen. They, as a team, are banded together for an Irish purpose.[34]

Therefore, there was little reason for second-generation Irish to feel anything other than Irish. Hobsbawm, however, would remind us of another more positive legacy, one that provided the British working classes with a 'cutting edge of radicals and revolutionaries':

> It is no accident that an Irishman, Feargus O'Connor, was the nearest thing to a national leader of Chartism, and another, Bronterre O'Brien, its chief ideologist, that an Irishman wrote 'The Red Flag', the anthem of the British labour movement, and the best British working class novel, *The Ragged-Trousered Philanthropist.*[35]

The Irish were to be at the cutting edge in the development of dock unionism at Glasgow too and their role was vitally important throughout the period of this study.[36]

## Early Dock Unionism and the New Unionism, c.1850 to the 1890s

Over the past years several historians have shown a particular interest in the affairs of the dock labour force. Despite the fact that these studies almost entirely concern the experiences of English dockers, at the principal ports of London, Liverpool or

---

[32] E. Hobsbawm, *Industry and Empire* (1986 edn.), p. 311; D. Woods, 'Community Violence', in John Benson (ed.), *The Working Class in England, 1875–1914* (New York, 1985), pp. 182–3, 186.

[33] Various reports on the Irish in Scotland contained in Scottish Census materials speak in this fashion, but this is less evident after the 1881 Census and absent thereafter, except in the most objective terms.

[34] *North British Daily Mail*, 7 Mar. 1893.

[35] Hobsbawm, *Industry and Empire*, p. 311.

[36] Kenefick, 'Irish Dockers' and 'A Struggle for Recognition'.

Hull, for example, they do nevertheless provide a good platform upon which create an understanding of the attitudes and aspirations of the ordinary docker. When these experiences are then compared with those of the Scottish dock labour force generally, a better understanding of the main similarities and differences can be clearly seen. John Lovell's *Stevedores and Dockers*, is one publication which created great interest in the working lives of dockers. Its main aim was to fill in the central features of London unionism, by arguing that the system of casualism held back trade union organisation at the port, as did the initial dynamic of steam. While his investigations are almost entirely focused on London, many factors of his research can relate to the dock labour force generally, despite the differences that obviously emerge between different ports, both in operation and in historical tradition. One principal factor identified was the disputes that arose regarding the question of control over employment. If trade unions could ensure preference in employment terms through membership of a particular union that would encourage dockers to join. Lovell has shown that the employers felt differently, however, and not only denied recognition, but also actively fought to undermine trade union organisation.[37] This analysis also holds good for Clydeside, the main difference there, being that employers were perhaps even more anti-union (as will be shown in Part Three of this study).

Lovell illustrates the problems of forging solidarity among the dock labour force when the divisive tendency of the skill factor is introduced. For example, the London employers latterly granted recognition to stevedores (considered the most skilled of the dock labour force) while resisting similar recognition for the great mass of ordinary dockers – historically the cause of much sectional division. Lovell expanded on this theme in a later article in 1987, noting also the radical changes that had affected British ports through the arrival of steam power, and the way in which this dynamic, as well as casualism and sectional strife acted to stem the development of dock unionism.

Another historian who contemplates the theme of division is Eric Taplin. In the article, *Liverpool Dockers and the Seamen*, he considered inter-union rivalry at the port, and in his book, *The Dockers Union* (which considers the NUDL from a distinctly Liverpool perspective), other divisions appear evident between dockers and different labour organisations, as well as those divisions that were all too familiar within the ranks of the dockers themselves. In part, this may be explained in terms of locality, and the parochial divisions that existed in these areas. For example, Taplin notes the considerable enmity that existed between the NUDL and the Liverpool Trades Council, who were accused of doing little to further general unionism in the city.[38]

In Glasgow the situation was very different, with the Trades Council there working alongside the seamen's union to actively encourage the formation of a dockers' union at Glasgow in the late 1880s. Indeed, the connection between Taplin's study of the NUDL and Scotland – despite the fact that it focuses on the

---

[37] Lovell, *Stevedores and Dockers*, see chaps. 3, 4 and 5.
[38] Taplin, *The Dockers' Union*, p. 33.

union at Liverpool – is that the union was successfully formed at Glasgow in February 1889, although two years later it was to move to its new headquarters at Liverpool. Ironically, in Henry Pelling's first edition of *The History of British Trade Unionism,* it is noted that the NUDL was formed on Merseyside and later 'spread to Glasgow', but in his edition of 1992 he correctly notes that it was in fact the other way round.[39] Perhaps Pelling recognised this error after Eric Taplin's work on the history of the NUDL was published? Whatever the reason, it does offer some evidence of the inaccuracies and inconsistencies relating to events concerning dockers on Clydeside.

Factual errors are also to be found in the work of David Wilson. In his book, *Dockers: The Impact of Industrial Change,* he stated that the SUDL eventually joined the TGWU in 1926, when in fact they had transferred their membership to that body as early as January 1923. Such inaccuracies show the lack of detail relating to the Scottish dimension of dock life. Lovell and Taplin, as well as Gordon Phillips and Noel Whiteside, *Casual Labour* (1985), offer us a more detailed analysis of events in Scotland, but they are not principally concerned with Scottish affairs. Nevertheless, they all recognise that Glasgow and its dock labour force were very important to the development of dock unionism, not only in Scotland, but in the British context too.[40]

It is also essential to test the thesis of others to ascertain whether their general conclusions about the port transport industry are applicable to the Scottish docks or in the context of dock life and work at Glasgow. For example, according to Taplin one of the main factors of division at London, Liverpool and Glasgow was religious sectarianism. At Liverpool the docks were geographically divided – north and south – into Catholic and Protestant populations.[41] Lovell too notes some lesser sectarian tendencies in London, but this was due to the fact that the Irish cornered specific areas of dock work, particularly corn portering and stevedoring work, where the first trade unions were formed. It was these unions that were unsupportive of wider docker unionism at the port, and it may be the case that sectarianism in London became institutionalised in the sectional divide between stevedores and dockers.[42] Indeed, Taplin notes that this tended to occur at most cities where the Irish joined the ranks of the dock labour force in large numbers.

[39] H. Pelling, *A History of British Trade Unionism,* see 1965 edn. p. 101, and new edition (1990), p. 91.
[40] Trades Council Minutes and the Trades Council *Annual Report* of 1889–90, show the significant support that was offered by the Council in Glasgow. Newspaper reports of the period also note that the support for the formation of a union among the dockers of Glasgow was evident before and after the National Union of Dock Labourers' actual formation during Feb. 1889. Indeed, from this period onward the *Glasgow Herald* and the *North British Daily Mail* ran frequent reports on the 'New Unions' progress. The *North British Daily Mail* produced a weekly column on Trades Council Meetings, reporting that by 4 Apr., 1889, the 'new society' had upwards of 1,200 men and was rapidly increasing in numbers. The following week it was reported to the Trades Council that the membership was 1,300 and that the NUDL 'had formed branches in several other seaports'. The Trades Council followed the development of the NUDL with considerable interest, very different to the attitudes of the Liverpool Trades Council, which the NUDL purposely did not affiliate to until 1906; see Taplin, *Dockers Union,* p. 54.
[41] Ibid., pp. 23–4.
[42] Lovell, 'Irish and London Dockers', pp. 16–18.

Despite Taplin's argument that there were similar sectarian tensions in Glasgo and at other major ports where there was a 'high proportion of Catholic Irish dockers', it seems clear, from the evidence gathered for this study, that religion was not to prove as big a problem on Clydeside as it so evidently was at Liverpool. This then poses the question, why? Joan Smith has attempted to explain this, and the other main differences between Glasgow and Liverpool, in terms of the historically different 'labour tradition' at Glasgow and Liverpool'. One reason why the trades councils of both cities acted differently towards the cause of New Unionism, states Smith, was that 'Old Unionism' was not so infected by anti-Catholicism in Glasgow as it was in Liverpool. The craft unions of Liverpool would have been overwhelmingly Protestant, and while the situation may not have been too different in Glasgow (as noted by Joseph Melling[43]), the sectarian division there was bridged through the development of what Smith terms 'municipal socialism and communism'.[44] Glasgow was, therefore, a more 'Liberal city' in contrast to the religious and political conservatism of Liverpool.

Was Glasgow a more proletarian city? Was this the major difference between it and Liverpool or London? Tom Gallagher believes so, adding that Liverpool developed a far deeper attachment to Orangeism than Glasgow. Liverpool lacked 'a strong co-operative movement and other working-class organisations that signified the existence of a strong proletarian culture'.[45] While this study makes clear that many Irish flocked into Glasgow docks, it will also be shown that no geographical and sectarian division emerged within this group, as occurred at Liverpool, and that this can partly be explained by Smith's, or Gallagher's theory of the growth of 'municipal socialism'. Smith, for instance, cites one example where the May Day celebrations at Glasgow in 1909 attracted some 30,000 people, whereas in Liverpool the May Day parade consisted mainly of carters, who were predominantly Protestant. The greatest show of labour solidarity in Liverpool was seen in a mass meeting of between 2,000 and 3,000 transport workers in 1912, the year following the historically important transport workers' strike there. In September of the same year, however, the *Liverpool Forward* was to report a turn-out of 15,000 Orangemen in a demonstration against Irish Home Rule.[46] It should be recognised, however, that Liverpool did not have the massive industrial base which was evident around Glasgow at that time. Therefore, Liverpool lacked Glasgow's significantly larger proletarian base, which, it may be argued, helped weaken the potential for sectarian division (a point that will be returned to in later chapters).

Throughout the literature on dock work there is evidence that the Irish were the single most important group in relation to the dock labour force of principal British ports. This was undoubtedly the case at Glasgow, particularly during the period of the New Unionism, with the great majority of Irish dock workers based in the west of Scotland. This may explain why there was such a pronounced division in terms of

---

[43] Melling, 'Scottish Industrialists', p. 92.

[44] J. Smith, 'Labour Traditions in Glasgow and Liverpool', *History Workshop*, 17, 1984, p. 50.

[45] T. Gallagher, 'A Tale of Two Cities: Communal Strife in Glasgow and Liverpool Before 1914', in R. Swift and S. Gilley (eds.), *The Irish in the Victorian City* (1985).

[46] Smith, 'Labour Traditions', p. 32.

...ism between the east and west coast ports, particularly from the
...nrest of 1910 to 1914, but may also explain the formation of
...Glasgow two decades earlier during the period of the New
...many dockers along the west of Scotland seaboard were Irish,
...or helped forge a distinctive brand of occupational solidarity which was
...ldom seen elsewhere along the British waterfront.[47]

The role of the Irish has recently been reappraised in an article by Derek
Matthews, '1889 and All That: New Views of New Unionism', and here Matthews
refutes, among other things, the earlier conclusions of John Lovell on the extent of
Irish involvement at London. He argues, for example, that the percentage of Irish
dockers in London was significantly lower than Lovell previously suggested. While it
does not seem to be his intention to in any way devalue the role of the Irish as trade
unionists, Matthews does argue that those who would have been active at the time
of the New Unionism would have been drawn from around the rural hinterland of
London, rather than from the immigrant Irish community.[48] This point will be
returned to in Chapter 5, but the evidence of this study clearly shows that Matthews
is wrong in relation to Glasgow.

Building upon this revisionist interpretation, Matthews also argues that the New
Unions, whether it was the matchgirls', the gasworkers', or the dockers' unions,
were not as militant as previously thought. When assessing the leadership of these
and other new unions, Matthews concludes that they were more moderate and
cautious in their approach to industrial relations than the literature currently
suggests. He also argues that the roots of the New Unionism cannot be traced to
changes in the labour process – factors of change such as extensive mechanisation,
or speed-up at the point of production – and that these factors were less applicable
in relation to dock work. Yet elements of all these factors were of some importance
at Glasgow. For example, in the 1880s, before the development of general unionism, Glasgow introduced grain elevators, which meant that six men could then do
the work of fifty.[49] There were, therefore, identifiable changes in the labour process
at Glasgow, which would have caused significant labour displacement. Glasgow was
also a port which was very much a product of steam and the rise of bulk cargo
handling. Moreover, as Gordon Jackson suggests, much of the port's late nineteenth century growth and the success of Glasgow as a port can be traced to these
very factors.[50]

Matthews' analysis of the composition of London's dock labour force, or his re-
appraisal of a non-militant New Unionism, may have some validity in specific cases,
but not in all cases. Matthews is correct, for example, to note the conciliatory nature
of the dockers' leadership, but he fails to consider the rank and file and the
militancy manifested by them, often in direct opposition to the leadership. Indeed,
at Glasgow this very factor was perhaps one reason why dockers were leaving the

[47] Kenefick, 'The Irish'.
[48] D. Matthews, '1889 and All That: New Views of New Unionism', *International Review of Social History* (hereafter *IRSH*), xxxvi, 1, 1991.
[49] R. Bean, 'The Liverpool Dock Strike of 1890', *IRSH*, xviii, 1, 1973, p. 59.
[50] Jackson, *History and Archaeology of Ports*, pp. 113–7.

ranks of the NUDL in great numbers by 1910 – a problem that had been threatening for some time. This became symbolised in the different approaches to industrial relations adopted by Jim Larkin on the one hand, and James Sexton on the other, causing a distinctive break between the two by the early 1900s.[51]

Frank Broeze, in his investigations into the 'militancy and pragmatism' of maritime labour', noted that this dichotomy in terms of industrial strategy often soured relations between the dock unions leadership and the rank and file.[52] This may help explain why both these strands were adopted by the seamen's and dockers' unions. Indeed, this dual approach became their industrial relations *modus operandi*. The reasons are simply put: the leadership took the long-term view, seeking to build and strengthen the union generally and convince employers that they could deliver agreements that the labour force would adhere to. The rank and file, on the other hand, took the short-term view. If they had any industrial relations problems at the place of work, that was where the problem had to be solved. Once a ship had been discharged or loaded, it left the dock. Any problems associated with it or with its cargo, therefore, had to be solved while it was in the port, not after it had left. Direct action was thus a necessary industrial strategy for the docker, but it was one that the leadership had to control in order to show the employers that they in turn could control the dock labour force.[53]

The work of Taplin and Lovell illustrates the importance of the New Unionism to dock labour organisation, and this is borne out by the investigations of Raymond Brown on Hull, R. Bean on Liverpool, and M. J. Daunton on Cardiff.[54] They note that in some ports dock unionism was virtually wiped out in the employers' counter-attack in the early 1890s (both Hull and Cardiff, for example). A similar situation was to occur at Glasgow at that time. However, while the employers there were successful in weakening the NUDL at the port, the union survived. Indeed, Glasgow's two dock unions emerged intact from the period of counter-attack at the port. Trade unionism was sustained in most other ports too, but the forces of division within the dock labour force often made survival difficult and rivalry inevitable. At Cardiff, for instance, Daunton noted the extreme acrimony that existed between the coal tippers' union and the coal trimmers' union, and that tippers worked alongside blacklegs when the trimmers were on strike, with the opposite being the case when tippers were in dispute. There was also friction between those trimmers regularly employed and the more casual trimmers, a situation open to exploitation by the employers in times of dispute, when they too were used as blackleg labour.[55]

---

[51] Taplin, *Dockers Union*, chapters 5 and 6; see also Kenefick, 'A Historiographical and Comparative Survey', pp. 60–1.

[52] F. Broeze, 'Militancy and Pragmatism: An International Perspective on Maritime Labour, 1870 to 1914', *IRSH*, xxxvi, 3, 1991.

[53] Ibid., p. 165, see also W. Kenefick, 'The Struggle for Control: The Importance of the Great Unrest at Glasgow Harbour, 1911–1912', in W. Kenefick and A. McIvor (eds.), *The Roots of Red Clydeside 1910–1914: Labour Unrest and Industrial Relations in West Scotland* (Edinburgh, 1996).

[54] See Bean, 'The Liverpool Dock Strike of 1890'; M. J. Daunton, 'Inter-Union Relations on the Waterfront at Cardiff 1888–1914', *IRSH*, xxii, 3, 1977, and R. Brown, *Waterfront Organisations in Hull 1870 to 1900* (Hull, 1972).

[55] Daunton, 'Inter-Union Relations', pp. 362–3.

In all the battles with the employers, the docker always had to face the added problem of imported labour. Geoffrey Alderman, in his article 'The National Free Labour Association', notes that there was always an army of unemployed who, desperate for a job, were to be seen waiting around the fringes of any port. This is what the association's leader, William Collison, called the 'human material' necessary for strike-breaking.[56] Indeed, an attempt was made to split New Unionism on the Clyde, by using the old Harbour Labourers' Union as a type of free labour organisation during the employers' counter-attack there between 1890 and 1892. As the work of Kenneth Buckley has shown, survival was not assured at this time, and dock unions such as the Aberdeen Shore Workers were non-existent by the end of 1893, after less than ten short years in existence, and a similar fate befell the Aberdeen branch of the Seamen's Union.[57] The Shore Labourers Union at Aberdeen, as reported by the secretary J. C. Thompson to the Registrar of Friendly Societies in February 1893, had been 'defunct nearly twelve months' by then.[58] Around the same time the dockers' union at Hull was under serious attack from the combined forces of the Shipping Federation and the Free Labour Association and, as noted by Raymond Brown, was almost wiped out by the end of the 1890s, with Hull thereafter becoming a 'strong centre for free labour'.[59]

The rot was not to stop during the first decade of the twentieth century, for the situation got much worse. A severe cyclical downturn in the economy meant that the dockers' union in Scotland was under severe strain. Glasgow had its problems, as did Aberdeen, but it was Dundee which was to become Scotland's equivalent of Hull, when it emerged a free labour port around 1904–5.[60] What is clear, however, is that national organisations had emerged from the New Unionist period, and these would be more difficult to dismantle. Moreover, as William Beveridge touched on in 1909, perhaps the greatest legacy of this period was that the dockers would not forget this period in their history and 'the measure of respect that [they] gained from it'.[61] Once ordinary workers had found strength in combination, it would be difficult for them to give that up and so they would attempt once more in the future to rebuild their trade unions. This is what occurred at the time of the labour unrest in the years leading up to the First World War.

## The Labour Unrest, the First World War and the Interwar Years

By the time of the labour unrest of 1910–14 dockers' trade unions were again to become a force to be reckoned with after a period of considerable calm. According to John Lovell, the years between 1899 and 1907 for trade unionism in general,

---

[56] G. Alderman, 'The National Free Labour Association: A Case Study of Strikebreaking in the Late Nineteenth Century and Early Twentieth Century', *IRSH*, xxi, 1, 1976.

[57] K. Buckley, *Trade Unionism in Aberdeen, 1878 to 1900* (Aberdeen, 1955), p. 43.

[58] Scottish Record Office (SRO), FS, 7/86, Aberdeen Shore Labourers Union, report by J. C. Thompson to Registrar of Friendly Societies in Scotland, Feb. 1893.

[59] R. Brown *Waterfront Organisations in Hull 1870 to 1900* (Hull, 1972), pp. 90–1.

[60] *RC on the Poor Law 1909, evidence,* Mr John Malloch, Clerk to the Harbour Trustees, Dundee, p. 66.

[61] Beveridge, *Unemployment: A Problem for Industry*, p. 32.

were 'the quietest in the whole period from 1891'.[62] But it was the years 1911 to 1913 that were to mark the end of the industrial peace along the waterfront and again set in motion a series of national strikes similar to the period of the New Unionism some two decades before.[63]

The literature relating to the labour unrest and the waterfront is quite extensive for this period. All the works noted previously by Lovell, Taplin, Brown and Bean illustrate the central importance of the unrest to developments in labour relations along the British waterfront and to dock unionism in general. It is often argued that the main reason for the rise in unrest was the growth in trade experienced by the port transport industry from around 1910 onward. Philip J. Leng illustrates this with reference to the Welsh ports of Newport, Cardiff and Swansea,[64] and also indicates a considerable contribution to the unrest was made by the syndicalist movement in these locations.[65] However, it is difficult to assess the importance or significance of syndicalism elsewhere along the British water-front, particularly as E. J. Hunt argues that it had little support outside South Wales.[66] Indeed, even in South Wales, notes Leng, 'most rank and file dockers were more concerned with gaining higher wages than overthrowing capital', although clearly the same could not be said of their leadership (one Alf Cox being known locally as 'Tom Mann the Second').[67]

Hunt's position can be contrasted with that of Richard Price, who argued that syndicalism was by no means of negligible importance and 'had made deep inroads into virtually every major trade union by 1914'.[68] In relation to the waterfront, however, the cause of the unrest would seem to be an amalgam of factors, including political considerations. First, the period before the war was not only one of increased economic activity, it also created an extremely tight labour market. Thus, as Bean suggests, unemployment was no longer considered 'the best card in the pack' for keeping dock labour in its place.[69] In other words, strikers could not be so easily replaced by imported labour when tight labour conditions generally prevailed. This is what helped the employers in their counter-attack of the 1890s, but it was never really an option during the labour unrest.[70] Moreover, as Bean further suggests, the employers by that juncture wished to enter into joint negotiation with the trade unions. Therefore, for the first time in their history,

---

[62] J. Lovell, *British Trade Unions, 1875–1939* (1977), p. 41.

[63] Much literature has been published in relation to the 'labour unrest' of 1910–14, and all note the part played by the dockers and their allies the seamen. The following are just a few: Pelling, *History* (1992), pp. 126–9; J. Hinton, *Labour and Socialism: A History of the British Labour Movement, 1867–1974* (1983), chapter 5, 'The Labour Unrest', pp. 83–95; H. A. Clegg, *A History of British Trade Unions*, Vol. II (Oxford, 1985); J. E. Cronin, *Industrial Conflict in Modern Britain* (1979), chap. 5; E. Hobsbawm, *Labouring Men* (1968).

[64] P. J. Leng, *The Welsh Dockers* (Ormskirk, 1981), pp. 57–71.

[65] Ibid., p. 64.

[66] E. J. Hunt, *British Labour History* (1981), p. 329.

[67] Leng, *The Welsh Dockers*, p. 51.

[68] R. Price, *Labour in British Society* (1986), pp. 153–7.

[69] R. Bean, 'Employers Associations at the Port of Liverpool, 1890–1914, *IRSH*, xxi, 3, 1976, p. 366.

[70] W. Kenefick, *Ardrossan: The key to the Clyde. A Case Study of the Ardrossan Dock Strike, 1912 to 1913* (Irvine, 1993), pp. 15–18.

the employers moved to embrace a system of labour relations that they had previously and unequivocally rejected as an industrial strategy.[71]

Secondly, between 1900 and 1910 there was a period of prolonged recession, which caused considerable unemployment on the waterfront, and helped push down wages. Stagnating wages and the increased cost of living was regularly cited as one of the major causes of discontent – the verdict arrived at by the Parliamentary Committee of the STUC in 1913. Other bodies, such as the Board of Trade and the Glasgow Trades Council, argued similarly and produced statistics which illustrated these conclusions.[72] Therefore, as Eric Hobsbawm argued, stagnation or decline in real wages was probably one of the root causes of the unrest experienced in the years before the First World War.[73] It may prove to be the case that the combination of rising wages and greater employment opportunities along the waterfront contributed significantly to growth in trade union membership between 1910 and 1914, and that this was the main reason behind the rapid increase in membership. The dock unions were to become much stronger organisations than ever before and this seems to have been the main attraction to the rank and file, as well as low entry fees and a small weekly contribution. Their internal organisational structures, however, had changed little since the New Unionist period, particularly the relatively poor quality of benefits available to members.

Thirdly, as will be shown throughout this study, there was a considerable degree of solidarity shown between waterside workers at this time, and between the dockers and the seamen in particular. Hobsbawm sees the role of the seamen as the one enduring link between the New Unionist period and the labour unrest, with the seamen proving the 'main force of unity in both cases', a good illustration perhaps of strong political and inter-occupational solidarity.[74] This is a theme that is particularly significant throughout the period as a whole and in relation to the port transport industry in general. On Clydeside this theme seems to be even more important, with the Glasgow Trades Council and the seamen's union having particularly influential roles in the process of union building. It is probably the case, however, that all these factors, when combined with localised demands around the various ports throughout Britain, became welded into an aggregate cause of unrest, as illustrated in J. E. Cronin's analysis of the period.[75]

Whatever the reasons for the unrest during the years 1910 to 1914, there is little doubt that the development of trade unionism on the docks would never suffer a similar set-back to that experienced during the 1890s. As argued by Hobsbawm, 'after the great strikes and lockouts of 1911–12 trade unionism on the docks would never again relapse into insignificance'.[76] Indeed, in Glasgow it led to the rise of a

---

[71] Bean, 'Employers Associations', p. 366.
[72] Cited in R. Duncan and A. McIvor (eds.), *Militant Workers: Labour and Class Conflict on the Clyde. 1900–1950* (Edinburgh, 1992), pp. 86–9.
[73] Hobsbawm, *Industry and Empire*, p. 159.
[74] Hobsbawm, *Labouring Men*, p. 217; see also W. Kenefick, 'The Dock Strike: The Labour Unrest of 1910–1914, with particular reference to the Ardrossan Dock Strike, 1912–1913' (University of Strathclyde, unpublished B. A. dissertation, 1990).
[75] Cronin, *Industrial Conflict*; see also Kenefick, *Ardrossan*, pp. 19–20.
[76] Hobsbawm, *Labouring Men*, p. 204.

new union, the SUDL (who developed into a formidable organisation, and between 1911 and 1923 came to represent all the west of Scotland ports, including Bo'ness and Dundee on the east coast, and several north-west English ports.)[77] It also signalled a new and more positive phase in the continued development of Clyde-side dock unionism, and this is in no small measure due to the emergence of joint-collective bargaining arrangements between employers and the dock unions: the first time in the industrial relations history of the port transport sector of the British economy.

The effect of the Labour Unrest and the impact of the First World War proved a watershed in port transport history. According to Jonathan Schneer, the docker had made 'unprecedented improvements all round' during the war years, and there were substantial rises in wages, and a further increase in trade union membership. But most importantly, argues Schneer, by the end of the war the dockers' reputation had risen significantly in the estimation of the general British public.[78] The ease with which the Shaw Court of Inquiry in the Wages and Conditions of Dockers was set up – similar to the Sankey Commission on Mining – was in many ways an example of society's more positive view of the dockers. And this was further enhanced by the performance of Ernest Bevin throughout the Inquiry.[79] The most immediate gain in the industrial relations sphere was the establishment of a national joint agreement and joint regulation of the port transport industry.

It may be argued that another reason why the dockers were drawn into such agreements (or alternatively, were presented by the threat of wholesale state intervention if they refused) was due mostly to their industrial relations track record before war broke out. According to Schneer, it was during this period that many dockers were seen to be responding to syndicalist appeals by joining both the National Transport Workers Federation and what on face value seemed a formidable amalgamation of the Triple Industrial Alliance with the miners and the railway workers.[80] This tends to undermine Hunt's thesis regarding the effects of syndicalism, suggesting perhaps that Price is more correct in his analysis and that syndicalism did have 'widespread currency during the period 1912 through to 1922'.[81] Before the war the dockers' reputation for militancy was well-established, although there had been no further national conflicts along the British waterfront after 1912.[82] However, it must be stressed that the might and potential of the Triple

---

[77] Kenefick, *Ardrossan*, for brief biography of Joseph Houghton, General Secretary of the Scottish Union of Dock Labourers, pp. 22–3.

[78] J. Schneer, 'The War, the State, and the Workplace: The British Docker During 1914–1918', in J. E. Cronin and J. Schneer (eds.), *Social Conflict and Political Order in Modern Britain* (1982).

[79] As noted by K. Coates and T. Topham, *The Making of the Transport and General Workers Union*, Vol. 1, Parts 1 & II (Oxford, 1991), p. 728. Historians have properly accorded Bevin the credit for a notable triumph at the Enquiry. The references to his achievement at the Inquiry are extensive and because of this he earned the title 'the Dockers K.C.' (King's Council). This is referred to in many publications, not least F. Williams, *Ernest Bevin, Portrait of a great Englishman* (1952); A. Bullock *The Life and Times of Ernest Bevin* (1960), and Hobsbawm, *Labouring Men*, p. 218.

[80] Schneer, 'The British Docker During 1914–1918', pp. 97–8.

[81] Price, *Labour in British Society*, pp. 153–7.

[82] Pelling, *History*, p. 128.

Industrial Alliance was never tested and when the opportunity for a general strike finally presented itself the Alliance collapsed in failure, in April 1921, in the aftermath of the event known as 'Black Friday'. This episode exposed the NTWF's supposed syndicalist credentials because it had failed to mobilise support for the striking miners. Indeed, even if it could be argued that before 1914 the NTWF had syndicalist overtones, this position was soon abandoned, particularly in the light of its central role as a force for conciliation and arbitration during the First World War.

From 1911 onwards, however, the employers themselves were gradually moving towards embracing the idea of joint negotiation and conciliation. (Prior to the period of the labour unrest the employers had openly repudiated trade unionism.) Arthur McIvor has argued that this new strategy was intended to placate the labour force and 'to prevent workers being taken *en masse* by growing socialist and syndicalist ideologies'.[83] Many believed that such a tendency was very much in evidence at Glasgow, and was particularly apparent during the strikes of 1911 and 1912. Sometime earlier the *Glasgow Herald* reported on the words of William Raeburn, a Glasgow shipowner, that these were times during which 'syndicalism, accompanied by rioting and anarchy, had swept over the land'.[84] Within a few short months of Raeburn's statement the Glasgow docks were embroiled in a serious dispute. It brought the port of Glasgow to a standstill and was reported to be 'a slightly varied form of the old question of shop management'.[85] Thus McIvor's argument has some validity, even if we can argue today that the employers' fears then were more apparent than real.

It has been argued that the movement towards joint regulation stemmed from the need to control the workforce. As Bean suggests, one way strikes could be averted was to control the rank and file through procedural agreements. In this system, however, negotiated procedures not only differed between ports, but within ports, between different docks and wharves, and between different gangs handling different cargoes.[86] This multifarious system of regulation was thus particularly prone to strike. Therefore, as Bean argues, national joint negotiation was sought to 'reduce the incidence and unpredictability of strikes through the acceptance of procedural agreement'. This was done with the intention that the dock unions themselves, tied to the ideal of joint negotiation, would police the dock labour force and ensure that the spirit and intent of such agreements were not broken. To do this the dock unions would have to keep the rank and file's instinctive desires to strike in check.[87]

It would seem that before the war, despite some of the major conflicts that did take place between capital and labour during the labour unrest, industrial relations

---

[83] A. McIvor, 'Employers Organisations and Strike Breaking in Britain, 1911 to 1914', *IRSH*, xxix, 1, 1984, p. 12.

[84] *Glasgow Herald*, 23 Nov. 1911.

[85] *Glasgow Herald*, 29 Jan. 1912.

[86] J. Bean, 'Custom, Job Regulation and Dock Labour in Liverpool, 1911–1939', *IRSH*, xxvii, 3, 1982, pp. 272–3.

[87] Bean, 'Employers Associations', p. 377.

along the waterfront generally stabilised before 1914. After the outbreak of the First World War this trend continued as did the further development of 'bilateral and joint regulation' of the industry, which placed relations within the industry on a 'much more orderly and stable basis' than ever before.[88] Joint negotiation at this juncture existed in most major ports. Eric Hobsbawm notes that this development with the dockers' closest allies, the Seamen's and Firemen's Union, saw that union rapidly convert 'into a virtual company union', even before the war years.[89] It may be argued, in the aftermath of a particularly extended period of militancy, that the same was occurring within the dock unions.[90] Despite the previous criticisms of the NTWF, however, it did unite the majority of transport workers under the auspices of one central organisation, and for the dock labour force in Britain helped them to develop a national perspective. This was to prove strategically important for 'nearly every organised docker in Britain'. It was a constant reminder to the government that 'labour's support during the war remained crucial'.[91]

## The Problems of the Interwar Years

In 1920 the Shaw Court of Inquiry delivered their condemnation of the abuses of the port system – specifically the casual system of employment – and the failures of the employers on profits, wages and working conditions. This Enquiry also further illustrated the central importance of the NTWF to the docker and the role of Ernest Bevin. He presented a formidable case on behalf of the dock workers as the representative of the NFTW, and leader of the large Dock, Wharf, Riverside and General Labourers Union (DWRGLU). This public Court of Inquiry was to prove of considerable value to the docker generally, but to Bevin's reputation in particular. Ken Coates and Tony Topham argue strongly that the enquiry was 'a triumphant affirmation of the demands for civilised standards and bargaining rights in the port transport industry' – a conclusion which was generally accepted by both the state and the public at large. At this point, public support for the dockers had never been so strong.[92] The main objectives of the NTWF were first, to force the industry to recognise the need for the registration of dockers (primarily to cut the number of men swelling the dockers' ranks and who operated along the fringes, or in the margins, of the industry, thus exacerbating underemployment along the waterfront); secondly, to force the employers to pay maintenance to the workforce when not employed (in order to support the numbers, they argued, were necessary to operate the port transport industry efficiently); and finally, to put an end to the system of casualism which, it was argued, was at the root of the unemployment problem haunting the industry.

The Shaw Inquiry report found in favour of these aspects of the NTWF case, but

---

[88] Bean, 'Employers Associations', pp. 358–9.
[89] Hobsbawm, *Labouring Men*, p. 217.
[90] Kenefick, *Ardrossan*, pp. 17–18, which analyses the similarities between the developments taking place within the seamen's union and those of the docker's unions, particularly on Clydeside.
[91] Schneer, 'The British Docker During 1914–1918', pp. 108–9.
[92] Coates and Topham, *Transport and General Workers Union*, p. 727.

future events and the attitude of the dock labour force itself dictated that they would only ever be partially implemented. It was only by the outbreak of World War Two that registration, for example, was finally introduced in any compulsory form, and other outstanding anomalies finally laid to rest. Another important plank of the NTWF case, however, was the attempt to win favour for the concept of Joint Industrial Council (NJC) status for the industry, and to insist that the employers themselves be coerced into a national association for the purposes of agreeing nationally negotiated guidelines. Both these ends were achieved and were arguably to prove the most long lasting legacies of the Shaw Inquiry of 1920.[93]

The first National Agreement was signed on 5 May 1920 under the auspices of the Joint Council of the Transport Industry, and negotiated between the National Council of Port Labour Employees and the NTWF. Thereafter, this agreement was to accommodate all further changes relating to port work and dockers' pay from then on until the last agreement was signed on 5 June 1967 (which preceded the final and complete decasualisation of the dock labour force in September 1967).[94] Between the findings of the Shaw Inquiry and the signing of the First National Agreement, further impetus gathered towards the ideal of amalgamating all the transport unions, particularly the dock unions. This was achieved in 1922, and by 1924 the TGWU had assumed the mantle of the leading, and for a time the only, negotiating body within the NJC for the port transport industry. This development in turn inevitably led to the decline and eventual disintegration of the NTWF.

If it can be argued that 1920 was to prove a 'pivotal' year in the history of the dock labour force in Britain, therefore, it can be claimed with some certainty that this year was to prove an equally important bench mark for the dock labour force at Glasgow. The headlong push towards amalgamation was to create a bitter legacy at Glasgow which was destined to seriously sour relations between, what became, the Glasgow Docks Branch of the TGWU (previously the Glasgow members of the SUDL) and the executive of the TGWU, during the years 1920 to 1932.

But was it mere coincidence that this period of instability followed the amalgamation of the individual dock unions within the Transport and General Workers Union during and after 1922? Indeed, in many of the strikes and disputes of this period, Ernest Bevin himself was often portrayed as the leading offender in denying the docker greater democracy and autonomy at local level. This was very much the case at Glasgow and the issue of trade union democracy was to prove the catalyst for the eventual secession of the Glasgow dockers from the TGWU. Other problems arose because of the issue of registration and decasualisation, which Bevin was endeavouring to impose on the docks nationally during the interwar years, but more generally it was concern over London interference in local affairs that was the cause of most difficulties.

The problem with the literature on the dock industry is that such incidents are not considered in great detail in relation to Scotland, even in such seminal works as

[93] Ibid., p. 728.
[94] *National Agreement*, 5 May 1920, 'and subsequent Agreements in modification thereof between the National Association of Port Employers and the TGWU and other Signatory Unions' (1969); see First Schedule, Part 1, p. 6, for list of ports covered by agreement.

David Wilson's *Dockers: The Impact of Industrial Change* (1972), or Gordon Phillips and Noel Whiteside's excellent study, *Casual Labour: The Unemployment Question in the Port Transport Industry 1880–1970* (1985). It is true that these are industry-wide investigations and perhaps their greatest contribution to the historiography is that they recognise the significance of the British docker's own concept of history, and how this was to dictate the docker's reactions to the changes taking place within the port transport industry. It is also the case that the literature that does exist seldom strays far beyond the formation of the TGWU in 1922. In Eric Taplin's book, for example, he finishes with the amalgamation of the NUDL into the TGWU, while John Lovell's study concludes some time earlier in 1914, and many other books and articles noted in this chapter follow a similar chronology.

It is clear that a separate study of Clydeside and the Port of Glasgow is necessary in order to redress the imbalance in the literature which favours English-based accounts. The many themes that have emerged through these investigations have shown that there are common threads running right through the port transport system as a whole, and that these links unite the great majority of dockers across the many ports, harbours, docks and wharves spread extensively across the great length of the British waterfront. Individual studies have also shown, however, that there is much to divide the docker, not only from port to port, but within a given port, and within similar areas of occupation. What we are ultimately witnessing is an illustration of the manner in which each distinctive dock group could and did generated its own set of cultural values. This is what happened at Glasgow with the Irish and the Scottish Highlanders, which is not part of the equation in any English context, and this fact alone is justification enough to pursue an investigation of the Scottish dimensions of dock life and work. In the final analysis, this study should be seen as an attempt to generate a counterweight to the present Anglocentric line of historical enquiry that is all too apparent within the current historiography of docks and dock labour in Britain.

# CHAPTER TWO

# The Port Industry in Britain: A General Overview

Before studying dock life in Glasgow and Clydeside, it is first essential to understand the nature of the industry, and to consider opinions upon dock life and the operations of the port transport industry in general. Several factors must therefore be considered, particularly those that helped unite the dockers, but also those that created division among them. In this sense, dockers from London often shared much with those from Glasgow, or Liverpool; they in turn shared much with others outside Britain from Antwerp to Marseilles, or from Hamburg to New York. However, not all ports operated on the same basis. For example, at London and Hull much of the work was executed overside a ship onto lighters or barges tied-up alongside on the riverside. Thereafter the goods handled were taken along the river to be transferred into warehouses for sorting and storage before they reached their final destination. We can contrast this with Glasgow. According to the testimony of one Glasgow stevedore in 1920:

> The port of Glasgow has no docks with gates, the tide flows in and out of the docks, and ships are affected by the rise and fall of the tide continually. Cargo is all loaded from the quay, with a few exceptions; there is practically no barge work; there is a little, but it is a mere trifle. The cargo is delivered and taken away from the quay when discharged, or brought previously to loading by cart and partly by rail in the case of general cargo. Mineral traffic is brought in entirely by rail. The sheds are purely transit sheds. There are no warehouses adjacent to the docks. The docks themselves are open to the roadways, whereas in other ports the docks are often enclosed. There are no dock gates for the most part and where there are gates they are seldom closed. Therefore the men go into the docks and to the ship on which they know they are going to be employed – they do not assemble outside the docks themselves. Only Rothesay dock is the exception.[1]

This was considered to be the main difference between Glasgow and other ports. The biggest problem was the tide, which could rise and fall anything between 12 and 15 feet. This not only made loading or unloading more difficult, and dangerous, but it could also increase turn-round times. Special staging equipment was available (essentially planks 36 foot-long, 18 inches-broad and 6 inches-thick)

---

[1] Shaw Inquiry, i, testimony, J. S. Spencer, Glasgow Stevedore, Principal of James S. Spencer and Company, p. 269.

which helped compensate for the varying water level but was thought more useful on smaller classes of vessels. On larger vessels this type of equipment was too dangerous, as the angle of rise was often too great for it to be effective. In short, the method was both hazardous and ineffectual.

The difference in ship size was also important as this determined the type of operation prevalent at a particular port. For example, large liners ran to strict timetables and therefore required a more regular workforce to service their needs, in contrast to the coasting trade, which did not run on regular lines. The latter, however, usually accounted for the bulk of employment in most ports and Glasgow was no exception. But as the Standing Advisory Committee of the Port Transport Industry pointed out, the irregular nature of the trade also meant irregularity of employment, and employment in the industry depended on many factors, chiefly:

> The uncertain and irregular arrival of vessels due to climatic conditions and unforeseen detention in other ports, the seasonal and cyclical fluctuation of world trade, the actions of tides, and the delays in the delivery of cargoes for shipment; and the necessity for a "turn-round" of vessels in the shortest possible time which frequently arises from these causes.[2]

There was competition for labour, resources and quayspace, and with a great variety of goods requiring different handling methods (and these differed depended on conditions peculiar to a particular port), in turn created an industry which at times verged on virtual chaos.

The nature and growth of the port transport industry was neither uniform nor consistent, and the same can be said of the historical growth of particular ports. Time lags are apparent, some ports having a longer operational history than others, or diminishing in status as other ports experienced greater growth – such as Greenock, for a time, in relation to Glasgow by the late nineteenth century.[3] Much of this can be attributed to the erratic and irregular nature of the economy as it developed over time, and the demand for different goods. This also affected investment and improvement (or the lack of it) and the extent of modernisation and mechanisation within a given port at particular points in time. When steam power became the dominant motive force in the economy, it led to increased demand for coal and the construction of coal ports to handle such goods. The combined needs of rail and steam, for example, virtually created the ports of Methil and Hartlepool.[4]

Steam power also allowed for the construction of larger seagoing vessels and the gradual replacement of the sailing ship. All such developments had a marked effect on Britain's ports and dock life in particular, and over time this combined dynamic created an incredible diversity. Thus, the dockers who worked in particular ports, or particular locations within a port, could develop practices peculiar to those

---

[2] PRO, LAB 101/18, *Port Transport Memorandum*, 'Introduction', para. 1. p. 1.
[3] Jackson, *Archaeology of Ports*, see preface.
[4] Kenefick, *Ardrossan*, p. 2.

locations. Greater diversity arose also from the product that some dockers generally handled; many became specialisms, such as timber and grain, which in turn saw the generation of further customs and practices peculiar to those trades.

## Diversity of Employment and Casualism

The waterfront did in fact create an endless array of specialisms and, as argued by John Lovell, this also led to a tradition of immobility among the dock labour force. This would have been even more the case in a port such as Glasgow, where there were no dock gates and the labour force simply gathered alongside the vessel they hoped to work on: very different from a port such as London where the men gathered at specific points around the harbour. In other cases the dockers began to work with one product and seldom any other, which in turn not only fostered a feeling of security, but more importantly promoted a notion of status. According to Lovell, this development was 'broadly true of port workers as a whole'. The docker who tended to work with one product became attached to the employer who handled that commodity, and thus generally remained within the sphere of influence of that product – whether it was contained within one dock, wharf, quay, or even a particular berth. This attitude was shared by much of the labour force, and had an impact on the work process at an extremely localised level, which in no small part accounted for dockers well-earned reputation for immobility. Port life in this way became stratified into what amounted to a caste system based on definition of function, a basic example of which would be the division between ship and shore work, or the product handled, such as coaltrimming, and the specialisation ascribed to that.[5]

Further consideration has also to be given to the ports which operated on a seasonal basis, like Dundee, and those which operated more regularly, such as Glasgow. Similarly, some trades operated more regularly than others. The timber trade was severely hampered by winter weather and the freezing over of the Baltic and Canadian sea-passages, which seriously affected the work done by the timber dockers.[6] Steam propulsion did, however, smooth out some of the irregularities in this trade. As well as helping to level out the work available along the waterfront throughout the year, it also favoured quay work over ship work, particularly in the preparation of cargo for loading, or the second phase of discharging cargo from quayside to wagons, or storage.[7] Steam also brought about change in relation to the size of ship that was to be worked on, and lent itself easily to mechanical adaptation, which led to the rapid expansion in bulk handling of cargoes such as coal, minerals or grain. However, this affected the deep-sea lines much more than the coastal trade.

Those who worked on the smaller vessels were considered to have greater skills, particularly in loading. The coal trimmers, for example, worked mainly on the

---

[5] Lovell, *Stevedores and Dockers*, pp. 33–4.

[6] *RC on the Poor Laws*, 1909, paragraph 266.

[7] Lovell, *Stevedores and Dockers*, p. 41.

smaller vessels and their skill was to ensure that the vessel remained well balanced. The more mechanised areas of the trade did not require these skills to the same extent, and the coal trimmers only boarded a vessel once it had been mechanically loaded up to a given level. The stevedore, or shipworker, was also considered to be more skilled as his task was to ensure the safe stowage of goods within the hold of a vessel, while also ensuring it was in good trim.

It can be argued that the development of the bulk trades created more employment in the long term – in as much as new handling methods and larger vessels produced a significant rise in tonnage shipped in absolute terms. Conversely, it can equally be argued that it displaced labour in the short term, led to a degree of de-skilling within that group of dockers who traditionally handled such material, generated speed-up at the point of production, and exacerbated the worst effects of the casual system of employment. Technological changes in the use of steam power, or the implantation of hydraulic and electrical appliances (just even one appliance such as the crane) did replace large numbers of men.[8] The introduction of the grain elevator in Liverpool in the late 1880s and early 1890s, noted R. Bean, could mean an eightfold reduction in the numbers who previously worked this particular cargo.[9] In Glasgow, in the first decade of the twentieth century, the picture was little different, and machinery was to prove a major cause of unemployment on the docks. For example, one 'hydraulic windlass' with one operator could do the job previously executed by a dozen men.[10] However, such innovations, as Gordon Jackson has pointed out, were unevenly applied and were introduced in different ports at different times. Their impact was thus not uniformly felt throughout the industry as a whole, or, indeed, one particular point in time.[11]

The general experience of dock work differed considerably from port to port, dock to dock, between ship and shore, and in the handling methods associated with different products. Indeed, the historical development of the port transport system made this unavoidable. It may well be that this 'organised chaos' was the only way in which the system could expect to operate. As Jackson argued, if the needs of the industry were geared to the needs of the economy, and firmly linked to irregularity in patterns of demand, then the port industry was, in a sense, the capitalist enterprise economy in microcosm.[12]

With a rapid expansion of trade in the nineteenth century, and the growing dynamic of steam, the industry was set to develop further its complicated system of operation, and from this would develop an irregular pattern of employment based on the casual system. And the development of industrial relations within the industry was to prove no less complicated. As noted by David Wilson:

[8] Ibid., p. 41.

[9] Bean, 'The Liverpool Dock Strike of 1890', p. 59.

[10] *Royal Commission on Poor Laws Relating to Unemployment, Minutes of Evidence*, ix (*PP*, 1910, xlix, Cd 5068), testimony of James Ferguson, Indoor Assistant Inspector of Poor for the Parish of Glasgow, p. 50.

[11] Jackson, *Archaeology of Ports*, pp. 96–103.

[12] From discussion with Gordon Jackson, University of Strathclyde, Sep. 1993.

the shape of industrial relations in dockland has been determined by the haphazard growth of the ports and the correspondingly haphazard structure of employment and trade unionism.[13]

What follows in this chapter is an analysis of the development of the casual system and the generation of traditional values and the customs and practices that sprang from it. It also investigates how this was to affect the port transport industry as a whole. Other factors are important, such as the impact of mechanisation, the cultural characteristics and ethnic composition of the dock labour force – and its numerical growth and function. But these will be addressed in later chapters. Much of the analysis in this and subsequent chapters is drawn from sources and materials which illustrate the experiences of English ports and English dockers. This raises the question of whether such an approach helps to shed some light on the experience of the Scottish docker? Indeed, given the lack of good documentary sources concerning the Scottish dock labour force, a comparative approach may be the only way to proceed with this type of research. The fact that many studies do not focus principally on Scottish port life does not mean that nothing can be gained from such an analysis. Some factors will affect all dockers, others differentiate them, but, in the final analysis, it is only through a comparative approach that such factors become clearly distinguished.

## The Dock Labour Force: An Occupational Community

According to a recent study by Stephen Hill, the docker formed part of a 'distinct, closed, isolated mass, almost a race apart, living in their own separate communities – the coal patch, the ship, the waterfront district'.[14] Moreover, 'they were typically inward looking and isolated' and, being insulated from the dominant social ideology, 'often generated their own sub-cultural values in opposition'.[15] Hill defined this type of social structure as an 'occupational community'. Even by the 1960s, when Hill's investigations took place, he recognised that this tendency was still very much apparent within the ranks of the dock labour force. For example, the dock community was still based largely on kinship ties, and that 'direct father-son inheritance' in terms of employment accounted for 67% of the dockers he had interviewed, and among foremen accounted for 75%.[16] Furthermore, other categories of relatives were apparent, such as 'brothers, fathers and brothers-in-law', who accounted for a large number of the remainder of Hill's survey.[17] Thus, he suggested, this type of 'occupational community' linked through kinship also helped 'the transmission of occupational values and norms, particularly in the past when the docking community was even more closely knit'.[18]

John Lovell found the same patterns at London docks. Partly, this 'occupational

[13] David Wilson, *The Dockers: The Impact of Industrial Change* (1972), p. 29.
[14] Stephen Hill, *The Dockers: Class and Tradition in London* (1976), p. 163.
[15] Ibid., p. 164.
[16] Ibid., p. 174.
[17] Ibid., p. 175.
[18] Ibid., p. 200.

community' (as defined by Hill) could, in the London context, be defined too as a 'cultural community', and much of this was due to the influence of the Irish within the dock industry. Even as early as the mid-eighteenth century, Lovell estimated that around two-thirds of the men discharging coal boats at London were Irish. A century later the Irish were still main players in the 'loading and discharging of ships, and the principal hard work further down the river'. Lovell also noted the 'clannish' nature of the Irish, that they gravitated to specific localities around London docks, and passed their work on from father to son:

> They lived and worked in self-contained communities, quite apart from other workers in neighbouring districts and trades . . . they accentuated the tendency for the waterside labour force to become fragmented into little isolated groups, between whom there was little contact or co-operation . . . no doubt the Irish immigration contributed also to this effect.[19]

The question of the Irish and their influence on dock life will be considered at some length in Chapter 5. Their role is acknowledged here in order to argue the case for the ease with which certain groups of dockers could develop an virtual homogeneous insularity of character.

'Solidity of institutional and occupational conservatism': this is how Gordon Phillips and Noel Whiteside described the dockers' community, in their study of casualism and its attendant problems. They argued that the dockers' attachment to the traditions of the past was based on casualism and that this attachment then became the hallmark of the industry as a whole and the docking community in particular.[20] In many respects, the whole matter of the waterfront and the docker's life revolves around this question and can be seen from two different points of view. On the one hand, there is the view of those from outside the industry who attempted investigations of dock work and the docker and, on the other, that of the docker himself in relation to his own work and social environment. The differences are clear in the docker's defence of the system and his reactions to the proposals of outsiders attempting to introduce change.

Casualism as a method of recruitment only finally changed at the time of Stephen Hill's survey in the late 1960s. Prior to that it had always been the main method of recruitment, and many of the traditions, customs and practices that were generated by this system of engagement essentially became codified in the general philosophy of the industry as it developed in the latter half of the nineteenth century. It was embraced by the dock labour force and became the basis for their way of life. As noted in another investigation of the dock community in the 1950s: 'It has been generally recognised for many years that the social characteristics of the docker are intimately related to the system of casual employment'.[21]

The docker was highly suspicious of those from outside the industry, but also of some within the docking community. For Lovell, the port worker was justified in his

---

[19] Lovell, *Stevedores and Dockers*, pp. 57–8.
[20] G. Phillips and N. Whiteside, *Casual Labour: The Underemployment Question in the Port Transport Industry 1880–1970* (Oxford, 1985), p. 5.
[21] Simey, *The Dock Worker*, p. 5.

resentment of the public's perceptions of waterside society. However, he also stresses that it was not always easy for the public to distinguish the regular worker from the loafer, as the position of each had become blurred over the years.[22] It is entirely possible that one reason for this confusion was a lack of understanding of what dock work was and ignorance of how the docker actually functioned. This then raises another important point: what is dock work and what conditions of employment describes a man who classifies himself as a "docker"? A clear definition can be found within the terms of reference for The Shaw Court of Inquiry, 1920, where dockers are defined as, 'all workers loading and discharging general cargo and handling same at quays, wharves, overside and in warehouses, and at docks and wharves'.[23]

The Shaw Inquiry made a specific distinction between the dock worker and others employed in port work, such as cranemen, warehouse men, machine operators, checkers and weighers (of cargo) and necessary maintenance staff. Dock work can, therefore, be narrowed down to those who actually handled cargo and goods – either on ship or on shore, or overside onto lighters or barges. Others excluded from dock work along the quays would be carters and porters. As Charles Booth was also to note, there was a considerable gulf between those who serviced the dock industry, such as the porter, or the craneman, and those who laboured in it. The main differences between the two were not only gauged in employment terms (the docker was casually employed, the dock servant was permanently employed), but in social terms too. The latter had a different code of dress from the docker and lived in better-quality housing, in districts more distant and distinct from the general docking community.[24]

Booth's definition of dock work differed little from that of the later 1920 enquiry. The question of skill is another matter entirely, however. But Booth's distinction of function, in his description of the structure of the dock industry at London in the 1880s, is probably an adequate illustration of the basic nature of dock work and one that can be applied to other ports. The basic structure of a dock labour force of the type employed in a port such as Glasgow would not differ much from that of Liverpool or London. In many respects these different ports share this common characteristic, although in London there would be more work done on the river, which was generally known in the trade as lighterage. While it is essential to note the differences from port to port, it is also useful to note the similarities.

Charles Booth's outline of the structure of the dock labour force can be seen in Table 2.1. But Booth also noted other categories of work that were not generally undertaken by dockers at London. One was the stowage of export cargo, work that was executed by the stevedores, undoubtedly the most skilled of the dock labour force. Another was the handling of coals for export and ballast. For the most part this structure holds well for a port such as Glasgow, but there are some major

[22] Lovell, *Stevedores and Dockers*, p. 32.
[23] Shaw Inquiry, i, p. iii and xviii.
[24] Booth, *Life and Labour*, p. 394.

differences. As there was less warehousing along Glasgow's waterfront, most cargo was discharged onto the quays, or loaded from the quays. It also had to be dealt with quickly in order to avoid quayside congestion. In these circumstances there would have been a greater need for more onshore, or quayside, labour.

---

**Table 2.1:** *Definition of the Function of the London Docker*

---

(1) Import Through Docks.
    [a]   Discharging from onboard ship in dock.
    [b]   Receiving on quay and passing into warehouse.
    [c]   Receiving and stowing into lighters.
    [d]   Handling in warehouse.

(2) Imports Through Wharves (same as above).
    [a]   Discharging from onboard ship in dock.
    [b]   Receiving on quay and passing into warehouse.
    [c]   Receiving and stowing into lighters.
    [d]   Handling in warehouse.

(3) Import "overside" from ships lying in stream.

(4) Export work – both dock and wharf – Handling goods on quay in preparation for the stevedores.

---

**Source:** *Life and Labour of the People of London* (Vol. vii, Part v, p. 400).

The other major difference between London and Glasgow – one which Glasgow shares with Liverpool – was the function of the stevedore. While there is no disputing the skill ascribed to the work done by this class of worker, there are significant variations in function to be found between the two ports. The stevedore in Glasgow was in fact an employer in his own right (or a Principal Employing Agent for the larger shipping firms), who would take on dockers to handle particular cargo. The stevedore was paid by the ton, and he was responsible for paying the men he engaged. He was not a sub-contractor, although this class of employers existed at Glasgow as elsewhere, but a licensed employer of men. The men he regularly employed were known simply as shipworkers and this was the main distinction as it operated in Glasgow.[25] In London, while the stevedore was still considered to be the most skilled of the dock labour force, he was nevertheless employed in the same way as the docker, although the London stevedore may have occasionally functioned as an employing sub-contractor.

Despite the differences that existed between them, all dockers were viewed as a singularly distinctive group in relation to other port service workers. The *Report into*

---

[25] *RC on Poor Laws*, ix, 1910, evidence, William Hannay Raeburn, Q. 89785.

*the Earnings and Hours of Labour*, 1906, illustrates perfectly this perceived division as viewed by those from outside the industry. The report only ever considered the conditions of the service section of the industry, stating categorically that 'dock and wharf labour, employed in the loading and discharging of ships', were not included in any calculations regarding hours worked and related earnings.[26] Thus the great mass of ordinary dockers were left out of such considerations and, despite the fact that this group accounted for a massive majority of dock workers, they never received the recognition they deserved, not until the First World War and the subsequent Shaw Inquiry. Up until this time the docker could be said to be something of a mystery to the average citizen. This being so, it is little wonder that dockers' communities became isolated and the dockers distrustful and wary of all except those with whom they shared their lives and work.

In industrial relations terms there developed another peculiar (but not wholly unpredictable) response by the dockers to all the forces that touched on their spheres of interests. Whether it was to be in relations with government bodies (as occurred during the First World War), employers' organisations or trade unions formed to defend the docker, the docker gained a reputation for being a rather ambivalent and mysterious creature. This was commented on, possibly unintentionally, in Booth's investigations, where he described the ordinary docker as 'a somewhat unimaginable mixture of English and Irish blood'. As for the organised docker, he was 'ultra democratic' on the one hand, while clinging to 'an absolute conservatism of old custom and local privilege' on the other. Not only did they battle with their employers, and among themselves, 'they were ever jealous of the authority of their leaders'.[27]

What Booth unwittingly recognised was the independent nature of the docker, and that this was born out of the gamble for employment demanded of the docker because of the casual system. What he also implicitly touched on were some of the major difficulties which would become the hallmark of the docker's relations with both his employer and his union; difficulties that placed industrial relations at the docks on a three-cornered footing. For example, to the docker industrial relations amounted to a defence of his way of life, against all comers, whether is was the employers, the dock trade unions, the state, or even wider society itself. These were the distinguishable characteristics associated with the docker around the early twentieth century and, as noted by Simey in his survey of the 1950s, 'over fifty years later they still retained their colour and vitality'.[28] Very little had in fact changed in the intervening period except, perhaps, that the dock labour force was even more committed to the defence of its traditions, customs and privileges.

Even the changes imposed on the dock industry by the state during the Second World War, or the Dock Labour Scheme introduced in 1947, never fundamentally altered the basic structure of industrial relations or the system of labour recruitment. The period after the Second World War brought about 'modest change', but

---

[26] *Report of an Enquiry by the Board of Trade into the Earnings and Hours of Labour of Working People in the United Kingdom*, viii, Harbour and Dock Services, 1906 (*PP*, 1912–13, cviii, Cd 6556), p. 259.

[27] Booth, *Life and Labour*, p. 404.

[28] Simey, *The Dock Worker*, p. 4.

in general much remained the same.[29] In order to better understand why change within the port transport industry was 'so modest' it is necessary in the first instance to place it in a firm historical perspective; and, secondly, to consider the nature of the casual system of employment and how the system operated. It may then be possible to offer an explanation as to why the system was to survive almost intact throughout the period under investigation.

*The Problems with the Casual System: Citizenship and Conformity versus Individual Liberty*

The dock industry has always attracted a degree of attention from society at large. Writing of the 1960s and 1970s, Michael P. Jackson noted that at that time academics, politicians and the public alike seemed intrigued by the question of labour relations on the docks. 'Hardly a week has gone by', he commented, 'without one or other of these groups noting the position at the docks.' Some observations considered the propensity for unofficial strike activity, the extent of inter-union conflict in the industry, and the dockers' attitude to modernisation; all of which were interminable causes of dispute. Top of this list, however, was the nature of employment in the industry.[30] At this juncture decasualisation had only recently been achieved after many years of striving to change the system, stretching back to the first real attempts to regulate employment at Liverpool docks in 1912.[31]

Arguments for change to the system of employment at the docks, however, had a longer history than the implementation of the first working scheme to decasualise at Liverpool in 1912. Nevertheless, even when fundamental changes did take place (wholesale decasualisation was finally imposed on the industry in 1967), many traditional features of dockside work were still preserved. According to Phillips and Whiteside, such a situation made the whole question of work and industrial relations on the docks 'difficult to understand':

> It represents, to the student of social policy, a signal failure of social reform, and to the student of industrial relations an equally outstanding instance of the failure of organised collective bargaining.[32]

Historically, no matter what account of the docks is considered, the main problem associated with the industry was invariably identified as stemming from the system of employment: casualism! And there is little deviance from the central theme. Put simply: 'the casual system [was] the root of most of the difficulties experienced in the dock industry'. The underlying factor associated with casualism, and therefore a

---

[29] Phillips and Whiteside, *Casual Labour*, p. 4.
[30] M. P. Jackson, *Labour relations at the Docks* (Westmead, 1973), p. 1.
[31] Hilton, *Are Trade Unions Obstructive*, p. 126. The Liverpool Scheme was the oldest in the country. Its main aim, among other purposes, was to 'restrict the supply of dock labour to those who genuinely followed the trade'. Thus the numbers seeking work at the docks would be cut back and a greater degree of regularity of work for the 'genuine dock labour force' would ensue. This scheme therefore, offered one model of decasualisation.
[32] Phillips and Whiteside, *Casual Labour*, pp. 4–5.

major reason for advocating change, was that it rendered those who worked in that manner inefficient and unable to discharge their duties as proper citizens.

This concept of 'citizenship' embodied the values held by those who investigated the docker's world.[33] But the docker cared little for society's concept of 'citizenship', particularly if this meant tampering with the casual system and all the traditions and customs that were generated by it. Casualism was viewed by the docker, in the words of Eleanor Rathbone, 'as giving him a sense of being his own master'.[34] This theme was later taken up by the Shaw Inquiry, when it reported 'that many dockers had come to view day labour as a sign of independence' and that this 'habit of thinking' had to be changed and the system of casualism 'torn up by the roots'.[35]

As Phillips and Whiteside argue, however, any social or economic critique of casualism was bound to founder on the rocks of conservatism and tradition. Extending the argument previously developed by Rathbone, and the later Shaw Inquiry, they described the dockers' attachment to casualism in the following terms:

> The casual system freed the docker from the necessity to work a continuous six day week, at the same time offering him the opportunity of relatively high earnings for irregular spells of employment. To many men these arrangements had a strong appeal. A traditional, almost pre-industrial rhythm of work and leisure persisted on the waterside, the more prized because it allowed the labourer a measure of control over the disposition of his time and effort.[36]

It was this 'pre-industrial rhythm' that upset most of the investigators of dock work. This in turn generated the idea that as long as this persisted the docker was not a fully functional citizen, in so far as his life and work did not conform to recognised social norms.

It must also be stressed that many dockers could live well on irregular earnings, when these were supplemented by frequent spells of overtime. Others had traditionally more regular access to work and, as stated by Ernest Bevin to the 1920 Shaw Inquiry, 'expected and received most work in any case'. In this instance he was speaking directly of the wages and work at the port of Glasgow. Bevin also stressed, however, that these estimates were based on the earnings of the ten most regularly employed gangs of dockers (of indeterminate size) and could not be accepted as evidence of average earnings. In many respects, Bevin was correct in as much as these ten gangs could have numbered anything from forty men to around 200,[37]

[33] Ibid.

[34] Simey, *The Dock Worker*, p. 10.

[35] Shaw Inquiry, i, paragraph 17.

[36] Phillips and Whiteside, *Casual Labour*, p. 33.

[37] Shaw Inquiry, ii. Estimates of gang sizes vary considerably from between 4 to 8 on average, for stevedoring work, to gangs of 19 and upwards in the mineral trade: see *Appendix* No 75 p. 85 (Clause 43), Agreement between J. S. Spencer, Stevedore, and the Scottish Union of Dock Labourers, for the Port of Glasgow (Apr. 1919), for estimates involving stevedoring gangs. For mineral gangs, see *Appendix* No 91 p. 105; statement by Mr D. Hopkins, Mineral Traffic Superintendent of the Clyde Navigation Trust.

depending on the cargo handled and the size of gang normally associated with that type of work.[38] The question of wages will be considered later, but while it may be argued that extensive poverty within the dock labour force was often more apparent than real, there is little doubt that for many poverty was a regular condition. This would be even more the case in times of economic depression, when even more men would be found seeking work at the docks. When this happened available employment was even more thinly spread.

## *Defence of the Casual System of Employment: The Problem of Changing an Industrial Consensus*

Society could not accept the casual system or the economic and moral corruption created through its operation. It was also clearly linked with poverty and this led Sydney and Beatrice Webb to conclude that casualism was the 'main cause of pauperism'.[39] Thus we find growing support for the decasualisation of the dock industry from the late nineteenth century onwards, in as much as 'the implications of the problem upon the social and industrial well-being of the community in general were becoming more and more recognised.'[40] But these were for 'purely social reasons', rather than arguments based on any specific economic rationale: except to note that the burden of the casual system was being borne by the national economy and not by the industry itself. Consequently, the Shaw Inquiry, in a sense codifying the problem based on the evidence presented to them by Ernest Bevin, concluded accordingly:

> The Court [Shaw Inquiry] is of the opinion that labour frequently or constantly underemployed is injurious to the interests of the worker, the ports, and the public, and that it is discreditable to society . . . If men were merely the spare parts of an industrial machine, this callous reckoning might be appropriate: but society will not tolerate much longer the continuance of the employment of human beings along these lines.[41]

But who was to blame for the development of this system? The Shaw Inquiry noted that the system was a 'convenience' to the authorities who operated the ports, and the employers who operated within them, and that it was they who needed an 'easily tapped reservoir of employment'. The employers for their part had always argued that the casual system was necessary to the efficient operation of the port system. Indeed, there is some justification for this line of argument and this point is accepted by most observers. Lascelles and Bullock, writing in the early 1920s posited:

> that the port system necessarily depends on the existence in each port of a pool of available labour sufficient to meet the demands of the port on the

---

[38] The total dock labour force at Glasgow in 1920 was estimated at 8,470, see Ibid., *Appendix* No 77 p. 90.
[39] S. and B. Webb (eds.) *The Public Organisation of the Labour Market*, p. 194.
[40] PRO, LAB 101/18, *Port Transport Memorandum*, 'Introduction', para. 2. P. 1.
[41] Shaw Inquiry, i, pp. 8–9.

busiest day, with the result that on all other days there must be a necessary margin of labour available for work, but unoccupied.[42]

It was also argued that the employers not only preferred and encouraged this system, but they also made matters worse by pursuing their individual recruitment drives. The Minority Report on the Poor Law Commissioners 1905–9, published in 1909, noted that such employers' practices worsened the condition of the labour market. Beveridge also reported that 'it was not at all unknown for employers and foremen to prevent those whom they employed by preference, though not regularly, seeking work with a rival in off times'.[43] Beveridge concluded:

> The main force keeping together this underemployed reserve of labour is the casual demand of a multiplicity of individual employers. Each employer has his own group of hangers-on at his gate, instead of all employers sharing a common reserve drawn from one centre.[44]

This type of diversity would have been more evident at larger ports such as London or Glasgow, which handled many different products. Therefore, multiplicity of function created a greater problem at ports such as Glasgow, Liverpool and London than it did elsewhere.

It was a multiplicity of employers, and the often irregular nature of their business, which developed the tendency for them to surround themselves (at all times) with as large a group of workers as suited their needs at their busiest periods of business. The more widely scattered these separate businesses, and the more affected by fluctuating patterns of trade, the greater the tendency was towards a further accumulation of labour. In effect, this created an ever-increasing reserve of surplus labour.[45] For many observers, therefore, the blame for the operation of this system was placed forcefully at the door of the employers. R. Bean outlines the main reason for the employers position on labour recruitment:

> The system of distributing dock labour was in many respects haphazard and near chaotic. Each employer held his stand at the same time . . . if not required there was no time to go to another.[46]

This was the very point that Beveridge was making in his 1909 study, and that a multiplicity of employment outlets only led to increases in the reserve of labour. This was also the main reason for the dockers' immobility. As a first step he proposed the reduction in the number of available stands. This would introduce a degree of regulation of employment and one tentative measure which would lead to the eventual decasualisation of dock work.

The Liverpool scheme of 1912 reduced the number of stands from around 'eighty or ninety' to thirteen main stands each centred in seven 'clearing house

[42] Lascelles and Bullock, *Dock Labour and Decasualisation*, p. 1.
[43] Beveridge, *Unemployment*, p. 86.
[44] Quoted by Webb, *The Public Organisation of the Labour Market*, pp. 199–200.
[45] Beveridge, *Unemployment*, p. 104.
[46] Bean, 'The Liverpool Dock Strike of 1890', p. 56.

areas' around the port. Although it was known that the practice of convening 'unofficial stands' developed, the general policy proved acceptable to the vast majority of employers at Liverpool after the scheme's initiation in 1912.[47] It was in this manner that the mobility of dock labour would be improved.[48] By contrast, Glasgow's dock labour force was still mostly recruited at the shipside. While by 1920 there does seem to have been a more regulated system of stands (although this is far from clear), there was no established clearing-house system similar to that in operation at Liverpool.[49]

The clearing-house scheme, despite its shortcomings, argued Taplin, 'pioneered the concept of registration and was a fundamental step towards decasualisation'.[50] Dockers were, however, still engaged through the call-on, and the practice of giving first preference to certain men, or groups of men, was still rigidly adhered to.[51] One by-product of such a system was that it was open to incomers and corruption. Concerning the latter, Beveridge noted that this attitude was most prevalent among the hiring foremen, that there were 'grave abuses associated with the system', and this gave the foremen considerable power:

> patronage to the foreman, which sometimes leads to the extraction of bribes, and is often, we are informed, the real obstacle to reform . . . [the] men responsible for getting the work done are afraid to give the men security of tenure, for fear it would weaken their power over them . . . The system undoubtedly lends itself to much abuse of patronage and encourages convivial drinking as a means of 'keeping-in' with the foreman.[52]

The pub, as Beveridge's testimony intimates, was the one place where such recruitment and 'convivial drinking' took place. Indeed, according to oral testimony the practice of buying drinks for the foreman was still very much in evidence well into the second half of the twentieth century.[53] Beatrice Potter painted an altogether different picture of the position and role of the foreman. Somewhat naively, Potter stated that she felt the practice of patronage did not seem so widely

---

[47] For fuller description of the Liverpool Dock Scheme see Phillips and Whiteside, *Casual Labour*, chap. 3; see also PRO, LAB 101/18, *Port Transport Memorandum*, pp. 1–16.

[48] Keeling, 'Casual Labour Problem', pp. 7–9.

[49] Shaw Inquiry, i, evidence, J. S. Spencer, Glasgow Stevedore, p. 272.

[50] Taplin, *Dockers Union*, p. 157.

[51] Hilton, *Are Trade Unions Obstructive*, p. 95.

[52] Beveridge, *Unemployment*, pp. 200–201, pp. 247–8, and pp. 97–8 – references to the building trade which shared many of the casual characteristics of the docks.

[53] Discussions with ex-dockers Gordon Banders (Tuesday 16 Jun. 1992: Glasgow Dockers Annual Trip to Kirkcaldy. Gordon began working at Glasgow Docks in 1924); Charles Ward, Glasgow Docker (Partick, in Glasgow, 95 Thursday Jun. 1992. Charles entered Glasgow's docklands in 1942); Tom O'Connor (Thursday 4 Mar. 1993. Tom entered the dock work in the late 1950s) All three noted the practice of 'keeping in with the foreman' by buying drinks. Many other dockers commented on this practice also. One main method other than buying a drink directly was to pass the foreman a matchbox within which was a 'half-crown'. Thus the giver would hope that his face would be remembered next day at the call-on. It was also not unknown for the foreman to phone certain pubs to recruit extra men. It was stated, on several occasions, that the men taken-on would be those who had left a drink behind the bar for the foreman to consume later.

spread as some thought, and that the foreman basically had 'the interests of his trade at heart'. The one thing that united him with 'all grades of dock labour', she suggested, 'was his faith in protection'. Only a small 'unprincipled' section of this group, and some 'small contractors . . . or corrupt managers', would give preference to those 'who stand a drink or pay over a percentage of their wage'.[54]

Potter also suggested that increased competition among those employers who handled imports or exports played a significant role in generating 'spasmodic and strained demands for labour' (which perhaps encouraged the habit of holding on to 'habitual employees'). She did not simply wish to lay the blame for the problems of the system wholly on the shoulders of the shipowners and merchants, but she did argue that they showed 'no sign of wishing to organise their business so as to give as regular employment as is practicable'. In the final analysis, however, Potter felt that all involved were victims:

> They were made so by the dislocated state of metropolitan life. In the 'individualism run wild', in the uncontrolled competition of metropolitan industry, unchecked by public opinion or by any legislative regulation of employment, such as the Factory Act.[55]

It was an impossible situation, argued Potter, for she thought it impossible that any group of individuals, masters, trade union officials or men, would ever be able to change this voluntary situation unless it was by forming a Public Trust (of which the trader, the dock labourer and the consumer would be a part) to act as a watchdog over the industry.

As the Webbs were later to argue (Beatrice Potter of course becoming Beatrice Webb upon her marriage to Sydney Webb), it was not only the 'selfishness of the employer or the corrupt interests of the foreman' that helped perpetuate the system of casualism. They noted that many of the men preferred the system and that neither side wished to 'disturb a practice which suited them both'. At times, as noted above, they could earn sufficient wages over two or three days to take time off for the next two or three. However, even when there was little work, or their earnings went down to the point where they were actually in distress, they still clung to the system.[56] As Eleanor Rathbone noted, the docker came to see this pattern of employment as a kind of liberty, a system through which he controlled his time, effort and leisure.

This was stated clearly in evidence given to the Shaw Inquiry in 1920. Joseph Houghton, the General Secretary of the SUDL, stressed this very point, when explaining why the Glasgow dockers had rejected both registration and the principle of weekly employment (in essence decasualisation). To put it simply, he argued:

> The men of Glasgow were afraid of losing what they called their liberty and their freedom so far as selecting their work is concerned . . . at the present time they have the right either to work or not as they see fit.[57]

---

[54] Potter, cited in Booth, *Life and Labour*, pp. 23–6.
[55] Ibid., pp. 33–4.
[56] Webbs, *The Public Organisation of the Labour Market*, p. 201.
[57] Shaw Inquiry, i, p. 158.

Nevertheless, there is no mistaking the consequences of operating such a system, particularly when it could be continually infiltrated by outsiders from other walks of life. This could be partly blamed on the nature of the industry, and on the attitudes of the employers, but it could be traced to problems in the wider economy too. Potter noted that a large proportion of the 'hereditary casuals' (as she defined them) drifted into the docks from other trades, and some of these men thereafter became established there. There were also the occasional groups of outsiders brought in at times of labour disputes, and some inevitably remained in dock work.

Indeed, it was at times of dispute that the employer encouraged the influx of new labour in order that they could keep the regular workforce in its place, or to 'freshen up the existing reserve'. According to Potter, such a man could be taken on straight from jail 'if he be remarkable for sinew and he strikes the quick eye of the contractor or foreman'.[58] But this meant that the regular dockers were pushed aside. This prompted Booth to report:

> The earnings of the professional docker are shared by a considerable number of incomers from all trades who seek work at the docks, not because the docks are busy, but because their own trades are slack, and therein lies the peculiar difficulty of the dock industry.[59]

'Whatever the number of competitors for work, each has some chance', and, as Beveridge argued, 'the more casual the employment the more equal the chances.'[60] There were, of course, always those who would be taken on more regularly than others, but they represented the minimum requirement of a port, a dock or a wharf, or a particular employer. These men were usually known as 'first preference' men. They were in a better position to exploit the advantages of the casual system and their 'first preference' status was probably recognition of their 'higher' level of skill, or because of their unswerving loyalty to one employer or foreman.

## Casualism, Dock Labour and Poverty

Those dockers less regularly employed by the industry, more often on the fringes of dock work, were nevertheless men accustomed to dock work and conditions. This meant that they had a good working knowledge of the industry and its needs, and, by definition, accepted the rationale of engagement and the code of conduct that went with it, and the traditions that had built up along the waterfront. There seems little doubt that this suited the employers, and had done for many years, despite the fact that the system also generated a significant degree of impoverishment for a sizeable minority of the dock labour force. It would seem that the Shaw Inquiry also saw poverty as a problem for many – after considering evidence to that effect given

[58] Potter, cited in Booth, *Life and Labour*, p. 28.
[59] Ibid., p. 422
[60] Beveridge, *Unemployment*, p. 107.

by Ernest Bevin – despite other evidence offering proof of high earnings, particularly at Glasgow around 1919 and 1920. They felt that 'idleness, poverty and neglect' were still very much associated with dock work and that the docker himself was 'prey to the temptations' which sprang from experiencing these conditions. While they accepted that the docker had generally gained in relation to wages throughout the war years, they still felt that the experience of poverty was never far away. Booth's survey of the 1890s gave evidence of the fact that the docker was in relative poverty when compared to other categories of workers – as seen in Table 2.2 below.

Table 2.2: *The Dock Community and Accommodation – London in the 1890s.*

| Numbers to a room | Total | % total Dockers |
| --- | --- | --- |
| 3, 4 or more to a room | 12,296 | 28.5% |
| 2 and under 3 to a room | 14,792 | 34.0% |
| 1 and under 2 to a room | 10,646 | 24.5% |

**Source:** *Life and Labour of the People of London* (Vol. vii, Part v, p. 391).

Booth found that there was general evidence of 'impoverishment' within the docking community, with some 62% living in overcrowded housing. While this situation was to improve in the early twentieth century, particularly in London, there was arguably still much overcrowding elsewhere in Britain – not least in Scotland. Indeed, as noted by R. J. Morris, 'over-crowding was not exceeded in Scotland, by any English town, with the exception of London and Plymouth'.[61] Conditions in Scottish port towns and cities such as Glasgow may have been much worse given Glasgow's legendary reputation for chronic overcrowding. Indeed, even by the early twentieth century, notes Morris, 55.1% of the population were still living in houses of one or two rooms. Only Dundee experienced higher levels of overcrowding. By comparison the highest English figures for overcrowding were Plymouth and London with significantly lower levels of 30.3% and 22.2% respectively.[62]

This raises the question, if poverty was such a problem for dock workers, why did they remain in that occupation? It may well be the case that many were afraid to venture far from the docks, particularly if they had never known any other environment, and in any case, as we have seen, dock work was to many a way of life and not just an occupation. The dockers also chose not to work weekly, even when the opportunity was there, because 'permanence was devoid of liberty'.[63] In many respects, it can be argued, the docker was not only trapped in a system he had

[61] R. J. Morris, 'Urbanisation and Scotland', in W. H. Fraser and R. J. Morris (eds.), *People and Society in Scotland, Vol II, 1830–1914* (Edinburgh, 1990) p. 83.
[62] Ibid., p. 84.
[63] Shaw Inquiry, i, pp. 8–9.

grown to understand and accept, but through a life-time's work, or family connections possibly spanning several generations, had invested too much in the
system. The more attached they became to this system of employment the more
difficult it would be to make a clean break from it.

For some time there had been a recognised link between the casual system and
levels of poverty. *The Royal Commission into the Poor Laws*, noted that there was
considerable evidence drawn from the dock districts which showed the 'real evils of
casual labour' and the considerable distress it caused. Regularisation of casual
labour, or its decasualisation, was proposed as a remedy better than any other for
the diminution of pauperism among the dock labour force.[64] It was not so much
that the system was wrong, but that it allowed the free movement of outsiders into
the trade, particularly in times of cyclical depression when men from other walks of
life descended upon the docks: 'thus depriving the *bona fide* docker of what he
considered to be his regular work'.[65] In Liverpool, the permanent surplus of labour
was increased during winter when 'out of work building labourers came into the
docks'.[66] As we have seen, the employers encouraged and exploited this situation in
order to keep the regular docker in his place. They not only preferred the casual
system as a means of providing for their labour needs, but they also used it to
discipline the workforce, as Ernest Bevin argued before the Shaw Inquiry (1920):

> I am convinced that the employers have always had at the back of their heads
> that economic poverty producing economic fear was the best weapon for
> controlling labour.[67]

This is borne out in the investigations of Bean, noting that employers at Liverpool considered unemployment 'the best card in the pack for keeping labour in its
place' (at least in the period before 1914). But this also had the effect of keeping
many dockers in a near permanent state of poverty.[68]

### Registration, Regulation and the Relief of Poverty

Poverty and its control was one reason why some observers, such as Frederic
Keeling, felt that the registration of all *bona fide* dockers was essential, not only to
help the industry modernise itself, but to control the influx of outsiders seeking
work in the industry. As Keeling predicted, however, any attempt at registration was
bound to bring 'opposition from the men'.[69]

At Glasgow, the dockers would have nothing to do with any proposal for
registration. Indeed, so strong was the mood at Glasgow in February 1920 the
*Glasgow Herald* reported that the Glasgow men would 'divide' the NTWF (which
until that point they had supported unswervingly) rather than accept registration.[70]

[64] *RC on Poor Laws*, ix, 1909, paras. 540 and 542.
[65] *Glasgow Herald*, 10 Mar. 1908.
[66] Bean, 'The Liverpool Dock Strike of 1890', p. 54.
[67] Quoted in Bullock, *Ernest Bevin*, p. 125.
[68] Bean, 'Employers Associations', p. 366.
[69] Keeling, 'Casual Labour Problem', p. 8.
[70] *Glasgow Herald*, 14 Feb.; see also Shaw Inquiry, i, evidence, Joseph Houghton, p. 167.

Casualism had formed the docker's 'gamble for employment' for many years. He had become accustomed to the system and the traditions that came with it. He was now being asked to freely give this up simply to suit the convenience of the employer, or the social theorist such as Keeling.[71] Society had come to view casualism as a 'social evil', but it was an 'evil' that the docker had learned to live with. And from the docker's standpoint: 'better the Devil you know than the Devil you don't'.

In Scotland, a campaign of 'anti-registration' was to develop to the point where it threatened to shatter trade unionism there, and at Glasgow and Aberdeen the movement was to hold out until the Second World War. However, the anti-registration movement was to find its voice raised loudest at the port of Glasgow, where proposals for registration and decasualisation were rejected in 1912, 1917 and again in 1919 (proposals that in each case were drawn up by the their own union – the SUDL – and the employers).[72] Resistance to registration plagued the Glasgow dockers' relationship with the Transport and General Workers' Union from 1922 through until the early 1930s.[73] The following 'proclamation' was issued after a mass meeting by the Glasgow Dock's Branch of the TGWU in March 1930. The dockers' position was clear and unequivocal:

> It is the opinion of this meeting that despite the well meant promotion in the first instance of dockers' registration by amateur social reformers, dockers' registration is not, and cannot ever be, a step towards the solution of poverty associated with the general under-employment of casual dock labour . . . It is our opinion that from the employers' point of view registration has long resolved itself into a mere instrument of coercion, and that from the point of view of our Trade Union officials . . . registration provides a solution to the vexed problem of stabilising the union among the Glasgow dockers . . . The proposed maintenance scheme we regard as palpable bait to involve us in the toils of the slavery of registration.[74]

The dockers were determined to 'protect [their] rights and status against any outside influence'. And at Glasgow, stated Phillips and Whiteside, the anti-registration movement revealed much about the 'history and tradition of industrial relations there'.[75]

As argued by Glasgow stevedore J. S. Spencer in 1920, the differences between dockers at Glasgow and dockers elsewhere had 'real reasons for their existence', based as they were on traditions built up over time. He concluded that in practice 'it would be difficult to wipe them out' and it would be difficult to impose any equality on the industry without due 'regard for past history . . . or past traditions'. This

---

[71] Keeling, 'Casual Labour Problem', p. 15.

[72] PRO, LAB 101/18, *Port Transport Memorandum*, noted that the Glasgow proposals were very comprehensive, but tha they were still rejected by the men, section i, para. 8, p. 3.

[73] Shaw Inquiry, i, evidence, Joseph Houghton, p. 158; and Shaw Inquiry, ii, *Appendix* No 80, 'Proposed Scheme for better Registration of Dock Labour at the Port of Glasgow', p. 91

[74] *Glasgow Herald*, 4 Mar. 1930.

[75] Phillips and Whiteside, *Casual Labour*, p. 33.

philosophy could be applied to well-established workplace practices, to differentials in the rate or method of payment of wages, to gang sizes, or to proposals for further mechanisation. But the issue of registration came to be viewed as the most direct and dangerous contravention of the docker's concepts of tradition and history: enshrined as it was in the system of casualism itself.[76]

Casualism was the main factor that united the whole operational system of the port transport industry, not only throughout Britain, but in other areas of the world. It was a system which was accepted by both the employer and the employed. Its development was dictated by the erratic nature of the growth in the port transport industry nationally, and was intimately linked to the needs of the national economy and the vagaries of local and international trade. The casual system lay at the heart of the transport industry. It generated a complicated system of tradition and custom, influencing the nature and the development of dock trade unionism as well as dictating the general well-being of the dock community.

Investigation of such factors reveals that the system also worked to ensure that traditional differences between specific locations, or within particular ports, persisted well into the late twentieth century. This can be explained in terms of the historic growth of a port, and the specific factors which promoted that growth. Clearly, the overall development of the port transport system was not a uniform one: it differed from one location to another and across time as well as space.

One force which bound all together was casualism. The principal purpose of this chapter was to illustrate and explain the nature and function of the casual system of employment and how it helped mould the docker's life, and how this in turn affected the process of industrial relations. Thereafter, these developments would dictate the manner in which the docker would defend that way of life against any force – the employers, trade union official, or, as stated by Glasgow's dockers in 1930, the 'amateur social reformer'. It is in this sense that Stephen Hill's argument is borne out. The dockers did generate their 'own sub-cultural values' in direct opposition to a more 'dominant cultural perspective' held by a wider community of interest.[77] Thus, according to David Wilson:

> The docks represent a far broader social microcosm than most industries and attitudes were deeply rooted in historical conflict. Dockers' communities were built around the place of work . . . jobs were kept in the family and the inter-action of social and working life did produce loyalties and protective practices which were based on casualism and justified by its perpetuation.[78]

The blueprint for the docker's attachment to casualism was not one based on a design of his own making, but it would be defended at all costs. And the most pertinent example of this was to be seen at Glasgow during the 1920s and early 1930s.

---

[76] Shaw Inquiry, i, evidence, James Spencer, p. 282.

[77] Hill, *The Docker*, p. 200.

[78] Wilson, *The Dockers*, p. 15.

# CHAPTER THREE

# The Trade and Development of the Port of Glasgow

*The Early Growth of Glasgow in the eighteenth and nineteenth centuries*

Glasgow's trading environment and area of commercial influence was expanding rapidly as the nineteenth century wore on. By the turn of the twentieth century Glasgow became more intimately linked with Govan, Partick and Clydebank. The main factors of expansion were first, the advent of steam power and the spread of new technology, which created a significant increase in trade; secondly, an increase in foreign and transatlantic trade; and thirdly, the rapid development of the mineral trade (of both foreign and coastwise traffic). But without the early improvements of the River Clyde – directly attributable to 'the enterprising spirit of Glasgow's merchants from the second half of the eighteenth century onward' – this trade could never have been exploited so efficiently along the length of the Glasgow waterfront.[1]

Each of these phases in the early period created increased employment opportunities at the port, in both dock construction and dock work. The numbers of those seeking work in Glasgow grew steadily and they began to settle in areas around the main quays and docks, mostly centred in Glasgow and Govan and to a lesser degree at Partick. Some of those who came to be involved in this work came from the Highlands and Islands of Scotland, but the Irish were predominant, while other aspects of dock work, better described as porterage, were dominated by lowland Scots. While dock work did create specialisms, particularly in relation to shipwork (discussed later in this chapter), work along the quay was always relatively important to Glasgow, the first small quay having been built at the port around 1668.[2]

Around 1760 Glasgow was still considered to be a provincial port town, with a population of about 32,000. Greenock at that time was considered the most important west-coast port and was to remain so up until the mid-nineteenth century. T. M. Devine has described Greenock as the 'archetypal port town of the western lowlands', and it was better suited to handle waterborne traffic and trade than Glasgow. By the 1820s, however, Glasgow was beginning to catch up with Greenock, helped by a rapid increase in population which had risen to

---

[1] *The New Statistical Account of Scotland (NSA)*, vi, (Lanark, 1845), p. 131.
[2] *Abridged Statistical History of Scotland* (Edinburgh, 1855), p. 669.

147,000 by 1821.[3] Glasgow had by then accumulated massive amounts of urban capital and labour. According to R. J. Morris, much of this was invested in the textile areas in the east end, which had been growing steadily from the eighteenth century onward. But in the meantime, new quays had been constructed along the Broomielaw, and further improvements made to quays and piers on the upper Clyde.[4] The erection of quays, and the deepening of the Clyde, began around the Broomielaw as far back as the 1770s, and by the 1830s the deepening and dredging of the River Clyde had become an industry in itself. At this time it was noted that there were four permanent 'dredging machines', two diving bells and 'powerful steam apparatus', which ensured further deepening particularly around the all important Broomielaw landing areas. While Glasgow, like other ports, had operated cranes for many years, it was around this time that Glasgow introduced cranes designed to lift heavy loads (in connection with the shipping of steam boilers). These were reputed to be able to handle 'articles of thirty tons'.[5] Glasgow's love affair with new technology and the improvement of her landing facilities had its foundations in this period.

The city of Glasgow began to grow in response to the process of industrial change taking place in her economic hinterland, but also because of the growing opportunities evident in the transatlantic trade. But the major breakthrough came around the mid-nineteenth century with the rapid deployment of steam technology. This further promoted the already considerable expansion of the factory-oriented economy centred around the cotton textiles and iron industries, and from the second quarter of the nineteenth century steel production was also becoming more important. In terms of employment, by 1841 37.5% of the city's labour force were engaged in textiles and clothing, although only 7% were employed in the metalwork, engineering and toolmaking industries. The metal trades were geared towards the export markets, however, and this meant that they had an impact disproportionate to the numbers the industry employed. Indeed, this trade was vital to the growth of the Glasgow port, and the increased demand for raw materials compounded this trend.

Between the late eighteenth century and the 1880s the physical growth of Glasgow was phenomenal. A great many of Glasgow's workers were to be housed in areas stretching along both sides of the river Clyde, mostly south and south-west, north and north-west, as well as the city centre area and the east end. Glasgow's population not only expanded rapidly, but by the turn of the twentieth century Glasgow's labour force also underwent a significant shift in composition. By 1911 those engaged in textiles had fallen from 37.56% to 16.86%. The engineering and metal industries by then accounted for around 16% of the workforce, and there was also a steady growth in employment associated with the food, drink and tobacco industries.[6] There was

[3] T. M. Devine, 'Urbanisation', in M. Devine and R. Mitchison (eds.), *People and Society in Scotland, Vol. I, 1760–1830* (Edinburgh,1988), p. 35.

[4] Fraser and Morris, *People and Society, Vol II*, p. 75.

[5] NSA, p. 197.

[6] G. Gordon, 'The City of Glasgow', in J. Butt and G. Gordon (eds.), *Strathclyde: Changing Horizons* (Edinburgh, 1985), pp. 58–60.

also a marked, if less spectacular, decline in those employed as general labourers, but this is compensated for by increased numbers engaged in other more category-specific labouring duties in timber, shipyard, foundry, tramway, engineer and dock and quay work. After the boundary changes of 1912 Glasgow's population grew to over 1,000,000, accounting for one-fifth of the total population of Scotland.[7]

This was a time of considerable expansion in the transport industry generally and the port transport sector in particular. From the late 1840s onward Glasgow entered a new and more significant phase of dock construction, and between then and the 1860s and 1870s employment opportunities increased significantly. According to Anthony Slaven and Sydney Checkland, official statistics for the period 1871 to 1901 suggest that employment in transport doubled, and from then until 1931 sustained some modest growth. Thereafter, this trend stabilised 'more or less in line with the stagnation in total Scottish population and employment'. Importantly, they note too that there are problems with these statistics, particularly with the re-categorising of 'general workers' in 1871 as transport-specific workers. In other words, these workers were now designated docker, stevedore, wharfinger and quayworker, whereas before they were simply lumped together as 'general labourers'. But there were many problems associated with the classification of workers specific to the port industry and, when linked to the confusion in employment practice witnessed by the operation of the casual system, the growth indicators for this industry may well have been 'over-inflated'. However, there is little doubt, argue Slaven and Checkland, that this was also a period when there was 'a considerable and strong growth in the volume of goods moved'. Clearly, this would have required extra labour.[8]

Economic expansion, however, had a significant effect on the operational and employment structure of the port, leading as it did to an increase in traffic and a greater diversity of cargo, particularly from the 1880s onward. Thus 'Glasgow became a very cosmopolitan sort of place' and its port came to handle, in the words of one Glasgow shipowner and employer, 'more different kinds of trade . . . more different lines of ships . . . more different classes of vessels discharging and loading . . . than at any other port . . . anywhere!'.[9] But such diversity meant that the labour force would become broken up into distinctive groups, handling different cargo, using different methods, creating different specialisms and skills.

### The Height of Prosperity, 1870–1914

In general the nineteenth century proved a lucrative period for the Scottish ports and the dock industry as a whole. George S. Pryde noted that between 1820 and 1913 the growth in Scottish trade was truly remarkable; with the value of imports rising from £3,146,000 to £49,938,000, and the value of exports rising from £2,670,000 to reach £47,361,000 during that period – a seventeenfold increase in total value from

---

[7] Ibid., p. 60.
[8] A. Slaven and S. Checkland (eds.), *Dictionary of Scottish Business Biography*, ii, (Aberdeen, 1990), p. 245.
[9] *RC on the Poor Laws*, 1910, evidence, W. H. Raeburn, Q89.877.

£5,816,000 to £97,599,000.[10] Ports such as Leith and Dundee fared particularly well from this profitable expansion in trade, but none more so than the port of Glasgow, which had enjoyed an almost uninterrupted pattern of growth from the height of the tobacco trade in the mid-eighteenth century until the First World War. Between 1850 and 1914, however, total revenue increased tenfold, rising annually from £69,244 to £633,758 (this had risen to £1,077,998 by 1920 – see Appendices Table II).

From 1887 onward the total number of ships arriving at the harbour never fell below 15,000 *per annum* and numbers were often considerably greater.[11] Between 1900 and 1913, total tonnage of vessels had increased from 8,761,193 to 13,469,191, while the total tonnage of goods rose from 7,215,368 to 10,418,324. This made Glasgow one of Britain's largest ports behind London and Liverpool.[12] Indeed, according to Gordon Jackson, Glasgow shared with London 'immense productive capacity with vast distribution services which made her the "Second City" of the British Empire'.[13] Indeed, in terms of total value of trade, Glasgow's share was to reach almost £55 million before 1914[14]. This accounts for over 56% of total Scottish value of trade (using Pryde's Scottish figures, as noted above), and by 1913 Glasgow was Britain's fifth leading port – as can be seen in Table 3.1. below. The main statistical analysis of the Clydeside region and particularly the port of Glasgow will be charted more fully in the latter parts of this chapter. What must be stressed at this juncture is the important and pivotal role played by the west-coast and Clydeside ports between *c*.1850 and 1914. The ports in this area of Scotland were by far the most important in trading terms, with six out of Scotland's nine principal ports located in a tight geographical area, as shown in Figure One.[15]

In terms of trade only the east-coast ports of Aberdeen, Dundee and Leith could challenge the six main west-coast ports and only Leith mounted any significant challenge to Glasgow. It should also be noted that the statistics shown in Tables 3.1. and 3.2, based on value of trade and on cargoes in ballast, do not offer the best illustration of labour needs. It is volume of trade rather than value which gives the best indication of labour needs, and cargo in ballast requires less labour than cargo only. However, at Glasgow, cargo in ballast was diminishing rapidly by the late nineteenth century and the coastal trade provided much of the dock work undertaken at Glasgow in any case. Value of trade, however, is also important. This indicates the income and wealth generated by Glasgow and other Scottish ports, and an indication of the revenues available to modernise and upgrade the harbour and its facilities.

Table 3.2. gives some indication of the main differences between Glasgow and Leith and illustrates how close both were in the 1880s in terms of trade entering the ports. By 1910, however, Glasgow's trade had risen significantly when compared to Leith.

[10] G. S. Pryde, *Scotland from 1603 to the Present Day* (1963), p. 211.

[11] J. D. Marwick, *The River Clyde and the Clyde Burghs* (Glasgow, 1909), see *Appendix*, Table III.

[12] Noted in W. M. French, *The Scottish Ports: Including Docks and Harbours* (Glasgow, 1938), pp. 107–8.

[13] Jackson, *Archaeology of Ports*, p. 134.

[14] Shaw Inquiry, ii, see *Appendix* 129, ix, p. 165 (also Board of Trade Summaries, 1913, Cmd 758).

[15] *The National Joint Agreement for the Port Transport Industry*, pp. 6–7 (May 1969 edn.), which notes 43 principal ports in Britain, including 9 located in Scotland; Aberdeen, Dundee and Leith on the East Coast, and Ardrossan, Ayr, Glasgow, Greenock, Irvine and Troon on the West.

**Table 3.1:** *Imports and Exports Through Individual Ports in Money Value, for twelve individual ports, for 1913. (£ millions)*

|  | Imports | Exports | Re-exports | Total | %U.K. |
|---|---|---|---|---|---|
| London | 253.9 | 99.1 | 58.8 | 411.8 | 29.3 |
| Liverpool | 175.5 | 170.1 | 25.2 | 370.8 | 26.4 |
| Hull | 48.8 | 29.2 | 5.5 | 84.6 | 6.0 |
| Manchester | 35.3 | 20.6 | 0.5 | 56.3 | 4.0 |
| Glasgow | 18.5 | 35.9 | 0.3 | 54.8 | 3.9 |
| Southampton | 25.5 | 20.7 | 7.4 | 53.6 | 3.8 |
| Grimsby | 15.8 | 21.9 | 0.1 | 37.8 | 2.7 |
| Newcastle | 11.3 | 13.2 | – | 24.6 | 1.8 |
| Cardiff | 6.7 | 17.2 | – | 23.9 | 1.7 |
| Leith | 15.7 | 6.9 | 0.3 | 23.0 | 1.6 |
| Bristol & Avonmouth | 18.0 | 4.0 | – | 22.0 | 1.6 |
| Dundee | 8.0 | 1.0 | 0.3 | 9.4 | 0.7 |

Source: Shaw Inquiry, ii, *Appendix* 131, pp. 173–5; from Board of Trade Summaries, 1913, Cd 7616 (*PP*, 1920, Cmd 937).

**Table 3.2:** *Net Tonnage of Overseas Vessels Arriving with Cargoes and Ballast for Scotland and Scottish Figures as percentage of UK, and totals and percentage (brackets) of Scottish Trade for Glasgow, Leith and Other Scottish Ports 1880 to 1938 (millions of Tons).*

| Year | Scotland | %U.K. | Glasgow | Leith | Others |
|---|---|---|---|---|---|
| 1880 | 2.5 | 8.5 | 0.8 (32%) | 0.6 (24%) | 1.1 (44%) |
| 1890 | 3.7 | 9.9 | 1.1 (29%) | 0.7 (20%) | 1.9 (51%) |
| 1900 | 5.4 | 11.0 | 1.5 (28%) | 1.1 (20%) | 2.8 (52%) |
| 1910 | 8.9 | 13.3 | 3.1 (35%) | 1.6 (18%) | 4.2 (47%) |

Source: Calculations based on figures from Slaven and Checkland, *History of Scottish History Biography, Vol. II*, (pp. 248–9.)

There would seem little doubt that Glasgow dominated Scottish trade during this period. How far can this be said of the west-coast ports as a whole, and can the same be said for export trade too? Table 3.3 shows one comparative example of the combined totals for cargo entering west-coast and east-coast ports for the year 1913. (It can be argued that 1913 is an unrepresentative year. However, it is only used here to offer an illustration of the balance of trade between these two parts of the country.) The east-coast ports are favoured in terms of total tonnage and numbers of vessels arriving, and saw around 14% more traffic in terms of total arrivals. The greatest amount of overseas trade came into the west-coast ports in fewer vessels than the east, while the east-coast ports took the bulk of the coastal trade.

**Table 3.3:** *Net Tonnage and Numbers of Vessels with Cargoes Arriving from Foreign Countries and British Possessions and Coastwise, with Totals for 1913, for the West- and East-coast Ports in Scotland.*

|  | Overseas | | Coastwise | | Totals | |
|---|---|---|---|---|---|---|
|  | Vessels | Tons | Vessels | Tons | Vessels | Tons |
| West of Scotland Ports | 1,778 | 3,320,750 | 16,545 | 2,843,759 | 18,323 | 6,163,509 |
| East of Scotland Ports | 5,236 | 2,892,481 | 16,071 | 3,414,789 | 21,307 | 6,307,270 |
| Sub Totals | 7,012 | 6,213,231 | 32,616 | 6,258,548 | 39,630 | 2,470,779 |

**Source:** Shaw Inquiry, ii, *Appendix* 131, pp. 173–5 [Note: the above figures were calculated from Board of Trade Summaries, 1913, Cd 7616], (*PP*, 1920, Cmd 937).

Several important factors emerge from this simple statistical illustration. First, it can be seen that the greatest traffic arriving at Scottish ports was in the coastal trade, accounting for over 82% of all vessels carrying cargo entering Scottish ports for 1913. There was thus some considerable commercial activity within the port structure nationally in the coastal trade, which proved equally important in terms of employment. It will be argued that those employers servicing the needs of coastal trade and traffic were without doubt the most numerous within a given port dealing in general cargo, and also employed the greatest numbers of dock workers in the majority of ports.

Even in ports such as Leith, or more significantly Glasgow, where there was a considerable trade in overseas traffic, the coastal firms would arguably still employ more labour. The ports handling overseas cargo invariably worked on larger vessels, and there is evidence to suggest that it was this part of port operations which was more mechanised. While these larger ships carried greater loads, they needed fewer hands to work them and more of the work would be undertaken by mechanical appliance. This may have been less the case at the lesser ports, however, where the average size of vessels was much smaller.

Because of the continual improvement of the River Clyde, the largest vessels trading at Glasgow before 1914 could be 570 feet long, having a draft of 30 feet and weighing around 14,500 tons.[16] Thus the operations on this type of ship would be very different from smaller vessels – not least the smaller vessels involved in the coastal trade. The irregular nature of coastal trade would also have made further requirements in terms of labour, and to ensure adequate supplies of labour on the busiest day each firm would have to have its own individual supply. While the overall effect of this employment structure meant that there were too many men when trade was slack, it also shows that most dockers would have been engaged by the smaller employers, thereby underlining the significance of the small employer within the overall port structure.

[16] Shaw Inquiry, ii, p. 100, *Appendix* 85, Table H/17 (1b).

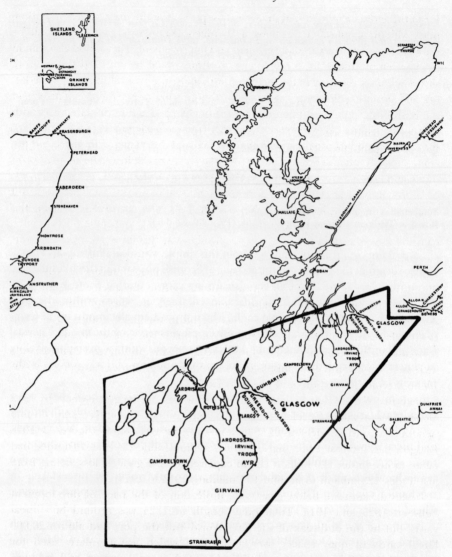

**Figure 1.** Scotland's Ports with Clydeside Ports inset.
**Source:** W. M. French, *The Scottish Ports,* 1938.

The main purpose of this brief analysis, however, is to illustrate the central importance of the west-coast ports – stressing the pivotal role of Clydeside and the port of Glasgow. While the totals shown in Table 3.3. are about evenly split, the balance of trade still favours the west-coast ports. These totals represent figures for cargo entering thirty-one Scottish ports for 1913, and only eight of these were west-coast ports. This underpins the importance of the west-coast in terms of trade and justifies investigating this region in relation to Scotland and its port transport system as a whole.

It can therefore be argued that the west-coast ports were the most successful trading ports, with the significant exceptions of Aberdeen, Dundee and Leith, and would be most likely to gain in terms of investment and improvement. They would also gain in terms of employment, in as much as more firms would be attracted to the more successful ports, resulting in the further growth in the numbers of shipping, stevedoring and portering firms operating within the growing port structure. This would obviously bring about a considerable degree of change as a port prepared itself with new facilities, and increased its water space and quayage – depending on the needs of the economy and its proximity to local, national and international markets, and the commercial dynamic at work within its hinterland. There would also be an increase in trade, and an ever greater diversity in the types of goods handled.

As the west-coast ports were nearest to Scotland's industrial heartland and geographically well placed to exploit trading links with the rest of Britain, the Empire and other transatlantic routes, it is not surprising that these ports were to gain the ascendancy over other ports in Scotland at this time. However, did this geographical advantage also favour the west-coast ports in terms of export trade? Table 3.4 offers one illustration of comparative advantage in terms of exports. In this example it can be seen that throughout this period the seven east-coast ports accounted for 52% of exports, Glasgow and Greenock accounting for the remainder. Indeed, Glasgow's average over this period in total was around 40%, while Leith's share fell from a high point of 22% in the 1870s to level off around 16% thereafter. The combined totals for Kirkcaldy (with Methil and Burntisland) increased significantly to compensate for Leith's loss in trade, rising from about 7% to around 20% by the end of this period.

In terms of the value in total trade Glasgow was the biggest earner. In 1913 Glasgow's total value of trade was almost £55 million, whereas the combined value of both Leith and Dundee was £32.5 million – 40% below Glasgow's figures. By 1918 Glasgow had increased her share to £96.5 million, while Leith and Dundee had fallen to just under £20 million (Leith experienced the greatest loss, falling from just under £23 million to around £14 million *c.*1913 to 1918).[17]

Tables 3.5 and 3.6 below give some indication of the pace of development between 1825 and 1914. Total quay length in 1825 was around 865 lineal yards, but by the outbreak of the First World War the port had almost 20,000 lineal yards of quay space; over a third of which was regularly used for the berthing of liners, and one fifth 'devoted to coal export and iron-ore imports'.[18] Capital expenditure rose from £104,000 to reach almost £10,000,000 during the same period, while the largest ship trading at the port rose in tonnage from 3,400 to 14,500. In all these cases the greatest leap forward came in the period between 1875 and 1914, during which time Glasgow had grown to encompass three principal harbours and four main docks with all quays belonging to the Clyde Navigation Company.[19] This is what Gordon Jackson

---

[17] Ibid., *Appendix* 129, ix, p. 165.

[18] Jackson, *Archaeology of Ports*, p. 134.

[19] *Report on Dock Labour in Relation to Poor Law Relief,* by the Hon Gerald Walsh (*PP*, 1908, xcii, Cd. 4391), p 17.

**Table 3.4:** *Net Tonnage of Vessels Clearing Selected Scottish Ports for Foreign Parts and Share of Scottish Totals and Scottish Share of UK Total, 1870–74 to 1910–13 (with cargo and ballast 000s tons).*

*West-coast Ports*

|  | 1870–4 tons % | 1880–4 tons % | 1890–4 tons % | 1900–4 tons % | 1910–3 tons % |
|---|---|---|---|---|---|
| Glasgow | 670 (37.5) | 1,286 (44.4) | 1,694 (40.3) | 2,503 (41.2) | 4,032 (41.0) |
| Greenock | 203 (11.3) | 207 ( 7.1) | 199 ( 4.7) | 106 ( 1.7) | 1,024 (10.3) |
| Sub total | 873 (48.8) | 1,493 (51.5) | 1,893 (45.0) | 2,609 (43.0) | 5,056 (51.0) |

*East-coast Ports*

|  | 1870–4 tons % | 1880–4 tons % | 1890–4 tons % | 1900–4 tons % | 1910–3 tons % |
|---|---|---|---|---|---|
| Leith | 389 (21.8) | 478 (16.5) | 692 (16.5) | 945 (15.5) | 1,599 (16.2) |
| Bo'ness | 151 ( 8.4) | 199 ( 6.8) | 202 ( 4.8) | 278 ( 4.6) | – |
| Methil* | – | – | – | – | 1,143 (16.2) |
| Kirkcaldy* | 124 ( 6.9) | 428 (14.7) | 728 (17.3) | 1,366 (22.5) | – |
| Burntisland* | – | – | – | – | 818 ( 8.3) |
| Grangemouth | 159 ( 8.9) | 221 ( 7.6) | 664 (15.8) | 818 (13.5) | 1,064 (10.7) |
| Dundee | 95 ( 5.3) | 83 ( 2.7) | 88 ( 2.1) | 59 ( 1.0) | 203 ( 2.1) |
| Sub total | 918 (51.2) | 1,409 (48.5) | 2,311 (55.0) | 3,466 (57.0) | 4,833 (49.0) |
| Scot/Total | 1,719 | 2,902 | 4,204 | 6,075 | 9,889 |
| % UK Total | 8.4 | 9.3 | 11.0 | 12.0 | 13.3 |

*relates to all three ports Methil, Kirkcaldy and Grangemouth.

**Source:** G. Jackson, *The History and Archaeology of Ports* – calculations from statistics for selected UK ports.

**Table 3.5. Progressive Statement of (a) Revenue, (b) Tonnage of Vessels, (c) Tonnage of Goods, (d) Total Capital Expenditure, and (e) Total Outstanding Debt, Since 1825 at Twenty-Five Year Intervals to 1900, and Pre-War Year of 1914.**

|  | (a) | (b) | (c) | (d) | (e) |
|---|---|---|---|---|---|
| 1825 | 8,367 | – | – | 103,964 | 55,757 |
| 1850 | 64,243 | 2,893,212 | 1,023,216 | 1,175,104 | 678,659 |
| 1875 | 196.326 | 4,499,714 | 2,346,842 | 3,684,312 | 2,910,027 |
| 1900 | 441,419 | 8,723,194 | 7,215,368 | 7,430,702 | 5,790,187 |
| 1914 | 633,758 | 13,821,425 | 10,067,502 | 9,789,191 | 7,196,575 |

**Source:** Shaw Inquiry, ii, *Appendix* 85, pp. 173–75, Table H/17–1a; from Clyde Navigation Trust, Treasurer's Office Report, February 1920 (*PP*, 1920, Cmd 937).

**Table 3.6:** *Progressive Statement of (a) Length of Quay, (b) Depth of Water in River at High Tide, (c) (d) and (e) Dimensions of Largest Vessels Trading at Port of Glasgow, since 1825 at Twenty-Five Year Intervals to 1900, and Pre-War Year of 1914.*

|      | (a) Lineal Yards | (b) Depth/feet | Largest Trading Vessel [c, d, & e] | | |
|      |                  |                | (c) Length/feet | (d) Draft/Feet | (e) Tonnage/Tons |
|------|------------------|----------------|-----------------|----------------|------------------|
| 1825 | 865              | 16             | –               | 13             | –                |
| 1850 | 3,391            | 20             | –               | 16             | –                |
| 1875 | 6,708            | 26             | 370             | 21             | 3,400            |
| 1900 | 15,115           | 33             | 490             | 27             | 8,300            |
| 1914 | 19,234           | 36             | 570             | 30             | 14,500           |

**Source:** Shaw Inquiry, ii, *Appendix* 85, Table H/17–1b; from Clyde Navigation Trust Treasurer's Office Report, February 1920 (*PP*, 1929, Cmd 937).

has termed the 'Height of Prosperity' for the British port transport industry. This was most definitely the case at Glasgow. Even before the boundary changes of 1912, which officially extended Glasgow geographically, Glasgow harbour was then considered to encompass Govan and the new mineral port of Clydebank.[20]

The influence of the Clyde Navigation Trust extended from the centre of Glasgow to Port Glasgow (some 12 miles down-river), divided in three stages. Stage one stemmed from the stretch of river co-extensive with the old harbour area around Victoria Bridge to a point 600 yards east of the Renfrew Ferry (see Map 1) and covered the riverside quays of Broomielaw, Anderston, Lancefield, Finnieston, Stobcross, Meadowside, Merklands, and the extensive Queen's Dock – all on the north side of the river. On the south were Springfield, Windmillcroft, Mavisbank and Plantation quays, and Princes and Kingston Docks. Stage one also contained the animal lairage and slaughter houses of Merklands, numerous timber yards, Shieldhall Wharf and its shed area, and several shipbuilding yards including the large Govan yard on the south side. Stage two stretched from that point to the Dalmiur, and encompassed the extensive coal and mineral site of Rothesay Dock on Clydebank, as well as several shipbuilding yards and quays. The third stage ran from Dalmiur to Port Glasgow, incorporating the harbours of Bowling and Dumbarton.[21] Much of the timber trade would be located along this stretch of the River Clyde. But stage one was by far the most important in terms of the volume of goods handled, in both the deep-sea and coastal trades, and the great bulk of the dock labour force would have been employed in this area too.

Other trade conducted along the Clyde Trust's geographical sphere of influence consisted of mineral, timber, and general cargo, as well as meat, wheat and flour (sited at Meadowside), and textiles for export. Added to this trade was the

[20] *RC on Poor Laws*, 1910, evidence, Raeburn, Q 89796.
[21] Glasgow City Archives (previously Strathclyde Regional Archives (GCA), T-CN Coll, Clyde Navigation Trust Papers (CNT).

export of iron and steel goods, heavy machinery and railway engines (much of this trade passed through Finnieston). Vessels leaving and arriving in Glasgow traded all over the world, namely Australia, Belgium, Canada, China, France, Japan, New Zealand, South Africa, South America, Spain, the United States and the West Indies.[22]

Foreign trade was thus very important to Glasgow's success. According to one source, the spectacular expansion of Glasgow, like Liverpool, 'was almost entirely a function of foreign trade'.[23] Foreign trade was of great importance too, accounting for almost 66% of the total value of trade at Glasgow before 1914 (Table 3.7 gives a breakdown for six principal export articles to illustrate this case). The values for trade in 1918 are also shown here, in order to illustrate the shift that occurred in the trade pattern during the war years. However, while imports and exports changed places in order of importance during this period, the trend was to remain more or less the same thereafter (and was to continue likewise throughout the interwar decades). Foreign trade was therefore more important before 1914 and was particularly so to the continued profitability of Glasgow as a port at this time, while also acting as a barometer of the extent of economic activity within Glasgow's industrial hinterland.

A natural corollary of this increased development in trade was the expansion of shipping at the port and an increase in the number of shipping firms operating at the port. In 1913 there were 128 shipping firms who had their 'sole or main offices' in Glasgow[24]. By the 1930s this had fallen to around seventy-six, and this compared favourably with Liverpool, which at that time had some eighty such firms. Twenty of these companies in Glasgow managed ten or more ships, which accounted for some 341 vessels in all. When this is compared to Liverpool, however, the differences can instantly be seen. The companies there which managed ten or more vessels had a total of 763 ships, while London had 1,794. While in tonnage handled, Glasgow lagged behind Liverpool and London, this did not reflect the heavy involvement of Glasgow in terms of world shipping, particularly before 1914.[25] Scottish enterprise was to the fore in the area of shipping throughout this period with the founding of well-known firms such as the White Star (1825), the Clan (1845), the Anchor (1852) and the Donaldson (1858) Lines, which augured well for the early period of development.[26] In employment terms the shipping lines were a significant source of work, taking on their own men, who were more regularly employed than others taken on by the stevedore contracting firms. As their business expanded, so too did employment opportunities.

In terms of employment and multiplicity of function, however, the coastal trade arguably accounted for the greatest level of activity around Glasgow and Scotland's ports as a whole. The coasting trade was extremely important to

[22] Ibid.; see also F. Mort, *Lanarkshire* (Cambridge, 1910), chap. 13, 'Shipping and Trade'.

[23] P. Deane, *The First Industrial Revolution* (Cambridge, 2nd edn, 1986), p. 71.

[24] H. Paterson, 'Seamen on the Clyde, 1887–1914: Work and Industrial Relations in the Clyde Shipping Industry' (University of Strathclyde, unpublished M.Phil. thesis, 1992), p. 14.

[25] Slaven and Checkland, *Business Biography*, ii, p. 257.

[26] Pryde, *Scotland from 1603 to the Present Day*, p. 239.

Glasgow, particularly in terms of employment. Coasting vessels may not have carried vast cargoes, nor have provided work for large gangs of dockers, but they did sail regularly and operated numerously, and thus gave regular work to a large body of men over the trading year as a whole. Consider again Table 3.3. and it will be noted that over 82% of all arrivals at Scotland's ports were connected to the coastal trade, and for the west-coast ports it was around 90%. Statistics relating to Glasgow for 1913 show that out of a total of 8,881 arrivals, 7,595 (or 85%) were involved in coastal trade. However, in total tonnage terms coastal shipping accounted for just under 36% of Glasgow's total in 1913. Nevertheless this work was fairly regularly spread over the year as a whole and therefore was very important in employment terms. Such statistics give some sense of the importance of the smaller coastal steam-tramp services, and while the larger shipowners of the regular deep-sea lines became the most powerful voices speaking on the affairs of the port transport industry as a whole, this is no indication of their importance in terms of employment and industrial activity around a port such as Glasgow.

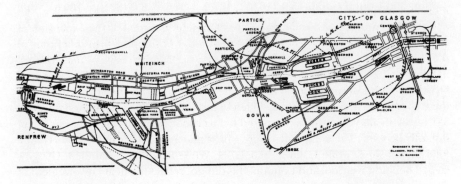

**End of Stage One**

**Map 1.** The City of Glasgow to Renfrew, *c.*1935
(Showing Stage one of The Clyde Navigation Trust Jurisdiction).

**Source:** W. M. French, *The Scottish Ports* (1938).

Glasgow's trade in general cargo was therefore very important and extensive. It was also the main thoroughfare for the passage of goods demanded by the populations of the city of Glasgow and its environs, and the much wider geographical spread of the west central belt of Scotland. In terms of tonnage, arrivals and clearances in coastal traffic between 1841 and 1912, Glasgow was never out of the top ten coastal ports in Britain. Moreover, in terms of arrivals alone Glasgow was third only to London and Liverpool (between 1876 and 1896 the Clydeside port of Greenock was fourth behind these three). Glasgow was therefore a great port in terms of foreign trade, but also in the coastal trade, and the latter is very often overlooked. As P. S. Bagwell and J. Armstong have argued, this is not unusual in so far as both historians and economists alike tend to regard coastal trade as 'inferior' to 'real trade', or foreign trade. The main reason for this is that the latter is considered more exotic and of 'higher value', but by concentrating on this aspect of trade, it is possible to overlook the very important part played by coastal trade in British trade development and, by definition, the development of the British port transport system.[27]

**Table 3.7:** *Value of Six Principal Articles of Export, All other Exports and Transit Trade, Percentage of Each in Relation to Glasgow's Total Export Value, and Total UK Value and Glasgow Percentage of UK, for 1913 and 1918. (£ millions)*

| Articles Exported | Glasgow 1913 (%) | UK | % | Glasgow 1918 (%) | UK | % |
|---|---|---|---|---|---|---|
| Metals and Manufactures | 6.2 (17.0) | 67.6 | 9.2 | 2.7 (10.3) | 46.0 | 5.9 |
| Cotton and Cotton Goods | 5.9 (16.2) | 127.2 | 4.6 | 8.6 (32.8) | 180.0 | 4.8 |
| Machinery | 5.1 (14.0) | 37.0 | 13.8 | 2.8 (10.7) | 16.1 | 17.1 |
| Coal | 1.4 ( 3.9) | 53.7 | 2.6 | 1.9 ( 7.2) | 52.4 | 3.5 |
| Food | 0.7 ( 1.7) | 29.2 | 2.4 | 2.3 ( 8.8) | 8.5 | 26.8 |
| Wool and Woollen Goods | 0.6 ( 1.7) | 42.3 | 1.4 | 0.8 ( 3.8) | 51.6 | 1.6 |
| All Other Goods | 16.1 (44.4) | 168.3 | 9.8 | 6.8 (26.0) | 146.8 | 4.6 |
| Transit Trade | 0.3 ( 0.8) | 109.6 | 0.3 | 0.3 ( 1.1) | 30.1 | 1.0 |
| | | | | | | |
| Totals | 36.3 (100) | 634.8 | 5.7 | 26.2 (100) | 533.4 | 4.9 |

Source: **Shaw Inquiry, ii,** *Appendix* 129, Table no xii and xiv, pp. 166–9 (*PP*, 1920, Cmd 937).

There was also a considerable trade in live cattle, sheep and pigs, discharged at the extensive lairage at Merklands Dock at Glasgow. This trade dated back to the 1870s, but had only moved to Merklands in 1907. Between 1881 and 1896 the trade in animals at Glasgow began to expand significantly, with cattle and sheep initially proving to be the most lucrative element of this area of activity, rising from a total of 32,264 animals to reach 126,006 before the turn of the twentieth century.[28] By the outbreak of war in 1914 there was accommodation for 2,800 cattle, 2,000 sheep (and pigs), with facilities for slaughtering, chilling and cooling. Merklands wharf was the only one in Scotland at this time at which foreign animals could be landed, but it was not an extensive employer of dock labour.[29] The men who worked there, while they were still drawn from the regular dock labour force, worked longer hours

---

[27] P. S. Bagwell and J. Armstrong, 'Coastal Shipping', in M. J. Freeman and D. A. Aldcroft (eds.), *Transport in Victorian Britain* (Manchester, 1988). See Table 6, 'Top Ten Coastal Ports' in 1841, 1855, 1875, and 1912, pp. 176–178 and pp. 207 to 210.

[28] GLA, CNT Papers TC-N-6 Coll.

[29] Report by D. R. Campbell, manager of foreign animals wharf at Merklands, in *Municipal Glasgow: Its Evolution and Enterprises, 1911 to 1914* (Glasgow, 1914), pp. 145–7.

than their counterparts elsewhere in the docks, an average of twelve hours per day as opposed to the standard ten hours. The 1920 Shaw Inquiry noted that the largest employers of labour at Glasgow were in fact an amalgam of employers operating across the entire structure of the port as a whole and were a combination of deep-sea, middle-size tramp and coastal lines. However, out of a group numbering twenty-one separate firms, of one type or another (who accounted for over 80% of all employment), over half were stevedoring firms.[30]

Because of the diversity and variety of goods handled at Glasgow a great many employers were to be found operating within the port. These ranged from the great shipping lines, down through the middle stevedore contracting group, to the labour-only sub-contractor who often employed only a handful of men on an occasional basis. The sub-contractor usually tendered for work from the larger stevedoring, lighterage and porterage contractors; within the latter there were many variations in the actual size of the firm, product, or products, handled, and the numbers of men regularly and occasionally employed. Berth occupation in 1911 gives some indication of the number of potential employers within the port at this time, the type of cargo handled and the places of destination. Some twenty-seven firms are represented on the 1911 berthage list – by no means definitive – and they would generally be regarded as some of the bigger employers operating in the port at this juncture (see Appendices Table I).

There seems little doubt that the smaller shipping firms (not the deep-sea firms) provided the bulk of employment opportunities at this time. According to the evidence given to the *Royal Commission on the Poor Laws* (which reported in 1910), the Allan Steamship Line, for instance, could employ between 125 and 600 men in one twenty-four hour period; while the City Line (not represented in the table below), could employ 500 men for a few days and on other days fall back to their twenty or so permanent workers when there was less work.[31] On a good day these two firms could, therefore, employ over 1,000 men between them and these were only two of the many large firms and shipping lines operating from Glasgow in 1911. Information regarding the actual numbers who worked at the docks is difficult to determine, but as the Shaw Inquiry indicated there are several facts that can be generally agreed on. First, the casual dock labour force at this time numbered some 8,470, which discounting 520 grainweigher and wharfinger staff, leaves 7,950. Secondly, there were twenty-one main employers who accounted for around 80% of this workforce, but these did not include the Allan Steamship Line and City Line, for example, or indeed another regular employers such as the Cork S. S. Line.

Table 3.8 attempts to give some illustration of how many dockers worked for a particular employer, and in what area of operation that employer was involved. What this shows is that the greatest number of men were involved with the tramp and coastal lines, and were employed by the master stevedores; that is, 5,200 out of a

[30] Shaw Inquiry, ii, *Appendix* 75 – table H/16.
[31] *RC on Poor Laws*, 1910, evidence, Colonel J. Smith Park of the Allan Line, p. 26; see also *Appendix* cxxxv, statement by Mr W. S. Workman, of George Smith & Sons, of the City Line, p. 1,111.

total casual dock labour force of 7,950 (which includes a shortfall of 100), or around 66% of the casual dock labour force. This rises to about 77% when all dockers not directly involved with deep-sea or foreign trade are taken into account. Thus it can be argued that by 1919–20 the great bulk of employment within the port of Glasgow was concentrated in coastal traffic.

Other shipping lines, or shipping firms, were represented at the port by agents, and according to the Glasgow Post Office Directory their numbers were not inconsiderable – they are arranged over some twenty-two columns covering nine pages. The Directory contains an entry for the City Shipping Line, for example, listed under shipping agents. Every one of the agents listed, as well as the individual shipowners and almost thirty stevedoring firms, were potential employers. Table 3.8 offers a flavour of the diversity. In the first column we have the names of those employers, but divided into four main groups (the transatlantic or deep sea lines; the tramps and coastal lines, and agents and stevedore firms; the coal employers, and those involved in the timber trade). The second column outlines the area of operation, and the third gives an indication of the numbers involved (also as a percentage of the Glasgow totals). What Table 3.8. also illustrates is that despite the diversity of operations there was still a coherent over-arching structure. In a sense, what is being shown here are the key features of port operation and function at Glasgow.

The multiplicity of employers is often difficult to comprehend, particularly in a large port such as Glasgow. In part this development can be attributed to the ascendancy of steam over sail, in so far as steam led to the evolution of much larger ships, generating ever-increasing loads as well as a greater complexity of cargoes. This led directly to the appearance of the master stevedores and wharfingers, as well as warehousemen, to handle such goods. Other aspects of the operation of a port would depend on the activity around its hinterland, as well as previous historical developments over time and space.   A good example of the extent of diversity in firms operating around and within a port can be seen more clearly, perhaps, by considering a smaller port such as Ardrossan on the Clyde and Ayrshire coast. For example, before 1914 it is known that this port employed around 250 men. Around 150, or 60%, were employed by the Ardrossan Harbour Company, who controlled the port. The remainder of these men were employed by six separate companies, one of which was G. & J. Burns who operated out of Glasgow, another being William Christie & Co. of Tilbury and Grangemouth. Around 100 men, therefore, were employed by six firms dealing with various cargoes, ranging from coal (bunkering), mineral and timber work to some general cargo duties. This not only illustrates the relatively small ratio of men to employers, but the manner in which a great many employers could congregate around a given port, specialising and functioning alongside specific cargoes. In a larger port such as Glasgow, this pattern was intensified and exaggerated. This may help explain why so many men could enter port work quite easily and why the casual system of employment persisted with equal ease: it was ideally suited to the system that it serviced and suited all involved, including the employee and the employer.

**Table 3.8. Employment Structure at the Port of Glasgow, 1919/20, Showing name of Firm, Area of Operations and Numbers Employed and percentage of Total.**

| Name of Line or Firm | Area of Operation | Numbers Employed |
|---|---|---|
| *Deep Sea Lines* | | |
| Anchor Line | | |
| Canadian Pacific | Deep Sea and General- | |
| Donaldson Line | Cargo Men, Coalmen | 1,800 |
| Cork S.S. Co* | (Bunkering) – discounting | (22.9) |
| Allan Lines* | Grainworkers and | |
| J&P Hutchison Ltd | Wharfinger Staff | |
| | | |
| *Tramps and Coastal Lines* | | |
| City Line* | | |
| George Smith & Sons | | |
| G&J Burns and Sons | | |
| Clyde Shipping Co | | |
| Laird Line | General Cargo men for | |
| William Sloane & Co | Smaller Lines and Tramps, | |
| (Master Langlands and Sons | Coastal Lines and Coalmen | 5,200 |
| Stevedores) James Spencer & Sons | (Bunkering) for Coasting Trades | (66.2) |
| Clutha Stevedoring | discounting Grianweighers | |
| William Craig | and Wharfinger Staff | |
| Main Pearson & Co | | |
| James MacLiver | | |
| Macormick & Fraser | | |
| | | |
| *Coal and Ore Stevedores* | | |
| Stewart & Shaw | | |
| Honeyman & Co | Coalmen (300) | 650 |
| George Monro | Ore workers (350) | (8.3) |
| | | |
| *Timber Stevedores* | | |
| James Macgreor | | |
| & Fergusson | Timbermen | 300 |
| Smith and Leishman | (upper and lower docks) | (3.8) |
| | Sub-total | 7,850 |
| Total Labour Force (including 520 grainweighers/wharfinger staff) | | 8,370 |

**Source:** Shaw Inquiry, ii, *Appendix* 76, Table H/16 – Glasgow 2, and 77, Table H/16 – Glasgow 3 (*PP*, 1920, Cmd 937).

Glasgow was dealing with hundreds of different types of goods, ranging from bricks to bolts, cement to corn, hay to herring (salted and barrelled), timber to tobacco, and preserved meats to a profitable trade in live animals, and many more items classified as general cargo. However, it was coal, minerals, iron and steel that accounted for over 60% of all total tonnage, particularly so in the decade before the outbreak of war, as seen in Table 3.9.

**Table 3.9:** *Net Tonnage of Coal, Iron and Steel, Iron Ore and total tonnage, Glasgow 1905–14.*

|  | Net Tonnage of Coal/Iron/Steel/Iron Ore | Net Tonnage of all Goods | % of total | Coal as % net tonnage |
|---|---|---|---|---|
| 1905 | 4,711,062 | 9,025,806 | 52 | 38 |
| 1906 | 5,620,634 | 9,256,218 | 61 | 36 |
| 1907 | 6,085,011 | 9,795,218 | 62 | 37 |
| 1908 | 5,820,603 | 9,530,693 | 62 | 38 |
| 1909 | 6,165,574 | 9,618,563 | 65 | 41 |
| 1910 | 6,563,766 | 10,097,283 | 65 | 40 |
| 1911 | 6,725,864 | 10,359,292 | 65 | 40 |
| 1912 | 5,914,092 | 9,524,662 | 62 | 39 |
| 1913 | 6,582,146 | 10,418,324 | 63 | 39 |
| 1914 | 6,328,511 | 10,067,502 | 63 | 40 |

**Source:** Clyde Navigation Trust Papers, GCA, T-CN 6/5/.

This work did not require a large workforce in relation to tonnage handled. By 1919 the number of men associated with this work accounted for just over 12% of the total estimated casual dock labour force. What is clear, however, is that while coal and minerals required fewer quayside and ship workers, more railway workers were required in the back-up services. As an employment multiplier, therefore, the coal and mineral trade was of particular importance to the Clydeside economy in general and to those who were to become intimately involved in this trade.

It was this lucrative trade that prompted the building of a dock at Clydebank specifically to cope with the expected continued increase in demand for these products. Consequently, Rothesay Dock came into operation in 1907 and in a few short years began to focus as the centre of the coal and mineral trade along Clydeside. Between 1907 and 1913–14, the coal and mineral trade began to move from the first stage of the River Clyde to the second stage. Previously, this trade had been concentrated upriver around the centre of Glasgow itself, on both the north and south sides of the Clyde. Before 1907, Queen's Dock, the General Terminus, Springfield and Mavisbank quays on the south side, and Princes Dock on the north side, had previously handled the great bulk of the coal and mineral trade in Glasgow.

The increase in traffic and trade through Rothesay between these years seems, at first glance, quite considerable. However, according to Jackson, the problems associated with the construction of Rothesay Dock, which was officially brought into commission in 1907, meant that the year 1913 may actually have been its first full trading year.[32] Nevertheless, when the Dock did come into operation, it took over from those other outlets where coal and iron ore were exported and imported. Consequently, the focus of this trade moved to Rothesay Dock. In terms of profit to those companies who dealt in coal, and in terms of employment, Glasgow's coal trade was thus very important. Up to the outbreak of the First World War therefore, according to one Glasgow shipowner, coal had been 'one of the most lucrative trades on the Clyde'.[33]

## The Role of The Clyde Navigation Trust

It is clear that coal tonnage handled at the port of Glasgow peaked before the First World War. But hitherto the Clyde Navigation Trust had invested heavily in the Port of Glasgow, as the building of Rothesay Dock illustrates. From its formation by an Act of Parliament in 1809, after the transfer of control from municipality to Parliamentary Trustees, Clyde Navigation Trust continued to expand the harbour area by constructing docks, wharves, harbours and quays. It financed all of these projects solely by its own credit, without any government, or municipal, finance. According to T. R. Mackenzie, the general manager and secretary to the Clyde Trustees, who reported the Trust's progress in 1900, the Trust never had difficulty raising the necessary capital. The confidence of the general public, wrote Mackenzie, 'was well supported by the steady and continuous progressive increase in the revenue of the port'.[34]

Investment was also considerable when it came to 'canalising' the River Clyde. After 1809, noted one observer, 'to all intents and purposes Glasgow became connected to the sea by a ship canal', particularly the 10 mile stretch from the centre of Glasgow to the Erskine Bridge.[35] This was a particular stimulus to the expansion of Scottish shipping, and as early as 1830 the Clyde was in every sense of the word an ocean seaway.[36] Once again it can be seen that this process had begun in the early part of the nineteenth century, particularly in the deepening of the River Clyde. For example, it was noted in 1768 that the river at Old Kilpatrick was in places only 2 feet deep (Old Kilpatrick came to be the midway point dividing stages one and two of the Clyde under the jurisdiction of the Clyde Trust). Some seven years later this had been increased to a depth of 6 feet – measured at the time of the spring tide.

[32] Discussion with Gordon Jackson, University of Strathclyde, Jul. 1992.
[33] *RC on Poor Laws*, 1910, Raeburn, Q 89789.
[34] 'Clyde Navigation', by T. R. Mackenzie, General Manager and Secretary to the Clyde Navigation Trustees, in Angus McLean (ed.), *Local Industries of Glasgow and the West of Scotland* (Glasgow, 1901), pp. 283–8.
[35] Paterson, 'Seaman on the Clyde', p. 6; see also A. W. Kirkaldy, *British Shipping: Its History and Importance* (1914).
[36] Pryde, *Scotland from 1603 to the Present Day*, p. 238.

By 1820 the average available depth was 9 feet and by the 1850s average depth was around 16 feet. Indeed, during the spring tides the greatest available depth by the 1850s was 19 feet in total. This shows the significance of the changes that had taken place in the first half of the nineteenth century, and laid the foundations upon which later developments were to be built.[37] Thus, between 1863 and 1907 the available waterspace had increased from around 70 acres, within the old harbour, to 207 acres in total.[38] The River Clyde was to be continually and extensively dredged to allow ever-larger ships to sail to and from the port, as well as to allow ships constructed on the Clyde to be built and launched.

What was occurring before 1914 was the steady increase in the size of ships, rather than a rise in their numbers. This prompted one observer to argue that therein lay the 'remarkable and long survival' record of the sail ships, as they too experienced a steady increase in size, although by the end of this period they were rapidly decreasing in numbers.[39] In the 1860s the average size of a ship entering Glasgow was 179 tons, and at that time sailing ships still outnumbered steam ships by ten to one.[40] By 1914 the average size of ship had risen to 719 tons, and the use of ever-larger ships resulted in an increased demand for regular expansion and improvements of docks, wharves and piers and dock equipment. These larger vessels were steel built and steam powered.

Larger ships often resulted in the increased use of machinery, principally because of the need for quick turn-round times. Before 1914, the Trust had invested some 10 million pounds in the Port, of which £7,196,575 had been borrowed – which accounted for around 30% of total revenue raised.[41] Nevertheless, with the increased emphasis on modernisation and mechanisation, a significant rate of investment would have to be forthcoming if the Port was to survive as a viable commercial interest. The period between the wars was one of mixed fortune for Glasgow, as it was for many ports at this time. The trade in coal and iron ore meanwhile never again reached pre-1914 levels. By diversifying into other products, however, Glasgow was to ensure its long-term survival.

*Mechanisation and Modernisation*

There is little doubt that the Trust were convinced advocates of change, principally in the continual update of machinery within the docks, and in particular in the use of new machinery to promote greater speed-up in loading and discharging of bulk cargo (as discussed in depth in Chapter 6, which considers the effect of such innovations on the workforce).

When factors such as innovations in mechanical handling are introduced and are considered alongside others such as changing product markets, the effect on the

---

[37] *Abridged Statistical History of Scotland*, p. 669.
[38] Jackson, *Archaeology of Ports*, p. 134.
[39] Pryde, *Scotland From 1603 to the Present Day*, p. 244.
[40] Ibid., p. 238.
[41] GCA, CNT, T-CN 6/5/ Vol. 7, 'Comparison of Revenue and Expenditure; Wages, Working and Maintenance and Local Assessment for 1914, year ending 30 June'.

dock labour force could be significant. This would be seen not only in terms of the difference in the type of product being handled, but also in tonnage rates – which, for most dockers, dictated average earnings. A product that commanded a higher value would have meant little to the docker, who relied on a good tonnage ratio to ensure a reasonable return for his work. But the increases in both imported minerals, such as limestone and to a lesser degree iron ore, and imported scrap iron, would still have provided a lucrative trade for dockers who regularly worked with these products. However, it would seem that the most common method of payment at Glasgow was by the hour. Thus the dockers could often expect to be paid in different ways depending on the cargo and the circumstances of loading or discharging.

Indeed, gangs of dockers working on the same ship could often encounter different levels of payment depending on the cargo that was being handled. According to oral testimony, even in the 1950s and 1960s there was no 'pooled rate' for goods handled by dockers, a situation that did not change significantly until decasualisation in the late 1960s. For example, if a ship with general cargo (various types of products) was being loaded or unloaded, different gangs of workers would receive different wages depending on the particular product they were handling. If two gangs out of five on a five-hatched ship were loading heavy steel or scrap, their wages could often be much higher than those loading lighter toilet porcelain; despite the fact that loading the latter could take longer as it demanded the safe stowage, or careful extraction, of a fragile and lightweight product.[42] The other three remaining gangs would also probably be on a different wage depending on the product they were handling.

Another factor to consider would be the degree of difficulty experienced when handling different types of cargo when they were stowed, or were to be stowed, in the hatches nearest the bow and the stern. It was generally accepted that these would be the most difficult holds to work in. However, any significant change in products handled, as with relocation of product, significantly affected the life of the docker, and in discussions of trade, trade statistics, rates and product location, this symbiotic relationship should be borne in mind. It should also be borne in mind, that many of the practices in the 1950s were little different from those practised at earlier times.

With the opening of Rothesay Dock came the introduction of Britain's first electrically operated coal hoists which, with the other large cranes for loading heavy materials and those associated with the shipbuilding industry, became an integral part of the Glasgow skyline.[43] Clyde Navigation Trust not only invested heavily in the building of new docks and quays, and in the successful dredging and canalising of the River Clyde, it also invested heavily in mechanised equipment, even in the early part of the nineteenth century, and maintained this development thereafter. Indeed, according to Jackson, the Clyde Trust was constantly 'reviewing and

---

[42] Discussion with Charles Ward, Glasgow Docker, 25 Jun. 1992. This information was verified by other retired dockers who were present.

[43] Jackson, *Archaeology of Ports*, p. 148; see also Marwick, *The River Clyde*, p. 228; and J. F. Riddell, *Clyde Navigation* (Glasgow, 1979), p. 234.

renewing its equipment' throughout this period as a whole,[44] and was continually shifting to suit changes in the pattern of trade.

As early as the 1870s the crane was becoming a well-known feature of the Glasgow docklands. Plantation Quay on the south side of the river was the site for a 60–ton crane with a height of lift of around 59 feet, and was capable of lifting 60 tons at 3 feet 10 inches per minute. Finnieston Quay on the north side of the river had a crane capable of lifting 30 tons, while Kingston boasted a 5–ton crane and 'eleven of a lighter sort . . . placed in less important parts of the harbour.'[45] Such lighter cranes may have been placed in 'less important' parts of the port, but this type of mechanisation would have had important implications for the workforce, increasingly so as the march of mechanisation continued. The level and extent of mechanisation, however, depended on the type of cargo being handled, and its adaptability to mechanical methods, and these tended to be located within the bulk trades. In the coastal trade, mechanisation would not have been as effective, due to the smaller size of vessel.

In an article printed in the *Glasgow Herald* in March 1910, George Baxter, Mechanical Engineer for the Clyde Navigation Trust, committed himself to a comprehensive analysis of dock equipment and its uses. He argued that modernisation was determined by the description and quantity of goods to be accommodated; by local custom and practice; open and closed docks; the rise and fall of the tide and the nature of the ground surrounding the docks, and so on. He also stated that the increased size of vessel demanded quick turn-round and that this was one of the most important considerations for the Trust in relation to the application of new mechanical equipment. General cargo, for example, needed large transit sheds 'for the sorting, consignment and the speedy removal of large vessels in a short period of time'. Coal and ore needed large sidings, ample room for wagons and areas for temporary deposit of such cargo, if wagons were not readily available. Thus, 'ships could be turned around quickly and their spaces taken by another'. This would have been the case for any port handling such goods if they wanted to carry on trading.

Baxter went on to outline the levels of mechanisation within the port as a whole, thus offering an excellent insight into the extent of penetration of new equipment before the First World War. Queen's Dock on the north side of the river was hydraulically powered and operated coaling and cargo cranes, capstans and a swing bridge. Queen's Dock also had steam-driven cranes – all having a capacity of between 20 and 30 tons as well as eleven 5 ton cranes at that time. Princes Dock on the south side of the river combined steam, hydraulic and electric power (the latter for lighting and driving electric cranes and capstans). Rothesay Dock was entirely electric. Some appliances were specially designed to handle coal and iron ore.

There were still many steam appliances to be found at other parts of the harbour. The General Terminus, and Plantation Quay, both on the south side, operated steam cranes and capstans, and many small lightweight cranes were to be found at

[44] Jackson, *Archaeology of Ports*, p. 134.
[45] R. Gillespie, *Glasgow and the Clyde* (Glasgow, 1976), pp. 94–6.

Springfield and Mavisbank quays. Within the docks as a whole there were to be found some 219 capstans. These were mostly electric and hydraulically powered, having a hauling strength of between 1 and 5 tons, the smaller ones having speeds of up to 2,000 feet per minute, and the latter speeds of between 25 feet and 100 feet per minute. Baxter's report covered such details in significantly more elaborate terms, but it does help us form an appreciation of the level and penetration of mechanical operations at the docks before 1914. The writer also noted the Trust's plans to extend the quay at Meadowside in order to cater for the growing demands of the grain trade. This would entail the creation of special facilities and berthage, in order that they could pursue the 'expeditious and economical conduct of that trade'.[46]

The plans for the new granary were to be outlined in a later report in the *Glasgow Herald* in 1910, where it was revealed that the new facilities would have a turnover of 250,000 tons annually and a total capacity of 31,000 tons. It was to be extensively mechanised and was to have two main storage areas; the first would have large silo storage areas and the second was to be divided into nine separate floors. All transference of grain, whether bulk or sacked, was to be by conveyor and elevator, both to and from the quayside. Grain could be discharged directly onto wagons or carts from loading bays in the second storage area. Coastal steamers could also be used for the distribution of grain and this could be redirected back to the quayside in the same manner as it was first unloaded. Facilities were also available for the loading of vessels via lighters. All loads were to be automatically weighed when discharging and loading.[47] (Meadowside grain operation was to be periodically enlarged thereafter, with one of the main periods of change occurring 'most notably in 1960'.[48])

For many who worked in the docks before 1914 mechanisation had become identified as yet another cause of unemployment. According to Treble, machinery 'undoubtedly raised productivity, but at the same time reduced the demand for certain kinds of workers'; further noting that the introduction of equipment which allowed for the transference of grain by suction halved the number of jobs available for grain porters in London.[49] Although the same process was not taking place at Glasgow at this time, there is no mistaking Clyde Navigation Trust's commitment to the modernisation of the Port of Glasgow and the grain trade. It would seem likely that such initiatives would be implemented, or at least would be under consideration. Indeed, the dynamic of the trade demanded that in order to make bulk cargo more profitable, greater loads would have to be moved more quickly.

Mechanisation would be particularly effective with cargoes such as grain, flour, minerals, coal, iron and steel, or, indeed, any commodity that could be bulk handled. Nevertheless, the positive effects of increased investment in mechanisation, and the modernisation of Glasgow as a port, have to be assessed and considered in relation to the workforce too. In short, what needs to be considered

[46] *Glasgow Herald*, 8 Mar. 1910.
[47] Ibid., Sep. 13 1910.
[48] Jackson, *Archaeology of Ports*, p. 134.
[49] J.Treble, *Urban Poverty in Britain 1830–1914* (1979), p. 58.

is the possible displacement effect mechanisation and modernisation may have had on the labour force generally, and on certain groups of dockers in particular. However, in the final analysis, while mechanisation may have forced down gang sizes, larger ships, with more hatchways, would have increased the number of gangs working a ship. Moreover, it may also have increased the numbers needed to clear the quaysides of cargo due to the speed-up caused by the quick turn-round time for vessels.

This chapter has outlined some of the main factors which prompted the geographical growth of the port of Glasgow, and the increasing influence of steam power in the developing fortunes of Clydeside. It has been shown that the port was ably managed and improved, particularly by the canalisation of the River Clyde. Indeed, the management of the Port of Glasgow by the Clyde Navigation Trust was applauded by none other than dockers' leader Ben Tillett, when noting the 'immense growth of trade' which followed the Trust's control of the Clyde.[50] In 1911 the *Glasgow Herald* too confidently praised the role of the Trust and its record to that date, 'one of steady progress at a rate that promised well for the future'. The article also reported that the Trust had its critics, such as the shipowners and employers at the port. At that time they were arguing against the building of a new graving dock at Renfrew, some way down river, which was to be financed entirely from the revenue from the previous year. The *Herald* noted how similar criticisms had been levelled against the building of Rothesay Dock, but that it was now one of the busiest parts of the port. It was felt that the Trust were simply 'anticipating the requirements of the future', and thus far 'each new improvement and each new scheme of extension had been justified by a corresponding growth in the trade of the port'.[51]

Without such investment and foresight the harbour of Glasgow could never have expanded or enticed the growing passenger vessel trade to use Glasgow in ever greater numbers before 1914. If such a trade had been envisaged in terms of natural endowment, this valuable trade would have been located in the natural deep waters further down river at Port Glasgow, some 12 miles distant, rather than located within the centre of Glasgow itself. Clearly, as the Port of Glasgow developed it began to handle an ever greater diversity of cargo and this hastened its geographical expansion further from the centre of Glasgow. As noted by T. R. Mackenzie in 1901:

> The Clyde Navigation Trust, which is not worked for profit, has done immense service in furthering the development of the commercial and industrial interests of the city of Glasgow and West Scotland. It has been administered on the most liberal lines for the conduct and expansion of trade . . . From this retrospect can be seen how the commercial instincts of the men of past

---

[50] Ben Tillett succeeded in putting a resolution through the TUC Conference in Edinburgh in 1896. The resolution stated that 'private ownership was economically unsound, injurious to the community generally and prejudicial to the workers involved'. In essence he was advocating the municipilisation of the Port of London, in view of the success of municipilisation elsewhere (ML Lib C. 92448).

[51] *Glasgow Herald*, 6 Sep. 1911.

generations led them to persevere and succeed in the high aim of making their inland city a great seaport.[52]

The Clyde Navigation Trust was a significant riverside landowner. As such it controlled and influenced the location of many industries around the port including shipbuilding and repair, the timber trade and a profitable trade in live animals both in lairage and slaughtering, as well as owning the land where numerous and varied small works were sited. While little land was given over to warehousing along the riverside, or within the docklands area generally, this trade became centred within the City of Glasgow itself. In this manner the docks could expand without the necessity for the type of physical expansion normally associated with a port which saw such a volume of trade as Glasgow.[53]

The nature of Glasgow's overall development, however, meant that particular parts of the port were not suitable for certain types of traffic and could be better suited to modernisation than others (certain types of docks were only suitable for specific classification of vessels, or sorts of cargo, and this meant that different handling methods developed). This not only complicated the operational structure and engendered a significant degree of diversity and function, it also complicated employment patterns. This arguably helped to maintain greater numbers within the docks than would have been the case otherwise, as well as generating a strict system of job demarcation and specific functional lines of occupation, which centred around a particular dock, cargo, or employer. This is why a port such as Glasgow by the twentieth century could at once be a good example of modernisation and efficiency, and at the same time retain many of the practices more closely associated with another age and the previous century: a microcosm perhaps of the port transport industry as a whole.

[52] Mackenzie, 'Clyde Navigation', p. 288.
[53] Discussion with Gordon Jackson, Sep. 1993.

# CHAPTER FOUR

# Port Operation, Employment Patterns and Occupational Variation before 1914

*The Question of Skill – Theory and Definition*

What constitutes dock work and how can the question of skill be measured in relation to the dock labour force? Phillips and Whiteside argue that one primary reason for the perpetuation of casualism was the 'diverse and elusive quality of skill among port workers'.[1] However, they also note that the dockers considered that their work demanded both 'skill and specialism'.[2] From the dockers' standpoint, dock work was skilled, but we cannot accept that such skill exists simply because the docker believes this to be the case.

In general, then, how do we define skill? Charles More argues that skill can be measured in two ways. First, the type of skill that is considered genuine: 'skill which is usually taken to mean an alliance of manual dexterity (skill) and knowledge'. For example, the carpenter uses manual skills, such as sawing and planing, with his specialist knowledge of different woods, types of joints and so on. But if skill is defined in these simple terms, the combination of some manual skill and some knowledge, then all workers possess skill. When we consider that there are varying levels of skill this definition is rendered somewhat deficient. Therefore, More provides us with a second measurement of skill that is rather more precise: that genuine skill is, 'any combination, useful to industry, of mental and physical qualities which require considerable training to acquire'.[3]

Clearly, the question of training is fundamental to the acquisition of a genuine skill and the most potent example of this would be the 'labour artisan'. But More also notes that much of the strength of the artisan class is derived from their trade unions' control of apprenticeships, and specifically in prescribing the length of the 'training' period necessary to acquire the requisite skills for a specific occupation. In other words, skill as defined by the artisan workforce itself. But is this an adequate explanation of skill? Is skill only acquired through training, or can it be ascribed to certain groups of workers because their work is 'useful to industry'? More would argue that the artisan's skill was genuine, 'acquired by an apprenticeship or some other method of training', and this training was by definition instructive. And it was the skills that the artisans possessed which gave strength

---

[1] Phillips and Whiteside, *Casual Labour*, pp. 25–6.
[2] Ibid., p. 274.
[3] Charles More, *Skill and the English Working Class, 1870–1914* (1988), p. 15 and chaps. 1 and 11.

to their trade union organisations, rather than their skill being derived from the strength of their unions.[4]

This provides us with an acceptable model of what skill is and a more than adequate definition of how the artisan acquired his skill. But More would admit that there are exceptions to his general conclusions. The cotton spinners had a powerful union which gave them considerable strength in the marketplace and kept their wages at a level 'usually associated with workers who had served long apprenticeships'. Thus, the cotton spinners were able to 'socially construct skill' and maintain a high level of wages commensurate with other groups of workers who had genuine skills – skills attained from a prolonged period of training or apprenticeship. In the case of the cotton spinners, therefore, it was their pivotal position in the production process, combined with the strength of their trade union, that enabled them to function along artisan lines. Such bodies of workers maintained their dominant market position by protecting their skill, particularly by the late nineteenth and early twentieth centuries when such skills could be significantly diluted by increased mechanisation, or by increased managerial control at the point of production.[5]

Social attitudes can play a role in deciding what is, and what is not, considered skilful. For example, if we adopt a 'Weberian' economic viewpoint of increased, or decreasing, market capacity, we discover a method by which skill can be ascribed to a certain group of workers (the cotton spinners, for example), and devise a method to observe how such ascribed skills change as society itself undergoes industrial and economic change. In other words, definitions of skill alter over time and are dependent on the needs of the market at a given period in time – skills 'useful to industry and society'. The genuine scarcity value that certain workers held helped to define their status and skills, and, in the final analysis, their usefulness to the economy. An example of this type of fluidity in the definition of skill can be seen with the changing fortunes of the handloom weaver between the late eighteenth century and the mid-nineteenth century. The emergence of the factory system of production and the increased use of machinery gradually diluted their skills, and changing market conditions further hastened their demise. This occurred at a time when the weavers' unions, unlike the cotton spinners or the engineers in the later period, lacked the organisational and political strength to resist such change. As a result their skills were devalued and in time the weavers became superfluous to the requirements of industry. However, in this changing industrial landscape new groups of workers, such as the engineers and the boilermakers, had established themselves, and by the second half of the nineteenth century they were the new aristocracy of labour. Moreover, they had developed trade unions that could speak

---

[4] Ibid., pp. 226–8, see too G. Crossick, *An Artisan Elite in Victorian England* (1978), and R. Q. Gray, *The Labour Aristocracy in Victorian Edinburgh* (Edinburgh, 1976). Gray and Crossick did not argue that all the power of the artisan derived from their unions, but Crossick in particular suggested that it was 'hardly relevant to enquire whether it was the union that gave them strength, or their strength that gave them their union'. What was important, was that both these tendencies grew out of the 'craft culture', p. 157.

[5] More, *Skill and the English Working Class*, pp. 20–1.

on their behalf and defend their interests against managerial attempts to control apprenticeships, the dilution of their trades, or the introduction of mechanised methods of production. Their scarcity value was thus artificially maintained at a time when they could easily have been replaced with new technology.

If skill could be defended and maintained because of the organisational strength of artisanal trade unions, could we expect to see a similar development take place within the trade unions representing the non-artisan workforce? Consider again the cotton spinners. Eric Hobsbawm would define them as at best being 'semi-skilled', but their status and position in industrial society was derived from the pivotal role they played in the production process:

> Their aristocratic standing depended on defending a limited number of strategic positions in the work process which enjoyed some bargaining-strength, against the potential competition of a large number of men quite capable of replacing them.[6]

Thus, Hobsbawm argued, the cotton spinners were 'contrived aristocrats', and, in line with More's thesis, they did not have much in the way of genuine skills.[7]

In the earlier part of the nineteenth century the situation was quite different, as the example of the handloom weavers illustrates. From a Marxist perspective, this would provide an ideal example of the division of labour within the labouring classes and the inevitable de-skilling of at least one part of it. This perspective also recognises, however, that the introduction of machinery necessitates operators who in turn become the new skilled of the future, and thus, as Marx intimated, the dilution of one skill can in turn promote another. Weber's theory is also relevant in this instance, in so far as the definition of skill changes in accordance with the needs of industry and changing patterns of demand within the economy. While More's definition of skill is still valid, it can perhaps be added that skill is also economically defined and that this definition changes over time. From this standpoint, therefore, skill is socially constructed, and it is this socio-economic recognition that gives skill legitimacy and status within society. This is evidently more likely to occur within the artisanal labour force, but it can also occur at a more 'contrived' level when certain groups of workers are seen to have a pivotal role in the production process.[8] The question is, however, did the dockers function in a similar fashion?

### Defining Skill Within the Dock Labour Force

Phillips and Whiteside described dock work as 'amorphous and diffuse in nature, involving many modes of, primarily, manual work'. The range of work and variety involved, when coupled with the constant threat of underemployment and dis-placement (either by the introduction of newcomers, or machinery) saw the docker

---

[6] Hobsbawm, 'The Aristocracy of Labour Reconsidered', *Worlds of Labour*, p. 235.
[7] Ibid., p. 220.
[8] More, *Skill and the English Working Class*, pp. 17–19. For basic theories of the market value of labour for Marx and Weber see, Tony Bilton (et al.) *Introductory Sociology* (1984 edn.), pp. 58–63. For Weber see H. Gerth and C. W. Hills (eds.), *From Max Weber: Essays in Sociology* (1948).

respond by developing 'a strong sense of demarcation and a jealous and proprietorial attitude to job territories'. Thereafter, the dockers began to convert 'their specialist function' in relation to particular cargoes into 'constructed skills'.[9] When considering More's analysis of what skill is, it could be argued that dock work is not 'genuine skill', but 'a contrived skill'. Therefore, the dockers developed the ability to both 'create and maintain privileges' similar to that of the artisan unions (aided by the close kinship ties typical of this type of 'occupational community'), and given the 'strategic position' they commanded in the economy, and, latterly, through the increased power of the dockers' unions, they could, in line with Hobsbawm's argument, 'enjoy some bargaining-strength, against the potential competition of a large number of men quite capable of replacing them'.[10] In this manner the docker was little different from the cotton spinner.

The docker required very little training and certainly did not serve any apprenticeship. However, certain groups of dockers did require to have some considerable experience in their particular line of work. In the *Fifth Report of the Select Committee on the Sweating System*, in 1890, it was argued that casual dock work was 'open to everybody without apprenticeship or training'. But the report also noted the testimony of the manager of Millwall Docks, Colonel Birt, who suggested that the matter of defining skill was not that simple. Birt argued that the docker's status could be reduced by the introduction of outside men, who entered into competition for employment with the 'trained dock labourer'.[11] Even the casual labourer, noted Birt, 'soon picks up more or less skill as a casual, and he will by degree work into a higher class'. Therefore, the docker did undergo some degree of instruction and if he stayed in dock work by necessity had to commit to a learning period. Moreover, Birt was also conscious that dock work had its 'aristocracy' of labour. In relation to the Port of London these were the dealporters and cornporters.[12] Clearly, many of the tasks executed within the docks, whether on ship or on the quayside, demanded physical strength as the first main condition, but dockside tasks often demanded a degree of skill and a period of training in order to further hone and develop these skills. The Standing Advisory Committee for the Port Transport Industry evidently accepted this position in their report of December 1936:

It was (and, indeed, is) commonly but wrongly assumed that dock work was entirely unskilled and could be performed efficiently by any person who managed to secure an engagement . . . but it was uneconomic because it was often so inefficient.

The report added that the there was a real risk to life and limb 'due to the employment of men who were unaccustomed to the work'. Therefore, dockers

---

[9] Phillips and Whiteside, *Casual Labour*, pp. 274–8.

[10] Hobsbawm, 'The Aristocracy of Labour Reconsidered', p. 235.

[11] *Select Committee of the House of Lords on the Sweating System, 5th Report, Minutes of Evidence* (*P.P.*, 1890 (169) xxi, pp. lxxii-lxxvii).

[12] *Select Committee of the House of Lords on the Sweating System, 2nd Report, Minutes of Evidence*, testimony of Colonel G. R. Birt, General Manager, Millwall Docks (*P.P.*, 1888 (448) xxipp. 279–80).

did need to aquire a degree of training and skill in order to avoid accident or injury.[13]

How, then, is skill measured within the dock industry and what groups, or categories, of dockers possessed it? Such judgements are not as easy to make within the general dock labour force as they would be in other areas of port work, particularly in the 'service sector'. For example, a craneman or a capstanman are precisely that: in short, they have a specific job title, a definitive area of specialism and could be easily identified as having skills, particularly by the outside observer. In Glasgow they were also permanent employees, working for the Clyde Navigation Trust, and they were not considered part of the casual dock labour force. But generally speaking, it was the shipworkers who were considered the most skilled of the dock labour force. While a good number of dockers could claim to have a degree of speciality in the handling of specific goods, it was generally accepted that stevedoring was a recognised skill, and the stevedores generally constituted 'a relatively small proportion of the total number of shipworkers' (and at the Port of Glasgow they were a recognised and licensed employer of labour).[14] As noted in Charles Booth's study of London: 'the stevedore [was] a skilled stower of cargo, whereas the mere docker . . . engaged both in discharging and loading . . . does not require to have very great skill'.[15] It would seem clear that the stevedore in Glasgow functioned as an employer of men, or, if he worked for the large shipping concerns, was an employing agent or foreman. The men he employed, however, functioned as an unofficial stevedoring class under the more general title of shipworker. At Glasgow they were considered to be the most skilful.

According to Booth, 'to stow cargo to the best advantage for the ship as well as the merchandise, demands science as well as care'. [16] And this fits in well with Colonel Birt's assertion that the docker did have skills, and that the casual docker was learning these skills while he was working within the industry. It was in shipwork that the first dock trade unions were to emerge around the mid-nineteenth century, and thereafter they continued to develop along craft lines in a fashion not too dissimilar to the artisan unions of the same period. Indeed, this occurred at the Port of Glasgow in 1853. The Glasgow Harbour Labourers' Union was known as a stevedoring body, but it was very much a union of shipworkers. That the employers viewed the membership of the GHLU as skilled is clear too, in that they openly entered into formal working agreements with them at Glasgow (the first agreement of its kind at the port). Had the shipworkers not played such an important role in the loading and discharging of certain quality goods the employers would certainly not have recognised their union.

There was, therefore, some degree of skill and training needed in order that a ship could be stowed with goods safely and 'scientifically'. Thus the shipworkers, in this instance, could be said to have 'genuine skill'. The coaltrimmers too had to have considerable skill, and while they only worked with one cargo, their expertise

---

[13] PRO, LAB 101/18, *Port Transport Memorandum*, 'Introduction', para. 4, pp. 1–2.
[14] Lovell, 'Sail, Steam and Emergent Dockers' Unionism', p. 236.
[15] *RC on the Poor Laws*, 1910, evidence, Colonel J. Smith Park, Q. 89617.
[16] Booth, *Life and Labour*, p. 428.

lay in the even distribution of coal around the hold in order that the vessel remained in good trim and thus safe for sailing. Likewise, when discharging a ship a similar practice was devised, but executed in reverse order. If not done correctly a vessel would simply keel over, and if not secured correctly, badly stowed cargo could make a ship list so dangerously as to cause it to sink.

In the early years of shipworkers' trade unionism it would seem that one of the primary functions of the organisation was to ensure the control of entry into the trade, and by initiating procedural agreements with the employers the union took over many of the tasks of management. In this sense, the GHLU was acting in a similar manner to the cotton spinners' union. Lovell would also subscribe to the notion that the organisational strength of the dockers was linked to 'craft principles of administration'. Given the lack of managerial structure at the docks the docker was left with 'a high degree of control'. The dockers themselves filled this managerial gap and like the cotton spinners performed a 'sub-managerial and supervisory' role: they also maintained 'shop floor discipline', argued Hobsbawm.[17] The dockers had come to exert a significant degree of control over their working environment in a likewise fashion, and the promise to maintain discipline would have been one reason why the port employers at Glasgow entered into agreement with the GHLU so quickly after their formation in 1853. In this way, 'unskilled workers can sustain autonomous regulations associated with craftsmen'.[18] It was a model the dockers were quick to adapt to their industrial relations strategy.

It would seem clear that the main division within the ranks of the dockers at any port, not least Glasgow, was between those who worked the ships and those who worked off-ship. The distinction was fundamental and the reason was quite straightforward: 'the purely casual, irregular, unskilled labourers were invariably confined to shore operations; employers put their regular workers on the ship'.[19] The level of skill thus ascribed to a particular docker was important as it dictated regularity of work over a given period. The more skilled a particular worker was, the more he could hope to work. Conversely, if the worker was less skilled, then the regularity of his work was affected considerably.

For shipworkers this differential was essential, and it was their perceived skill, and thus their regularity of employment, which in turn dictated the extent of average weekly earnings, rather than simply hourly remuneration for the work done. For example, the ship worker who worked below the deck stowing goods, or other cargo, was considered to have greater skills than the ordinary quayworker, but there was very often little differential in the average hourly rate paid generally at a port, as shown in Table 4.1. After the amalgamation of the shipworkers' union and the quayworkers' union in Glasgow around 1899, however, these two specific areas of specialism did become somewhat blurred, although there was still a significant degree of demarcation between certain types of dock work.

---

[17] Ibid., p. 220.
[18] Lovell, 'Dockers' Unionism', p. 231.
[19] Ibid., p. 235.

**Table 4.1:** *Shift rate and average weekly wage of section of Glasgow Dock labour force,*
*1908.*

| Employment Status | Shift Rate | | Average Weekly Wage |
|---|---|---|---|
| Class | Day | Night | |
| A – Permanent | 7*d.* | 8*d.* | 27*s* |
| B – Regular Casuals | 7*d.* | 8*d.*-10*d.* | 25*s* |
| C – Irregular Casuals | 7*d.* | 8*d.*-10*d.* | 12–15*s* |

**Sources:** Gerald Walsh, *Report on Dock Labour in Relation to Poor Law Relief,* 1908.

As will be shown in Chapters 7 and 8, during the 1890s both the shipworkers and
the quayworkers began to work in areas previously dominated by the other. Indeed,
by 1890 the Glasgow Harbour Labourers' Union Rules specifically stated that
'members are not restricted from taking part in any kind of work, either on board
or ashore'.[20]

*Employment Patterns and Occupational Variation*

Evidence presented to the Shaw Inquiry gives some illustration of the way in which
the dock labour force was employed and the differences which existed between
those who handled different types of cargo on board ship or along the quayside.
Those who worked on ship were the general cargo men, the coaltrimmers and the
ore men who discharged mineral cargo. The quayworkers generally remained
onshore and prepared materials for loading or landed cargo onto the dockside, or
directly onto carts and railway wagons waiting alongside. They also stored materials
in transit sheds or other storage areas around the docks.

The grain trade also employed dockers. Grain was discharged from larger vessels
to the smaller coasting vessels in several different ways. The dockers always worked
in gangs (of varying size depending on the size of the ship carrying the cargo), and
worked conveyor belts in order to aid in the discharging of grain from the hold of a
ship onto carts or wagons (later it would be discharged using suction hoses). On the
smaller steamers, where the use of conveyors was not always practical, or where the
stevedore did not have access to such equipment (some docks were not suitable for
their use), grain was discharged using a winch operated by a docker, and directed
out of the hold by a hatchman, who was also a docker. Similarly, grain could also be
bagged and weighed (although grain weighing was not a function of the ordinary
docker) on board ship before it was discharged, then physically taken to the
hatchway and placed on wooden palates to be winched, or lifted out by crane, or
carried up and across gangways to the quayside. Once on the quayside it was loaded

---

[20] SRO, Constitution and Rules of Glasgow Harbour Labourers' Union, FS 7/ 81 (May 1890,
Section II, Part Two, Clause 11.).

onto vans or carts, or open railways wagons to be taken to the grain stores, or again loaded onto smaller vessels for coastal distribution.

General cargo often needed a greater degree of skill and was handled on both the quayside and on board ship. This type of cargo came in several different shapes and sizes and many dockers came to handle only a few articles of this type. Thus, there was a significant degree of diversity in this type of work. Some work demanded great physical strength, particularly cargo such as cement (which was packed in barrels for transit), creosote oil or molasses in casks, or nitrate or guano in bags, all examples of 'dirty cargoes'. By 1920 the average gang size in this type of work was between four and eight. Both general cargo dockers, and grain workers, were paid by the hour and worked on both deep sea vessels and coasting ships and steamers. A higher rate was also paid for working on coasting vessels; further differentials in payment were made for working with special cargoes, such as refrigerated and frozen meats.

Other dockers worked only with timber and only worked either on the upper docks, from Meadowside and above, or on the lower docks of Merklands, Shieldhall or Rothesay Docks. The Shaw Inquiry noted that the timber men were also paid by the hour and that a higher differential was paid to all work undertaken within the lower docks area. The timber itself was discharged in a variety of different ways; either lifted by crane after being bundled and slung, or separated and carried physically when pieces were too small for lifting by crane. Apart from such information, however, the evidence placed before the Shaw Inquiry gave few other details of this type of work.[21] At the Clydeside port of Ardrossan on the Ayrshire coast, for example, timber was discharged overside, while the timber ships were in the tidal basin. At high tide the dock gates were opened and the timber was punted across the water to the sleeper factory, where it was lifted up on to the quayside by the dockers.[22] It is unlikely, however, that the overside method was used at Glasgow because the port had no dock gates or tidal basins. Therefore, the great bulk of this work would have been executed between ship and quayside.

At the port of Greenock in the late 1890s timber was discharged overside and 'rafters' were employed to assist the dockers in this type of unloading. Onboard ship, however, the docker handled all timber and gang size would vary depending on given factors. Gang size was increased from three to four, for example, when timber was discharged from the larger ships, as opposed to smaller steamers, and it was on the ships that the rafters were employed (one rafter and four dockers to each winch used for discharging). Rafters were, however, paid 1s per hour at all times, whether rafting or otherwise, whereas the dockers were paid 7s per hour. No mention of rafters is made in connection with the timber trade at Glasgow and this may have been the major difference between the two ports.[23]

---

[21] Shaw Inquiry, ii, *Appendix* 75, 'Terms and Conditions of Dock Labour at Glasgow, 1920' (including evidence from Clyde Trust Engineer George Baxter, reported in the *Glasgow Herald*, 8 Mar. 1910).

[22] Kenefick, *Ardrossan*, p. 3.

[23] SRO, Rates and Regulations of Greenock Dock Labourers' Union, FS 7/106 (Rule 38, 26 Oct. 1897).

The other method of payment in operation at most ports handling bulk cargo was by piece rate or payment by tonnage. While it is known that this method of payment was prevalent at Glasgow, it is one factor that was not considered in Gerald Walsh's report. The discharge tonnage rates for cargo also varied considerably, depending on the goods handled. As noted in the previous chapter, different goods were handled at different rates and by different methods of payment. For example, at the Clyde port of Ardrossan in 1912 the rates paid for the discharge of copper and sulphur ores was 4d. per ton, whereas for iron ore and limestone the rate was 3½ d. per ton, and the average rate for loading coal was 1¼ d. per ton. Not only were there variations between the rates for products handled, but there was also a variation between different ports handling the same products. While the tonnage rate at Ardrossan for coal was 1¼ d., at the another Clyde port of Irvine it was 1¼ d. per ton, while at Manchester, Liverpool and Cardiff, the rate was reported to be 2d. per ton.[24]

While there is no specific breakdown of payment and method of payment for Glasgow at this time, some indication of the type of structure that may have been in place can be determined from later joint agreements between employers and the union representing the dockers. For example, in the 1920s and 1930s it is clear that dockers were paid in a variety of different ways ranging from day wages to piecework rates, with a separate section for the payment of permanent workers at the port. There were also different levels of payment and agreements on overtime dependent on the type of cargo handled. Thus, special recognition was given to London Ocean Shipowners' piecework rates, or London coastal, short sea and Baltic food trades.[25]

The agreements also covered payment for different types of cargo, specifically the handling of general cargo loaded or discharged from the deep-sea berths around the port of Glasgow. Citing the actual rate of payment is, for the purposes of this comparison, unnecessary at present (as it without doubt bears little resemblance to the level of payment in the period before the War), but the comparison and the definition of the different types of cargo handled, arguably changed little during this period. General cargo was paid as day wages, but there were varying payments for grain weighers, grain wagon loaders, timber workers, coal workers, ore workers and other mineral workers (as shown in Table 4.2). There were also separate agreements for those working on the same cargo on the coasting vessels.[26] There were also lists of items which were noted as dirty cargo and carried a higher premium rate. Such items ranged from creosote oil in casks, asbestos or guano in bags, seal oil and whale oil in barrels and cases (drums excepted), to the handling of live animals, all of which were paid on an hourly basis.[27]

After the Great War the agreements that came into operation amounted to the codification of the traditional methods of payment, including historical differen-

---

[24] *Ardrossan and Saltcoats Herald,* 24 Oct. 1912.
[25] *Scottish Transport and General Workers Union, General Agreement with Glasgow Docks No.1 Branch,* Jan. 1932 (based on a modification of the National Agreement of May 1920), see pp. 3 to 8.
[26] Ibid., pp. 9–13.
[27] Ibid., pp. 14–17.

tials, such as those seen in the timber trade. The lower harbour rates were higher, because they were further away from the areas where the timber workers lived. There were also other traditional differentials established between the coasting and deep-sea trades. All these differentials, the Shaw Inquiry were informed, were based on 'traditions built up over time, with most having real reason for their existence'. According to the Glasgow stevedore who submitted this evidence, these differentials would in practice 'be difficult to wipe out'.[28]

What may have changed during the war years was the extent and penetration of mechanisation, particularly in the bulk trades, and in this line of work discharging methods varied considerably. Ore could be discharged by loading it into buckets suspended from a crane, as was most often the case at Rothesay Docks. However, time rates could be paid in this trade also, especially when grabs were used for discharging cargo. But all ores discharged from coasting vessels were paid by piece rate. Working with the bucket was considered to be less of a problem than with the grabs. According to the report of Clyde Trust engineer George Baxter, the grabs had to drop in free fall from an optimum height above the hatch so as to penetrate the cargo below. Thereafter the cargo was lifted from the hold and discharged onto waiting railway wagons, which when filled would immediately leave the dockside. It may have been the case that time rates were used with grabs because gang size was reduced by this method. In the case of the grabs, the pace of production was dictated by the rate of entry and exit from the hold. When the bucket was used the rate of entry and exit was dictated by the rate at which the dockers loaded the ore. The piecework method would, therefore, have been used in this instance to encourage speed of discharge.

Men working in the coal and ore trades, noted the Shaw Inquiry, were paid similarly. But coal was loaded in different ways, depending on the vessel. On a small vessel it could be transported in buckets to the end of the quay and then tipped into the hold of a ship berthed alongside. This method would also be affected by the rise and fall of the tide, particularly in a port like Glasgow, and the varying level of the ship in the water as cargo was discharged from its hold, as well as the effect on the smaller ship as its hold was filled. Special staging would have to be erected when the tide was high and the tippers would then push the coal 'bogies' up the incline and over into the hold. In the majority of cases, particularly at Rothesay Docks, a quayside crane would be used and buckets would be tipped mechanically into the hold. After a certain height was reached the coal would be spread evenly around the hold by the coaltrimmers. In this instance, the coal would be loaded and paid at an hourly rate, and only when the coaltrimmers boarded the vessels would the rate of payment change to piece rate.

Coal could also be loaded by the use of the coal hoist, or by lifting full railway wagons over the hold and the coal directed into the hold via a chute fixed to the end of the wagon. The discharge of coal would have been executed in a similar way to the ore trade, depending on the size of the vessel and the dock alongside which the vessel was berthed. Indeed, coal was important in other ways too, in so far as it

---

[28] Shaw Inquiry, i, testimony of J. S. Spencer, Glasgow, p. 271.

required significant numbers of railway workers, as well as dockers. At Glasgow the same wagons could have been used to ship in coal and ship out minerals – but this did not always happen. It was not unusual for the coal and mineral merchants to deny each other the use of their wagons. These conflicts of interest between traders at the port would doubtless have been better resolved had the Clyde Trust controlled the supply of wagons.[29] The operation of cranes, hoists and capstans were considered specialist functions managed by the employees of the Clyde Trust.

What the Shaw Inquiry illustrated was that the structure of the dock labour force in Glasgow had not changed significantly after the First World War. It had remained more or less the same as it had been at the close of the nineteenth century, after the amalgamation of both the shipworkers and the quayworkers within the same trade union organisation. But, like so much associated with dock work conclusions can be impressionistic. It is true that the Shaw Inquiry sustained the findings of Gerald Walsh's earlier enquiry of 1908, but it is equally true that there are many weaknesses in both these studies, not least in connection with dockers' wages.

## Employment Structure – Gerald Walsh's Investigation, 1908

A good starting point in any attempt to analyse the structure of the dock labour force in Glasgow is Gerald Walsh's Report on Dock Labour published in 1908. The results of enquiries made between 1905 and 1907, his account concentrates on the shipworkers and their employers, rather than the occupational considerations of the quayworker and others. But this need not pose a problem, insofar as both the shipworker and the quayworker at Glasgow were, by that time, more or less united under the generic title of 'docker'.

Despite weaknesses in his analysis, particularly in relation to the actual numbers working at the port, Walsh did raise some interesting points. For instance, he stressed that the term 'dock labourer' was open to many interpretations, but for the purposes of his investigation it was still the most 'convenient' title for describing the different classes of workers at the docks. He felt that the labour force, as it operated in Glasgow, could essentially be broken into three distinctive component parts, or classes, which he termed A, B and C men. Within this structure lay the whole occupational spectrum, ranging from the permanent employees (but not those employed by the Clyde Trust), to the stevedores who loaded the ships, down to the quay porters and carriers, and 'the casual labourer who obtained an occasional day's work'.

The A class docker was considered an experienced man, attached to a foreman almost permanently, working either day or night. These men were, to all intents and purposes, permanent (permanency meant employed on a weekly basis, or occasionally by the fortnight), mostly in the private employ of the Allan and Donaldson Shipping Lines. They received the highest weekly wage of around 27s and were not members of any trade union.

The second group, the B class, were considered to be equally experienced, but were not attached to a particular foremen. Rather, they followed a particular firm,

[29] Shaw Inquiry, i, *Appendix* 75; see also Baxter's article, *Glasgow Herald*, 8 Mar. 1910.

shipping agent, or master-stevedore contractor (although they always worked under a designated foreman). This group did not as a rule work day and night like those in group A, but were employed on a casual basis. Their basic rate, if they should secure a full week's work, was estimated to be around 25s. They answered to the foreman who was a permanent employee, 'placed in supreme command' of a particular vessel. Under the foreman was a sub-foreman, or ganger, who would supervise one hatch on a vessel and a gang of between fourteen and nineteen men, depending on the cargo. These men were considered to have a significant degree of specialism and generally worked for a particular contractor. Walsh stated that they were 'organised' and so would have been members of the National Union of Dock Labourers.

The B class were, in times of increased activity, supplemented by men drawn from the ranks of the class C men. It may be presumed that these men were the out-and-out casuals and were most probably quayworkers. Their wages were on average half that of those of the other classes – between 12s and 15s per week. These men, stated Walsh, were not members of a trade union.

Walsh felt that this was a reasonable picture of the employment structure at Glasgow. He stressed that the work did see 'all kinds and classes of men drift into the docks', but that men worked there because the work was essentially 'intermittent and more congenial [than] working in more regular employment'. The Glasgow dock labourer confined himself to dock work only and sought work nowhere else. Walsh felt it only necessary to add:

> that the men appear to possess an accurate knowledge of the arrival of vessels, the class of cargo, and the number of men likely to be required: and labour is fairly distributed between classes A and B.[30]

It would seem that both the class A and class B men were mostly shipworkers, as most of his references are to descriptions of this type of work. However, given the great amount of work done along the quayside at this time, this distinction is by no means clear. Indeed, by the time of Walsh's investigation the lines of demarcation between work done on the quay and that done off the ship may have been so eroded as to pose no great problem of definition. It may have been more of a problem in the earlier period, particularly in the late 1880s and early 1890s. But by the later period there was less confusion over function. In the period well before Walsh's study, there is evidence which suggests strongly that the shipworkers were a minority within Glasgow's dock labour force. The Glasgow Harbour Labourers' Union had a membership of around 900 in 1872 and from then and up until the late 1890s numbers settled at around 600. At the same time Glasgow Trades Council reported that the National Union of Dock Labourers had a membership of over 4,000.[31] Thus,

---

[30] G. Walsh, *Report on Dock Labour in Relation to Poor Law Relief*, 1908, pp. 17–18.

[31] For membership figures of the GHLU before 1889 see Lovell, 'Dockers' Unionism', pp. 232–7. For 1889 figures, consult S. and B. Webb, *Industrial Democracy* (1913), pp. 120–1. Averages for GHLU membership in the 1890s are taken from Registrar of Friendly Societies Reports, SRO. For NUDL estimates of membership for 1889 see *Glasgow Trades Council Annual Report*, Nov. 1888–89, p. 8.

even at their highest level of organisation, the shipworkers of Glasgow constituted at most perhaps 20% of the dock labour force. Clearly, by the 1890s the greatest number of port workers in Glasgow were employed as quayworkers.

Of the last class, the C class, Walsh says little. Walsh stressed in his report, when discussing the workings of the Poor Law, 'that the docker proper did not come upon the rates'. Evidence from this study would that it was among the category C dock workers that the worst extremes of poverty would have found. In short, they were the most irregularly employed class of dock worker. Lastly, Walsh intimates that the A men were 'mostly permanent' and that the dock labour force generally (estimated in his terms at around 5,000) was more or less evenly split between A and B men. This would mean that around 2,500 were 'mostly permanent'. However, employers at Glasgow, with the exception of Clyde Trust, only maintained a relatively small permanent force. Therefore, Walsh's use of the term 'permanent' is somewhat problematic and proves as ambiguous as his own reservations over the usage of the term 'dock labourers'.

Walsh's analysis essentially follows the general philosophy and logic of Colonel Smith Park of the Allan line, one of only two employers canvassed during his investigations in Glasgow, particularly in relation to the class C men. Smith Park described the class C men as, 'inexperienced, generally physically unfit and [they] never exerted themselves [sufficiently] to secure regular employment'. He further stated that this class seldom filled the vacancies in the second class, and that when such vacancies arose they were generally filled by the able-bodied from other occupations who quickly adapted themselves to dock work. He also argued that there were not many men in the third class who were 'permanent frequenters of the docks'.[32]

Smith Park arguably underestimates the size of this third class. He also under-estimated, perhaps intentionally, the levels of distress encountered by them and the other classes of docker in times of economic downturn. The 1900s were time of significant depression on Clydeside, yet Smith Park hardly considers the effect of this, or the unemployment that followed in its wake. Indeed, like Walsh himself, Smith Park seems to be suggesting that the majority of dockers had in fact escaped it. If someone was suffering it was generally the class C men, and they brought much of that on themselves. Thus, he could argue that it was not the industry itself that caused an unemployment problem, but the general attitude of those who operated within the third class group. The problem of distress within this group, he argued, 'lay in their own hands'. It seems clear that this is a view accepted by Walsh and that this may be why he did not consider this group in his survey.

*Redefining the Structure – The Observations of James Larkin c.1907*

Within the crude employment structure constructed by Walsh, little account is taken of the role of the sub-contractor, usually a docker himself, probably but not necessarily a foreman of casual status. In 1906, James Larkin, as General Organiser

---

[32] *RC on Poor Laws*, 1910, evidence, Smith Park, Q. 89620

of the NUDL, noted the plight of those employed by the sub-contracting middle man. This was around the same time that Walsh conducted his investigation. Larkin observed that this 'contract labour' (as he called it) was a 'most degraded, harassed body of men'. Larkin, in this instance, was speaking of the iron-ore workers at Govan in 1907, who were, he noted:

> Mostly North of Ireland men who lived in model lodging houses . . . engaged by the hour, and at all hours of the day or night . . . They might work one hour . . . then stand by for two or three . . . may be half a day – get one or more hours work, [and] draw a few coppers.[33]

Larkin observed that these men were 'in a continual state of semi-starvation and drunkenness', and they were the first human beings he had ever seen 'drinking methylated spirits'.[34] They often preferred to sleep in the holds of the ships they were working rather than pay the 4*d.* per night charged by the 'doss house'.[35] It may have been these men that were viewed by Walsh as the 'out-and-out casuals'. Thus, safely accounted for, they were easily dismissed from his investigations because they were not viewed as 'dockers proper'. This may suggest that the more regular dock jobs in Glasgow were kept for the better qualified members of the dock labour force, or those part of a well recognised kinship group. What Larkin described, therefore, was the effect of a policy of importing workers into areas of dock work which were too irregular to attract a more settled labour force.

There may have been another reason behind the employers' importation of Irish labour in this instance. It was shown through the evidence presented to the *Royal Commission on Labour*, 1892, that the employers at Glasgow had actually 'smashed' the Glasgow Harbour Mineral Workers' Union (GHMWU) in 1888, after only one year in existence. A letter written by the ex-secretary of the union, in May 1889, confirms this. The GHMWU had been caught up in a very costly dispute with the employers, and after being 'locked out by the masters', it was recorded that men from Belfast were brought in to take their places. As a result of the employers' action the strike collapsed and so too did the fledgling GHMWU.[36] Here was a ready-made workforce willing to work in the mineral trade on a regular basis, but the employers were clearly happy to operate this trade on a sub-contract basis. To have an organised group of workers associated with this trade, however, attempting to exert control over how it operated, would have undermined the employers managerial prerogative. The operation of the sub-contracting system was clearly the most inexpensive way for them to operate the mineral trade in that section of the

---

[33] Emmit Larkin, *James Larkin, Irish Labour Leader 1876–1947* (1965), pp. 18–19.

[34] Ibid.

[35] It is true that the iron-ore trade was one particularly and frequently affected by adverse weather conditions. Most of these shipments came from Spain through the port of Bilbao and across the Bay of Biscay – notorious for bad weather. Shipments were regularly held up, and more often than not several shipments would come into Glasgow at the same time.

[36] SRO, Letter from James Coulan, secretary of the Glasgow Harbour Mineral Workers' Union, May 16 1889, to the Registrar of Friendly Societies in Scotland, FS 7/73. This letter was an explanation as to why the union had failed to register for 1889, and the ex-secretary explained that the union was financially ruined and therefore had gone out of existence.

port and the employers would not accept any other. As a result, the men who sought employment there became out-and-out casuals and the worst paid of the Glasgow dock labour force.

David Wilson also looked at this sub-contracting group in his more general investigation of the docker in Britain. He noted that these types of employers normally performed small-scale jobs and that their profit margins were extremely tight. As a result, the men who worked for them were also 'squeezed mercilessly'. Wilson actually drew on Larkin's observations to illustrate the iniquities of the system as it existed, principally at Glasgow, before 1914, although it could be expanded to cover almost any port. He also argued that it stemmed directly from the casual system itself:

> The reliance on casualism multiplied the number of employing companies . . .
> With the multiplication of small employers, the malpractices of casual hiring
> worsened. Most involved foremen accepting favours from the men who were
> driven to pay for the privilege of being employed.[37]

The operational structure of the port, therefore, dictated the type of work available and affected the employment conditions of the men attracted to it. The 'contract labour' men, as described by both Larkin and Wilson, were employed by the hour, paid by the hour and often laid off by the hour. They were also paid below accepted port rates. While Wilson notes that their employers were often 'more amenable to industrial pressure', they still nevertheless symbolised the worst excesses of the casual system.[38] Larkin wished to see this contract labour, hourly-rate system, eradicated entirely, and replaced by a 'piecework system' of payment. He felt that the contract labour system only worked in the interests of the shipowners and not the sub-contracting middlemen. This was a situation that was very much against the interests of the dockers they employed.[39] In certain respects the practice of sub-contracting, or 'sub-taking' as it was known at Greenock, was another offshoot of the casual system of employment. Indeed, although one of the main aims of the Great London Dock Strike in 1889 was to eradicate this practice it was to survive for many decades to come.

There is little doubt that 'sub-taking' was a real problem. It was recognised by some early organisations of dockers that this was part of the very fabric of port life, but through their trade union rules they attempted to exert some sort of control over this method of employing men. It would seem that the practice of 'sub-taking' a vessel was often entered into with little prospect of the sub-contracting docker actually having the money to pay the men he employed. Hence the Greenock Dock Labourers' Union incorporated a rule outlawing such practices by members of their society. They also stated that no member of the society would undertake sub-contracting duties, without first attempting at all times to recruit union members. If they were found to be flouting these rules, they would be expelled from the society.[40]

---

[37] Wilson, *Dockers*, pp. 33–4.
[38] Ibid., p. 37.
[39] Ibid., p. 33.
[40] SRO, Rules and Regulations of Greenock Dock Labourers' Union, Oct. 1887, FS 7/106 (Rules 34 and 35).

The 'sub-taking' system was still in place after the First World War, but in a redefined form, and the men who worked for the sub-contractors in such circumstances came to be known as 'snappers'. In essence, they managed to secure work at the docks fairly regularly, but could be dropped very quickly when a *bona fide* docker came to claim his rightful position. In other words, the 'snapper' took work knowing that at almost any moment he could be replaced. This precarious situation persisted well into the second half of the twentieth century and remained one of the few methods of entering dock life on a more permanent (ex-snapper) basis, without familial connections. Oral evidence, however, would suggest that the 'snapper' was not always someone from outside the dock community, but possibly a second or even a third son of a regular docker. In a system almost akin to the practice of primogeniture, where the first son automatically followed his father into the trade, second sons could also regularly gain entry, but only by the active sponsorship of the union. A third son would usually only gain entry in very particular circumstances; if, for example, his mother was a dock widow and found herself struggling financially.[41] It would seem clear that this was also a method in which the docking community itself could control entry into dock work, but this did not occur in any widespread sense until the interwar period.

## Dockers' Wages

The basic three-tier employment structure in Glasgow operated throughout all areas of dock work, with the addition of a 'lower class' of docker, who worked casually for the sub-contractor. The main areas of employment at the port of Glasgow, in this instance, were in coal, grain, mineral, timber and general cargo trades – the largest being general cargo.

Despite problems associated with attributing 'skill' to dock work, hourly and daily rates of pay were not affected. Rather, the skill factor affected regularity of work. Moreover, the differences between shipwork or quaywork that may have existed did not affect rates of pay either. Indeed, like the skill factor, regularity of work, rather than any fundamental differential in pay rates, would again be more important.

Information regarding the wages of casual dock labour before 1914 is poor and unreliable. Indeed, there was no systematic investigation of the wages of dock labour, even in the 1886 and 1906 government wages census. Partly this arose from the difficulty of properly estimating the numbers of dock labourers. Men were simply taken on to work on a particular cargo, and no qualitative statistics were kept on the actual numbers employed in any given period before 1914. When the port

---

[41] Taken from a non-recorded conversation with ex-docker Tom O'Connor of Glasgow, who entered dock work in the late 1950s (4 Mar. 1993 ). The position of the 'snapper' left an indelible image in Tom's mind. Regarding the system of internal recruitment, Tom argued that this had been the practice for many years and one which the dock community doggedly retained. The relaxation of the rules to allow 'third son' was also considered to be serving a welfare function, ensuring that members of the community could be offered some sort of safety net in financial terms. A third son would usually enter the docks in these circumstances at a reasonably young age, thus his wages would become part of the budget of his mother's household.

transport industry was considered, therefore, in such government surveys they collated figures relevant to 'harbour and dock services', those in receipt of a weekly wage, but not the casual dock labour force. Thus, dock and wharf labour 'employed in loading and unloading ships' was excluded from such calculations.[42]

Even by the end of World War One it was still relatively difficult to estimate with any certainty just how many worked at Glasgow docks. In relation to wages earned, the situation was even more difficult. Glasgow stevedore James Spencer noted in 1920 that 'there was no accurate statement of wages'. This was because Glasgow had neither a clearing-house system (central points positioned around the docks, where all dockers received their wages weekly, as in Liverpool) so that the numbers seeking work could be reliably counted): nor did it have a system of registration (as initiated in Liverpool in 1912, and in many other ports, such as London, by the end of the war in 1918), which was another reliable method of enumerating the dock labour force. Thus, as Spencer concluded, 'there was no means [to] get the correct information' regarding number or wages.[43] In short, there are few reliable statistics regarding either the wages received or the numbers [even] included'.[44]

It is therefore necessary to keep such problems in mind when attempting to build up some picture of the wages structure at Glasgow, particularly between the late 1880s through to 1939. To average out what one particular docker was actually paid at any time throughout this period as a whole would be difficult. Daily rate and weekly averages of pay were dictated by product handled, the frequency of a particular cargo entering or leaving a port, and the status of the dock worker involved in a particular trade, or the general state of the cargo. The term 'piece-work' was never used in Gerald Walsh's investigation of Glasgow in 1908, only the hourly rate and the average hours worked per week by the various categories of docker are referred to. This excludes the sub-contracted workers. It is also unclear whether the quayworker was paid at this average rate too, and it is important to recognise the role played by bulk cargo in Glasgow's trade at this time, normally paid at tonnage rate, yet again not referred to as such in Walsh's investigation.

It is clear from the information gathered from the many strikes that occurred between the late 1880s and 1914 (most strikes invariably centred on wage demands) that dockers at Glasgow were paid at different rates and by different methods, and that this was in part dictated by the employer. In the 1890s, for example, the shipping lines paid a day rate of 6*d*. and a night rate of 7*d*. per hour.[45] The stevedore was generally paid higher rates, but these varied between 5½ *d*. and 8*d*. on day rate and between 5½ *d*. and 10*d*. per hour on night rate,[46] the average being 7*d*. and 10*d*. respectively. It should also be recognised that between this period and the

[42] *Report of an Enquiry by the Board of Trade into the Earnings and Hours of Labour of Working People in the United Kingdom*, viii, Harbour and Dock Services, 1906 (*P.P.*, 1912–13, cviii, Cd 6556), pp. 236–59.

[43] Shaw Inquiry, i, evidence, J. S. Spencer, p. 272.

[44] *Report of an Enquiry by the Board of Trade of the State of Employment in the United Kingdom in October 1914* (*P.P.*, 1914, xi, Cd. 7703), pp. 13–21.

[45] *Royal Commission on Labour, 2nd Report*, Group B – Minutes of Evidence, ii (*P.P.*, 1892, xxxvi, Part iii, C. 6795–11), evidence, Smith Park, Q. 12,769.

[46] Ibid., Monro, Q. 12,675.

first decade of the twentieth century the hourly rate was relatively stable – as noted in Walsh's figures for 1908, when compared with Table 4.1.

It was generally accepted that the stevedore worked his employees harder, hence the higher wages. He also worked with smaller gangs than those employed by the shipping companies. The shipping lines also varied their method of payments. The Allan Line, for instance, while employing its quayworkers by the hour, also employed men involved in their coasting vessels on a weekly basis. The size of the squads varied considerably, ranging between twelve and twenty, employing a sub-foreman at each hatch and an employing, or travelling, foreman, who chose the men taken on at the call-on points, to oversee the whole operation on the one vessel.[47] The Allan Line also practised the piecework payment system, but only for those employed in grain weighing, another point omitted in Walsh's report. This was paid as a whole to a squad of five and divided according to their function within the squad.

**Table 4.2:** *Piece Work Rate for Grain Workers Based on Squad Tonnage Rate Payment of 8s 3d. per ton in 1892 and Average Weekly Wage for Employees of the Allan Shipping Line.*

| Squad-members | Payment per Ton | Average Weekly Wage. |
|---|---|---|
| Weigher (one) | 1*s* 11*d*. | 32*s* 6*d*. |
| Backers (one) | 1*s* 10*d*. | 30*s* |
| Filler (one) | 1*s* 6*d*. | 25*s* |
| Bag Holders (two) | 1*s* 6*d*. | 25*s* |

**Source:** *Royal Commission on Labour, Second Report*, 1892, evidence from M. J. Smith Park of the Allan Shipping Line (Q 12,783–5).

Those who worked in this trade, when not employed with grain, were said to have worked in hourly employed tasks and were able to earn 'large sums of money in a day',[48] probably working in the limited shed areas on the south side of the river.

However, at Glasgow the rates paid seem generally to have been structured by the hour, or on a daily shift basis, broadly in line with Walsh's observations (noted in Table 4.3). What is particularly interesting about these figures is that they do not seem to have changed significantly in almost twenty years. It was estimated in 1892, for example, that the average weekly wage 'for those willing to work' was around 27*s* 6*d*. By the first decade of the twentieth century a docker from the 'first class' group was able to earn around 31*s* 6*d*. for a fifty-one-hour week, while a 'second class' docker could earn around 26*s* to 30*s* per week on estimates based on yearly averages.[49]

There was also a lower average in operation of 15*s*,[50] which compares favourably

[47] Ibid., Smith Park, Q. 12,770–6.
[48] Ibid., Q. 12,785.
[49] *RC on Poor Laws*, 1910, evidence, Smith Park, Q. 89620.
[50] *RC on Labour*, 1892, evidence, George Monro, Q 12,747 and 12,749.

with data gathered by Walsh around the same time. Based on the lower level, there was little advance in wages between 1890 and 1909. It was only during the period 1910–14 that a major attempt was made to rectify this position – with the greatest advances being made between then and 1920.

**Table 4.3:** *Average Weekly Wages at the Port of Glasgow for the Years 1892, 1908, 1913 and 1920.*

| Year | Hourly Rate | Weekly Average |
|------|-------------|----------------|
| 1892 | 7*d*. | 27*s* 6*d*. |
| 1908 | 7*d*. | 25*s* to 27*s* |
| 1913 | 8½*d*. | 40*s* |
| 1920 | 1*s* 9*d*. | 80*s* |

**Source:** *Royal Commission on Labour* (hourly and average rate of payment as noted in *Glasgow Harbour Labourers Union Rules*, 1890), 1982; Gerald Walsh's Report, 1908; Shaw Inquiry, 1920 (for both 1913 and 1920 estimates – calculations of average hourly rate and weekly wage from selected individual occupational).

The above table gives some impression of the pattern of wages over this period, but this is all they offer. The figures for the later period are perhaps more reliable than those for 1892 and 1908, but there is, in fact, little between them. Overall, however, the rise in wages between 1892 and 1920 is quite significant and this is even more the case if consideration is given to the average hourly rate in the 1880s, which was estimated to be between 5*d*. and 6*d*. per hour. During the period up to 1913, there seems little upward movement in wages, but, generally, real wages were on the increase from the early 1880s up until around 1907 – when wages stagnated and began to fall behind prices. Indeed, real wages did not exceed the figures for 1907 until the post war boom year of 1921.[51] Bearing this in mind, Table 4.4. does give some indication of the movement in wages before and after the First World War. But the main purpose of this table is to illustrate the differences between certain groups of dockers, rather than increases in wages.

The Shaw Inquiry also estimated individual earnings for specific groups of dockers who worked with specialist cargo, giving comparisons with the pre-war rates of payment and average hours worked. What Table 4.4 shows is the remarkable resilience of the differential within each occupational group, which was not seriously eroded over the period 1914–19. The average weekly rate of increase over that period also remains much the same over each occupational group, once again showing that the differential between each remained more or less intact. It was only after the formulation of the first National Joint Port Agreement of May 1920 that the differential was eroded somewhat. But even after this time there were so many

[51] J. E. Cronin, *Industrial Conflict in Modern Britain* (1979), see Appendix Table B.7, pp. 224–7.

**Table 4.4:** *Comparison of Wages Paid to Dock Labourers, (a) hourly rate, (b) weekly average, and (c) increase between August 1914 and November 1919 and numbers of men employed in each Category for 1919.*

| | 1914 | | 1918 | | Increase |
|---|---|---|---|---|---|
| (Job title and numbers) | (a) | (b) | (a) | (b) | (c) |
| **General Cargo Men** | | | | | |
| Coasting lines (1,000) | 6*d*. | 28*s* 0*d*. | 1*s* 6½*d*. | 67*s* 10*d*. | 39s10*d*. |
| Large Lines (1,800) | 8*d*. | 37*s* 4*d*. | 1*s* 9*d* | 77*s* 0*d*. | 39s 8*d*. |
| Other Lines and | | | | | |
| Tramps (4,200) ** | 8*d*. | 37*s* 4*d*. | 1*s* 9*d*. | 77*s* 0*d*. | 39s 8*d*. |
| | | | | | |
| **Timber Men (300)** | | | | | |
| Upper Harbour | 8½*d*. | 42*s* 0*d*. | 1*s* 9½*d*. | 82*s* 6*d*. | 40*s* 6*d*. |
| Lower Harbour | 9*d*. | 42*s* 0*d*. | 1*s* 10½*d*. | 82*s* 6*d*. | 40*s* 6*d*. |
| | | | | | |
| **Coal men (300)** | 10*d*. | 46*s* 8*d*. | 1*s* 11½*d*. | 86*s* 4*d*. | 39s 8*d*. |
| | | | | | |
| **Ore Men (350)** | 10*d*. | 46*s* 8*d*. | 1*s* 11½*d*. | 86*s* 4*d*. | 39s 8*d*. |
| | | | | | |
| **Grainweighers (120)** *** | 1*s* 5*d*. | 74*s* 7*d*. | 2*s* 9½*d*. | 123*s* 2*d*. | 48*s* 7*d*. |

*Average working week in 1919 is 44 hours, in 1914 it is 56 hours.

**The overtime rate for smaller lines and tramp line workers was 1*d*. higher than that paid by the large lines. This differential was maintained throughout the war years.

***The grainweighers were paid by piece work. The hourly figure equivalent is calculated from the piece rate 9*s* 1*d*. per 10 tons (assuming an average output of 720 bags per 9–hour day) for 1914. For 1919 the hourly figure equivalent is calculated from the piece rate 17*s* 6*d*. per 10 tons (assuming an average output of 640 bags per 8–hour day).

**Source:** *Shaw Inquiry, ii, 1920, Appendix* 78, Table H/14 and H/16–Glasgow.

local variations and practices of payment accommodated within the national agreement, that many of these traditional differentials remained more or less in place: only then they had become codified in the procedural agreement.

According to the evidence presented to the Shaw Inquiry, the dock labourers in Glasgow were better paid than men in other types of general labouring work, both before and after the war. The general labourers' hourly rate was around 5*d*. in 1914, rising to 1*s* 4*d*, per hour by 1919. The rate for sawmill casuals went from 6*d*. per hour to 1*s* 6*d*. over the same period. The highest paid labour at this time was in the building trade where masons' and bricklayers' labourers were paid a rate of 7*d*. per hour, rising to just over 1*s* 7*d*. between 1914 and 1919. As already noted, dock labouring rates rose from around 8*d*. per hour to 1*s* 9*d*. over the same period. The dockers also experienced the greatest reduction in average weekly hours worked, when compared to other groups of labourers during the same period, including shipyard labourers and regular labourers working in the many sawmills around Glasgow at this time.[52]

It would also seem to be the case that Glasgow's dockers fared well in relation to wages paid at other ports. According to the Majority Report of the Shaw Inquiry, by 1919 the average rate of pay in Liverpool was 12s per day, whereas in London for dock work it varied between 11s 8d. and 13s 9d. at the higher end of the scale. But in Glasgow, it was noted, 'the general rate of pay was 14s per day'. Indeed, other evidence given to the enquiry illustrated that the highest rate of pay paid by 1919 was 14s in London (stevedores only), Bristol, Goole, Grangemouth, Greenock, Plymouth and West Hartlepool. But the great majority of ports paid less and often substantially less. Only Port Talbot and Swansea paid higher, with rates of 15s 1d. and 15s 6d. respectively.[53]

On the basis of these estimates, wages at Glasgow were on average higher than at most other ports, and dockers at Glasgow fared well in relation to other dockers around Britain. However, it must be emphasised that these are estimates. What the outside observer is left with is an indication of wages and conditions during this period. It cannot be assumed that such high wage levels were enjoyed by all casual dockers. This very point was argued strongly by Ernest Bevin, and pressed home to great effect during the Shaw Inquiry when James Spencer first produced the above noted estimates. Bevin argued cogently that such estimates were based on the earnings of the most regularly employed gangs and that these gangs constituted Glasgow's 'first preference men . . . who expected and received the most work in any case'.[54] Such evidence must therefore be viewed with a degree of scepticism, offering, as it does, illustrations of dock work that are perhaps more apparent than real.

*The Royal Commission on Labour*, 1892, also attempted to argue that Glasgow's wage structure was relatively stable. The report stressed that there was little seasonal fluctuation at Glasgow, particularly in the liner trade. And, as noted by the representative of the Allan Line, sailings between April and November were generally between three and four per week, dropping-off slightly to between two and three sailings per week for the remaining part of the season.[55] However, bad weather could often seriously affect certain trades, particularly the iron-ore trade, and although it was not to prove a seasonal problem, it was, nevertheless, a regularly recurring one.

### The Clyde Trust as an Employer

Glasgow did not have extensive dockside warehousing and therefore there would have been a considerable flow of traffic along the docks. This would have meant significant quayside handling, which would most certainly have created the im-

---

[52] Shaw Inquiry, ii, *Appendix* 81, Table H/16 – Glasgow 7, 'Comparison of Wages of Various Classes of Labourer in Glasgow District in Aug. 1914 and Dec. 1919'.

[53] Shaw Inquiry, i, 'Majority Report', p. 5; and Shaw Inquiry, ii, *Appendix*, 130, Table H/40.

[54] Shaw Inquiry, i, pp. 272–80.

[55] RC on *Labour*, 1892, Q. 12,765.

pression of great industry. It certainly necessitated the Clyde Trust's engagement of cargo handlers (arguably little different in function from the ordinary docker) when normally this would not occur. This was the conclusion of one Royal Commission in 1909:

> At some [Ports] the work is done by shipping companies having stevedoring staff of their own; at others, by merchants, dock and railway companies, crews of ships, master stevedores and porters; only in a few cases is it done by a harbour trust.[56]

It is important to note that the Clyde Navigation Trust did play a significant role in providing work and in directly employing its own staff. While this particular commission reported that 'trustees did not normally take on their own men', they patently did so in Glasgow. Indeed, those stevedores who employed a large body of dock labourers at any time of the year only did so by licenses, which were granted by the Clyde Trust and renewed on a yearly basis.[57] This again underlines the important role played by the Trust, both in the operational sphere and as a major employer in its own right.

Both the shipowners and the stevedores had a pool of 'permanent men'. It can also be argued that, as a percentage of the dock labour force as a whole, their numbers were fairly small. In the absence of any significant details of these workers, it may be impossible to construct any real definition of the nature of 'permanency' as it operated in Glasgow. For the most part, permanency meant employment through the Clyde Navigation Trust, which maintained a reasonably large permanent labour force. Essentially, the permanent labour force was engaged on a fortnightly basis throughout a given year. Using fragmentary evidence drawn from the years 1909–12, it is evident that average numbers employed in any one of those years could vary considerably, as can be seen in Table 4.5 below. These figures represent a myriad of occupations, such as cranemen, capstanmen, maintenance engineers and mechanics, various tradesmen including electricians, divers, ferrymen and bargemen, as well as Trust employees who discharged materials between ship and the dock. These are only a few of the different occupations that would have been in the employ of the Trust.

It would have been in the traffic department that the Trust's own employees would regularly discharge goods, primarily from a ship to the railway wagons waiting alongside the quays. According to the *Second Report of the Royal Commission on Labour*, 1892, the Clyde Navigation Trust employed around 500 such workers – engaged and paid on a weekly basis – for such tasks. Furthermore, testimony suggests that the railway companies in Glasgow also employed men for the discharging of certain materials[58]. While these men were not considered dockers, their work obviously centred around the port and its activities. It was argued that these men were 'constantly employed'.

---

[56] *RC on the Poor Laws*, ix, 1909, Part vi, para. 261.
[57] *RC on Labour*, 1892, evidence, Mr George Monro, Q. 12,668–9 (Monro was one of 40 stevedores granted such a license in 1892).
[58] Ibid., Monro, Q. 12,725–32.

**Table 4.5:** *Average Numbers of Employees Engaged Yearly between 1909 to 1912.*

| Year | 1909 | 1910 | 1911 | 1912 |
|---|---|---|---|---|
| Average Number of Employees | 1,444 | 1,493 | 1,617 | 1,581 |

Source: GCA, T-CN 6/7, Clyde Navigation Trust Papers. Statement of the Number of Accidents to Employees and Amounts of Compensation paid (Workmen's Compensation Act 1906) 1909–1912.

It may be argued that the great majority of men employed by the traffic department were in fact those engaged in the discharge of cargoes, of the type described above, and the regularity of that employment was naturally and directly related to the level of trade within the port of Glasgow, which meant that they shared some degree of commonality with the casual docker. Nevertheless, if the year is taken as a whole and the actual fortnightly figures are viewed against fortnightly averages for the year, the fluctuations in employment are still significant. The average numbers employed for 1912 were 1,794, while the highest numbers employed in any fortnight were 1,924 against the lowest number of 1,467. While these figures correspond with the interruption of trade through industrial action, quite dramatic fluctuations can also be seen within the four major employing departments, particularly in traffic.[59]

What is significant in these figures is the fact that these employees represented that part of the workforce considered to be permanent and who, by definition, enjoyed a greater degree of regularity and security than their mostly casual counterparts – the dockers. It is true that the jobs of the central core of these permanent workers were probably relatively safe. Nevertheless, the fact that the numbers required by a given department could vary from one engagement period to another causes us to re-evaluate the term 'permanent'. Even this situation, however, would compare favourably with that of the ordinary docker, who was often employed only by the day, or half day, or who at 'good times' could possibly expect to be working for a whole week.[60] But the basis of his recruitment remained the same – casual. If there could, therefore, be such fluctuation within the ranks of the 'permanent' worker at this time the situation for the casual worker was many times worse.[61]

By the time of the Shaw Inquiry, the Clyde Navigation Trust were employing 1,400 workers in total, with 334 employed directly in the loading and discharging of goods. The great majority by far were composed of capstanmen, some 177 in all, with around 105 cranemen, who operated steam, hydraulic and electric cranes (numbering forty-three, thirty-seven and twenty-five respectively). There were also around twenty-five workers operating mechanical grabs around the docks. All were

[59] For example, numbers employed went from a low point of 362 employed (fortnight ending 19 Apr. 1912), to the highest period of employment where 557 were engaged (fortnight ending 10 Oct. 1912): the average for this department for the whole of that year was 510.
[60] *RC on the Poor Laws*, 1909, Part vi, paras. 258–304.
[61] J. Treble, *Urban Poverty in Britain, 1830–1914* (1979), p. 55.

regularly employed and were paid a weekly wage 'whether or not there was work for the cranes'. They also had around 159 permanent staff employed in the grain trade, seventy-four of whom were weighers.[62] By 1920 the majority of the granary men (who numbered around seventy), a number of the Trust general labourers (who with lamplighters and platelayers numbered 237), and some 100 casual employees employed in the granary and grain sheds, were members of the Clyde Trust Branch of the Scottish Union of Dock Labourers (SUDL). However, it would seem that there were strict lines of demarcation between the Trust men and the casual dockers. The rules of the society state that on no condition could a Trust employee take up a position as a casual docker, unless he was to be sponsored by the Union (perhaps as a second son of a regular docker) and gave up his employment with the Trust, especially if he were regularly employed.[63] Without doubt, casualism was a way of life for the docker and not simply a system of employment.

As can be seen from the above analysis – by considering port operation, employment patterns and occupational variations – there was still much that bound the dock workers together, if only because of the distorted perceptions of those who did not understand the industry and viewed all who worked on the docks as 'thriftless, hard drinking gamblers'.[64] It can also be seen that many elements of port life served to place formidable barriers between dock workers – not least at London, considered a less 'centralised' port. But at Glasgow, while there are examples of the strict demarcation of function, such as existed between Clyde Trust men who were considered permanent employees, and ordinary casual dockers, and despite a considerable degree of diversity of function, the dockers there seemed to forge strong alliances with each other, which were not evident at other ports.

The development of alliances is seen to particular effect with the amalgamation of both the shipworkers and the quayworkers within the same trade-union organisation in the late 1890s (despite a hitherto strong history of 'bad blood' between the two, as will be shown in later chapters). This does not mean, however, that Glasgow did not experience the same barriers to trade-union organisation as existed at other ports, barriers whose erection was aided by the attitudes of employers and the workforce generally. In ports with longer and more illustrious histories, such as London, these divisions became the basis of considerable sectional difference and lines of demarcation. This not only affected regularity of work and earning differentials, but collective bargaining advantages also.[65]

In Liverpool, the problem was not of the same order of magnitude as it was in London, but formidable barriers existed nevertheless. These differences came to be enshrined in the traditions that developed within a particular dock, or wharf, and dictated work practice through an often complicated system of custom and practice. In Liverpool there was a considerable degree of naked sectarianism (the

[62] Shaw Inquiry, ii, *Appendix* 87, Table H/17–Statement 2 (furnished by Clyde Navigation Trust).
[63] Mitchell Library, SF. 331.8811 3871, Sco. Manuscript, C.372148, Scottish Union of Dock Labourers' Executive Minutes, 1919–22.
[64] Lovell, *Stevedores and Dockers*, pp. 30–2.
[65] Lovell, 'Dockers' Unionism', p. 234.

port divided geographically as the upper dock and lower docks along strict Protestant and Catholic lines). This did not happen in Glasgow to anywhere near the same degree as it did in Liverpool, despite the West of Scotland's well chronicled sectarian traditions. But the development of custom and practice, and localism, was little different there from other ports. It was a problem that existed generally along the entire waterfront.

From the study of Glasgow it can be seen that, as the port developed geographically, so too did the systems of custom and practice, which centred around the issue of cargo handled, becoming ever more discrete to the outside observer, but considerably more important to those who worked within the port transport industry.[66] When James Sexton took over as leader of the National Union of Dock Labourers in 1893, he classified himself as one who was overseeing what amounted to a collection of 'innumerable small clubs and societies all hostile to each other'.[67] In building up some picture of the working life as it pertained to the Port of Glasgow, we have seen how such 'small clubs' could, and did, emerge. Furthermore, by offering some comparisons with other ports – both English and Scottish – we have seen too, in contrast, the significant similarities which existed between different ports. It is also clear that major problems are encountered at various levels in this investigation. There are difficulties associated with the composition of the labour force, and differences in status; between permanent and casual, shipworkers and quayworkers. There are also problems in determining the differentials in both skill and regularity of work, not discounting the matter of estimating the actual size of the labour force, or, indeed, estimating the wages of the dock labour force over time.

We have also seen that the employment structure is not always easily defined, and even where there ostensibly exist specific lines of demarcation, as noted by Eric Taplin, these can often become blurred. Furthermore, there are problems with official reports into dock life, and with Gerald Walsh's report in particular. While his report is of considerable use, it nevertheless fails to show the whole picture. He does not seem to have considered the quay worker, without doubt an integral part of the dock labour force in Glasgow, particularly from the 1890s onward, and considers mostly the role of the shipworker. While it would be quite wrong to suggest that there were no remaining differences between the two at the time of Walsh's investigation, it would also seem to be the case that shipwork and quaywork, by that time, were executed by men who worked under the more readily recognisable generic term 'docker'. Any differences that did remain were essentially expressed in terms of payment differentials, rather than separate spheres of function.

Over and above such weaknesses Walsh fails to account for others employed in dock work, such as the sub-contracted labourers noted by James Larkin. However, by including the observations of Larkin and the investigations into dock life by

---

[66] For a fuller analysis of the problems of custom and practice in job regulation and labour organisation see R. Bean, 'Custom, Job Regulation and Dock Labour'.

[67] J. Sexton, *Sir James Sexton, Agitator* (1936), p. 109.

historians such as Wilson, Lovell and Taplin, a clearer picture has begun to emerge. This provides a context in which to better judge the experience of the Glasgow dock labour force. It can also be seen that Glasgow, like many other ports, developed in other directions and began to experience her own rise to prominence at a different point in time and in relation to different products, when compared to other ports such as London.

Glasgow also had a workforce which was arguably less complicated than that which existed in London, principally, perhaps, because its labour force did not have the same length of time to develop along sectional lines. In many ways Glasgow was a very modern port that was able to expand more quickly than others during the second half of the nineteenth century. It could, therefore, embrace the impulse to modernise in specific areas, such as in the grain trade, or in the handling of bulk coal cargo, without the problem of resistance, as occurred in London from a well-established body of men with an already well developed system of control. The pace and penetration of technology and mechanical appliances also helped to shape a different type of employment structure to that which existed in London. Moreover, it generated a different type of response by the workforce.

Glasgow's development is just the story of one port, but illustrates why, when compared to other ports, such as London or Liverpool, the port transport industry in Britain could develop into a complicated industrial institution. It also helps to explain why ports could operate at different levels of mechanisation, modernisation, geographical spread, and trade. This in turn dictated employment policy, industrial relations strategies and the development of customs and practices specific to a particular port, while moulding the general experience of the dock labour force. Other factors in this equation would be the numbers involved in dock work in Glasgow; the density and concentration of the workforce along the waterfront; the racial composition of the workforce, and how these in turn would help to mould attitudes to the work process developing locally.

# Part Two

# CHAPTER FIVE

# Numerical and Racial Composition of the Dock Labour Force: Roots and Origins

*The Numerical Growth of the Dock Labour Force before 1914*

One of the most problematic areas in the study of port life is attempting to estimate the actual numbers engaged in port work throughout the period as a whole. As noted by Glasgow's Harbour Master in the 1830s, early estimates of the Glasgow dock labour force stood at around '1,000 or so men'.[1] By the 1890s, according to the evidence of licensed stevedore George Monro, numbers had risen to 5,000 or more,[2] and remained at more or less the same up until Gerald Walsh's survey between 1905 and 1907.[3] But thereafter, according to the testimony of another licensed stevedore Mr McCulloch Graig, numbers began to rise again to a level between 6,000 and 7,000 by 1910.[4] By the time of the Shaw Inquiry, Glasgow's casual dock labour force was estimated to number 8,470.[5]

Official census figures (see Table 5.1) conflict significantly with these estimates, particularly between 1891 and 1921, but there is still little doubt that there was a considerable expansion in the numbers working on Clydeside between 1861 and 1911. Indeed, if the combined official totals for both Glasgow and Govan are considered, the dock labour force increased almost fivefold in fifty years, rising from 1,197 to 5,586 (nearly 470%). As a percentage of the total Scottish dock labour force, Glasgow and Govan combined constituted 42% in 1911 (as opposed to 34% in 1861). Therefore, according to official statistics from 1891 onward, four out every ten dockers in Scotland were to be found working on Clydeside (discounting Port Glasgow, Greenock and the Clyde Coast ports of Ardrossan, Irvine or Ayr).

From an employment standpoint the port of Glasgow was thus expanding rapidly and continued to grow up to 1911 and beyond (reaching a high point during the war years). Thereafter, on a decennial basis, official numbers began to fall, but so too did the Scottish figures as a whole. As a percentage of the Scottish total the Glasgow dock labour force was still the largest in Scotland. Because of the casual nature of the work, however, it may never be possible to adequately

---

[1] W. Sloan, 'Assimilation of the Highland and Irish Migrants in Glasgow, 1830 to 1870' (Strathclyde University, unpublished M.Phil. thesis, 1987), p. 47, see also *NSA of Scotland*, Appendix G, evidence of Glasgow's Harbour Master, p. 117.

[2] *RC on Labour*, 1892, evidence, Mr George Monro, Q. 12,644.

[3] Gerald Walsh, *Report on Dock Labour*, 1908, p. 17.

[4] *RC on Poor Law*, 1910, evidence, Mr F. McCulloch Graig, Glasgow (stevedore), p. 1,098.

[5] Shaw Inquiry, i, testimony, James Spencer, Glasgow (stevedore), p. 270.

enumerate actual numbers employed in dock work before 1914.[6] This means that
official statistics, extrapolated from the census figures, offer us a general impression. But when compared with employers estimates a clearer picture does begin to
emerge.

---

**Table 5.1:** *Number of Dock, Wharf and Harbour Labourers in Scotland, Glasgow, Govan,
totals for Glasgow and Govan combined, and Greenock between 1861 and 1931: including
percentages of Scottish totals (in brackets).*

| Year | Scotland | Glasgow | Govan | Glasgow/ Govan | Greenock |
|------|----------|---------|-------|----------------|----------|
| 1861 | 3,487 | 1,008 (29%) | 189 ( 5%) | 1,197 (34%) | 567 (16%) |
| 1871 | 3,867 | no breakdown of figures for this year | | | |
| 1881 | 5,258 | 1,545 (29%) | 181 ( 3%) | 1,726 (33%) | 723 (14%) |
| 1891 | 6,781 | 2,361 (35%) | 633 ( 9%) | 2,994 (44%) | 379 ( 6%) |
| 1901 | 9,601 | 2,851 (30%) | 982 (10%) | 3,833 (40%) | 446 ( 5%) |
| 1911 | 13,147 | 3,973 (30%)* | 1613 (12%) | 5,586 (42%) | 577 ( 4%) |
| 1921 | 12,337 | 4,890 (40%)** | — — | 4,890 (40%) | 610 ( 5%) |
| 1931 | 10,682 | 4,153 (39%) | — — | 4,153 (39%) | 406 ( 4%) |

*1911 includes the Police Burgh of Kinning Park within the boundaries of Glasgow – previously
Kinning Park returned a total of 115 men who were identified as dock workers.
**1921 includes the Police Burghs of Govan and Partick which were incorporated within the city
through the boundary changes of 1912. The numbers noted for Glasgow in 1921 and 1931 thus
include those who worked in the docks in both these districts thereafter.

**Sources:** Census of Scotland, 1861 to 1931.

In short, it appears that there was more than a fivefold increase in numbers
employed at the docks between 1861 and 1891, and more than a sixfold increase
between 1861 and 1911. In any terms, this is a significant expansion in employment.
As noted previously, Port Glasgow functioned as Glasgow's main trading artery with
the Atlantic. But once a direct channel had been built between Glasgow and the
open sea, the bulk of this trade began to locate up river in the city of Glasgow. This
also affected Greenock. The rise in the numbers employed at Glasgow against the
sharp decline of the dock labour force at Greenock, would certainly seem to bear
out this point.

In 1861 Greenock had a dock labour force around half that of Glasgow and
Govan, but by 1881 it had fallen to 42%, and fell further to reach 12.6% in 1891. In
terms of a percentage of Scottish totals, there was a fall from 16% to 5% in the

[6] *Home Office Statistics of Compensation under the Workmen's Compensation Act* (1906) *and Employers
Liability Act* (1880), 1911 (*PP*, 1912, lxxv, Cd 6493), p. 9. Home Office statistics on compensation claimed for accidents in the industry after 1906, for example, clearly illustrate the difficulty
in adequately enumerating actual numbers employed in dock work. It was stated categorically
that numbers were 'perhaps hardly capable of exact calculation'.

period. Therefore, the decisive turning point for both ports, in terms of numbers employed, came in the 1880s. However, the roots of this shift dated back to the 1840s and the deepening and widening of the river Clyde from Glasgow to Port Glasgow, and the relocation of some of the growing shipping firms to Glasgow such as the Allan Line, which moved to Glasgow from Greenock in 1846 (and by 1880 could boast was the 'seventh largest shipping concern in the world').[7] It is also clear that quaywork employed more than shipwork, and by the late 1880s and early 1890s quayworkers had gained the ascendancy at Glasgow. This can be seen first and foremost through the membership figures of the NUDL, for the shipworkers were to remain, for the most part, with the older society of the Glasgow Harbour Labourers' Union, until they amalgamated in 1899.

By the 1880s and early 1890s much of the work being carried out in the Glasgow dock area was executed on the dockside, and in this respect Glasgow was little different from Liverpool. For instance, the Royal Commission on the Port of London, which gathered evidence in 1901 (published in the 1902 volumes of Parliamentary Papers) noted that in Liverpool 'business was more centralised', with more goods discharged onto the quays, or into the warehouses, *en route* to their ultimate destination. At London, on the other hand, while the docks played an important role, more ships discharged or loaded at their moorings, or at wharves along the river frontage. The actual dock and quay labour force was therefore smaller at London.[8] At Glasgow, business was likewise more centralised, but the main difference between Glasgow and Liverpool and, to a greater degree, London, was that much of the warehousing was executed away from the docks.

After the war, however, dock work had become much more regulated. Dock workers were still employed through the 'call-on', but the numbers of men employed on the fringes of the system had decreased. J. E. Cronin suggests that considerable progress was made during the war to place restrictions on the size of the dock labour force.[9] Indeed, it can be argued that there was a professional and dedicated dock labour force at Glasgow, made up from those committed to dock work, and drawn almost entirely from an identifiable dock community. Those who did gain entry did so mostly through familial connections and always through sponsorship of the union (a development that gathered pace throughout the interwar years, and from 1945 onward became a firmly established principle of dock work generally). This would thus aid the development of a group culture, which, as Cronin would argue, helped nurture and inflame militancy within the group, but that this stemmed primarily 'from the economic forces impinging upon the industry'.[10]

---

[7] Slaven and Checkland, *Business Biography*, p. 257; see also pp. 262–4 for brief biography of Alexander Allan, who with his father and 4 brothers founded the Allan line in the early nineteenth century.

[8] *Royal Commission on the Port of London, Minutes of Evidence*, 1901 (*PP*, 1902, xliii, Cd 1151), paras 39 and 40.

[9] Cronin, *Industrial Conflict*, p. 182.

[10] Ibid., p. 187.

*The Role of the Irish: Growth and Racial Composition, 1871 to 1891*

By the first decade of the twentieth century the Glasgow and Clydeside dock labour force contained a large Irish element. Joseph Houghton, the leader of the SUDL, in answer to a question raised by the Shaw Inquiry in 1920, about the numbers of Irish working at the port, noted that there were 'just as many Scotchmen as Irishmen at Glasgow docks'.[11] This suggests that the Irish-born dockers constituted about 50% of the dock labour force.

The role of the Irish was stressed in the 1911 census of Scotland, in a report on occupations of the Irish in Scotland and Glasgow in particular. Official estimates of Glasgow's dock labour force at this time show that the Irish accounted for about 47% of that body of workers. Prior to 1911, however, there was no industrial breakdown of favoured Irish occupations in relation to dock work. Should we therefore accept that the Irish were always as heavily involved in dock work? Or was this a recent phenomenon? There is evidence that suggests otherwise. On the basis of evidence gathered in a study of London docks at the time of the 1891 census, Matthews would argue that the Irish were not major players during the labour disputes of the period. He then extrapolates from his London investigations to impose the same conclusions on both the ports of Glasgow and Liverpool. However, as will be shown below, in relation to Glasgow Matthews is clearly wrong. Indeed, as far back as the 1830s Glasgow's Harbour Master estimated that out of the '1,000 or so men labouring at the harbour, the great majority were either Irishmen or Highlanders'.[12] William Sloan, in his study of the Irish and the Highlanders in Glasgow between 1830 and 1870, estimated that around two thirds of the quay labourers in 1851 were Irish, mostly from the North, particularly Donegal.[13]

The Irish and the Highlanders were also well represented in the business of harbour porterage, accounting for 17.7% and 33.7% respectively in 1834, and by 1869 the Irish and the Highlanders accounted for 50% of porters' licenses issued by the City of Glasgow. It was stated that the Irish constituted over half of that number (and that 25% of the total Irish contingent were drawn from the eastern and more industrialised areas of Ulster, suggesting that they were more likely to be Protestant.[14] Even before the great boom in employment at Glasgow, therefore, which took place between 1871 and 1891, there was already a high Irish involvement in the port transport industry at Glasgow. Moreover, if Lovell's analysis of early dock unionism is valid, then this section of the labour force would have been in a position to exploit what would be considered the more skilled areas of dockwork. As will be shown in the following chapters, they were to form part of the first organisation of dock workers at the port of Glasgow, similar to those Irishmen in London who had after 1851 dominated the 'better paid work', and whose sons 'inherited the pick of the work along the waterfront'.[15]

---

[11] Shaw Inquiry, i, testimony of Joseph Houghton, p. 160.
[12] Ibid., p. 47; see also the *New Statistical Account of Scotland*, Appendix G, p. 117.
[13] Sloan, 'Highland and Irish Migrants in Glasgow', p. 43.
[14] Ibid., p. 51.
[15] Lovell, *Stevedores and Dockers*, pp. 57–8.

What were the major changes that were to take place during the period 1871 to 1891? First, there was a substantial increase in the labour force, but was there a corresponding increase in the Irish contingent, and, if so, were they drawn from the same industrialised background as the Irish licensed porters already settled in Glasgow? This point is an important one as it could supply some evidence to explain the conflict that was to take place between the old-established dock union and the NUDL once it became established in 1889.    According to census returns, by 1891 the Scottish dock labour force had increased by over 75% when compared to the levels recorded for 1871 (see Table 5.1). In Glasgow, between the 1881 and 1891, numbers increased by 50% from 1,545 to 2,361. In Govan, on Glasgow's southside of the river, the percentage rise was an even more pronounced 250%. But where did the dock labour force come from in the first instance? Can we construct a 'place of birth' profile of those officially recognised as dock workers? It may prove fruitful to begin this investigation by considering how increased employment vacancies were filled. The increase in trade around the port of Glasgow, and on Clydeside generally, saw the port being rapidly developed and expanded.    It would seem very likely that the men who laboured in the unskilled tasks associated with the building of the quays and wharves during this period stayed behind after construction was completed. In short, the 1870s and 1880s saw a great influx of extra labour into Glasgow with many remaining behind to work the quays and wharves that they had helped to build. Given the time-scale associated with this type of construction, these men had already acquired an intimate knowledge of the surrounding area, both in regard to the working environment and the local communities that lay around the recently completed docks. David Wilson, has noted that in London, Liverpool, and even New York, the men who built the docks settled in the communities that surrounded them and thereafter confined themselves to working those same docks. Moreover, Wilson states that it was the Irish who became the new dock labour force in these particular locations.[16] Was this was the case in Glasgow?

The evidence from this study shows clearly that the dockers who came into Glasgow between the 1880s and the 1890s were predominantly Irish-born, despite Matthews' arguments to the contrary. Matthews asserts that throughout the 1880s the dock labour force in most of the major ports were being drawn in ever increasing numbers from the rural hinterlands surrounding centres such as Glasgow, Liverpool and London. The main flaw in Matthews' argument, however, is that his conclusions are based almost entirely on his London study. This was 'a small though random sample' of 200 dock and wharf workers at London, 100 from the old dock area and 100 from the new dock area. Within the old areas of London docks, Matthews' sample showed that only 18% of the dock labour force were Irish-born, but that 19% were drawn from the rural hinterland. The remainder were born in London districts (no indication is given that they were second generation Irish). The other sample, of the 'newer' dock area further down-river, showed that the Irish accounted for only 1% of the dock labour force, while 51% were drawn from rural areas mostly south of London. Matthews thus concluded, 'it would seem a safe

---

[16] Wilson, *The Dockers*, p. 29.

assumption that rural labour was a major source of additional workers in the London docks up to and during the 1880s, and that rural areas were a major source of labour in the Glasgow and Liverpool docks also'.[17]

It may well prove to be the case that Matthews' thesis is correct in relation to London – although such a small sample (accounting for barely 1% of the estimated total dock labour force) is insufficient to firmly validate his conclusions. As the evidence from the present study illustrates, however, he is quite incorrect in relation to Glasgow. According to official census returns, the total number of dockers employed in Glasgow and Govan in 1891 was 2,994. By sampling four in every ten of those defined in the individual enumerators' returns as dock or quay workers at the time of the 1891 Census, it can be seen that the Irish overwhelmingly dominated the industry. The survey accounted for 1,191 dock or quay workers, of whom 796 were located on the north side of the river and 395 on the south side. Of the north side sample those of Irish birth numbered 541, or 67.96%. On the south side, out of a sample of 395 those of Irish birth numbered 208, or 52.65%. Therefore, out of the total sample of 1,191, the Irish-born numbered 749. This suggests that something in the region of 63% of the Glasgow dock labour force of 1891 were Irish-born. This occurs well after the high point in Irish immigration in 1851.[18]

A complete survey of the dock workers in the parishes of Ardrossan and Stevenston on the Clyde coast perhaps offers another view of the structure of the dock labour force at this time (Ardrossan constitutes a geographical midpoint demarcating the Clydeside area). The total number of dockers working in these two parishes numbered 331. Out of this total, the number of Irish was 193, or 58% of the dock labour force. The biggest grouping of workers was in the town of Ardrossan itself, with the most of the remainder living in the town of Saltcoats. In Ardrossan 122 out of a total of 235 dockers were Irish-born. In Saltcoats the number was sixty-one out of a total of eighty-three, which is 52% and 73% respectively. Within this group can be seen the usual familial connections often associated with the docking community, either related by blood (fathers, sons and brothers), or through marriage. The remainder were either resident in the three towns (including Stevenston), or were living with a relative who was a resident.

There was also a strong representation from other areas in Scotland, particularly from the Highlands and Islands. In total, fifty-one dockers, 15.4% of the dock labour force, came from outside the area, mostly from Argyllshire, Ross-shire, Inverness-shire and the islands of Skye, North Uist and Lewis. There was also a

[17] Matthews, '1889 and All That', *IRSH*, xxxvi, 1, 1991, p. 46–7.
[18] This is not a scientific survey and no recognised scientific sampling method was used. The areas that were most closely considered lay around a highly populated area of Glasgow and Govan nearest the docks, quays and wharves. On the North side of the river this meant the Anderston District, which covered Anderston quay, Finnieston, Lancefield, Broomielaw as well as those areas serving Queens Dock, such as Kelvinhaugh. The South side included the Gorbals, Plantation, Mavisbank and that area around Govan serving Princes Dock. The List of Enumerators reports are as follows: North side; 644(10) 1–24 Anderston District; 644(10) 25–40 Anderston District; 644(7) 1–24 Blythswood; South side; 646(1)17–43 Plantation; 644(12) 1–24 Gorbals; 644(12) 49–72 Gorbals.

contingent from Glasgow, Dumbarton and Paisley. In addition, there were twenty-nine men from England who constituted almost 9% of the dock labour force around Ardrossan port. These figures account for 82.2% of the labour force there, the rest being drawn from the surrounding community.[19]

The position at Glasgow may not have been too much different, although, being a major port, many men from further-flung areas of the globe were to be found. Nevertheless, there would seem to be little doubt that the Irish were the biggest single grouping, particularly among the newest recruits to dock work. As noted through the testimony of William Raeburn of Glasgow to the Royal Commission of Labour in 1892, the recently formed NUDL 'consisted mostly of Irishmen' who worked the 'rougher sorts of cargo'.[20] By this Raeburn meant the bulk cargoes, such as coal or minerals. Raeburn does not refer to the Irish who, as has been shown, formed a significant section of the older dock labour force.

According to the Census for Scotland in 1911, the total number employed at Scottish docks who were categorised as dock and quay workers was 13,147. Of this number it was estimated that some 2,985 were Irish-born, which was almost 23% of the Scottish dock labour force. Dock work was thus regarded as one of the most favoured occupations of the Irish-born population in Scotland at this time. In Glasgow the situation was even more pronounced than it was in Scotland generally, where percentages were considerably higher than the national average. It was shown that of the 3,973 dock workers in Glasgow (discounting Govan and Clydebank), 1,861 were Irish-born, constituting nearly 47% of Glasgow's dock labour force. When compared to total number of all the Irish-born engaged in dock work in Scotland, we find that 62% were to found working in and around the Port of Glasgow. It should come as no surprise, therefore, to discover that dock and quay work were listed among the principal occupations for Irish males in Glasgow in 1911.[21]

Even taking the census figures at face value, it can be seen that there were a great many Irish involved in the docks, particularly in the West of Scotland. If the figures for the Irish employed in dock work in the Clydeside counties of Lanarkshire, Renfrewshire, Ayrshire and Dumbartonshire are taken as a whole, that is 2,290, 165, 129, and 61 dockers respectively, it will be seen that they number 2,645. When calculated against the 2,860 Irish-born dockers working in Scotland we find that 88.6% were working along the Clydeside waterfront area.[22] Although the Census *Report on Occupations* tells us little about the composition of the remainder of the dock labour force, it is reasonable to assume that a considerable number would be second-generation Irish. There was an established tradition of the first, and often the second, son following his father into this type of work. The fact that those concerned were born in Scotland need not have diluted their identification with things Irish. For example, William Walker's study of the Irish in Dundee between 1885 and 1923 reveals that those who were second generation Irish, 'were often

---

[19] Ardrossan Local History Library, Census Enumerators Returns for the Parishes of Ardrossan and Stevenston, Ayrshire (on the Clyde Coast), 1891.

[20] *RC on Labour*, 1892, evidence, William Hannay Reaburn, Q. 13,417.

[21] *Census of Scotland 1911*, and *Report on Occupations*, Volume III, p. vi, and p. 28.

[22] Ibid.

more Irish than their forebears'.[23] This attitude seemed characteristic of the Irish wherever they settled. In Manchester in 1901 the Irish-born made up 3.6% of the population, but, similar to the Dundee Irish, 'many second, and third, generation Irish, whose social and political identities were formed by their national origins, also considered themselves to be Irish'.[24]

It is important to recognise that the racial composition of any group of workers could play a fundamental role in the attitudes, or developing attitudes, towards industrial relations. According to John Lovell, over the longer-term:

> The Irish element brought stability and cohesion to wide areas of waterside employment. In particular, the tradition of the son following father into dock work did much to raise the calibre of the labour force.[25]

David Wilson also notes similar links between the Irish and dock labour, and that their early influx into dockwork helped to engender 'a significant sense of community'.[26] Indeed, it was this sense of community which accounted for the solidarity of sections of the dock labour force during labour disputes, while also aiding the process and development of trade unionism.[27]

Cultural traditions can also dictate the politics of a particular group of workers. The process of building up a dock union in Glasgow was intimately linked with Irish politics, and this factor seems to have played a significant part in the formation of the first general and non-sectional union at the port. While this factor has yet to be compared with the impact of others, such as the role of the seamen's union and the solidarity that existed between them and the dockers, there is no disputing the role of the Irish-born leadership in forging the spirit of trade unionism between the dockers at Glasgow between 1889 and 1893.

### Irish Politics and the Formation of General Dock Trade Unionism at Glasgow

The thrust of the campaign towards the formation of a National Union of Dock Labourers was aimed at the quayworkers at Glasgow. During this period familiar names in Irish political history, particularly Daniel O'Connell and Henry Grattan, were used to further this cause and help strengthen the fledgling union in its first days and weeks of existence.[28] Recalling his childhood days in late nineteenth-century Glasgow, Harry McShane, who then lived in the Tradeston area on the southside of the River Clyde near the Gorbals, confirms that many dockers in Glasgow were not only Irish workers, but also Catholic, and he stressed the strong link between ordinary Catholics and Irish politics:

> All the Catholics I knew who had any interest in anything at all made themselves informed about their religion, and since in Scotland the Catholic

---

[23] W. M. Walker, *Juteopolis: Dundee and its Textile Workers 1885–1923* (Edinburgh, 1979), p. 115.
[24] S. Felding, 'Irish Politics in Manchester 1890–1914', *IRSH*, xxxiii, 3, 1988, p. 264.
[25] Lovell, *Stevedores and Dockers*, pp. 57–8.
[26] Wilson, *The Dockers*, p. 50.
[27] Lovell, 'The Irish and the London Docker', pp. 16–18.
[28] Reported in the *Glasgow Herald*, 5 Feb. 1889.

Church was closely connected with the Irish movement their interests in religion often took them towards politics. Politics, of course, meant Home Rule for Ireland.[29]

McShane noted that in the election of 1906, after the Liberals made it known that they would refuse to introduce a Home Rule bill should they win the election, many Catholics went over to Labour, because they were prepared to back Irish Home Rule, and so voted for the Labour candidate George Barnes. William Walker illustrated a similar dynamic at work at Dundee where the question of Home Rule similarly helped focus the attentions of the Irish community. Walker suggested that the machinery 'designed to win constitutional concessions in Ireland' also aided 'political organisation and the habit of protest' within the Irish community too.[30] Dundee also voted in a Labour candidate. These were the only two Labour MPs returned in Scotland in 1906.[31] It seems very clear that what governed the political attitudes of the Irish in Scotland depended to a great degree on current British political attitudes to Ireland, particularly the question of Irish Home Rule. It is true that in both these areas the Irish vote was not entirely united: a great many Irish still voted Liberal, as in the Blackfriars district in Glasgow and several areas of Dundee.[32] And the issue of Irish home Rule was not simply one that concerned the Catholic population. As McShane suggested, many Protestant Irish supported Irish Home Rule too.[33]

The relationship with Dundee is also important to this investigation, particularly after 1911 when the Scottish Union of Dock Labourers reorganised Dundee harbour after it had in effect become a free labour port sometime around 1905. Before then the only focus of organisation among the dockers in Scotland was the NUDL. However, the NUDL's foothold in the Scottish ports was weakening, and after 1910 they were totally excluded from the West of Scotland ports. Only the east-coast ports were to remain in the membership of the NUDL, but there were two exceptions to this east-west split. One was Bo'ness harbour and the other the port of Dundee.

Levels of Irish immigration to Scotland dropped significantly after 1851, but many of those who arrived after this period went to work in and around the 'canals, harbours, roads and railways' of Glasgow.[34] Irish immigrants to Scotland from around 1871 onward were mostly from Ulster. There were two main movements from this area at this time; the first between 1876 and 1884, and the second between 1899 and 1907. In 1876, for example, out of 8,807 Irish immigrants heading for Scotland, 8,191 were estimated to have come from Ulster, while in 1900, 1,646 out of a total of 1,968 came from there. It has been

[29] H. McShane and J. Smith, *Harry McShane: No Mean Fighter* (Edinburgh, 1978), p. 11.

[30] Walker, *Juteopolis*, p. 142.

[31] McShane, *No Mean Fighter*, p. 16; see also Walker, *Juteopolis*, pp. 280–4.

[32] D. B. Dick, 'Dundee: A Case Study in the Decline of the Liberal Party' (unpublished paper presented to 'Scottish Dimensions' Conference, History Workshop, Ruskin College, Oxford, Mar. 1995).

[33] McShane, *No Mean Fighter*, pp. 13–14.

[34] Pryde, *Scotland from 1603*, p. 251.

suggested that these were Protestant workers, although without firm statistical evidence.[35]

In between these two main phases, Irish immigration into Britain dropped even further, from 5,696 in 1888 to 1,352 by 1893, while in Scotland levels fell from 1,414 to 569 over the same period.[36] Therefore, the number coming into Scotland as a whole, and at the time of the formation of the NUDL in 1889, was minimal. This suggests that those of Irish birth who made up the dock labour force were already established in the trade beforehand, or had gravitated into that type of work from other areas sometime previously. It should be recognised, however, that there were significantly higher numbers coming into Scotland on a temporary basis at this time. For example, in 1891, the total of temporary migrants from Ireland to Scotland numbered 2,060, as compared to 1,614 who moved on a permanent basis in that year,[37] and the greatest number of these came from Ulster – some 1,451 in total.[38] It may well be that these temporary workers occasionally attempted to find work on the docks, particularly as this period coincided with a time of considerable prosperity and a significant degree of labour unrest – both of which came to an end with the depression of 1893.

### Religion and the Dock Labour Force at Glasgow

Did such demographic factors significantly alter the religious composition of the Irish who had come to be involved in dock work at Glasgow? In other words, could the dock labour force still be argued to be a mostly Irish Catholic group by the time of New Unionism on Clydeside? As was noted in Chapter 4, through the observations of Jim Larkin in 1906, some 'North of Ireland men' did find their way into dock work. But in this instance they were mostly taken on as sub-contract labour. Pryde's study would seem to offer evidence that some Irish Protestants were finding work in the docks at the time of the second major immigration phase between 1899–1907. During the earlier phase, however, their inclusion would seem less obvious. In February 1889, for example, when the Glasgow dockers were in the process of forming the National Union of Dock Labourers 1880s, it was noted that the dockers would all be Dan O'Connell's once their union was in a position of strength. The Catholic politician Daniel O'Connell was opposed by the Protestant Irish in the first part of the nineteenth century, and was anathema to those of the Orange Order who constituted a significant number of the Irish Protestants of the later immigration phase. Would this make it unlikely, therefore, that the reference to O'Connell would have been of any significance to the quayworkers if they had been predominantly Protestant?[39] This would, therefore, undermine Pryde's

[35] Ibid., p. 256.

[36] *British Parliamentary Papers Relating to Irish Emigration*, 1891, Irish University Press Series, Vol. 27, see table 'Destination of Emigrants – Native to Ireland', p. 663.

[37] Ibid.

[38] Ibid., see Table 'Destination of Migrant Labourers from the Provinces of Leinster, Munster, Ulster and Connaught', 1891, p. 473

[39] Mitchell, *The Irish in the West of Scotland 1797–1848.*

assertions that those Irishmen joining the dock labour force at this time were predominantly Protestant.

The work of both Lovell and Taplin shows that Irish involvement in the dock labour force often generated a significant degree of sectarianism, or anti-Catholicism, within the ports where the Irish came to be well represented. Eric Taplin provides the example of Liverpool Docks where the labour force were geographically separated, north and south, along determined Catholic and Protestant lines[40] and, as Lovell points out, the Irish at London were separated from others who worked at the port along sectional lines.[41] This may also have functioned as a sectarian division in as much as the Irish, and presumably Catholic, section of the labour force were to be found within the ranks of the stevedores. Sectarianism, in this context, therefore, was institutionalised through the sectional division that existed between the stevedores and the general dock labour force.

Despite the considerable numbers of Irish within the dock labour force on Scotland's west coast there does not seem to have been any comparable sectarian development. How, then, was this potential sectarian divide overcome at Glasgow? As noted in the introductory chapter, Glasgow's well-established tradition of 'municipal socialism' may well have been helpful in bridging the sectarian divide.[42] Whereas Liverpool developed a deep attachment to Orangeism, Glasgow (relatively speaking) did not. And Liverpool also lacked 'a strong co-operative movement and other working class organisations, which signified the existence of a strong proletarian culture'.[43] Glasgow was, therefore, a different type of industrial city to Liverpool. Glasgow's industrial base was far more extensive, and a stronger proletarian movement could, and did, develop there before 1914. This is clearly seen in the attitude and actions of the Glasgow Trades Council, in relation to assisting the New Unionist impulse from 1889 and in particular through the help offered to dockers when at the same time they were attempting to organise themselves. Liverpool Trades Council was criticised heavily for not doing more to develop New Unionism at Liverpool, or the dockers cause, so much so that James Sexton (who became leader of the NUDL in 1893) refused to have any dealings with the Liverpool Trades Council between 1894 and 1906.[44] At Glasgow, indeed, across Scotland as a whole, the opposite was very much the case. Glasgow Trades Council, like Aberdeen and Edinburgh Trades Councils, actively organised unskilled workers during the period of New Unionism.[45] And Glasgow Trades Council continued its commitment to organised dock unionism when in the aftermath of the decline of the NUDL in 1910, the Council took the initiative in forming a special committee to help reorganise the dockers. One of those seconded to that committee was Joseph Houghton, who went on to form the SUDL and became and

---

[40] Taplin, *The Dockers Union*, p. 24.
[41] Lovell, 'The Irish and the London Docker', pp. 16–17.
[42] J. Smith, 'Labour Tradition in Glasgow and Liverpool', *History Workshop Journal*, 17, 1984, p. 50.
[43] T. Gallagher, 'A Tale of Two Cities', in R. Swift and T. Gilley (eds.), *The Irish in the Victorian City* (London, 1985), p. 111.
[44] Taplin, *Dockers Union*, p. 54.
[45] As reported in the *Glasgow Herald* throughout Jan. 1889.

remained its leader between 1911 and 1923.[46] While Glasgow and Liverpool Trades
Councils were bodies composed mainly of skilled Protestant artisans, this did not
hinder the Glasgow Trades Council from actively supporting New Unionist causes,
or dockers' unionism at Glasgow between 1889 and 1914. At Liverpool the
situation was very different.

It can be seen through this analysis that race and religion are important in the
history of dock trade union organisation at Glasgow. It can also be seen that
because there existed a broader proletarian culture in Glasgow sectarian loyalties
could be tempered by feelings of occupational class solidarity. According to
available evidence, it would appear that the Irish never entered into competition
with Protestant Scottish workers on the docks. The docks were built by the Irish and
it was the Irish who remained to operate them once they were completed. This
meant that there were no traditions along the Clydeside waterfront of Scots born
Protestants working the docks. The field was thus left open to the Irish and they
accepted the work happily. Indeed, they made it their own. They thereafter shaped
the custom and practice in the workplace, influenced developments in the area of
industrial relations, and inculcated these within their vision of organised dock trade
unionism. In other words, they were in every sense of the definition, 'an occupational community'.

It was the case that the old society of dock labourers had a large Irish contingent
within their ranks. From this standpoint it may be argued that the majority of Irish
involved in the dock labour force at this time were most likely Catholic by birth and
that this was yet another reason why there was no serious sectarianism along the
Glasgow waterfront. The Irish also brought with them many of the traditions that
had developed out of their experiences in Ireland and these were thereafter
absorbed by subsequent generations born in Scotland. Indeed, it may not be any
accident that the developing casual system, which had already taken shape before
the Irish came into dock work, was to find favour with this group of workers. It may
be suggested that the attachment shown to the casual system by the dock labour
force stemmed from a tradition that had developed in a rural past, in the period
before immigration to Scotland. This tradition revolved around the idea of access
to land, however limited. The system was known as land sub-division. The employment structure along the waterfront was similar in so far as the system of casualism
equated with the sub-division of employment. The other significant grouping of
workers at the docks in Glasgow came from the Highlands and Islands of Scotland,
from the very areas where the sub-division of land was also commonplace.
Beveridge had defined casualism as a system that was at least a rough and ready
way of ensuring that all had some access to work. It seems fairly likely then that the
cultural characteristics of the Irish and the Scottish Highlanders, evident in the
rural past, became translated into the experience of the industrial present. Perhaps
this explains Phillips' and Whiteside's sense that 'a traditional, almost pre-industrial
rhythm of work and leisure' persisted along the waterfront,[47] and why the Glasgow

---

[46] Glasgow Trades Council Minutes, Dec. 20, 1910.
[47] Phillips and Whiteside, *Casual Labour*, p. 33.

dock labour force came to view dock work 'as a way of life', and was to defend its territorial and occupational sphere of influence at all costs.

There is no doubt that the dock workforce at Glasgow and along the west coast of Scotland included a large Irish contingent. This constituted a very large group who shared many common characteristics which, it may be suggested, contributed towards the development of trade unionism in the Clydeside ports (the roots of which rested in the rapid phase of Glasgow's rise to trading pre-eminence in the mid-nineteenth century). This same dynamic was perhaps working at other ports such as Dundee, and other Clydeside and Clyde coast ports such as Greenock and, in particular, Ardrossan. While other factors also helped in the development of dock trade unionism along Clydeside, not least the links with the seamen and the Glasgow Trades Council, the cultural factors which we identified at Glasgow provided its core.

This chapter has attempted to analyse the composition of the dock labour force in the late nineteenth and early twentieth centuries. The majority of the Clydeside and Glasgow dock labour force were Irish with a significant grouping drawn from the Highlands and Islands of Scotland. Dock work became a favoured occupation of the Irish, particularly in the West of Scotland, and they were linked with other waterside occupations. It has also been argued that, up until the the 1890s, the Irish were mostly Catholic, suggesting further linkages with other ports such as Ardrossan, Liverpool, or London.[48] However, there were obviously many more who were not Catholic, and this was often the cause of further division within the dock labour force at London. This was clearly the case at Liverpool too, which had a consistent record of 'sectarian sectionalism', at least until the labour unrest of 1910–14. But even these 'sectional quarrels soon reasserted themselves'.[49]

Another substantial group to become involved with dock work came from the Highlands and Islands of Scotland. Both these distinct ethnic groups shared some common characteristics: they had the experience and the memory of a specific rural past. The areas from which many of these men were drawn, whether Ireland or Scotland, had been characterised by a long and strong attachment to the land and particularly to land sub-division. It may have been no accident that the men who were to emerge as leaders of the first national union of dockers in Britain, the NUDL (formed in Glasgow in February 1889), were not only Irish, but also firm adherents of land reform. They argued for free access to land, the ending of the monopoly by landlords, and the end to what they considered 'rent robbery'.[50] The land question also acted to bring together Irish and Highland political issues and created a coalition of Irish Nationalists, the Irish Land League, and urban Liberal-Radical elements, during the 1880s and 1890s.[51] As Bernard Aspinwall has argued, 'Irish Nationalism, support for the Land League and Catholicism were part of a

---

[48] T. Mann, *Memoirs* (1923), pp. 28–93.
[49] Taplin, *Dockers' Union*, p. 101: see also Taplin, *Liverpool Dockers and Seamen* (Hull, 1974), for an analysis of the extent of sectarianism on Merseyside.
[50] *Report of Executive of the National Union of Dock Labourers*, Liverpool 1893, by Richard McGhee and Edward McHugh (President and General Secretary respectively), pp. 14–16.
[51] T. M. Devine, *Clanship to Crofters' War* (Manchester, 1994), p. 225.

complex mixture that could unite with Scottish Highland tenants in a critique of
the existing order'. The ideas of Henry George and the Land League, therefore,
could act to bind together the Irish and Highland elements of the Glasgow dock
labour force.[52] Each group still had links with a similar rural past, and their modern
relationship with Scottish industry developed from an earlier tradition of seasonal
employment within the dock industry, or railway construction, and, as we shall see,
dock and wharf construction at the port of Glasgow. Most of these men, particularly
in the later period, would have been recruited from the construction crews who
laboured in the docks during a period of extensive building in the 1860s through to
the 1890s. The men who joined the more recent ranks of the dockers were not only
Irish, but were mostly Catholic too.[53] There was, therefore, a significant cultural
dimension to the dock labour force at Glasgow, one that was shared with other
groups of workers who lived around the docks.

Our evidence also shows that Derek Matthews is wrong in his assertions that
Glasgow's dock labour force was drawn from its rural hinterland. However, there
are clearly recognisable rural connections when considering the role played by the
Irish and the Highlanders in the formation of the dock labour force at Glasgow.
The role of a non-Irish rural labour force in ports such as London in the 1880s, as
Matthews suggests, may be of some significance. Even if these men were introduced
into dock work during disputes, and were to remain within this sphere of employment afterwards, they may have contributed to the further development of dock
trade unionism thereafter.

The rural link was highlighted too by the TUC in the early 1890s, when they
reported on the procession of agricultural labour into Britain's docks whenever
there was an industrial dispute.[54] Indeed, some considerable time later, the Royal
Commission on the Poor Laws noted the preference of the employers at Britain's
docks for what they termed 'the fresh country bred men of Ireland'.[55] Therefore,
the Irishman and the Highlander in Glasgow shared some common ground with
some of the newer recruits to the dock labour force after the 1880s, and that was a
memory of a rural past. In Glasgow, however, the rural connection was between the
Irish and the Highlanders. The lack of any discernible sectarianism there suggests
that their common cultural links helped to bridge what elsewhere could be a
serious social rift.[56]

This chapter has also considered the impact of the expansion of employment at
Glasgow, and this is important for several reasons. First, many of the official reports
concerning dock work pivoted around the levels of poverty experienced by the
docker, because of the casual nature of his employment. From the late nineteenth
century onward the question of poverty and dock work was a continual theme. If

[52] B. Aspinwall, 'The Catholic Irish and Wealth in Glasgow', in T. M. Devine (ed.) *Irish Immigrants
and Scottish Society in the Nineteenth and Twentieth Centuries* (Edinburgh, 1991), p. 103 and p. 98.
[53] McShane, *No Mean Fighter*; see also Lovell, *Stevedores and Dockers*, and Wilson, *Dockers*.
[54] TUC *Annual Report*, 1890, Presidential Address, p. 25.
[55] *RC on the Poor Laws*, 1909, ix, Part vi, para. 264.
[56] W. Kenefick, 'Irish Dockers and Trade Unionism on Clydeside', *Irish Studies Review*, 19, 1997,
and W. Kenefick, 'A Struggle for Recognition', in Davies (et al.), *International History of Dock
Labour*.

official estimates of the numbers employed are incorrect, then the extent of the problem of poverty within this group of workers would also have been seriously underestimated, particularly between the period 1890 to 1914.

Secondly, incorrect statistics bring into question estimates of trade-union membership of dock workers. For example, Glasgow Trades Council stated at their annual congress of November 1890, that at Glasgow the recently formed National Union of Dock Labourers had over 4,000 men, which did not include the membership of the old Society of Harbour Labourers, who probably numbered around 600.[57] This suggests a total of around 4,600 at a time when the Glasgow labour force was officially estimated at about 3,000. The combined figures for both Glasgow dock unions at this time nearer those estimates submitted by the employers, which suggest a dock labour force of between 5,000 and 6,000. The employers' estimates of the dock labour at Glasgow are therefore probably more reliable than official estimates.

Thirdly, it can be argued that the rapid increase in the numbers employed at the port of Glasgow around the late 1880s actually aided the development of trade unionism. The same dynamic which aided the growth of the workforce also arguably created tension within the industry, creating further pressures in employment terms. Thus, the discontent felt by this growing body of workers was rapidly converted into an impulse towards trade union organisation. This impulse would have been even more obvious if the numbers were greater than official estimates suggested. Moreover, the great majority of these men would have been employed in the upper parts of the dock constituting a stretch of the river Clyde no more than 2 miles long. In other words, they were in much closer contact within the port of Glasgow than other than workers at other ports.

At ports such as Hull or London the workforce was more scattered. At Hull, for example, the operational waterfront stretched some 7 miles in all, and in London it extended some 16 miles in total. Moreover, Glasgow's trade was almost entirely executed on the quayside, whereas in London a significant amount of work was carried out on the River Thames itself. Glasgow's dock labour force was, therefore, a more clearly defined occupational community. Most dockers worked and lived within and around a very tight-knit area, and they therefore shared a more intimate working and community relationship. Such a situation would have helped to engender a significant degree of occupational solidarity and further aid the process of dock unionism. Around 90% of Glasgow's dock labour force worked in this area, as only the minority who were involved in the timber, coal and ore trades would have regularly worked outside it, mainly at Rothesay Docks. Indeed, even some of these men would have occasion to work up-river in both the timber and mineral trades.[58]

Fourthly, the rapid increase in numbers at this time could perhaps have been responsible for generating a 'siege mentality' within the ranks of the shipworkers'

---

[57] *Glasgow Trades Council Annual Report, 1888–89*, p. 8.
[58] W. Kenefick, 'The Impact of the Past Upon the Present: The Experience of the Clydeside Dock Labour Force, *c.*1850 to 1914' (unpublished paper, Economic History Conference, Nottingham 8 Apr. 1994).

union. It may well prove to be the case that the growing numbers of quayworkers were perceived as a threat to the older society. This in part might help explain the bitter sectional divisions that were to emerge in the early 1890s.

Lastly, it is important to recognise that the racial and cultural composition of any group of workers can play a fundamental role in their attitudes, or developing attitudes, towards industrial relations. Cultural traditions can often dictate the political characteristics of a particular group of workers. This may be one explanation for the high levels of solidarity that were to be seen at Glasgow in the later period of this study. Indeed, early Irish rural secret societies were, in the words of Sir George Cornwall Lewis in 1836, to be considered 'a vast trades union for the protection of the Irish peasantry'.[59] Therefore, in the Irish rural past there was already a well-established tradition of combination, one that was perhaps relatively easily translated into the industrial present.

[59] Quoted in W. P. Ryan, *The Irish Labour Movement from the Twenties to Our Present Day* (New York, 1920), pp. 15–35. It is well known that the Irish countryside had a long history of peasant combination and many protective groups emerged from the late eighteenth century up to, and beyond, *the Great Famine of 1845–1850*. These groups were often violent and resorted to intimidation and threat.

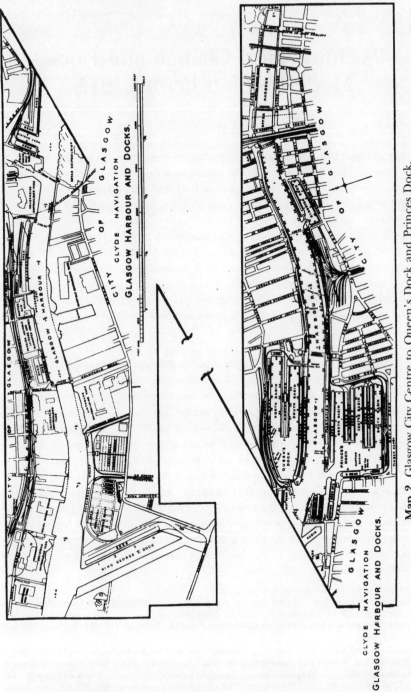

Map 2. Glasgow City Centre to Queen's Dock and Princes Dock.

Source: derived from W. M. French, *The Scottish Ports*, 1938.

# CHAPTER SIX

# Technological Change and Dock Modernisation before 1914

It is not always clear within the port transport industry just how the spread of technology affected the progress of the industry over time. On the one hand, it was only the handling of bulk cargoes such as coal and grain that was 'substantially affected by modern technology'. The pace of mechanisation was 'slow and limited in its effects', at least up to 1914.[1] On the other hand, mechanisation was to penetrate more deeply throughout ports that had a more recent trading history, such as Glasgow, than older ports such as London. While Glasgow had boasted harbour operations that stretched over several centuries, it was only in 1808 that Glasgow was first recognised as an official port of register. In the following year the Town Council of Glasgow was constituted as statutory trustees with separate finances. Thereafter the port began to experience greater levels of trade, as illustrated in Chapter 3.[2]

Due to the deepening of the Clyde many shipping businesses were encouraged to move from Greenock and Port Glasgow into Glasgow. In 1820, for example, there were only eighty-four ships, totalling 6,384 tons, registered at Glasgow, less than the other Clydeside ports of Irvine, Port Glasgow and Greenock.[3] By the second half of the century, however, Glasgow's expansion was evident, rising to 660 ships of 212,028 tons by 1860, and by 1900 reaching a high point of 1,605 ships, with a net tonnage of almost 1,600,000.[4] By 1914 many shipping firms had their headquarters, or offices, at Glasgow. This undoubtedly reflected the expansion in the deep-sea trade. In this sense Glasgow's rise to trading pre-eminence as a port took place from around the late 1860s and the early 1870 onwards. Glasgow's main phase of expansion, there-fore, was relatively recent and the labour force had less time to generate traditional work practices which would delay mechanisation. The London Port Authority, for example, attempted to introduce the grain elevator in the late nineteenth century, but the dockers were able to hold-up this process. Thus, the more ingrained

---

[1] Phillips and Whiteside, *Casual Labour*, p. 32.

[2] This can be seen in terms of total tonnage arriving between 1828, 1867 and 1900, when figures rose from 700,000 tons, 1,800,000 tons and 4,400,000 tons respectively, see J. Cunnison and J. B. S. Gilfillan (eds.), *The Third Statistical Account of Scotland* (hereafter *TSA*): *Glasgow* (Glasgow, 1958), p. 313.

[3] Ibid., Glasgow had 84 of 6,384 tons registered in 1820 as compared to 341 ships of 46,171 tons at Greenock; 114 ships of 18,225 at Port Glasgow, and 121 ships of 10,487 tons at the Ayrshire port of Irvine, p. 332.

[4] Ibid.; in 1938, for example, there were 1,060 ships with a net tonnage of 1,371,433, noted *TSA: Glasgow*, p. 332.

workplace traditions of ports such as London, which had a much longer history, were responsible for halting the spread of certain mechanical appliances. In Glasgow, probably because the trade was still relatively immature, there were few problems associated with the introduction of this type of equipment into the port.

## The Dynamics of Steam and Hydraulic Powered Equipment: A Cause of Labour Displacement and Speed-up?

As the work process became more mechanised, causing speed-up, increased productivity and reductions in numbers, did the docker simply cling more tenaciously to traditional practices in order to offset the impact of new equipment on their working lives? How far was the docker's ever-hardening position in the defence of custom and practice and the casual system of employment, therefore, a reaction to the forces of change caused by increased levels of technology?

Steam, or hydraulics, could cause considerable unemployment by the late nineteenth century.[5] Even at a more general level, Beatrice Potter argued, the 'substitution of steam ship for sailing vessels, while spreading work more evenly across a given period of time, also acted to increase uncertainty in employment terms'.[6] Eric Taplin suggests that before the First World War there was a genuine belief within the port transport industry that mechanisation was a major cause for concern. Robert Williams of the National Transport Workers Federation (NTWF) reported in 1913 that mechanisation was the cause of considerable speed-up in certain areas of dock work. He noted that 5–6,000 tons of grain could be discharged in two days by 'huge elevators' when previously it would have taken several weeks. Before the introduction of these elevators three to four hundred men were needed to discharge such a cargo. But by 1913, this was literally 'carried out without human intervention'. Thus, even at a very moderate estimate, 'up to 80% of the labour needed for this type of work was dispensed with'.

At Liverpool, over two decades earlier, it was claimed that there was 'more machinery, of the greatest variety, for expediting work and economising labour than any other similar area in the world'. In addition:

> The docks themselves were considerably modernised by the use of mechanical, often steam powered contrivances. Dock gates, capstans, moving bridges, pumping gear, sluice gates and the like were remodelled to speed up the movement of ships in and out of the docks and to save on labour.[7]

While Eric Taplin suggests that this may have been more a matter of 'civic pride' than practical innovation, he still notes that Liverpool was considered 'more efficient than London', in part a consequence of its more highly mechanised state.[8]

---

[5] This can be seen in relation to the crane and the elevator in the loading or discharging of certain goods, or specifically at Glasgow in relation to introduction of the 'hydraulic windlass' (see chap. 1).

[6] Hilton, *Are Trade Unions Obstructive?*, pp. 14–15.

[7] Taplin, *Dockers' Union*, p. 9.

[8] Ibid., p. 10.

In evidence presented to the 1892 Royal Commission on Labour, it was shown that Glasgow was similar to Liverpool in so far as its workforce was able to load and unload cargo more quickly than London. Does this indicate that there was a similar technological force at work at Glasgow? After 1870 the main technological change affecting the docks around Britain was the transformation from sail to steam propulsion. This not only meant a fundamental change in shipping technology, but an increase in the size of hold and, therefore, the carrying capacity of a ship. Steam power was not so dependent on the vagaries of wind and tide, which had the effect of ironing out the seasonality historically associated with the port transport trade. Colonel Birt, the General Manager of Millwall Docks stressed this very point when giving his evidence to the Royal Commission on Labour in 1892:

> In my early days the fluctuations were much worse and for weeks together the docks would be idle and a shift in wind would bring an enormous fleet in. That course is remedied [now] by the introduction of steam.[9]

The arrival of the steamship 'brought changes in methods of working which were universal in their application'. Ships could now sail on longer journeys and on more 'complicated routes', and even on short sea routes 'steam ousted sail fairly easily'.[10] The coastal trades felt the effects of steam foremost, but it was the attempts to reduce operating costs on the long-distance routes that caused the greatest changes in the work process. In this area, the ousting of sail was a 'more lengthy process', but when steam power eventually overtook sail:

> The time spent in port had to be kept to a minimum, and thus the rapid handling of cargoes became an absolute necessity. Mechanisation was one way of achieving the necessary speed-up in dock operations.[11]

These developments not only caused problems arising from speed-up, but were also 'seldom consistent with stable employment of dock labour'. With the advent of steam, argued David Wilson, 'came the intensification of the casual system and the need to increase the casual pool of labour'.[12] This was one of the major impacts of technological change. The ship owners sought to reduce units costs by using larger and more powerful vessels. On board, cargo could be handled quite quickly, but on shore the process was held back by the lack of modern mechanical handling equipment. Put simply, as the shipowners' resources were tied up in their ships, this meant that more men were needed to work on the quayside to keep up with the faster discharge and loading rates on the better equipped ships.[13] Steam technology exacerbated the worst effects of the casual system, therefore, because it resulted in more cargo being handled over a shorter period.

Despite the many references to the adverse effects of mechanisation made by commentators such as Potter, Taplin and Lovell, the overall progress of mechan-

---

[9] RC on Labour, 1892, evidence, Colonel Birt, Q. 6931.
[10] Lovell, Stevedores and Dockers, p. 26.
[11] Ibid., p. 27.
[12] Wilson, Docker, p. 32.
[13] Ibid.

isation within the industry as a whole was nevertheless quite slow.[14] Indeed, quick turn-round times did not always necessitate high levels of mechanisation. A pliable labour force, 'working long hours at high speed', in ports such as London or New York, could work faster than a well-equipped port such as Hamburg. As long as labour was plentiful 'there was little incentive to mechanise on a large scale'.[15] As Liverpool and Glasgow were said to have been more efficient than London, does this mean that their dock labour forces were worked even harder and over longer periods than their counterparts at London? And does this line of argument therefore undermine the proposition that it was the increased level of mechanisation evident at Liverpool, or at Glasgow, which was responsible for increased efficiency and quicker turn-round times?

That the spread of mechanisation within the port transport industry was slow has been explained by Eric Hobsbawm. He saw mechanisation as a means of rationalising the port industry, but stressed that it had to be tied up with a more flexible hiring system.[16] Indeed, we have already seen that the hiring system was drawing more men into the docks. Coupled with the casual system of employment, British dock labour employers simply exploited their comparative cheap labour advantage. Thus, as Lovell concluded, 'there was little incentive to mechanise on a large scale'.[17]

Nevertheless, there was an increased use of both on-board and quayside equipment, particularly steam-driven winches, with hydraulic and steam-powered cranes (and by the early 1910s the electric crane) emerging in ever greater numbers from around the mid-nineteenth century onward. But their implementation and penetration of Britain's docks was as haphazard as the historic growth of the dock system:

> Prior to 1914 the nature of dock work had not been substantially affected by modern technology; the pace of mechanisation had been slow and its scope confined. Only a few bulk cargoes – like coal and grain – could be easily moved by machinery, and only if ships had been built for its use. Other lifting operations could be performed by cranes or winches, but only in conjunction with a large amount of manual labour. The more expensive installations could not be afforded except by highly capitalised dock undertakings and shipping firms. For the most part, therefore, human motive force continued to rule on the waterside.[18]

Was this the case at Glasgow? As has been seen, vessels entering and leaving Glasgow were rapidly increasing in size before 1914 and came to be heavily involved in the coal and grain trades. These trades were also to become highly mechanised before 1914, and there was a considerable degree of research and development into new methods of handling such cargoes at Glasgow. As for the shipowners, from 1858 onward they and others with trading interests at the port figured prominently

---

[14] Taplin, *Dockers' Union*, p. 10.
[15] Lovell, *Stevedores and Dockers*, pp. 28–9.
[16] Hobsbawm, 'National Unions on the Waterside', *Labouring Men*, p. 213.
[17] Lovell, *Stevedores and Dockers*, p. 29.
[18] Phillips and Whiteside, *Casual Labour*, p. 32.

among the Clyde Trust's fifteen members (this was out of a total twenty-five, the remaining ten elected by Glasgow Town Council).[19] By 1905 the trustees numbered forty-two (at which level they remained), of whom eighteen were either shipowners, dock companies or shipping agents (a further six trustees had trading interests around the port). The amount invested at the port at that time illustrates the commitment to modernise before 1914, and given the representation of employers on the board of the Clyde Trust, it can be suggested that they too were equally committed to equipping Glasgow to meet the needs of a modern port.

## Mechanisation and its Effect at the Port of Glasgow

How did technological change affect Glasgow, and to what extent were trends at Glasgow similar to or different from those generally experienced around Britain's other major ports? Did Glasgow's relatively late development dictate a different trend in modernisation? One significant feature of this was product relocation within the port. For example, before 1914 much of the trade in coal and minerals, the bulk trades more prone to mechanisation, moved from the area near the centre of Glasgow around Queen's and Princes Docks to Rothesay Dock situated further down-river at Clydebank. This relocation would have seriously affected those dockers working at Glasgow, and as a result many would have become displaced. By relocating the bulk of this trade down-river, however, the Clyde Navigation Trust may well have avoided a costly dispute if they had attempted to introduce the same system of mechanisation within the area formerly used to handle the great bulk of that trade. This would not have been their sole reason for moving the trade down-river, or even the most important. By recruiting a fresh labour force at Clydebank, however, they did circumvent any possibility of a dispute arising out of the implementation of new technology. For there is little doubt that Rothesay Dock was the very model of what a modern mechanised dock should be, including the installation of the first electric crane on the British waterfront.

So was Glasgow a more mechanised port than others in Britain? To what extent did modernisation affect the workforce? Clearly, Glasgow had a well-deserved reputation for being a modern, and modernising, port, and this process affected the workforce in two distinct ways. First, as more docks and quays were built, more labour would have been needed to work them. Thus, modernisation initially created a greater demand for labour. Secondly, many of the recently built docks of the 1870s and 1880s had modern appliances already installed, such as cranes, capstans and winches, and various other types of powered equipment. The newest recruits to dock work at Glasgow, therefore, were already familiar with such equipment. This would also have been the case with the new breed of shipworkers, in so far as they would have been introduced to power-driven machinery on board the more modern steam vessels. Thus, the great majority of Glasgow's dock labour force would have matured alongside powered machinery of various types, both on-board ship and along much of the quayside. The main problems of mechanisation,

[19] NSA, vi, pp .10–12.

therefore, to the newest section of the dock labour force, or to those already well-established in given areas of trade such as grain and coal, would have occurred when subsequent appliances were introduced – as was to happen in the late 1880s and early 1890s.

### Technological Change, Unemployment and the De-skilling of the Dock Labour Force

It is generally recognised that increased mechanisation and other forms of technical progress not only dispensed with the need for special skills, but also increased irregularity of employment within the port transport industry (in so far as the cost of maintaining expensive capital machinery could be offset by laying off the workforce when trade was quiet).[20] It also affected levels of skill, demoting workers associated with skilled work within the docks to the ranks of the lesser skilled. This is a view which John Lovell believes carries much conviction[21] and can be argued from two perspectives. First, the impact of de-skilling and displacement by labour-saving machinery in other industries saw men drift towards the docks in the hope of gaining employment: this was in addition to the men from outside the industry who regularly descended on the docks during periods of temporary unemployment in their own trades.[22] Secondly, the de-skilling of certain areas of work within the dock industry itself caused by the introduction of labour-saving devices and technological change meant that even more workers were in competition for the lesser skilled jobs at the port, a point borne out by Lovell:

> The packing of cargo and the rigging of gear were special skills which fell within the sphere of shipwork, and generally speaking it can be said that their relative importance tended to diminish under the impact of technological change.[23]

By definition, mechanisation in this instance was still responsible for a degree of de-skilling and an increased rate of speed-up.

Phillips and Whiteside argue that the gradual spread of machinery before 1914 was lessening the manual skills demanded in some trades such as the coal and grain trades. As a result employers could recruit downwards and take on men of lower status within the industry.[24] There was a clear link also between this type of technological change and the de-skilling of elements of the dock labour force, which in turn increased levels of uncertainty about employment for the particular

---

[20] Christopher Saunders, *Seasonal Variations in Unemployment* (Oxford, 1936), p. 44.

[21] Lovell, *British Trade Unions*, p. 27.

[22] It is generally recognised that skilled men (or men of indeterminate skills for that matter), descended on the docks when trade was bad. One example of this is noted in the press coverage of a strike that took place in Glasgow over Jun. and Jul. of 1889. It was reported to a meeting of Glasgow dockers that the Trades Council there were not quickly coming to a decision to donate monies to the strike fund to enable the dockers to hold out against the shipowners. Dockers' leaders stated, '[but] we will know how to handle these tradesmen in future'! To which a body of dockers replied, 'Yes! When they come to the quays when trade is quiet!' Reported in the *North British Daily Mail*, 4 Jul. 1889.

[23] Lovell, *Stevedores and Docker*, p. 38.

[24] Phillips and Whiteside, *Casual Labour*, pp. 274–5.

group of workers involved. As Lovell cogently argues, the over-riding effect was to create demands for stronger men, where physical prowess was more important than the degree of skill they brought to the job. These men worked below decks, but they depended on the skills of others above decks, or on the quayside, to erect overhead rigging and safely deliver cargo into the hold. A degree of skill was thus necessary in relation to the safety of the gangs involved in shipwork below decks (a finer point in the discussion of skill, however, not readily accepted or recognised by employers):

> A mistake in slinging . . . could mean loss of life. A shipworker was thus obliged to rely absolutely on the proficiency of his workmates, and it was this atmosphere of mutual reliance which more than anything else bound shipmen together as a distinct group.[25]

It can be clearly seen that the link between technological change and safety is of great importance in relation to shipwork.

By the first decade of the twentieth century, it was argued that modernisation was causing unemployment on a large scale. Between 1905 and 1909 the Royal Commission on Poor Law and Relief of Distress heard evidence which considered the main causes of unemployment. From the *Minutes of Evidence* there developed a vigorous debate as to the causes of unemployment within the docks. One cause regularly cited was 'the abuse of alcohol'.[26] Without doubt the dockers had 'secured something of a reputation for hard living', notes Eric Taplin, but 'behaviour of this sort could be attributed more to those on the fringes of dock work, rather than the typical docker, many of whom enjoyed a stable family life'.[27] Another oft-cited cause of unemployment was the introduction of the Workmen's Compensation Act of 1906, which was alleged to have 'reluctantly' forced employers to engage only the fittest, healthiest and, by definition, the younger elements of the dock labour force, because of increased insurance costs.[28]

Nevertheless, there was also a considerable debate which centred around the issue of mechanisation as a force for change within the industry, and the effects of this on an industry with an already endemic unemployment and underemployment problem. There were those like Colonel J. Smith Park, who felt that mechanisation did not cause unemployment, but rather created *more* work. In certain respects this was true as machines provided work for operators and increased demand for the tradesman who would undertake any necessary maintenance. And here Smith Park was at least consistent, for he had offered evidence given to an earlier Royal

---

[25] Lovell, *Stevedores and Dockers*, pp. 39–40.

[26] *RC on Poor Laws*, 1910, *Minutes of Evidence*, statement by the Deputy Chairman of the Distress Committee in Glasgow, Mr William Fleming Anderson. p. 40,

[27] Taplin, *Dockers' Union*, p. 20.

[28] *RC on Poor Laws*, 1910, *Minutes of Evidence*, many of those questioned debated this matter, and there seemed to be a general feeling among employers, agents, owners and Distress Commissioners alike, that the Workmans Compensation Act was an important cause of unemployment at this time. Whether this was true or not is incidental; to the employing class it was real enough and it may well have forced them to alter their recruitment policies from that which existed before, to the detriment particularly of the older men who were members of the dock labour force at this time.

Commission in the early 1890s where he displayed a similar attitude. He did note that the introduction of grain elevators at Glasgow had caused resistance among the men, but that this had been overcome by bringing in operators supplied by the manufacturing company. He added, however, that this could not have been done in a port such as London 'as the resistance of the London men would be too strong'.[29]

Smith Park did not say why the London men would have shown such resistance, or indeed, why the Glasgow men attempted it. It may have been feared that the immediate effect of the introduction of this equipment would be the displacement of labour. R. Bean's analysis of the Liverpool strike of 1890 sheds some light on the reasons why labour would enter into dispute over such issues, particularly in the grain trade, where 'mechanisation now meant that one elevator and six men could do the work of sixty, thus discharging ships not only more quickly but also at less cost'.[30] Moreover, the reason that it could be introduced in Glasgow, and evidently in Liverpool, but not in London was that the trade was still fairly new to the port, and that the trade unions were not sufficiently well-organised, or strong enough, to fight such moves.

Phillips and Whiteside argue that in the 1940s the pace of further modernisation of British ports, in terms of improved facilities and mechanical handling, 'was very uneven and in the older centres, very slow'. These, where long-standing workplace traditions had time to harden, would be those very centres which would most resist change.[31] In the 1930s Glasgow would have been one such 'older' centre. However, in the later decades of the nineteenth century Glasgow's situation was somewhat different. Being a relatively new port, Glasgow would have been more amenable to change. Its equipment was already up to a modern standard, while its workforce was in no position to resist new implantation of technology in any effective manner until the time of the labour unrest between 1910 and 1914.

The introduction of new machinery did, in the short term at least, have the effect of causing some degree of labour displacement. This was the opinion of some who gave evidence before the Royal Commission on Labour of 1892, but who ultimately believed that mechanisation 'served positively to increase the demand for labour generally. Prejudicial, perhaps, in the short term, but not so in the long term.'[32] The General Manager of Millwall Docks in London in the early 1890s was convinced that the introduction of the 'Priestman's Bucket' in the grain trade had helped to reduce the average squad size from eighteen to six – the equivalent of an annual saving of £3,000 on the wages bill. However, using this apparatus resulted in an increase in the grain traffic through the port (because it allowed cargo to be landed which formerly could not support the cost of landing charges) which saw the wages bill rise by £9,000.[33] This could imply that the overall size of the

---

[29] *RC on Labour*, 1892, evidence, Mr J. Smith Park, Q. 12,788.

[30] Bean, 'The Liverpool Dock Strike of 1890', p. 54.

[31] Phillips and Whiteside, *Casual Labour*, p. 255.

[32] *RC on Labour, 1st Report*, 1892, *Précis of Evidence*, ii, evidence presented by Mr Josiah Griffen, Secretary and Manager of Surrey Commercial Dock Company (*PP*, 1892, xxiv, C. 6708 – II), p. 23.

[33] Ibid., evidence, Colonel Birt (General Manager of Millwall Docks), Q. 6935–6, Q. 6986, and Q. 7055 to Q. 7075.

labour force handling the grain cargo increased significantly (although, the rise may also be explained as an increase in overtime payments to a much reduced quantity of men).[34] Whatever the case, it is clear that the increased speed and volume of the grain cargo handled made this business very profitable and lucrative indeed.

But mechanisation did not stop with the Priestman Bucket. The grain elevator was the next major innovation, and the introduction of machinery which facilitated the transference of grain by suction, before 1914, arguably caused greater consternation among the dock labour force. One historian noted that the introduction of this equipment in London halved the numbers of grain porters previously needed to perform such tasks.[35] But much less technically advanced forms of mechanisation had their effect too, a point that *The Minority Report on the Poor Law* (of 1909) confirmed, when it reported:

> It is now increasingly true that machinery is displacing the purely unskilled labourer, and causing a demand for men of more general ability and reliable character . . . the steam crane, the grain elevator [at the docks] are materially diminishing the demand for unskilled labour.[36]

The introduction of the grain elevator and the Priestman bucket, just two of the many innovations that were being employed at this time, along with the newer hydraulic and electric cranes, or more powerful steam winches, turn-tables, and capstans, give some indication of the challenges facing the dockers between the late 1880s and 1914. The penetration of this equipment may have been further facilitated because organised labour was severely weakened by a trade depression that persisted throughout the first decade of the twentieth century, and which was particularly severe on Clydeside. Dock labour throughout the period as a whole was rarely in any position to halt the steady march of mechanisation.

In giving his evidence to the 1910 Royal Commission on the Poor Law, Colonel J. Smith Park seems to have overlooked the fact that the discussion was aimed at finding whether the causes of unemployment within the dock labour force were in any way linked to the introduction of new handling equipment. He concentrated on defending mechanisation by offering examples of the benefits to those involved in the construction, operation and maintenance of mechanical appliances.[37] His rationale does not seem to have been one with which other commentators

---

[34] Lovell, *Stevedores and Dockers*, p. 39. Lovell notes that due to the pressures of speed-up promoting faster rapid turn-round times, ships were subjected to 'long periods of continuous labour, often exceeding twenty four hours'. In this sense, then, the wages bill would be more representative of overtime payment, rather than automatically suggesting that more men were being taken on to execute the work. Similar evidence was put before the Shaw Inquiry, but because of the lack of empirical data – as to the actual numbers employed, due to the casual nature of employment and the fact that wage documentation was not kept on the casual labour force, only the permanent men – this area of investigation will always prove problematic. However, official enquiries strongly suggest that this was more generally the case.

[35] Treble, *Urban Poverty*, p. 58.

[36] Sydney and Beatrice Webb, *The Public Organisation of the Labour Market: Being Part of Two Minority Reports of the Poor Law Commission*, 1909, pp. 187–8.

[37] *RC on Poor Laws*, 1910, Q. 8,764.

generally agreed, however. William Fleming Anderson stated clearly before the same Commission his belief that 'the steady advance of machinery' did have a displacing effect on the labour force.[38] Mr James Ferguson, Indoor Assistant Inspector of Poor in Glasgow Parish, also argued that the introduction of machinery was a major cause of unemployment. Discussing the effects of the hydraulic windlass, Ferguson noted, 'at our harbour and docks modern machinery for the loading and discharging of cargo has been a means of displacing a large number of men'. He also observed that the use of hydraulic lifts and two or three cranes working at each hold of a ship, meant that the time it took to empty a large steamer had been reduced from between 'two or three days to two or three hours'.[39] Obviously, whether such a high increase in turn-around time was achieved would depend on the cargo being handled, especially if it were valuable and needed to be stowed in a particularly careful manner. However, quick turn-around times like these were entirely possible at this juncture.

The quest for the quick turn-around time had been sought for many years and for the most part was fought for successfully by the employers, until, that is, the dock labour force became stronger and more organised. Once the dock unions found themselves in a position to resist the blanket introduction of mechanical appliances, they fought gritty, and often successful, campaigns against it. Nevertheless, it was almost certainly the spread of mechanisation at Glasgow, and Liverpool for that matter, even in the early 1890s with the introduction of the grain elevator, that earned both ports the reputation for quick turn-round times. As noted by William Becket Hill, 'under no system in London do dockers there work as well as Liverpool or Glasgow men. Liverpool could discharge half as quickly as London'.[40]

Despite Hobsbawm's suggestion that there was little rationalisation evident within the port transport industry before 1914, the situation at Glasgow was notably different. It was not simply an example of the type of 'civic pride' exhibited at the port of Liverpool.[41] While it is possible to argue that there was no wholesale modernisation of the British port transport industry before 1914, this does not preclude the possibility that some ports experienced greater modernisation than others. The evidence of this study suggests that the Port of Glasgow was one such example.

## Research and Development: New Working Methods at Glasgow c.1910

Clyde Navigation Trust engineer George Baxter, meticulously chronicled the effects of modern equipment at the port of Glasgow in 1910, in an article in the *Glasgow Herald* in March of that year. Among the many instances of mechanisation evident at the port, he particularly noted the effects of the coal hoist. The

---

[38] Ibid., Anderson, p. 44.

[39] Ibid., James Ferguson, p. 50.

[40] *RC on Labour, 1st Report*, v, 1892, evidence, Mr William Becket Hill of Allan Brothers of Liverpool and London, p. 25; see also *Minutes of Evidence*, Q. 6,525 to Q. 6,530 .

[41] Taplin, *Dockers Union*, pp. 9–10 and p. 170; see also James Samuelson, *Labour Saving Machinery* (1893), pp. 66.

modern coal hoist (worked by hydraulics) was very economical, could move coal rapidly and 'required fewer men to work it' than the coaling crane. Baxter estimated that the coaling crane could at best lift between twenty-eight and thirty coal wagons per hour, whereas the hydraulic hoist, 'under favourable circumstances', could ship about fifty wagons per hour. However, the rate of loading was dictated by the speed at which the loaded coal could be trimmed, so it was only more effective than the coaling crane up to a certain point. The Clyde Navigation Trust also initiated research and experimentation into new techniques and modern appliances at the port. Baxter noted an example at Princes Dock where one vessel was loaded with '8,400 tons of cargo and bunker coal in 56 hours' using the coaling crane. At the purpose-built Rothesay Dock, Baxter praised the effects of the electric hoist, which could lift, lower, tip and empty cargo, and was even more economical than its hydraulic counterpart at Princes Dock. He reported one timed experiment where the electric hoist loaded thirty wagons of 253 tons each in 37 seconds – the equivalent of just over 48 wagons, weighing 12,308 tons, in one hour.

He also gave examples of the handling of Spanish ore, which he noted was hard and lumpy, and a hazardous employment as some cargo fell when the buckets were being hoisted away from the hold. This type of work entailed a considerable amount of manual labour, usually employing around eighteen dockers in the main hold of an ordinary vessel. He considered the findings of an earlier experiment at Queen's Dock some five years previously, when three different types of 'digger grabs' and one ordinary tipping bucket, were tested against each other. One grab needed special fittings, the other two required no alterations. The tipping bucket was worked by a similar crane to that using the grabs and the bucket weighed 24% of the gross load raised – 76% was thus raised as cargo. The grabs, on the other hand, accounted for 70% of gross load raised. With only 30% raised as cargo, speed, rather than volume, was the main aim. He further noted that one set of grabs required a drop of several feet in order to penetrate the ore. But it was found that by dropping the grabs in such a fashion damage could be inflicted on the tank top when nearing the bottom of the hold. There were obvious drawbacks to using the grabs. However, the results of the experiment were as follows:

Table 6.1: *Results of Experiments with different Grabs for the Discharge of Cargo.*

|  | Cost | Time Taken (Hrs) |
| --- | --- | --- |
| First Grab | £10. 4s 9d. | 35.7 |
| Second Grab | £14. 0s 0d. | 51.3 |
| Third Grab | £12. 2s 10d. | 43.1 |
| Tipping Bucket | £19. 11s 0d. | 29.4 |

**Source:** Article by George Baxter, Engineer to the Clyde Navigation Trust,'Dock Equipment: Appliances at Glasgow Harbour', *Glasgow Herald*, 8 Mar. 1910.

Baxter concluded that the grabs worked best on ships with hatches directly under-neath, but only maintained this performance level until the bottom was nearly reached. Thereafter, conditions were more favourable for working with the tipping bucket. The trials showed that the grabs at that point were of limited advantage, particularly in relation to ships which had small hatches, twin decks, and/or engines amidships. The writer did note the advances taking place elsewhere. On the Great Lakes, for example, specially designed ships were being used to facilitate unloading by grabs, taking almost all the cargo both economically and rapidly.[42]

While there was no particular use for the grabs in this instance, the grabs were of use on larger ships, where a combination of grabs and bucket were used for the unloading of ores. This example not only reveals the commitment of the Clyde Navigation Trust to modernisation and technological implementation, but shows also that they had considerable freedom about enforcing changes in working conditions. It would seem clear from the times recorded for the loading of coal, or the unloading of ores, that the method chosen must have had a significant effect on the pattern of work. Such an example shows the pressure that the dock labour force was under at this time, and it is entirely possible that these experiments aroused the wrath of a workforce increasingly determined to fight the introduction of such new methods.

It is evident that employers wished to introduced new methods by 1912 when, as reported by the *Glasgow Herald* (less than two years after Baxter's article appeared), they locked out Glasgow's dockers in their attempts to reduce gang sizes. They considered their action on this occasion as a 'necessary evil' as they could no longer tolerate the fact that 'six men were employed to do the work of four' and that this was now 'a common feature of dockside work'.[43] This dispute was the culmination of conflict over the question of squad sizes and coincided with the desires of both George Baxter and the Clyde Navigation Trust to further reduce turn-round times. In August 1911, a dispute arose around the question of 'too few hands to do too much work'.[44] And at the heart of many wage disputes of the period lay deeper concerns over the issue of work intensification and the impact of technological change. One example was the extra payment extracted from the employers by grainworkers for the bulk discharge of vessels using elevators.[45]

Such factors were thus the cause of a significant degree of unrest within the workforce, not least when the employers acted to force down squad sizes and intensify work-load.[46] This may have been one reason behind the decision to move the mineral trade down-river to Clydebank, a change of location being favoured

---

[42] *Glasgow Herald*, 8 Mar. 1910.

[43] *Glasgow Herald*, 21 Jan. 1912, one of various reports between 17 Jan. 1912 through to 22 Feb. 1912, noted that some 7,000 dockers were in dispute, principally over the employment of non-union labour, but also because of the drive to lower gang sizes and increase workload. The strike ended with squad sizes being reduced by 2, and thereafter there would be 8 men in the hold and 6 men onshore. Indeed, another related dispute during that period, reported in *Forward* weekly, from Jan. 17 to Feb. 22, was caused by employers attempting to further reduce shore squads sizes from 6 to 4; see also Kenefick, 'The struggle for Control'.

[44] *Glasgow Herald*, 2 Aug. 1911.

[45] Ibid.

[46] Ibid., Jan. and Feb. 1912.

over the attempt to change the resistant attitudes of the dockers at the upper docks. The only recognition that George Baxter offered the workforce was to note that the unloading of Spanish ore was 'hazardous', implying perhaps, that new methods were less so. But, in terms of speed-up, the pressure brought upon the docker arguably increased the dangers associated with this work, rather than the reverse. This was without doubt a major concern of the workforce. The dangers inherent in dock work, in relation to mechanised handling equipment, had been recognised almost twenty years before, when Mr Josiah Griffen, Manager of the Millwall Commercial Dock Company, admitted that for all the gains offered by mechanisation, 'accidents were inevitable'.[47]

## Mechanisation and Poverty – A Tenuous Link?

As noted by Richard McGhee and Edward McHugh, the leaders of the NUDL in the early 1890s, the link between mechanisation and poverty had been recognised for some time. They asserted that mechanisation was a tool used in the exploitation of the working class, where one man could do the work previously done by ten at the beginning of that century. Yet, workers as a whole, 'were worse fed, worse housed, worse clothed than were their forefathers'. McGhee and McHugh reported thus their opinions on the effect of mechanisation:

With the great increase of productive power – the struggle for existence grows keener. Labour-saving machines do not lessen as they ought to the daily toil of any worker. They are used as competitors to reduce his wages, and make the struggle for the opportunity to labour every day severer than before. In the proper solution of this paradox lies the only permanent hope for labour.[48]

Their report further stated that this was in fact only an 'artificial condition' generated by the 'cunning' of one class, and used against another. There was nothing natural in such a state of competition.

Despite the early recognition of the problems associated with the use of machinery on the docks, the subject was to plague the industry for many years to come. During the First World War the trade unions claimed that the employers advanced the spread of mechanical equipment by exploiting the loophole in the Excess Profits Tax and using the 'argument of national emergency' to achieve their aim, while 'greatly increasing output'.[49] Thus by the time war was ended the industry had changed significantly:

Methods of production have been improved, new machinery introduced, and the rate of production speeded up, but the person who profited is neither the worker nor the consumer, but the capitalist. Our regret is that our predecessors in this job did not keep records such as we keep.[50]

[47] RC on Labour, Précis of Evidence, 1892, p. 24.
[48] Report of the Executive of the National Union of Dock Labourers in Great Britain and Ireland, 5th Annual Congress, Oct. 1893, pp. 13–14.
[49] Hilton, Are Trade Unions Obstructive?, p. 117.
[50] Ibid., p. 113.

This was being reported in the 1920s and 1930s when once more dock labour did not seem to be in any position to defend itself against the further encroachment of technical advance. It was a time when dockers could not stop the introduction of more equipment, such as a new variety of crane, which could 'displace anything up to twenty men on one job' at a considerable saving to the employer.[51] The Shaw Inquiry stated that there were without doubt some problems relating to the introduction of machinery, but believed these were not insurmountable, particularly if such factors were raised and discussed through a Joint Industrial Council (an option that was not generally available before 1914 and the outbreak of war). The Shaw Inquiry concluded:

> To increase the output by the introduction of machinery is ultimately a benefit to the nation at large, in which those engaged in labour share, but it necessarily and almost always involved a displacement of labour, and thus, owing to the fact that the working men, like other classes of the community, are apt to take short views, causes a resistance to change and new methods and postponement of that benefit which they bring.[52]

The Hilton Inquiry of the 1930s revealed that the employers could argue that the trade unions were in fact holding out against the introduction of new equipment. As noted by one employers' representative:

> The Unions maintain that the advantages from the introduction of machinery should be labour aiding, not labour saving, and this attitude has to an extent limited the benefits derived from the installation of such machinery.[53]

Evidence from the Shaw Inquiry illustrated clearly that by the end of war in 1918, the dockers of Glasgow would not be prepared to accept further labour displacement. There had already been problems with the introduction of a new electric grain-weighing machine. One machine would replace three typical grain-hand-weighing-machines and would reduce the typical gang involved in this work from fifteen to six, leaving nine surplus to requirements. But the men refused extra payment to operate the machine, and as a result the intention to purchase a further two electric machines was abandoned.[54]

The main thrust of the Shaw Inquiry's conclusions was that working men should be consulted in matters concerning mechanisation, particularly if 'some provisions for positions being found for labour so displaced' were to develop as a result. If this were to be done, noted the Inquiry chairman, citing the evidence of Glasgow stevedore James Spencer, a 'new era of consideration, confidence, and co-operation' could be at hand. Unfortunately, this was not to be and the problems that were linked to mechanisation were to continue for sometime to come.

---

[51] Ibid., p. 116.
[52] Shaw Inquiry, i, p. 13.
[53] Hilton, *Are Trade Unions Obstructive?*, p. 108.
[54] Shaw Inquiry, i, p. 274.

# CHAPTER SEVEN

# Occupational Health and Safety

The question of occupational health and safety in relation to dock work is a difficult area of investigation, with little evidence of any thorough analysis of these issues in any of the major historical studies concerning dock work. Eric Taplin and John Lovell do make regular references to the dangerous nature of dock work, but they offer little or no quantitative, or qualitative, evidence to back up such references. Recent work by Taplin does offer some statistical treatment of known data, but the issue of occupational health and safety is at no time fundamentally addressed. This situation is not altogether the fault of the historians as there is a dearth of good documentary material, and statistical data, relating to health and safety along the waterfront throughout the period 1850 to 1914. This does not mean that the issue should be overlooked. An analysis of health and safety issues on the docks could begin by considering attitudes to the issue of occupational health and safety within British industry generally. It should be stressed, however, that there are problems associated with this line of enquiry too. This is borne out in an article written by Arthur McIvor, on the industrial health of manual workers, where he noted that it was not until the First World War 'that the debate on industrial health and efficiency was brought into the public arena'. Before 1914:

> physiological and psychological health at work was severely neglected by the vast majority of British managers and employers, most of whom were concerned only to stay within the legal limits of the Factories Acts.[1]

The roots of the health and safety debate stretch back to the mid-nineteenth century. In the *Fourth Annual Report of the Medical Officer to the Privy Council*, for 1861, it was stated that 'the canker of industrial diseases gnaws at the very root of our national strength'.[2] Anthony Wohl shows that even before the 1860s there had been a considerable debate on the effects of industry on the labouring population, evident in even earlier reports. Wohl notes that 'historians still argue about the accuracy of such reports', but recognising these were to 'provide the material for the factory reform movement', he also argues, perhaps more importantly, that there was 'no attempt to follow up such reports in order to pinpoint the incidence of occupational diseases'.[3] Identifying the incidence of occupational injury, there-

---

[1] A. McIvor, 'Manual Work, Technology, and Industrial Health, 1918–39', *Medical History*, 31, 1987, p. 161.

[2] A. S. Wohl, *Endangered Lives: Public Health in Victorian Britain* (1983), p. 257.

[3] Ibid., p. 259; Wohl notes several reports of the period dating from J. P. Kay's report on the cotton workers, 1832, P. Gaskell's *The Manufacturing Population of England* (1833), and C. Thackery's report of 1831 on *Health and Longevity in the Trades and Professions*.

fore, was, and still is, no less a problem for the historian. The 1833 Factory Act, notes Wohl, did introduce the novel idea of a state inspectorate for industry, but it did not consider how to prevent, or reduce, the hazards associated with certain industries; nor did it provide for reporting and collating the number of accidents and incidence of industrial diseases.[4] It was not until the 1864 Factory Act, and similar Acts passed throughout the 1860s and 1870s, that the first preventative measures were advocated for factory work, such as the introduction of proper ventilation. By the 1880s the Factory Acts were extended to cover a wider range of occupations, before then the Acts only covered the textile industry. It was not considered, however, that the Factory Act be extended to cover laundry work, or work on the docks.

It was not until the 1890s that legislation covering occupational health and safety began to be more vigorously applied. The 1895 Factory Act obliged an employer to notify the Factory Inspectorate of industrial diseases contracted by his employees, such as anthrax, or lead or arsenic poisoning, diseases which up until that point 'were simply an accepted part of working life'.[5] The extended 1895 Factory Act was also the first intended to cover the docks, but, as will be shown below, there were many problems associated with its application to the waterfront. Reports on the incidence of accidents, however, were to remain a problem for some time to come, not least in relation to dock work, and there were further difficulties in relation to litigation when compensation was sought by an injured worker. The Factory Act allowed for an injured worker to sue his, or her, employer, but the burden of proving the employer's liability lay with the employee. The 1897 Workmen's Compensation Act took away the need to prove liability, but it was still a costly business to enter into litigation against an offending employer.[6] Nevertheless, the Workmen's Compensation Act was seen as a major breakthrough. To John Munkman it was 'a new phase in the history of employers' liability' as well as the first extensive programme of welfare reform, little different in character, it was suggested, to those later introduced through the Liberal reforms of 1906 to 1911.[7]

In their book, *The Wounded Soldiers of Industry*, P. Bartrip and S. Burman, argue that the Workmen's Compensation Act was not perhaps the breakthrough that Munkman suggests. The Act did have 'numerous defects' in so far as it only covered a minority of workmen, and only after a qualifying period of fourteen days. The Act did not provide compensation, however, rather it offered a type of maintenance.[8] Another theme is the difficulty of establishing reliable figures for compensation paid, or details as to how exactly the system operated. They conclude that data on agreements and formal arbitration are incomplete as the return of accident statistics was only legally required after 1907 under a Home Office order.[9]

---

[4] Ibid., Wohl, p. 260.
[5] Ibid., p. 264.
[6] P. Bartrip, 'The Rise and Decline of Workmen's Compensation', in P. Weindling (ed.), *The Social History of Occupational Health* (1983), p. 162.
[7] Ibid., pp. 2–3.
[8] P. Bartrip and S. Burman (eds.), *The Wounded Soldiers of Industry* (1985), pp. 208–9.
[9] Bartrip, 'Workmen's Compensation', p. 164.

The Workmen's Compensation Act, 1897, did cover the docks, as did the Factory Act after the amendment of 1895, but the anomalies noted by Bartrip and Burman are even more problematic in relation to dock work. At a general level the 1897 Act had little effect on the working lives of the great majority of workers.[10] The main reason was that employers had no incentive to improve safety at the place of work. In order to protect themselves against the cost of paying compensation, note Bartrip and Burman, employers took out insurance, but the policies were not 'merit rated'. This meant that the cost of insurance against accident was not reduced if, for example, an employer introduced protective measures to improve the safety of the working environment.[11] The Workmen's Compensation Act was at best a compromise, and both employers and employees were 'equally unenthusiastic about it'. It failed to promote greater safety, and ultimately this issue was decided between masters and men.[12]

This chapter considers the development of health and safety regulations and how they were applied to the port transport industry. Careful consideration will be given to the problem of accident reporting; the level and extent of injury and accident, and the changing nature of safety standards over the period 1890 to 1914. Necessarily, the analysis will be speculative, as statistics on injury and accident were extremely unreliable.

## Health and Safety Provision along the Waterfront

If there were serious problems in the application and interpretation of health and safety legislation in relation to British industry generally before 1914, there is little evidence that the situation was any different along the waterfront. The evidence that does exist, although scant, suggests that the Factory Acts had a limited impact, and that dock work was in fact extremely dangerous when compared to other occupations. Moreover, the collection of accident and injury statistics were even more problematic in relation to dock work than many other industries before 1914. The first calls to deal with safety in the port transport industry stretched back to the early 1890s after the great majority of dockers became organised into various general dock trade unions during the period of New Unionism. At the Trades Union Congress in 1893, Ben Tillett argued that factory inspectors should be appointed to look after docks and wharves, underlining the need to make checks on machinery used in dock work. If this were to occur, argued Tillett, 'the percentage of accidents would be considerably decreased'.[13] The following Congress noted that the docks were to be included within a new bill of 1895, which extended the Factories Act, but that there were still major problems in applying the Act to dock work. The main problem was that work aboard ship was not covered by the Act, a point that will be considered at length below, therefore, the factory inspectorate had no jurisdiction beyond the quayside. Secondly, it was argued that

[10] Bartrip and Burman, *Wounded Soldiers*, pp. 207–14.
[11] Ibid., p. 214.
[12] Ibid., p. 221.
[13] TUC *Annual Report*, 1893, Belfast, p. 82.

the docks inspectorate should be independent of the industry and that they should have the sole responsibility to gather all the evidence relating to a particular accident. Thus, it was argued, 'the victimisation of witnesses, at work, at inquests, or, at courts of law, would be avoided'.[14] Moreover, the unions demanded an inspectorate who were 'practical and experienced men' drawn from the docking community itself. But both proposals were rejected.

The campaign to improve on health and safety regulations was stepped up towards the end of the nineteenth century. One resolution brought before the STUC conference in 1899 sought to deal with the still 'large amount of accidents taking place amongst dock labour':

> Because of the hurry and scurry entailed by the rapid discharge of steam and sailing vessels, tackle and plant were often erected without sufficient regard to safety. As a result accidents were a frequent occurrence.[15]

The reference to 'hurry and scurry' and to 'tackle and plant' indicates the effects of machinery, and more specifically the effects of steam, on the nature of dock work. This increased concerns over the extent of injury and accident.

The main problem for the port transport industry was the prevailing operational structure, and the difficulties associated with interpretation and implementation of Factories Act legislation as it related to the docks. A Home Office report of 1902 argued that the Factories Act could only apply to factories and not to the docks as it would 'be impossible to collect the returns from a multitude of different occupiers in any case':

> it appears to us to be very questionable whether, when returns were collected, the results which would be obtained from the classification and analysis of them would compensate for the trouble of collection . . . and that little useful information is to be derived from them.[16]

In 1904 a report into the working of the Compensation Act reiterated some of the problems with the workings of both the Factories Act and the Workmen's Compensation Act in relation to dock work. It noted that the 1895 Act was intended to bring this work under the jurisdiction of the Factories Department of the Home Office. The factory inspectorate, however, did not have jurisdiction aboard ship, that was the domain of the Board of Trade. This caused a serious problem when it came to litigation where compensation was paid for accidents occurring between ship and shore, but not on ship, or between ship and waterside, a legal ambiguity which the employers readily exploited. The House of Lords eventually decided the question at the turn of the century, when they categorically defined the dock as a 'factory'. There should have been no further problem, therefore, with the interpretation of the 1895 Act in relation to compensation cases, no matter where an

[14] TUC *Annual Report*, 1894, Norwich, p. 51.
[15] STUC *Annual Report*, Dundee 1899; resolution by Glasgow Harbour Labourers' Union, 'Danger of Dock Work'.
[16] *Home Office Report of Committee Appointed to Enquire into the Notification of Industrial Accidents (PP, 1902, x, Cd. 998)*, p. 18.

accident occurred within a dock.[17] But in reality it would never be that simple. With compensation causing such a problem in terms of litigation, it no doubt caused some injured dockers to think twice about instituting any claim. In such circumstances they might well have felt that it was too much bother to file an accident report, or take the matter further. Moreover, a firm caught up in such legal proceedings might well have ensured that the docker taking them to a tribunal would not work for them again. Even if the docker did not win his case, or was awarded very small sums in compensation, he would still be likely to suffer some form of victimisation.[18] This is again reiterated by Bartrip in his collaborative work with Burman. They argued that the man who sued his employer could find himself 'dubbed as a trouble maker' and thereafter, particularly in periods of high employment, would often find it difficult to obtain another job.[19] Eric Taplin stresses this forcefully in relation to dock labourers when he notes that 'working dockers' would not attend accident and compensation hearings, fearing that 'their future employment would be put in jeopardy'.[20]

It was not until 1908 that the new regulations came into force and closed many loopholes. But concern over inadequate safety inspection of dock work was still being expressed strongly.[21] A resolution sometime earlier, moved by an Aberdeen delegate of the NUDL in 1906 illustrated this by calling on the Parliamentary Committee of the STUC to once more press the government to provide 'more expert inspectors, preferably drawn from the class possessing practical experience of that type of work'.[22] By the time of the STUC conference of 1914 the General Secretary of the SUDL, Joseph Houghton, was raising issues such as sickness and injury within the industry. The main concern, however, was that the shipowners, stevedores and dock authorities were 'continually and systematically ignoring dock regulations'.[23] Thus, if Houghton's testimony is to be believed, port employers, at least in Glasgow, were not even attempting to stay within the legal limits of the Factory Acts. Thus, as suggested by both McIvor[24] and Taplin, safety regulations relating to dock work in effect 'meant very little in practice'.[25] Two years on and the problems related to dock regulations were still not solved. James Fulton, a delegate for the SUDL to the STUC in 1916, noted his 'humiliation' at having to come back to conference and submit again the same resolution that he had moved so many times before. 'It was degrading', he added, 'that they had to ask

---

[17] Report of the Committee into the Law Relating to Compensation for Injuries to Workmen, i, Report and Appendices (PP, 1904, lxxxviii, Cd. 2208), para. 118.
[18] Bartrip, 'Workmen's Compensation', p. 158.
[19] Bartrip and Burman, Wounded Soldiers, p. 28.
[20] E. Taplin, 'When is a ship a factory? Working conditions, accidents and compensation at the waterfront from the 1880s' (unpublished pre-circulated paper presented to the 9th British-Dutch Labour History Conference, Holland, 1994), p. 5.
[21] Ibid., p. 4 and p. 6.
[22] STUC Annual Report, Greenock, 1906; resolution by NUDL, Aberdeen Branch, 'Loading and Unloading of Ships'.
[23] STUC Annual Report, Kirkcaldy, 1914; see pp. 86–96 on 'Dock Regulations', and p. 75, 'Trade Unions and Political Action'.
[24] McIvor, 'Manual Work', p. 161.
[25] Taplin, 'When is a ship a factory?', p. 8.

for a common act of humanity, and argued that animals were treated better in injury than dockers.' He cited one case where a shunter at the docks had 'bled to death . . . because there was no place in which his injury could be immediately and temporarily treated'.[26] By the time of the Dunfermline Conference of the STUC in 1920, it was noted that the Home Secretary blamed the conditions of war for 'holding back reform and the extension of the Factories Act to the docks'. Thus, even by the 1920s there were still many concerns over the lack of improvement in health and safety conditions and there were still many unresolved legal issues outstanding. James Sexton, who was by then an MP, was still calling for further reform 'but without success'.[27]

The interwar years did little to change this situation and even by the late 1930s there was still great concern over the rate of accident and injury within the industry, not discounting the many serious legal anomalies that existed regarding payment of compensation for accidents. For example, in *The Scottish Transport and General Workers' Union General Executive Council's Annual Report* of December 1938, it was noted that the union's legal department had recently and successfully 'pursued some dozen Court of Session actions' necessitated by the Workmen's Compensation Act and the Employers Liability Act. The union had been forced to take a number of cases to the Court of Session in order to challenge lower court decisions because of what they felt were the obvious ambiguities in interpretation of the law. They blamed the employers for making a bad situation worse, when they reported:

> The occupation of a Dock Labourer is always a hazardous one, but the circumstances of the cases investigated by the Legal Department do not always disclose on the part of the masters of ships, or the owners of machinery or plant, or indeed, of the Stevedores themselves, a proper appreciation of the dangers and a satisfactory knowledge of the Dock Regulations. Too often they [show] a callous disregard of them.[28]

It would seem, then, that many of the problems complained of by members of Glasgow's dock labour force earlier, whether it was through membership of the NUDL in the 1890s and 1900s, or the SUDL during the 1910s, were still a problem for the industry by the end of the interwar period. The report went further:

> It is the breach of the most peremptory rules that have had the most serious consequences, particularly those regulations requiring safe means of access from the deck to the hold; efficient lighting; testing of lifting machinery, or the fencing and covering of hatches. Heavy damages have been recovered, but no amount of damages can compensate for the fatalities that are of far too frequent occurrence at the Port of Glasgow.[29]

[26] STUC *Annual Report*, Perth, 1919: resolution moved by the SUDL, 'Ambulances at Docks'.
[27] Taplin, 'When is a ship a factory?', p. 6.
[28] Mitchell Library, TU. S331 880941 Sco C. 372408, *Annual Report of the General Executive Council of the Scottish Transport and General Workers' Union*, Dec. 1938, p. 4.
[29] Ibid.

It would also seem clear that there was still something of a problem with the reporting of accidents around the docks at Glasgow, or at least the way in which accidents were recorded. The report concluded that all accidents 'had to be reported immediately to the nearest delegate of the union'. It was also noted that dockers often lost their legal right to compensation because they reported accidents too late.[30] This in itself would seem to provide evidence that an accident could take place and not be generally known about at the time it occurred. The interwar years, therefore, provided little in the way of improvement in the general health, safety and welfare of dockers around British ports. At the port of Glasgow it was no different. Indeed, it may well have been much worse.

McIvor notes that it has been argued that in the modern sector of the economy during the interwar years 'industrial health, safety and welfare, was qualitatively improving'. The 1937 Factory Act only enhanced this development, he argues. Indeed, in relation to dock work, as will be shown below, there is some statistical evidence to suggest that he may well be correct. But McIvor does sound a note of caution when claiming that there is also evidence 'of a growing dichotomy in health standards at work between the new industries and the older where working conditions deteriorated, and improvements in workers' health were negligible'.[31] Dock work was not a new industry:

> High rates of accidents and inadequate compensation persisted throughout the interwar years and it was not until the establishment of the National Dock Labour Scheme in 1947 that material improvements took place in that the Dock Labour Board and the local Boards in each registered port were charged with the provision of training and welfare facilities.

Even with the Dock Labour Scheme, 'dock work remained a dangerous occupation'.[32]

### The Hidden and Acceptable Dangers of Dock Work

Like the miner, the docker took pride in his work, and bred his son for the same, and the issue of safety became inextricably bound up with skill and status. In short, if a man was good at the job then he would avoid accidents. Nevertheless, as David Wilson argues, fatalities were five times more likely in dock work than in manufacturing, and two-thirds of all accidents in industry were associated with dock work – such as 'falling, striking against objects or being hit by them'.[33] Other injuries were almost entirely related to the peculiarities of dock work: dockers being bitten by insects or rodents in infested cargoes, or in one case where a docker died by contracting anthrax after handling a cargo of bones. The *Special Report upon the Causation and Prevention of Accidents on Docks* of 1900 also cites examples of dockers

---

[30] Ibid., p. 5.
[31] McIvor, 'Manual Work', pp. 188–9.
[32] Taplin, 'When is a ship a factory?', pp. 8–9: Taplin notes that between 1947 and 1977 1,041 dockers were killed, an average of 34 per year.
[33] Wilson, *The Dockers*, p. 116.

contracting anthrax, as well as lead poisoning,[34] and several cases of pneumonia related to handling dusty cargo.[35] 'Asbestosis, skin disease, rheumatism, osteo-arthritis and bronchial illnesses', noted one source, were all more prevalent in the docks than in other industries.[36]

Dock work, it would seem, was bad for an individuals' health. This is illustrated in one curious example of statistical manipulation, used in the 1904 *Report of the Committee into the Law Relating to Compensation for Injuries to Workmen.* Attached to the Appendices of the above report was a table which purported to give the compara-tive mortality rates of males aged between twenty-five to sixty-five in various occupations. It not only illustrated estimated annual mortality rates for each group, but the proportion of deaths due to accident for each group, as seen in Table 7.1.[37] What does this statistical exercise tell us? First, that dockers had the highest mortality rate, for all causes, out of all the occupational groups involved and that this illustrates the unhealthy nature of working in the dock industry. Only the mortality rate of unoccupied males is higher, suggesting that having no work at all was more dangerous to health. Secondly, the accident mortality rate for the docker was very high indeed, third after other waterside workers such as bargemen, lightermen and seamen.

Taking the docker as a high-risk group and comparing it to the average for all occupied males, the docker's life expectancy was much poorer than that of other occupational groups, particularly when compared to the factory labourer, or even the lead miner.

Anthony Wohl argues that high mortality in this case may have been an 'indication of general standards of living, and the hazards of working in an undernourished state outdoors, than simply related only to dock work'. He also notes that other causes of high mortality were 'consumption, pneumonia, and other respiratory diseases'.[38] Thus the linkages with the docker's living standards,

---

[34] Medical Records Office (hereafter MRO), Register of Deaths, HB 6/5/63, 1936; a brief survey of a Register of Deaths at Glasgow gives at least one example of a docker, John Houston, 56, dying of the effects of lead poisoning in 1936. The medical records of several major hospitals at Glasgow are now kept at Greater Glasgow Health Board Archive, held at the Mitchell Library, Glasgow. Unfortunately, this source proved to be of little use as there were few records which actually cited the occupation of patients, and death certificates only occasionally noted occupation from around 1936. There was no requirement by law for a medical practitioner to enter occupation, and neither was this information required for the death certificates. Some doctors, however, often wrote occupation on the reverse of a certificate.

[35] *Report Upon the Causation and Prevention of Accidents at Docks, Wharves and Quays,* 1899 (*PP,* 1900, Cd. 223), p. 97.

[36] Wilson, *Dockers,* p. 116.

[37] This process of statistical manipulation needs some explanation. Table 7.3 was compiled on the basis that during the years 1890, 1891 and 1892, 1,000 deaths occurred annually among 61,215 men aged between 25 and 65. They then generated 'comparative mortality figures' for all causes of death that would occur annually for 61,215 men engaged in a given occupation (almost 100 occupations were listed in total). They then calculated the number of mortalities that were caused by accident in each of those occupational groups, comprising 61,215 men. The table lists the top 15 (and 4 selected from the 89 lower mortality occupations) suffering high mortality rates and an accidental death rate of 100 or more per 61,215 men employed in that occupation – a rate of 0.16% or more.

[38] Wohl, *Endangered Lives,* pp. 279–81.

**Table 7.1:** *Comparative Annual Mortality of Males, Twenty-Five to Sixty-Five Years of Age, (a) all causes, (b) expressed as percentage of sample total of 61,215, (c) accident mortality rate, (d) expressed as percentage of sample total of 61,215, in 15 Selected Occupation, 1890–1892.*

| Occupational Groups | Comparative | | Mortality | Figures |
|---|---|---|---|---|
| | All Causes | (%) | Accident | (%) |
| Barge, Lighter and Watermen | 1,199 | 1.96 | 223 | 0.36 |
| Seamen | 1,352 | 2.20 | 202 | 0.32 |
| Dock and Wharf Labourers | 1,829 | 2.99 | 162 | 0.26 |
| Fishermen | 845 | 1.38 | 148 | 0.24 |
| Coal Heaver | 1,528 | 2.49 | 144 | 0.23 |
| Coal Miner | 925 | 1.51 | 141 | 0.23 |
| Railway Platelayer | 1,055 | 1.72 | 141 | 0.23 |
| Railway/Road Layer/Pointsmen | 825 | 1.35 | 137 | 0.22 |
| Slater and Tiler | 1,322 | 2.16 | 133 | 0.22 |
| Carman and Carrier | 1,284 | 2.10 | 128 | 0.21 |
| Stone, Slater and Quarrier | 1,176 | 1.92 | 120 | 0.20 |
| *(Selection from lower Group)* | | | | |
| Factory Labourer | 1,078 | 1.76 | 80 | 0.13 |
| Lead Miner | 1,310 | 2.14 | 43 | 0.07 |
| Cotton Flax/Linen Manufacturer | 1,141 | 1.87 | 26 | 0.04 |
| All Males | 1,000 | 1.63 | 53 | 0.09 |
| Occupied Males | 953 | 1.56 | 56 | 0.09 |
| Unoccupied Males | 2,215 | 3.62 | 81 | 0.13 |

**Note:** the above statistics were derived from data on births, deaths, and marriages.

**Sources:** Calculated from *Appendix*, Table viii, *Report of the Committee into the LawRelating to Compensation for Injuries to Workmen* ( *PP*, 1904, vol i, Cd 2208), p. 186.

low wages, and overcrowded housing conditions (as previously noted through Booths' survey), were all important to the docker's life prospects. Moreover, if his general health weakened him sufficiently, then he may have been more prone to accident, or injury, while at work.

It would seem clear that the docker's standard of living had a direct effect on his health, and perhaps this had an added impact in the workplace. But this was not the sole reason, or even the most important reason, for the dangerous reputation of dock works. Some felt that much of the blame could be laid at the doorstep of the docking community itself. The world of the docker was, in the words of James Sexton, harsh and brutal, but it could never be remedied 'while the men directly affected are so careless as to the conditions under which they labour'.[39] It should also be recognised that the industry generally was resistant to change, and that the system of casualism only served to reinforce such resistance. Casual workers were 'discriminated against' by the strict interpretation of the Workmen's Compensation Act in any case, particularly in relation to the very low levels of compensation awarded. The employers knew this and exploited this situation by assigning their foremen to 'pester' the injured docker to sign agreements accepting lower levels of compensation than they were legally entitled to because they were 'fearful of losing their jobs'.[40] Fear of loss of employment was therefore one reason that dockers did not report accidents, or claim compensation.

David Wilson notes one case of a tally clerk at Tilbury docks in London, who slipped and broke his ankle while below deck and under the orders of the foreman. In fact, he was not supposed to go below deck, but a company representative offered him an accident report that said he was injured above deck, and that he fell down a companion way. He did this, stated Wilson, to ensure that he would be taken back on once his injury was healed. It was six weeks before he was back at work, but he did not pursue the compensation claim that would have ensured him six weeks' wages.[41] This example illustrates the considerable influence of the hiring foreman and the power he possessed and exercised through the operation of the system of casualism.[42] Such malpractice often acted to 'ensnare' men in a poverty trap, argues Taplin, 'from which it was almost impossible to escape'. The docker thus accepted the dangers of dock work as he did the system of employment:

> Though dismissed with bravado, the risk of accident was high. There was enough disfigurement, disablement and death to make even the most carefree pause from time to time. Death or disability could lead to the total impoverishment of the family.[43]

Dock work was a physically demanding occupation, and 'a man's health could be broken effectively by continuous heavy lifting or handling of noxious cargoes'.[44] Nearly every aspect of dock work carried its dangers in some form or another, even something as basic as the use of chains in the preparation of cargoes for lifting. The docker could contract *erysipelas*, which resulted a deep red inflammation of the skin caused by the *streptococcus* bacterium that became attached to the chain during its production.[45] The physically deteriorating effects of dock work was recognised in a letter drafted by NUDL officials at Glasgow during the strike 1889. It was repro-

[39] Taplin, 'When is a ship a factory?', p. 7.
[40] Ibid., pp. 5–6.
[41] Wilson, *Dockers*, pp. 51–2.
[42] Beveridge, *Unemployment*, pp. 247–8.
[43] Taplin, *Dockers' Union*, p. 19.
[44] Wilson, *Dockers*, p. 117.
[45] MRO, HB 17/2/144, Jun. 1913, Register of Patients at City of Glasgow Fever Hospital, Shieldhall. James Brown, a 48 year-old docker from Govan, was admitted with *erysipelas* on 24 Jun. 1913, and spent 13 days in hospital before being allowed home. Apart from this entry in the admissions register, and the note of the patient's occupation, there are few examples thereafter of the occupation of patients being entered, with the exception of nurses in connection with conditions associated with their work.

duced in the *North British Daily Mail* in June and July of that year. Part of it read as follows:

> The work they [the dockers] have to do is so severe that to continue it for a few years brings upon them premature age. Their employment is irregular and uncertain, [and] on an average, one week with another, they hardly earn more than 12s.[46]

It was also reported that the dockers themselves understood only too well 'the laborious and dangerous nature' of their work,[47] and they had come to accept this as an occupational hazard.

Unlike their union officials they did not demand safer working conditions. Rather, they pressed for 'fair remuneration' for the work they performed.[48] The *Glasgow Herald* in May 1914 noted that the dockers were well aware, for example, that 'chemically treated' iron ore from Norway was a serious health hazard. Their answer to such dangers, however, was to strike for higher wage increases, rather than challenge the hazard.[49] This is possibly an illustration of what Stephen Hill described as the 'exercise in real power' that the docker had in such situations.[50] Cargo needed to be loaded or unloaded, and, if there were problems with it some arrangement would be arrived at quickly in order that operations could continue with as little delay as possible. In this situation the docker had considerable bargaining power and used it. But it was a principal factor 'contributing to the persistence of bitter industrial relations on the waterfront'.[51]

As noted by Eric Taplin, 'injury and death were commonplace in dock work, yet danger was accepted with equanimity by workers and ignored by employers'. In short, 'risk was part of the job'.[52] Thus the trade union leadership arguably had little option but to choose the legislative path to change, as one of their main problems was convincing the rank and file that improved health and safety was in their own best interests. Moreover, as argued by Bartrip, the issue of health and safety did not prove to be the 'profitable recruitment device' either, and did little to

---

[46] *North British Daily Mail*, 19 Jun. 1889.

[47] Ibid.

[48] *North British Daily Mail*, 4 Mar. 1893; a report on 'a well attended meeting' of the membership of the NUDL at Glasgow.

[49] *Glasgow Herald*, 18 May 1914.

[50] Hill, *The Dockers*, p. 200 (see also chap. 1); Hill argued that the dockers had a significant degree of control over the work process that very few other workers had, even into the second half of the 20th century. Because of custom and practice and the casual system, which the employers actively sought to maintain up until the interwar years at least, the dockers were able to exploit the system to their own benefit. By the time the employers wished to promote change within the industry, the traditions built in the past had become stubbornly ingrained. Forms of negotiation were to remain a hallmark of the industry, such as shipside bargaining on dirty cargo, or special rates for more dangerous cargo. Although these were ostensibly negotiated with the trade unions, the rank and file determined what was acceptable, or not. It is in this sense that Hill presents his argument: casualism may have had its problems, but many of these problems were bought off in the past and this gave the dockers considerable and direct bargaining power at the point of production – the shipside.

[51] Taplin, 'When is a ship a factory?', p. 8.

[52] Ibid., p. 1.

encourage trade union penetration within the dock labour force.[53] For the dockers, trade unionism was more closely linked to gaining preference in employment, and to protecting jobs from outsiders, than concerns over safety. In a sense safety was a non-issue along the Glasgow waterfront and this was typical for the industry as a whole.

### Accident, Injury and Dock Work

This final section concentrates on a statistical analysis of the data available, illustrating the extent of the dangers of dock work and the extent to which this changed over the period *c.*1890 to 1939. Despite the unreliability of the data, the following analysis, and the tables generated from related statistics, are an attempt to illustrate the extent of the problem of accident and injury within the port transport industry in order to present some picture of the dangerous nature of dock work. There is evidence contained in the *Executive Report* of the NUDL of 1983, but this was a very small sample (see *Appendix* Table V). It nevertheless offers us a snapshot of just how dangerous dock work could be. Out of forty-five reported serious accidents, twelve resulted in death, while other less serious injuries left the docker permanently injured and unable to work again. There were three incidents where men lost limbs, or had them crushed, two examples of concussion (not resulting in death) and five incidents where limbs were broken or fractured.[54] Many of the causes of accidents in this report were put down to defective gear and unguarded machinery, or incidents where men had fallen into hatches because of faulty staging. Numerous injuries were caused by breakages in lifting tackle, unsecured or damaged staging planks giving way, or by worn ropes and chains splitting and breaking. One accident reported a gas explosion caused by bad ventilation in a ship's hold and there were also examples of accidents occurring due to the incompetence of other dockers, supervisors and foremen.[55] It concluded by noting that the report had been commissioned in order to provide 'the Executive with some evidence' so that they could put pressure on the Government to bring in 'special legislation for the inspection of gear and machinery used in loading and unloading vessels'.[56]

The problem of accidents due to machinery was highlighted by Charles Kennedy, Glasgow's NUDL delegate to the TUC in 1898, who urged a reduction in this type of accident by extending the 'dangerous machinery clause' contained in the 1895 Factory Acts. This had been intended to cover all mechanical appliances and gear used particularly in the piece-work trades.[57] But this fell on deaf ears and to make matters worse the TUC Congress of 1899 was informed that there was no 'enforcement to return reports on the numbers of accidents at the docks' as there was no need for employers to make compulsory accident reports. A resolution called

[53] Bartrip, 'Workmen's Compensation', p. 162.
[54] *NUDL Executive Report*, Half Year, ending Dec. 1892, pp. 3–8.
[55] Ibid., detail of accidents described throughout, see pp. 3–8.
[56] Ibid., p. 2.
[57] TUC *Annual Report*, Bristol, 1898, p. 70.

for 'medical practitioners, dispensary, and institutions of surgical aid, to be called upon to make weekly reports' in order to rectify this situation.[58] Accidents would, therefore, remain unreported until such times as some independent body, armed with statutory powers, could oversee health and safety matters on the docks.

The case for improved safety at the docks should have been significantly strengthened by an important report of the Chief Inspectors of Factories and Workshops at the end of the 1890s. The two investigators were J. S. Maitland and Sydney Eraut, who had visited Liverpool, London, Hull, Glasgow, Leith, Dundee, Greenock, Belfast, Bristol, Southampton, and the coaling ports of South Wales and the north-east of England.[59] According to Taplin, this report 'graphically analysed the nature and extent of accidents at the docks and for the first time national statistics were published, and they made grim reading'.[60] Maitland and Eraut not only reported on the extent of accidents on the docks, but also offered practical advice as to how they could be reduced and prevented. They noted that the most common single cause of accident was associated with 'falls' (see Table 7.2), and that this was the greatest single cause of fatalities. Deaths from falls numbered forty-three in total, or just under half of all fatalities. This included dockers who fell into the water space between ship and shore, or between ships berthed alongside each other, and who drowned as a result, as well as those men who fell into the cargo bays.

---

**Table 7.2:** *Number of Accidents at Docks, Wharves and Quays, Fatal and Non-fatal, 1898.*

| Causes | Fatal | Non-Fatal |
|---|---|---|
| Total for docks, wharves and quays | 89 | 4,070 |
| Hoists | – | 3 |
| Cranes and other lifting tackle | 19 | 246 |
| Other machinery moved by power | 7 | 53 |
| Machinery not moved by power | – | 48 |
| Explosion | – | 1 |
| Escape of gas, steam, etc. | 2 | – |
| Falls other than those included above | 43 | 999 |
| Other causes | 18 | 2,178 |

**Source:** *Factories and Workshops: Annual Report for 1899, Appendix* 12, 'Report upon the Causation and Prevention of Accidents at Docks, Wharves and Quays' (*PP*, 1900, Cd 223, Vol xi 249), p. 99.

Of the non-fatalities, just under 1,000 accidents were caused by 'falls', which was just short of one-quarter of the total. Such incidents were usually related to poor gangway and staging provisions, or the use of ladders rather than gangways or staging, when carrying goods between ship and shore. They also made particular

---

[58] TUC *Annual Report*, Plymouth, 1889, pp. 81–2.
[59] 'Report Upon . . . Accidents at Docks', p. 98.
[60] Taplin, 'When is a ship a factory?', p. 3.

reference to this factor in relation to drownings at Glasgow and provided some statistical data to illustrate their case. The sample only involved twenty-four dockers but it was noted that of the number injured, only fifteen recovered, while seven drowned and another was fatally injured.[61]

Table 7.2. gives a clear illustration of the dangers associated with dock work, but still only offers a snapshot, and may prove to be a gross underestimate of the actual accident rate. This can be argued from two perspectives. First, at this juncture accidents on board ship would not have been collated, nor would accidents occurring between ships berthed alongside one another, because these were not covered by the Factory Acts. Those accidents reported, therefore, were not representative of the port transport industry as a whole. Considering that ship work was the most dangerous area of a docker's work, and that most accidents tended to occur on ships, this is a major omission. Secondly, we know that dockers frequently did not report accidents. Perhaps the above illustration helps to support the general contention of this chapter, that only the most serious onshore accidents were reported by dockers at this time.

The *Special Report* of 1900 not only illustrated the dangers of dock work, but stressed that many accidents could be prevented (see Figure 2) by bringing the inspection of safety at the docks under Government inspectors' control.[62] The report also noted correspondence from the Clyde Navigation Trust stating that some accidents could be prevented when the proper equipment was used, such as 'safe gangways', which the Trust provided 'free of charge' to all river passenger, channel, and ocean steamers. The Trust did not, however, supply gangways for tramp steamers, unless they paid a charge of one *shilling*, as there was no legal need to provide safe gangways. It was stated that other vessels 'at times used ladders' rather than gangways, and that 'this was a very dangerous means of getting from ship to shore, or *vice versa*'.[63] As McIvor argues, as long as the employers acted 'within the legal limits of the Factories Acts' then they were under no obligation to provide better equipment.[64] It is true that the Clyde Navigation Trust instituted a series of 'Regulations' governing the use of equipment, mostly gangways, linking ship and shore, between ships berthed alongside one another, and covering the provision of proper gangways 'inside vessels'. However, unless the Clyde Trust were willing to set up an internal inspectorate, through the Harbour Master's Office, for example, to enforce these regulations (and there is no evidence to suggest that they did), it may be supposed that their regulations were generally ignored. As long as other port employers were keeping within the letter of the law, the Trust had little jurisdiction over them, although the Trust could enforce their regulations on work done by their own employees.

[61] 'Report Upon . . . Accidents at Docks', see *Appendix* 12, 'Numbers of persons injured, fatally and otherwise, falling into Harbour of Glasgow while going onboard and coming ashore from their respective vessels by means of gangways, etc., between 1st Jul. 1895 and 1st Jul. 1896', p. 100.

[62] Ibid., p. 101: Brief report on 'Fatal Accident' at Bristol Harbour.

[63] Ibid., pp. 101–2: Letter from Clyde Navigation Trust, from Harbour Office, 5 Jan. 1895.

[64] McIvor, 'Manual Work', p. 161, and Bartrip and Burman, *Wounded Soldiers*, p. 214.

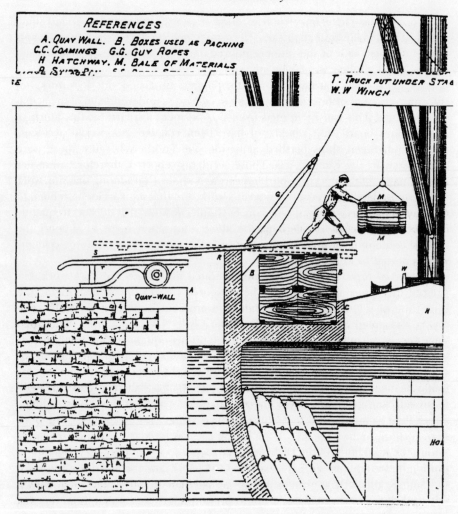

**Figure 2.** Sketch showing unsafe staging improperly supported.

**Source:** *Special Report Upon the Causation and Prevention of Accidents at Docks, Wharves, and Quays, Appendix* 12 ( 1900, Cd 223), pp. 87–99.

The report further stated that 'there were numerous methods adopted for the loading and discharging of vessels in docks, varying according to locality, and the class of cargo to be handled.'[65] Not only would this system be difficult to regulate, it would be costly, particularly at a port such as Glasgow which had no dock gates, and where ships were affected by the rise and fall of the tide. Cargo handling was, therefore, further complicated in such circumstances, and rendered all the more dangerous as a result.

[65] Report Upon . . . Accidents at Docks, p. 74.

Glasgow stevedore James Spencer reminded the Shaw Inquiry, gathering evidence in 1919, that Glasgow was a tidal port, and that this had specific implications for the loading and unloading of material between shipside and quayside. Because the tide could rise or fall by 12 feet or more, specialised gear and staging were of only limited use and, therefore, there was a greater degree of difficulty attached to the handling of cargo by workers there.[66] When cargo was physically lifted on board by shipworkers, they often had to take it over long planks, which moved with the tide. On the larger vessels, this method was more difficult, but nevertheless still used. As a result, stated Spencer, 'this type of equipment became too dangerous'.[67] More often, ladders were used in place of staging and planking. Spencer also testified that the men were expected to work long periods of time on one vessel, sometimes 24 hours or more.[68] As noted in Table 7.3. below, fatigue was cited as a major cause of accidents on the docks. Moreover, dockers would clearly be required to work over the period of the ebb and flow of the tide, and so the dangers of using any equipment, other than proper gangways, to load and discharge cargo were apparent on a recurring basis.[69]

There is a reference to the problems associated with the carrying of materials on board ship in a press report on a Glasgow Trades Council meeting during 1893. The meeting was probably only of interest because it involved the NUDL representative to the Glasgow Trades Council, speaking on behalf of a shipworker injured at the docks, who was a member of the Glasgow Harbour Labourers' Union[70] (as we shall see in the following chapter, the two unions were at that point in dispute with each other[71]). The report carried the headline 'Harbour Labourers and White Slavery', referring to the conditions the labourers worked under. The shipworker in question, Mr Hugh Latta, sustained a very serious accident while carrying a bag of flour weighing 2 cwt (the equivalent of 280 lbs – just over a tenth of a ton – or nearly 126 kilos). The docker's injuries were not detailed in the report, but it indicated the use of staging planks, rather than the use of proper gangways. Mr Soutar, the NUDL representative, argued that the best way to stop such overloading was by bringing in a law to prevent it. He also added, however, that members of his union would not have been injured in this manner because 'bags were trucked and not carried'.[72] Trucking meant that cargo was moved at all times by some means other than physically lifting materials, usually by pallet onto a bogey, trolley, or cart, to the point of loading, which usually meant that it went straight

---

[66] Shaw Inquiry, i. *Minutes of Evidence*, p. 269.
[67] Ibid., p. 270.
[68] Lovell, *Stevedores and Dockers*, p. 39.
[69] As strongly suggested in the 'Report Upon Accidents on Docks', p. 88 and p. 99, see also pp. 101–3 relating to gangways.
[70] Reported in the *North British Daily Mail*, 7 Sep. 1893; Report of Glasgow Trades Council meeting of that week.
[71] TUC *Annual Report*, Glasgow, 1892, pp. 49–50; the GHLU were expelled from the TUC at Glasgow in 1892 because they had been found guilty of blacklegging against members of the NUDL while on strike.
[72] *North British Daily Mail*, 7 Sep. 1893.

onto a carter's vehicle, or railway truck. As Glasgow had few storage areas or shed facilities, any cargo landed would have to be discharged from the quayside as quickly as possible.

At most ports shipwork would probably have been the most dangerous area of dock work. As noted by John Lovell:

> The men on the ship were compelled by machinery to work at speed, in cramped and precarious positions, for long hours. There was a constant risk of cargo coming loose from the 'sets' and falling onto the men in the hatchway below; there was an equal risk of men falling down unprotected hatches or overboard.[73]

The emphasis was placed on physical 'strength, competence and responsibility'. Even when dockers were often required to perform comparatively simple operations, they were expected to carry them out 'quickly and without error. Inexperienced shipmen put the men's lives in jeopardy'.[74] (A factor referred to in the NUDL and the later Advisory Committee report.[75])

This is not to suggest, that quaywork did not carry its hazards too. John Lovell does argue that quaywork was more of a continuous process than shipwork, and as such was 'generally conducted at a slower pace' and therefore of a safer nature. However, this would have been more common in a port such as London, where cargo had to be sorted and often only 'finally delivered long after the ship had left the quayside'.[76] Lovell does stress that as the goods moved faster over the ship's side because of mechanisation, this would also mean the need for quicker removal from the quayside and thus speed-up in the work process. At Glasgow, given that sorting for long term-storage was not an option, it would therefore have been imperative to clear the quayside as quickly as possible, and thus the pace of operation would have been much quicker. In such a situation accidents could occur with greater frequency.

Dock work, wrote Alan Bullock, 'had a well earned reputation for being hard and dangerous [where] safety was inadequate and frequently ignored, and the accident rate was second only to that of the mines'.[77] Better preventative measures were therefore needed. However, as we have seen, the reaction of the employers was predictable:

> The shipping interests blocked every proposal for reform as it would raise costs and delay the swift turn round of vessels in port . . . Although they were forced to accept new legislation they did so with reluctance and soon appreciated that it meant very little in practice.[78]

---

[73] Lovell, *Stevedores and Dockers*, p. 40.
[74] Ibid., pp. 39–40.
[75] PRO, LAB 101/18, *Port Transport Memorandum*, 'Introduction', para. 4, p. 1–2, where it was stated that 'the risks to life and limb due to the employment of men unaccustomed to [dock] work', was considerable.
[76] Ibid., p. 41.
[77] Bullock, *Ernest Bevin*, p .117.
[78] Taplin, 'When is a ship a factory?', p. 8.

---

**Table 7.3:** *Most common cause of accidents at docks, wharves, and quays*

---

(1) <u>Falls</u>
    (a)    Falling into ship's hold.
    (b)    Falling from stage to deck, or from stage to water.
    (c)    Falling from quay wall into water.
    (d)    Falls of goods which are being hoisted.

(2) <u>Accidents from Machinery in Motion</u>
    (a)    Limbs or clothes catching in cog wheels.
    (b)    Catching (*sic*) in ropes from winches, or from capstans.
    (c)    Defective machines, breakages of chains or ropes.
    (d)    Catching (*sic*) in or being injured by hoists.
    (e)    Steam from cranes.

(3) <u>Shunting Accidents from use of Locomotives</u>
    (a)    Injuries from moving locomotives, or wagons attached thereto, or from wagons attached to capstans –
        (1)    While coupling, etc.
        (2)    While crossing in front, etc.
    (b)    Wagons which have run away.
    (c)    Defective railway lines –
        (1)    High speed.
        (2)    Sharp curves.
        (3)    Dangerous crossings.
        (4)    Insufficient clearance room at sides.

(4) <u>Fatigue due to Excessive Hours of Work</u>

(5) <u>Handling of Dangerous Materials</u>
    (a)    Handling dusty materials (basic slag, etc.)
    (b)    Use of flammable paints –
        (1)    Danger from the vapour.
        (2)    Danger from fire.

---

**Source:** *Special Report Upon the Causation and Prevention of Accidents at Docks, Wharves, and Quays, Appendix* 12 ( 1900, Cd 223), pp 87–9.

The docks were incorporated within the Factory Acts in 1895, and were also included within the Workers' Compensation Act of 1897, so they now had a degree of protection and access to a system of compensation that was hitherto denied them. Dock union officials, however, continually stressed that 'they did not seek compensation for the loss of limbs, but facilities for keeping them'.[79] Table 7.4 represents the incidence of disablement and fatality for the United Kingdom as a whole, from 1909–14, and then from 1919–38.

[79] TUC *Annual Report*, Huddersfield, 1900, p. 53.

Table 7.4: *Number of Disablements and Fatalities in Dock Work for the UK and percentages of these in relation to the total numbers of Dock Workers estimated to be employed in the Port Transport Industry, for 1909 to 1914, and from 1919–38 at three yearly intervals.*

| Year | Disablement | (%) | Fatalities | (%) | Total Numbers for UK |
|------|-------------|------|-----------|------|----------------------|
| 1909 | 6,486 | 4.98 | 118 | 0.09 | 130,000 |
| 1910 | 11,950 | 9.27 | 174 | 0.13 | 128,878 |
| 1911 | 13,853 | 10.47 | 196 | 0.14 | 132,246 |
| 1912 | 16,937 | 10.67 | 225 | 0.14 | 158,598 |
| 1913 | 17,147 | 12.17 | 207 | 0.14 | 140,820 |
| 1914 | 14,602 | 11.70 | 196 | 0.15 | 124,708 |
| 1919 | 10,196 | 6.31 | 135 | 0.08 | 161,371 |
| 1922 | 9,843 | 8.06 | 92 | 0.07 | 122,030 |
| 1925 | 12,367 | 8.06 | 122 | 0.08 | 142,550 |
| 1928 | 13,381 | 9.36 | 87 | 0.06 | 142,835 |
| 1931 | 10,616 | 10.02 | 83 | 0.07 | 105,875 |
| 1934 | 10,362 | 10.44 | 76 | 0.08 | 99,161 |
| 1937 | 11,866 | 11.14 | 84 | 0.07 | 106,428 |
| 1938* | 10,672 | 9.55 | 74 | 0.06 | 111,655 |

(*1938 was the last year of this particular statistical run as calculated by the Home Office.)

**Source:** Home Office Workmens Compensation Statistics, 1909–38.

Despite the limitations of these statistics, not least that there are no data relating to accidents during the war years, they do provide some illustration of the trends in accident and injury within the dock industry. For example, it can be seen that the highest incidence of fatalities took place before 1914, and after 1919 both fatalities and disablements were down considerably on the pre-war levels. This would seem to indicate that dock work was less dangerous in the interwar period. Although there is also an increase in disablements by the 1930s, levels never exceeded those recorded in the last two years before the First World War. A significant weakness in these statistics, however, is that they compare incidence of injury against total numbers involved in dock work, but not against the actual number of man hours worked.

It should also be borne in mind that statistics relating to the numbers who worked in the port transport industry during the interwar period were more reliable than the estimates offered for the period before 1914. It was during the war and the interwar years that the great majority of dockers became fully registered, and estimates for the total numbers working in the dock industry were more reliable. There were still ports such as Glasgow and Aberdeen where there had been a failure to gain acceptance of any scheme of registration, until the Second World War.[80] Therefore, statistics measuring the incidence of accidents against total numbers employed are significantly more accurate post-1918, and this

[80] Aberdeen did in fact have a register during World War I, but rejected it in 1919.

may account for the seemingly improved health and safety record of the industry during the 1920s and 1930s (see *Appendix* Table VI).

There was no comparable statistical breakdown of Scottish figures for this period, although a brief statistical series was produced for the period 1909–13. The figures for Scotland have been left out for two reasons. First, the period 1909–13 can be considered too limited a time span to conduct a significant comparative analysis of Scottish against UK figures. Secondly, there are major discrepancies in the Scottish figures when compared to the UK totals. For example, the total number of all accidents recorded in compensation cases in Scotland between 1909 and 1913 was 522, or 1.14% of official estimates of the Scottish dock labour force. As can be calculated from Table 7.4, for the same period the total number employed on the docks for the UK was 66,373, or 9.6%. This means that Scottish averages for compensation were around 85% lower than national averages. Clearly, there are real problems associated with the compilation of Scottish figures. However, there may have been an even greater reluctance on the part of the Scottish docker to report accidents or pursue compensation when compared to his English counterpart.[81]

The last area to be considered is how the dock industry differed from the six other leading industries as categorised by the Home Office. A series of tables has been provided in the *Appendices* to give comparative data on these industries for the years 1909–14, and at selected intervals for 1919–38. But for the moment, by comparing tables 7.5 and 7.6 it can be seen that the accident rate fell significantly in all industries between 1913 and 1919, and this continues to fall, if only slighty, during the 1920s and 1930s (and this is in line with McIvor's general analysis of this period).[82] In considering the full list of tables for the interwar years we find that the rate of fatalities on the docks, as a percentage of the total workforce, remains in the top three with shipping and mining.

Table 7.5: *Number of Disablements and Fatalities and percentages of Total Numbers employed in seven selected industries for the year 1913.*

|              | Disablement | (%)   | Fatalities | (%)  | Total Numbers Employed |
|--------------|-------------|-------|------------|------|------------------------|
| Shipping     | 8,191       | 3.17  | 497        | 0.19 | 258,272                |
| Factories    | 208,949     | 3.91  | 1,091      | 0.02 | 5,342,625              |
| Docks        | 17,147      | 12.17 | 207        | 0.14 | 140,820                |
| Mines        | 195,387     | 17.53 | 1,312      | 0.11 | 1,114,210              |
| Quarries     | 6,001       | 6.85  | 66         | 0.07 | 87,541                 |
| Construction | 6,568       | 6.70  | 96         | 0.09 | 97,954                 |
| Railways     | 26,444      | 5.65  | 450        | 0.09 | 467,931                |

---

[81] *Home Office Workmen's Compensation Statistics for Scotland*, 1909–13; there were figures available for Scotland, 1909–13, but there was no similar separate breakdown for Scottish figures.

[82] McIvor, 'Manual Work', p. 188.

**Table 7.6:** *Number of Disablements and Fatalities and percentages of Total Numbers*
*employed in seven selected industries for the year 1919.*

|              | Disablement | (%)   | Fatalities | (%)  | Total Numbers Employed |
|--------------|-------------|-------|------------|------|------------------------|
| Shipping     | 3,867       | 1.82  | 309        | 0.14 | 211,422                |
| Factories    | 183,358     | 2.99  | 1,165      | 0.01 | 6,127,706              |
| Docks        | 10,196      | 6.31  | 135        | 0.08 | 161,371                |
| Mines        | 134,991     | 11.40 | 1,248      | 0.10 | 1,184,038              |
| Quarries     | 2,973       | 6.38  | 34         | 0.06 | 49,235                 |
| Construction | 3,107       | 3.12  | 52         | 0.05 | 99,547                 |
| Railways     | 16,536      | 3.14  | 324        | 0.06 | 525,864                |

**Source:** *Home Office Workmens Compensation Statistics,* 1913 ( 1914, Cd 7669), and 1919 (1920, Cmd 1185).

As for disablements, the docks record the greatest proportion after mining, until 1938, when the docks drop to third place following quarries.

What this meant was that by the end of the 1930s the docks would seem to be a safer working environment all round when compared to the often worsening records of other industries. Employers in other industries, noted McIvor, turned to slashing wages and increasing workloads in order to remain competitive, particularly after the major economic slump of 1929–33.[83] As a result, other industries' standards of health and safety stagnated or fell, thus allowing the docks, so to speak, to catch-up, giving the impression that health and safety standards in the port transport industry were improving. Eric Taplin would generally agree that there was improvement towards the end of the 1930s, but stressed that the difficulties of enforcing safety legislation along the waterfront were not satisfactorily dealt with until after the Second World War.

There is little doubt that there are real difficulties associated with any study of health in the port transport industry. The early trade union officials did not keep records of the nature and the extent of mechanical penetration before and during World War One,[84] and the same could be argued for accidents and injury. Employers, and even the Factory Inspectorate, likewise, did not systematically keep such data. Bartrip and Burman noted that the unions' task was made more difficult in that employers were not legally bound to report accidents, or return injury and accident figures. It is also true, as Taplin points out, that not all trade union leaders were concerned with safety as an issue, principally because it was hardly likely to be a great rallying call to attract more dockers into the ranks of the trade unions. It can be argued, however, that the biggest problem was that dockers themselves did not regularly report accidents at work. The statistical data must be considered carefully; and, in the final analysis, accept that the findings that do emerge from these

[83] Ibid., p. 184.
[84] Hilton, *Are Trade Unions Obstructive?*, p. 113 and p. 199.

disparate sources can only ever offer us a mere glimpse of the real and dangerous nature of dock work.

Many factors militated against the reliable reporting of accidents at the docks, but how far can it be said that much of this was due to the dockers themselves? Can it be argued that there was a reluctance on the part of dockers not only to report accidents, but also to make claims for compensation when injured? *The Compensation for Injuries to Workmen Enquiry*, in 1904, was informed by James Sexton that there were a 'very considerable number of accidents in the industry where no compensation was claimed'.[85] If a docker was injured and his claim was upheld, he was usually paid compensation on the basis of what he had earned with a particular employer up to the point of injury, even if he had been employed for a few hours, a few days, or a few weeks.[86] One of the main problems, therefore, was that an accident was compensated for on the basis of what a man had earned with the one specific employer, and any claim for accident was made against that particular employer. If he had worked for several days or even weeks and was injured, he would be compensated based on the amount earned with that employers. If he started with another employer on another day and then found himself injured his compensation was based on the money earned with the new employer. No account was taken of what he earned previously, even if he had worked continuously for days or weeks beforehand. The docker was a casual worker and compensation was paid on the casual basis: clear evidence, argued Taplin, that casual workers were 'discriminated against'.[87]

It seems clear that the docker felt there was little use in taking any legal action when injured unless it was absolutely necessary to do so. As Sexton himself argued, 'the men had a dislike of going to court, when there was a prospect of losing work'.[88] It would seem obvious why the men 'disliked going to court' – because of, as Bartrip suggested, 'the grossly inadequate payments that were awarded'.[89] In the case of the injured dock worker, as we have seen, compensation payments were considerably less. Going to court meant giving up the chance of a day's work, as well as perhaps losing a regular place in a dock gang. When all these factors are considered we see that there was much to discourage the docker from initiating and seeing through a compensation claim.

There is one other associated problem to be considered when using the statistics from compensation reports. Before the 1906 Compensation Act, it would seem that

---

[85] *Report of the Committee into the Law Relating to Compensation for Injuries to Workmen 1904*, ii, *Report and Appendices* (*PP*, 1905, lxxv, Cd. 2334), Q. 2492.

[86] Ibid., Q. 2,949 to Q. 2,505; Sexton gave one example to illustrate his case concerning a docker at Glasgow. The docker in question had been working on one ship for 5 days, and with overtime had earned 30s up to that point. On the Saturday, however, he did not secure work on the ship, but with another employer, a master porter, and was discharging cargo from the quayside when he was injured, within an hour of beginning work. He made a claim for compensation and his case was taken before the Sheriff Court in Glasgow during 1903. The Court declared that he was entitled to 3½d. per week, or 50% of what he would have earned in an hour up to the point he sustained his injury.

[87] Taplin, 'When is a ship a factory?', p. 6.

[88] *Report into Compensation for Injuries to Workmen*, evidence, James Sexton, Q. 2,556

[89] Bartrip, 'Workmen's Compensation', p. 167.

accidents at the docks were included with all accidents relating to factory work. Thus, there was no single industry breakdown. After the Act of 1906, by order of the Secretary of State, statistics relating to accidents and compensation within the port transport industry had to be recorded and presented separately. It is only after this time that some attempt can be made to measure the extent of accident and injury on the docks (although we do have the exception of the Special Report of 1900).[90]

Even after the changes made in 1906 the same problems still existed in relation to accident statistics. It was also difficult to measure the extent of accident and injury within the industry as a whole, principally because of the difficulties involved in actually enumerating the labour force. For example, Home Office reports on compensation, paid under the Workmens Compensation Act, stated clearly time and again that 'the casual nature of employment on the docks makes exact calculation improbable'.[91] Bartrip and Burman cogently argued that generally speaking there is no reliable statistical base from which to calculate the effects of the Factory Acts and the Workmen's Compensation Acts, at least not until the interwar years. As we have seen, in relation to dock work this factor proves even more problematic.

The process of gaining an award for compensation for the family of a docker who died, due to an accident at work, was as problematic and troublesome in terms of litigation as any other. In circumstances such as these the docker's family may not have considered taking a compensation claim to court, relying perhaps on a donation from the trade union, or more likely a trusted charitable agency. Indeed, it may well be that the family waived a possible compensation payment in order to ensure that the eldest son, or a second son, could enter into dock work to work alongside, or even as a replacement for, his father. Perhaps too this was a cultural phenomenon generated from the largely Catholic Irish base which formed the majority of the Glasgow dock labour force. As at Liverpool, the Irish in Glasgow were perhaps better served through agencies of welfare relief, such as the St Vincent de Paul Society, which, as John Belchem has shown, 'provided generous relief in case of need, with only minimal proof of religious observance'.[92] Indeed, Bernard Aspinwall has argued this case for the Irish in Scotland. He noted that 'the Irish were naturally distrustful of the state, and established their own self-help organisations, pre-eminently the St Vincent de Paul Society'. This Catholic society, and others, argues Aspinwall, 'engendered a small-scale Catholic cradle-to-grave social welfare system'.[93] It could well be the case that the dockers at Glasgow did not generally pursue compensation because they could survive without it, and, as in the case of Liverpool, there was a considerable degree of 'collective mutuality . . . within the Irish community, providing a framework of inclusive cover probably

---

[90] Referred to in *Home Office Statistics of Compensation*, 1909 (*PP*, 1910, lxxxii, Cd. 5386), p. 8.

[91] Ibid., p. 9; for a further example, see *Home Office Statistics of Compensation*, 1911 (*PP*, 1912, lxxv, Cd. 6493), where it was stated that the dock labour force at this time was 'perhaps hardly capable of exact calculation'.

[92] J. Belchem, 'Sectarianism, ethnicity and welfare: collective mutuality among the Liverpool Irish', (unpublished pre-circulated paper, 9th British-Dutch Labour History Conference, Holland, 1994), pp. 14–15.

[93] Aspinwall, 'The Catholic Irish', p. 96.

unmatched by other forms of voluntary endeavour'.[94] With family members around, you could be looked after while carrying an injury, or if you were ill. Your place could even be protected by a gang who had familial ties, whereas a stranger could expect no such assistance. This was the essence of the occupational community. For even without the St Vincent De Paul Society – which would not have been an option in any case if you were a Protestant docker – there was mutual support system for any docker who surrounded himself with family and other kinship connections.

Peter Bartrip argued that the trade unions were the main beneficiaries in the fight to take employers to tribunals for accident and injury hearings. Because of the cost of raising legal actions against the employers, the trade unions perceived a 'profitable recruiting device', which in turn expanded their membership. In relation to the docks, however, the opposite may have been the case. It would seem clear that the calls of trade union leaders for dockers to report accidents to union officials, whether it was James Sexton of the NUDL or Joseph Houghton of the SUDL, simply fell on deaf ears. Indeed, as late as the 1930s the leadership of the recently formed Scottish Transport and General Workers' Union were still calling on dockers to report and note accidents.

Perhaps the reason for the docker's reluctance to make accident reports arose from his view of the role of the union. The union was seen simply as a protective device to ensure that both the employer, and the foreman, could neither force down wages, nor allow the introduction of outsiders into the docks. In short, the union was never viewed, or used, as a friendly society. Thus the union exerted its authority only at the place of work, and within the wider community of interest the docker perhaps relied more on the extensive 'self-enclosed, Catholic Irish, network of charity and collective mutuality', as argued by Belchem. It was not until the Glasgow and Clydeside dockers had total control over their own trade union affairs in the 1930s that this attitude began to slowly change as the union itself adapted to suit the needs of that occupational community.

Even by the late 1930s, despite the probability that the industry was by then a safer one, Glasgow's dock union was still very much concerned with health and safety issues. Employers were disregarding regulations covering safety on the docks. Indeed, it seemed to some that many of the problems of the early 1890s were still of great concern even by the late 1930s. Without the direct intervention of the government in such matters little voluntary change would take place within the industry generally. The impact of government legislation is seen all too clearly during the Second World War and the post-1945 period. Such change was orchestrated by Ernest Bevin and was a significant achievement. But it took the full power of government and a considerable political will to force this change on the industry against the wishes and inclinations of both the employers and the dock labour force generally.

---

[94] Belchem, 'Sectarianism, ethnicity and welfare', pp. 17–18.

# Part Three

# CHAPTER EIGHT

# The Development of Trade Unionism on Clydeside

The previous chapters highlighted the main factors which significantly affected the everyday working lives of dockers. Part One considered the wider implications of life and work on the docks and wharves of Britain while Part Two examined related factors which were more specific to the port transport industry within the Clydeside region in general and the port of Glasgow in particular. It was shown that, when certain factors were brought together in combination they had a critical impact on dock work, and were a major influence on the developing outlook and attitude of dockers generally, while conditions particular, or peculiar, to individual ports exerted a more discrete influence at a regional and local level, and, in turn, affected the manner in which trade unionism and industrial relations strategies developed. The third part of this study, however, is concerned principally with the evolution of trade unionism on Clydeside, tracing the roots of that development, and the manner in which dock union organisation on Clydeside compared with, or differed from, the growth of dock unionism elsewhere.

The three chapters which make up this section will deal with each of the distinct phases of dock unionism on Clydeside. Chapter 8 considers the Glasgow Harbour Labourers' Union (GHLU), from its formation in 1853 up to its eventual amalgamation with the National Union of Dock Labourers (NUDL) in 1899. Chapter 9 investigates the effects of 'New Unionism' on Clydeside and the development of general unionism, with the formation of the NUDL at Glasgow in 1889 through to its decline and disintegration by 1910. Chapter 10 considers the renaissance of dock unionism on Clydeside with the formation of the Scottish Union of Dock Labourers in 1911 (which emerged during the period of the 'Great Labour Unrest' on Clydeside), and examines the short-term impact of the SUDL on dock unionism on Clydeside between 1911 and 1914.

We consider first the role of the artisanal GHLU (the Old Society) both before the formation of the NUDL and after, but will concentrate on the relationship between the two organisations over the decade 1889 to 1899. Particular attention will be paid to the factors that divided these two component parts of Glasgow dock unionism in the early 1890s, but also the reasons behind the eventual amalgamation of the two by 1899. Certain fundamental cleavages do emerge, such as the sectional divide based on the skill attributed to the members of the GHLU, and those of the lesser skilled quay workers who were predominant within the ranks of the new unionists at Glasgow. We also consider the role of the membership of the Old Society as strike-breakers in the early 1890s.

Certain questions naturally arise from this line of enquiry, the foremost being the GHLU's willingness to act as a strikebreaking force, not only on the Clyde but in many different locations around Britain. Did these activities account for the GHLU's rapid rise in membership during 1889 up to 1892 (and beyond)? Did GHLU members embark on the strikebreaking strategy in opposition to the NUDL's advocacy of militant action and the tyranny of their politically motivated leadership? Was this strategy also influenced by economic considerations, or craft consciousness, or cultural factors, and how could these be of importance if the shipworkers did indeed share the same racial antecedents as the quayworkers? Another variable was the changing employment structure, which aided the rapid increase of onshore workers, or quayworkers, in relation to those engaged in shipwork. Steamships and steam-driven technology might have been viewed as undermining their perceived status initially as they were skilled sail-ship workers. Thus, their actions might be viewed as protectionist in orientation. The aim of this chapter is to attempt to answer these questions and in doing so place the GHLU, and the artisanal phase of emergent dock unionism, in a firm historical context.

### The Roots of Trade Unionism: The Glasgow Harbour Labourers' Union, 1853 to 1899

As the work of Hobsbawm, Lovell and Bean has shown, prior to the rapid deployment of steam technology along the waterfront, unionism within the dock labour force was beginning to emerge in many of Britain's ports around the mid-nineteenth century. The first organisations were without doubt extremely sectional in outlook and formed from those groups of dock workers who had a degree of skill. This was a phase which Hobsbawm classifies as a period of 'highly developed separatism'. This was the artisanal phase of British dock trade unionism,[1] and one of the first of these organisations was formed in Glasgow in 1853. The GHLU was a rather exclusive organisation, which by the late 1860s was imposing an entrance fee of £5, which was increased later to £8. This figure, however, was likely to be reduced for the sons of those who were already members.[2] But when this entrance fee is compared to the 16 *shillings* charged by the Greenock Harbour Labourers' Union in 1889, it can be seen that this levy was intended to maintain exclusivity and act as a barrier against dockers from the lower levels of the labour force from attaining entry.[3] Many casual labourers who worked at the docks at this time could not hope to enter into the ranks of this society. The entrance fee levied was also a formidable barrier to further dock union expansion at the port.

There is little doubt that the GHLU took itself very seriously indeed and within a few years of its formation, in October 1858, they affiliated to Glasgow Trades Council (in the same year that the Glasgow Trades Council was formed). It was noted in the *Glasgow Sentinel* in October of that year that the Glasgow Harbour

---

[1] Hobsbawm, *Worlds of Labour*, preface p. viii.
[2] Lovell, 'Sail, Steam', p. 232.
[3] *Glasgow Herald*, 5 Feb. 1889.

Labourers had two delegates admitted to the Trades Council.[4] This occurred at a time when it was generally only the artisan trade unions which were strong enough to form themselves into protective societies. Despite the fact that they referred to themselves as labourers, however, they did conduct their society business very much in the style of the skilled artisan trade societies.

Between the early years and the outbreak of extensive labour unrest in the boom years of the early 1870s, the GHLU remained very much within their own sphere of interest. After 1872, however, for reasons that are not entirely clear, the GHLU ceased to be so highly exclusive and began to recruit downwards, presumably assisted by a reduction in the entrance fee. This period of recruitment also coincided with an extensive strike that took place at this time. The strike ended in defeat for the dockers, broken, in the time-honoured tradition, by the importation of outside labour. According to the testimony of one shipowner to the Royal Commission on Labour, reporting in 1892, the strike was also followed by a period of dullness in trade and this seriously undermined the GHLU's bargaining position at the port. After the strike was over, those who filled the places of the strikers remained employed at the docks (which was not at all unusual at this time), and thus the number of men was greatly increased. This no doubt further weakened the GHLU and perhaps accounts for their later distrust of general unionism in the late 1880s and early 1890s.[5] The immediate result of the dispute, however, would seem to have been a reversal in the fortunes of the GHLU and as a result membership levels fell dramatically between 1872 and 1889. Partly this development can be explained and linked directly to the growing and increasingly influential role played by the steamship owners from the 1870s onwards. According to Lovell, the large shipping companies 'were only concerned with preserving their perfect freedom of action'. They would not tolerate workers' combinations interfering with their business. As their influence began to take hold the steamship owners erected formidable barriers to the emerging dock unions of the time. Glasgow did not escape this particular development. Indeed, the ever-increasing number of steamship companies locating at and operating out of the port tended to make Glasgow even more anti-union than was the generally the case at other major ports.[6]

Employment opportunities were also changing rapidly as steam gradually began to replace sail as the main motive power, and this only acted to further enhance the steamship owners' grip on the industry. Those who worked for the shipowners after the strike of 1872 were not organised, on the insistence of their employers, and this factor almost certainly played a part in the decline of the membership of the GHLU from a high point of 900 around 1872,[7] falling to 230 by 1889.[8] Moreover, as the

[1] *Glasgow Sentinel*, 16 Oct. 1858.

[5] *RC on Labour, 2nd Report*, 1892, testimony, J. Smith Park, representing Glasgow Shipowners' Association and the Allan and State Line Steamers, Q. 12,789; and Mr William Hannay Raeburn, Chairman of Clyde District Committee of the Shipping Federation (also member of the Board of the Clyde Navigation trust, the local Marine Board, the Pilot Board, and owner of tramp and cargo steamers) at Glasgow, Q. 13,417.

[6] Lovell, *Stevedores and Dockers*, p. 85.

[7] Lovell, 'Sail, Steam', pp. 232–7.

[8] Webb, *Industrial Democracy*, pp. 120–1.

membership of the GHLU had been traditionally employed on sailing ships, and as the emphasis changed from sail to steam, their place within the existing port structure became less essential than before. Their status within the port structure had thus been in a sense down-graded. Between 1856 and 1899 the number of sailing ships fell from 5,779 to 1,268, a fall of almost 80% in terms of the numbers of vessels arriving at Glasgow, while their tonnage had fallen by half. By contrast, the number of steam vessels increased by over 32%, while the total tonnage of steam vessels increased by over 60% (see *Appendix* Table IV).[9] This may have convinced potential members that there was little economic worth in retaining, or applying for, membership of the union, and simply increased the power of the shipowners over labour affairs at the Port of Glasgow.

The dynamic of steam was providing new employment opportunities for a different class of worker, causing an increase in the numbers of quayworkers needed at the port. These men would, by the definitions adopted in Chapter 3, be considered less skilled than the men of the Old Society. But with the emphasis shifting from sail to steam it also meant that these men were now in competition with a greater mass of less skilled workers. The new workers were a potential source of alternative labour. In short, the shipworkers of the Old Society could in theory be replaced. Many of the men working on the docks after 1872 had been brought in during the strike of that year. Thus the potential threat of a growing number of quay workers, coupled with the attitude of the shipowners, along with the gradual shift from sail to steam power, may have combined to create a type of siege mentality within the ranks of the Old Society membership. If this interpretation is correct, these were the factors which promoted a developing and increasingly close relationship with the less anti-union stevedoring class of employer at Glasgow before 1889. It was in the loading of the sailing ships that members of the Glasgow society had acquired their skills and it was the master stevedores who operated mainly in this line of work.

As the number of steamships increased, however, the master stevedores began to work the smaller steam vessels, coasters and tramps, as well as continuing to work those sailing vessels which were still operating widely. For the reasons outlined above, between 1872 and 1889 the relationship between the employers and the Old Society membership was a reasonably stable one. Both seemed willing to enter into agreement with the other. On the employers' side, they accepted the rules of the society, including the requirement that 'foremen be members of the union and accord to unionists a preference in employment',[10] while the unionists were expected to 'adhere to the unwritten rule that they would not contract directly with sailing ship owners',[11] a possible reference to the growing influence of the shipowners in port policy matters. In short, they saw the larger shipowners as a potential threat to their pool of labour. Fearing that their regular men might be persuaded away from their line of work, the smaller employers agreed to recognise

---

[9] Calculated from statistical tables noted in Marwick, *The River Clyde*, pp. 238–44.
[10] Lovell, 'Sail, Steam', p. 238.
[11] Ibid., p. 240.

and accept the rules of the Old Society in return for what amounted to a mutual loyalty agreement.

Not all employers agreed with their foremen becoming members of any union (save perhaps a foremen's union), the argument being that they could not 'exercise proper supervision if subject to the same authority and liable to the same rules as the men under their charge'.[12] Indeed, the question of the union-isation of foremen was a fundamental feature the particularly confrontational dispute that was to arise between the dockers and the employers in the early months of 1912, which the employers viewed as a challenge to their managerial prerogatives.[13] In short, the foremen had to remain free from trade union influence and so be able to act in the best interest of their employers. However, this mutual agreement with the employers helped to preserve the Old Society up to 1889, and also guaranteed the stevedores an adequate supply of labour at the same time. Through such an agreement, the Old Society protected its position by creating a specific niche for its membership within the employment structure at Glasgow harbour. But, more importantly, it protected its members from the increased competition posed in the form of the growing number of quayworkers.[14] It seemed a fine arrangement, while it lasted.

During 1889 the Old Society at Glasgow enjoyed something of a revival when membership figures began to rise rather dramatically. Between then and late 1892 membership reached 1,100[15]. Membership fell again however until by 1898, the last full year of the Old Society's existence, the number settled at around 670.[16] However, numbers were generally well maintained throughout this period, and were certainly higher throughout the 1890s than the previous two decades. The initial rise in the membership in 1889 is somewhat intriguing in that it coincided with the formation of the NUDL in Glasgow from February 1889. But it also corresponded to a general upturn in trade at this time. Eric Taplin has shown that there was considerable rivalry between the Old Society and the NUDL, principally, he argued, because the former refused to become absorbed into the new union.[17] According to the Webbs, this was due to the GHLU's traditions of exclusiveness and privilege, clearly suggesting a strong sectional dimension. However, it is also clear that the employers at Glasgow recruited the GHLU as a type of strikebreaking force in an attempt to weaken, even to break, the NUDL and their close allies the Seamen's Union during a series of strikes which occurred at the port during the early 1890s.

---

[12] *RC on Labour, 1st Report*, 1892, evidence submitted by Mr William Egerton Hubbard, Chairman of the Joint Committee of the London and St Katherine and East India Docks Company, Q. 4624.

[13] *Glasgow Herald*, Jan. – Feb. 1912.

[14] It is difficult to separate the numbers of quay workers from those who worked ships at this time. However, Census returns do allow some indication of the nature of the overall increase in those employed at the ports of Glasgow and of Govan from 1861–91. It should also be noted that it was not until 1891 that dock workers were enumerated separately from other dock servants, such as permanent employees, officials and stevedores.

[15] TUC *Annual Report*, Glasgow, Sep. 1992, see affiliation list.

[16] Board of Trade Report on Trade Unions, 1899 (*PP*, 1900, lxvii, Cd. 422), pp. 74–7.

[17] Taplin, *Dockers' Union*, p. 29.

The Old Society patently had a knack of surviving. They had come through a period of significant restructuring from sail to steam, periods of downturn in the trade cycle, increased competition for employment as more men entered dock life, and at least one significant failure in terms of industrial dispute, namely the strike of 1872. Thereafter, the evidence would suggest that the Old Society's strike record remained more or less unblemished, with the exception of one year, 1887. Indeed, from around 1889 onwards a no-strike agreement was incorporated within the society rules:[18]

> No strike shall be organised unless decided by three fourths of a majority of the whole membership of the society, and that only after the matter in dispute has lain for one clear week before the Honourable Lord Provost of Glasgow, the Provost of Govan, and the Provost of Partick, as the Board of Conciliation to act between the two parties.[19]

It does seem, however, that there was a break in the history of the GHLU in Glasgow, and that its existence was not continuous for the whole period from 1853 to 1890. Although the preface to the New Rules and Constitution of the GHLU gives a brief history of the 'society', stating that it was established in June 1853, omitted was the fact that the union's Friendly and Protective Society was dissolved in September 1886 (according to the records of the Registrar of Friendly Societies in Scotland).[20] There is no other evidence to show any organisation in existence until around April 1889 (two months after the NUDL was formed), and the new constitution seems to have been drawn up sometime in May 1890. Indeed, it is only in 1890 that the GHLU is referred to at all in any contemporary reports. At the time of the lengthy and costly strike during June and July 1889, there is no mention of the GHLU. It is only after this strike was over that the GHLU seems to feature in the unfolding industrial story of life and work along the Clydeside waterfront. The *North British Daily Mail* in June 1890 gave some hint that perhaps the strike of 1889, and the re-emergence of the GHLU the following year, were connected. The GHLU were:

> well deserving the notice and encouragement of all employers of labour and workmen alike. Their constitution and rules, if properly carried out, will tend greatly to the alleviation of the working classes and to the prevention of strikes, which have in the past caused so much loss of trade, misery, ill-feeling, and disorganisation.[21]

Was it then purely a coincidence that the Old Society was resurrected at a time when the Clyde seemed to be under threat from industrial action on the part of the

---

[18] *RC on Labour, 2nd Report*, 1892, evidence given by Mr George Monro (unofficially representing the Free Labour Party (sic) at the Port of Glasgow), Licensed Stevedore through the Clyde Navigation Trust, principally with mineral cargo, Q. 12,700 – Q. 12,706.

[19] SRO, FS 7/ 81, *Glasgow Harbour Labourers' Union Rules* May 1980 (deposited with the Registrar for Friendly Societies in Scotland), see Second Part, Clause 14.

[20] SRO, FS 7/10, Glasgow Harbour Labourers, Friendly and Protective Society, note by Registrar of Friendly Societies in Scotland that the Society was 'dissolved 21/9/86'.

[21] *North British Daily Mail*, 26 Jun. 1890.

1. Workers at Clydeside Docks, c. 1890.

2. Sailing ships on the Broomielaw, pre-1914.

3. The building of Princes Dock, c.1870s.

4. Unloading the *Berenger*, Queen's Dock, 1870s.

5. S.S. *Hawnby*, the first vessel to discharge at Meadowside Granary, May 1914.

6. Portable sack conveyor at Meadowside Granary, c.1914.

7. Stevedores aboard the *Montreal*, Glasgow, 1912.

8. C.F. Crichton, Convenor, Traffic Committee, Clyde Navigation Trust, starting up new pneumatic elevator, 1922.

9. Steam coaling crane, North Quay, Queen's Dock, pre-1927.

10. Suction pipes discharging grain from vessel's hold, Meadowside Granary, 1925.

11. Workers at Clydeside Docks, 1930s.

12. Rothesay Dock, June 1937.

13. Tugs, South Basin, Queen's Dock, 1930s.

14. Discharging sulphur, Rothesay Dock, 1930s.

15. View from roof of Meadowside Granary, 1949.

16. Passenger ships at Yorkhill Quay, seen from Queen's Dock centre tower, 1940s.

NUDL? Indeed, how 'Old' was the GHLU at that time, in so far as the changes written into their 'New Rules' constitute a decisive break with the past? The 'no-strike' clause is a clear example of this and that it was received particularly well by the employers was evident for all to see. Licensed stevedore George Monro of Glasgow noted in his evidence to the Royal Commission on Labour in 1892 that he thought that the no-strike clause was 'a pretty good rule', adding that to date it had not actually been required. He suggested that no strike had taken place since the rule had been incorporated within the Old Society's constitution. And even then, prior to the incorporation of the new rule he could only recollect the society taking part in one strike.[22]

Monro's testimony confirms that the rule was, therefore, relatively new, and that it had only been in operation for around two years. It is clear that the old constitution did not preclude strike action and never once referred to the setting up of any 'Board of Conciliation', and there was no reference either to a special conciliation or arbitration role for the Lord Provosts of Glasgow, Govan and Partick. The old rules dealt with many things, such as the 'good moral character of every Harbour Labourer', and that they should be 'free from all constitutional and bodily disease'.[23] Regarding strikes, there was no one-week 'cool down' period as incorporated within the 1890 Rules, or any clause on conciliation. It simply stated that when a strike was called, there should be a roll call of all members who would then appoint a committee to direct the dispute and its outcome.[24]

It is also unclear who was actually directing the affairs of the GHLU in 1890. As will be seen below, the employers of Glasgow seem to have been closely connected with the GHLU from its resurrection around 1890, maintaining this link up until 1893 at least, but what has to be resolved is whether the GHLU was functioning as a type of company union. Glasgow stevedore Mr Monro, Mr J. Smith Park of the Allan and State Lines of Glasgow, and William Hannay Raeburn, Glasgow shipowner and chairman of the Clyde District Committee of the Shipping Federation, agreed that the Old Society was a worthy organisation. Indeed, they were convinced that the Old Society had in its membership 'a better class of dock labourer' when compared to the more aggressive and general NUDL, which, for the most part 'consisted of Irishmen who handled the rougher sorts of cargo'. This point will be returned to below, but did this reference to the Irish in the NUDL mean that there were no Irishmen within the ranks of the GHLU?

According to evidence presented to the 1892 Royal Commission on Labour, shortly after the formation of the NUDL, the Old Society was approached by representatives of the Allan line, primarily J. Smith Park, to give their assistance in breaking strikes, disputes and boycotts organised by the NUDL. Because the NUDL had 'threatened them with extinction, unless they amalgamate with them', the Old Society pledged to fight against the 'tyrannical methods of action' employed by the NUDL and so agreed to join with the Allan Line in 1890, during the company's

---

[22] *RC on Labour, 2nd Report*, 1892, evidence, Monro, Q. 12,696–12,700.

[23] *Glasgow Harbour Labourers' Friendly and Protective Society Rules*, Oct. 4 1880, second section para. 1, 'Guidance to Members'.

[24] Ibid., section 3, para. 1.

fight against the new union. J. Smith Park stated that they had 'worked pleasantly with them ever since' and that many 'of the best of their old men', encouraged by having the Old Society behind them 'have joined it and deserted the other'.[25]

It may indeed be the case that the Old Society was now viewed as a virtual 'company union', and men were thereafter permitted to join this body whereas before shipowners like Raeburn would not have had any dealings with official trade union organisations of any type. However, as some of the records placed with the Registrar of Friendly Societies in Scotland illustrate, the GHLU was happy that they had 'recognised an identity of interests between employer and employee alike' and that the union was making 'productive progress' because of this open agreement.[26] In short, membership had increased as a result of their new found friendship with the shipowners. William Glen, the spokesman for the GHLU, and probable architect of the 1890 rule change, noted, 'that he hoped that the union be looked upon as the parent of all good workmen, and the union ticket a certificate of competency and character'.[27] Through the encouragement of at least one large shipping company, the Allan Line, the Old Society saw its membership rise, and it had apparently survived an attempt by the NUDL to exclude its members from working at the port.[28] It also resisted a bid by the NUDL to enforce a closed shop at Glasgow. The NUDL boycotted ships that had been worked on at any time by members of the Old Society, and did try to force the stevedores to employ only NUDL men. Some stevedores who hired Old Society members to discharge vessels found that when they needed more men, invariably in NUDL membership, to load those same vessels, 'they could not get the men to work together'.[29] The NUDL strategy on this occasion, however, was unsuccessful.

Between 1886 and 1890, therefore, there was a major shift in the fortunes of the GHLU, and this was arguably achieved through their common bond of interest with the employers. Society financial records for the period between September 1885 and September 1886, for example, illustrate that the total funds for GHLU that year were just over £45, and membership contributions accounted for £17 18s of this total. By the end of April 1890 (April to April now being the union's financial year) contributions were up to £199 15s, and total income was £284 18s, an increase of well over 600%. Indeed the balance, after expenses were calculated against income, which showed an increase of just over £8 in September 1886, rose by a massive 1,375% to £109 19s 6d. in April 1890[30] Not only does the comparison of these accounts show a major change of fortunes of the GHLU, but as there were no returns made for the intervening period, the evidence would suggest that the GHLU did not exist during that period and that it only emerged again, principally because of the machinations of the port employers at Glasgow, following the

[25] Ibid., Smith Park, Q.12,803.
[26] SRO, FS 7/81, *Glasgow Harbour Labourers' Union Rules: New Rules and Constitution of the Society*, May 1890 (deposited with the Registrar for Friendly Societies in Scotland), see preface.
[27] Ibid.
[28] Webb, *Industrial Democracy*, p. 121.
[29] *RC on Labour, 2nd Report*, 1892, evidence, Monro, Q. 12,696.
[30] SRO, FS 7/10 and FS 7/81, taken from record of accounts as presented to the Registrar of Friendly Societies in Scotland.

formation of the NUDL in 1889. Their re-emergence was therefore calculated to disrupt the operation of the NUDL and, perhaps from the beginning, they were to function as a company union and act as a strikebreaking force along the Clydeside waterfront.

The open animosity between the Old Society and the NUDL may, however, have had significantly deeper sectional roots. The Old Society was composed for the most part of ship workers. These dockers would have been considered skilled workers in the eyes of the shipowners and other employers at Glasgow. Such workers probably regarded themselves as superior to the quay workers who constituted the majority of the NUDL. As the testimony of William Raeburn suggests, the members of the Old Society handled the better cargoes, whereas the 'mostly Irish members' of the NUDL handled the rougher materials. It may be inferred from this that the members of the Old Society, 'generally a better class of dock labourer', were not Irish by birth. However, this is far from clear. Many of the names noted in the various records of the GHLU's Executive Council suggest both Scottish and Irish (and perhaps even Catholic) surnames: Patrick Scullion, James O'Brien, Hugh Sharkey, James Kelly, William Kelly and Patrick Kerregan.[31] The sectarian factor may have played little part, therefore, in the division between the two dockers' unions at Glasgow, and the Irish dimension may have been as important in maintaining cohesion within the ranks of the GHLU as it did for the members of the NUDL

There is another factor which could explain the divisions that came to exist between the two societies. The shipowners only employed free labour prior to their honeymoon with the Old Society after 1889, whereas the stevedores employed the society men of the GHLU. The dichotomy of definition used, however, to describe the members of the Old Society in the early 1890s meant that on the one hand they could be members of a *bona fide* union, while on the other the society could be viewed as a free labour organisation – discussed further below. More pragmatically, the shipowners were in a position to offer workers the opportunity to attain permanent status within the industry. Not all dock workers were concerned about such issues, preferring the freedom to work when they wished, rather than the rigour of permanent work. The shipowners for their part had already argued a case against the use of organised labour on the docks, but came to use the services of the Old Society and applaud it in the aftermath of the formation of the NUDL in February 1889. Through questions raised during the second report of the Royal Commission on Labour, the role of the Old Society was explored in greater detail. George Monro, when asked if Glasgow had a Free Labour Association, categorically denied that they had, but he also conceded that by 1892 the stevedores recognised no union but 'merely employed men – free labour men'. But we know that the majority of these so-

---

[31] SRO, FS 7/10, Glasgow Harbour Labourers' Friendly and Protective Society, record of Dissolution on 1 Sep. 1886, and signatures of Executive Council Members; and SRO, FS 7/81 *Glasgow Harbour Labourers' Union New Rules*, 13 May 1890, and Glasgow Harbour Labourers' Union record of Dissolution, 31 May 1899 when GHLU officially amalgamated with the NUDL; see Executive Council list of signatories.

called 'free labour men' were in fact members of the Old Society. The employers knowingly recruited them on that basis and so in this instance they could be viewed as free labourers despite being members of a trade union. When compared to the antagonistic and aggressive tactics of the NUDL these men could reasonably argue that they were simply upholding a higher standard of behaviour expected of good trade unionists.

The 'very good rules of the society' which brought about a 'good relationship between employers and employed as to strikes' also saw the Old Society function as strike-breakers.[32] According to the Webbs, the Glasgow Harbour Labourers' Society frequently supplied labour to help the employers break other strikes at the docks in Glasgow and in Liverpool, well before the Shipping Federation, for example, had firmly established itself in Glasgow by around 1892 (under the chairmanship of none other than William H. Raeburn). One of the main shipping firms in Glasgow engaged the members of the Harbour Labourers' Union to take the place of strikers and this was repeated at Liverpool. This was noted by Glasgow Trades Council in the *Annual Report* for 1889–90 where it was stated that the NUDL had been making 'strenuous efforts to advance the general interests of the Dock Labourers, and came out at the beginning of that year, to help the Liverpool men in their fight against the Allan Line'. The report concluded that the strike had been 'broken by the Old Dock Labourers' Society', with the assistance of 'all the blacklegs that could be got'.[33] The Report on Strikes and Lockouts for 1890 confirms the employers' success in a series of campaigns along the Clyde, particularly after the strike of 6 March to 26 March when it was reported that strikers had in fact been replaced by members of a 'rival union'.[34]

This particular campaign was organised by J. Smith Park of the Allan and State Shipping Lines, who was also a representative of the Glasgow Ship Owners' Association. He told the Royal Commission of 1892 that he had organised 'hundreds of quay labourers in Glasgow in 1890 to break a strike at Liverpool'. Similarly, he brought men from Liverpool to break strikes in Glasgow at this time. The reason was simple, 'they could work without the same fear in a place where they were not known'. He noted that the Old Society helped them in this endeavour, particularly in breaking the NUDL boycott of Allan Line vessels, as instructed by the NUDL Executive.[35] Clearly, the GHLU membership had no such fears and openly broke strikes in their own back yard. This indicates that they perceived no moral dilemma as far as these actions were concerned, considering that their actions were legitimate, and commensurate with their higher status within the dock labour force. Thereafter, both the employers and the Old Society worked together to break other strikes, as the testimony of the Webbs suggests, and

---

[32] *RC on Labour, 2nd Report*, 1892, evidence, Monro, Q. 12,696.

[33] Glasgow Trades Council, *Annual Report 1889–90*, p. 14.

[34] *Report on Strikes and Lockouts for 1890, by the Correspondent to the Board of Trade* (*PP*, 1890–91, lxviii, C. 6476), see pp. 55–105, 'General List of Strikes' showing cause, date, result and mode of settlement.

[35] *RC on Labour, 2nd Report*, 1892, evidence, Smith Park, Q. 12,798 and Q. 12,801–802.

this line of action, they noted, 'was repeated whenever a dispute arose between the employers and any Union on the Clyde'.[36]

The high point of the GHLU's partnership with the employers, or as the Webbs put it, 'their ultimate degradation', came when they entered into an alliance with the Shipping Federation in 1892. In that year the TUC met in Glasgow, with the delegates from the GHLU being excluded from the proceedings for their part in the alliance, but only after it had been expressly brought to the attention of the Congress. It was noted that they had not only taken the place of members of the NUDL, but also members of the Londonderry Dock Labourers' Union, and had also replaced striking dockers in London. Congress finally concluded, after some considerable debate, that 'they were not a fit body to be represented at Congress'. The GHLU were thus forced to leave the Congress.[37]

It is entirely possible that the GHLU members' role as strike-breakers was engineered through the influence of the Shipping Federation, growing in many of Britain's ports from the early 1890s onward. In Hull, after the employers counter-attack of 1893, for example, the Federation coerced employers previously willing to recognise and negotiate with dockers' unions, to desist from such practices, and reject trade unionism outright. Indeed, after 1893 trade unionism at Hull was almost entirely replaced by a commitment to the ideals of the Free Labour Movement.[38] However, it is not entirely clear that the situation at Glasgow was similar to that in Hull, particularly when it would seem that the Shipping Federation failed to recruit many of the big shipowners of Glasgow on any long-term basis. Nevertheless, as noted by one source, the Federation did 'make its strike breaking facilities available without too much enquiry into the niceties of membership' when employers found themselves in conflict with the labour force.[39] As the testimony of George Monro suggests, he at least felt that the stevedores could control the actions and activities of the Old Society, whose members he regularly employed, and who were referred to by him as 'Our men's society'.[40] In essence, the GHLU members operated, and came to be viewed by many, as free labour, and from this standpoint they arguably fulfilled the function of a Free Labour Association in Glasgow at this time.

Nevertheless, there were those in Glasgow who not only exhibited more than a passing admiration for the men of the Old Society, but also voiced a considerable degree of support for the Shipping Federation. In evidence presented to the 1892 Royal Commission on Labour William Hannay Raeburn's affection for the role of

---

[36] *Report on Strikes and Lockouts for 1890*, the GHLU provided replacement labour after the NUDL refused to unload pig iron shipments, as it came from Barrow-in-Furness where the NUDL were in dispute during Oct. 1890. In Dec. of that year the Old Society helped break a strike concerning 4 stevedoring firms who demanded that their employees left the NUDL. It was also noted that the Old Society did not object to their members working alongside non-union labour, which was another reason for the dispute in the first instance. They also provided scab labour against a strike organised by the Scottish Railway Servants' Union.

[37] TUC *Annual Report*, Glasgow, 1892, pp. 49–50, 61, 64–6; see also *Report on Strikes and Lockouts for 1892 (PP, 1893–94, lxxxiii, C-6890)*, p. 70.

[38] R. Brown, *Waterfront Organisations at Hull 1890–1900* (Hull, 1972), p. 92.

[39] Patterson, 'Seaman on the Clyde', pp. 130–2.

[40] *RC on Labour, 2nd Report*, 1892, evidence, Monro, Q. 12,740–745.

the Federation seems unequivocal. He was at this time acting chairman of the Clyde District Association of the Shipping Federation, representing the interests of 'a very large number of Glasgow shipowners'.[41] And Raeburn was to maintain his affinity with the Shipping Federation well into the following century. Speaking some time later to the Royal Commission on the Poor Laws (which reported in 1910), Raeburn suggested that the 'Federation' had been used in more recent times as a defensive association more than anything else, and stressed his admiration of one of its primary functions. 'We have found by proper working it has been very helpful', specifically in its role as a 'labour bureau':

> For instance, trouble arises in Glasgow, Belfast, or anywhere else [and] a body
> of men have gone out, because they had disagreed with their employers; this
> bureau has a large number of men on its books from all parts of Great Britain,
> and in twenty four hours we have been able to put into Antwerp, for instance,
> lately, about 2,000 men in three days, so that shows what even one organisation
> can do with regard to that, that has only one bureau in London.[42]

There seems little doubt that Raeburn accepted that the Federation had some real authority in industrial relations matters, and his use of the word 'we' would seem to indicate that he felt considerable affinity with the Federation and their ideal. Ironically, a series of questions followed Raeburn's remarks on the achievements of the Federation, which led to an interesting conclusion on the part of one commissioner:

> If the Shipping Federation could achieve such considerable success in regards
> to labour replacement, could a similar show of resolve not achieve unanimity
> among employers to the setting up of central labour exchanges, and their use
> of labour through them [?][43]

This was a direct accusation that the employers, when they had a mind to, could work together to fight against organised labour at the docks, yet still argue that the industry could not be organised more efficiently in order to reduce the cause and irregular nature of dock employment and the problems of unemployment, the very reason why the Royal Commission had been set up in the first instance.[44]

The GHLU did eventually amalgamate with the NUDL in 1899,[45] but it is not entirely clear why this happened. It may have been that the employers needed the services of the GHLU less frequently as the 1890s wore on, particularly when this period saw a general downturn in trade. In this situation members of the GHLU may have felt that their needs were better served by amalgamating with their recently formed rivals, thus bringing together the two main parts of Glasgow's dock labour force. However, while it can be argued that between 1892 and 1895 there was a perceptible decline in economic activity, from 1896 the situation improved

[41] *RC on Labour, 2nd Report,* 1892, evidence, Raeburn, Q. 13,417.
[42] *RC on Poor Laws,* ix, 1910, *Minutes of Evidence,* pp. 36–7.
[43] Ibid., question to Raeburn by commissioner.
[44] Ibid., Monro, Q. 12, 736.
[45] *Board of Trade Report on Trade Unions in 1899,* pp. 74–7.

somewhat. Even before 1896 the situation along the waterfront may not have been as bad as generally experienced elsewhere.[46] Therefore, the economic component may not have been the overriding factor helping to promote amalgamation.

Ultimately, what was to occur at Glasgow was the amalgamation of two distinct but not mutually exclusive elements of dock trade-union representation. For a time they existed side by side, as indeed did similar bodies at London, Liverpool and Hull. Moreover, their relationship was one initially based on the mutual distrust of the other. But this was not unusual and was indicative of the sectional divisions that were apparent at other ports where competing groups attempted to exclude the other from operating freely. However, as the Webbs' testimony suggests, the NUDL attempted to amalgamate with the Old Society initially, and only after this was rejected did they attempt to force them out of existence.[47] Similarly, it is clear that the employers attempted to undermine the NUDL and thereafter courted the GHLU and perhaps even aided its resurrection from its former moribund state. It is not surprising then that the GHLU rejected a partnership deal with the NUDL. The dockers of the Old Society may have perceived that their status within the port was diminishing in relation to the growing numbers of quayworkers. They also began to take on new tasks and did more onshore work, which would previously not have been part of their remit. In their struggles against the NUDL they were to take on work that would have traditionally remained within the influence and control of the quayworker and, therefore, those dockers who were members of the NUDL. However, the sectional lines that previously separated the two organisations were also becoming blurred with such developments. It may well be the case that they had become so blurred that former differences were no longer the great barrier to amalgamation as they had hitherto.

The growth of new employment outlets, specifically in regard to bulk cargo such as coal and minerals, promoted a further increase in the numbers of quay workers, who had remained largely unorganised until the formation of the NUDL. Attempts had been made previously to organise bodies of dock workers at Glasgow. The Labour Protection League, for example, were reported to have made such attempts during September 1888, after a lock-out of quay labourers by stevedores in a dispute which had spread from Belfast. Indeed a report in the *North British Daily Mail* makes reference to a 'Labourers' Union' being founded in January of that year.[48] But no record of the foundation of this union was ever deposited with the Registrar of Friendly Societies in Scotland. It should be noted, too, that Glasgow Trades Council had attempted to organise and preside over the affairs of both mineral workers and quayworkers around the same time (as they did in a dispute in October 1888[49]). Indeed, it would seem that the Council gave assistance to a group of quay labourers around December 1888, in order that they could gain their licenses from Clyde Navigation Trust to act as stevedores, and it

[46] *Report on Relief of the Able-bodied Unemployed During the Winter of 1893–94* (Scotland), *Board of Supervision Report* ( *PP*, 1894, lxx, C-7413), pp. 11–12.
[47] Webb, *Industrial Democracy*, p. 121.
[48] *North British Daily Mail*, 20 Sep. 1888.
[49] *North British Daily Mail*, 4 Oct. 1888.

was reported that the Trades Council received the thanks of the new stevedores for their assistance in that matter.[50]

When the quay labourers were finally organised, however (lacking the traditions of the Old Society), they came to embrace a more antagonistic attitude to labour relations. The GHLU favoured formal agreements, some principled codes of practice, and conciliation, very much in the style of the artisanal Old Unionism of the period. By 1890, the NUDL embarked on the tactic of 'ca-canny' (their go-slow strategy), and further developed their antagonistic tendencies towards industrial relations through sympathetic strike action with the Seamen's Union and other workers at Glasgow and a myriad of other ports. The GHLU, in contrast, were formulating their no-strike clause, and pledged thereafter 'to encourage the settlement of all disputes by arbitration and therefore prevent strikes'.[51] Indeed, these two opposing tendencies conform well to the seemingly contradictory development of militancy and pragmatism within waterside trade unions, as outlined and argued by Frank Broeze.[52] That is, the militancy of the rank and file on the one hand, juxtaposed by the pragmatism and conciliatory nature of the leadership on the other. It may have been a grudging acceptance of the reality of dock work as it developed and changed in character towards the end of the century, that ultimately forced these two parts together. If not, each might well have cancelled out the effectiveness of the other in an internecine squabble, which could have seen them sufficiently weakened as to promote the extinction of both, as was to occur at Hull in the aftermath of the employers' counter-attack there in 1893.

Despite the animosity that existed between the two unions, it was through a combination of both quay workers and ship workers that dock unionism on the Clyde survived. The Old Society could have acted as a firm base for the founding of a 'Free Labour Bureau' in Glasgow, similar to that established by William Collison at Hull, and if this had happened it could well have proved a real threat to the continued existence of the NUDL. The GHLU certainly had links with the Free Labour Movement of this period. As the following chapter will show, they were to be recruited by Graham Hunter to break a strike in Dublin in 1892. Hunter was a close ally of William Collison, a leading strike-breaker of the period and one who continued to function in that role until 1914.[53]

After 1893, however, there are no further references to the Old Society acting as strike-breakers. And they never appear in the minutes of Glasgow Trades Council again as functioning in that role. With the continuing downswing in the economy throughout this period the employers may have felt that the NUDL no longer posed any serious threat to them. Thus the GHLU formed no part of the employers' long-term industrial strategy thereafter, neither did they automatically receive

---

[50] *North British Daily Mail*, 20 Dec. 1888.

[51] GHLU, *New Rules*, 1890, section II, clause 4.

[52] Broeze, 'Militancy and Pragmatism'.

[53] W. Collison, *The Apostle of Free Labour* (1913), reference made to Graham Hunter, pp. 267–7; reference also made in TUC *Annual Report*, Glasgow, 1892, p. 65; a further reference made to 'Boss Union Smasher', Graham Hunter, engaged to break a later dock strike at Ardrossan in 1912, *Ardrossan and Saltcoats Herald*, 8 Nov. 1912.

preference in employment as they had before. The Old Society's inclusion at the 1894 TUC Conference, with little or no notice being paid to their previous role and their expulsion in 1892, would suggest that they no longer functioned as a strike-breaking force on Clydeside. Like the prodigal son they were once more welcomed back into the fold.

Press reports after 1893 suggest that relations between the two bodies were improving. As was noted in the previous chapter, the NUDL made an appeal on behalf of a GHLU member to Glasgow Trades Council following a serious accident he had encountered at the docks there.[54] This occurred at a time when the two bodies were still in disagreement over the GHLU's role as strike-breakers, and shortly after their expulsion from the TUC Conference at Glasgow in 1892. Some time before this episode the NUDL had been attempting to get the GHLU expelled from Govan Trades Council, and requested that Glasgow Trades Council should assist in 'taking the Govan Council to task' for allowing the GHLU to remain affiliated to it. It was unanimously agreed that the Glasgow Council would do everything it could to 'squelch the union which had been blacklegging at Glasgow Harbour'.[55] The matter became even more complicated, however, by the counter-claims of the Old Society that it was in fact the NUDL men who were guilty of the crime of blacklegging and that this situation had been openly ignored by NUDL officials.[56] It was another year before matters were brought to a head, when Govan Trades Council were reported to have arranged meetings between themselves and the Glasgow Council to 'investigate the existing differences between the NUDL and the Harbour Labourers' Union'.[57]

The matter was again raised at the 1894 TUC Conference when a NUDL delegate, Mr Souter, asked what the GHLU had done 'to take the stain off their character since they were first expelled by the 1892 TUC at Glasgow'. He also requested, but seemingly failed to gain support for, a committee to be set up to 'investigate the whole matter and the conduct of the GHLU between 1890 and 1892'.[58] However, it would seem by this time that the TUC had washed their hands of the matter and that the actions of the GHLU no longer greatly troubled the NUDL. After a report of October 1894 in the *Glasgow Echo* there is no further discussion on the matter, and the problems that existed between the NUDL and the GHLU seem to have resolved themselves. The fact that they did operate as a strike-breaking unit, however, may not have been the most important barrier to amalgamation in any case. Blacklegging was not as important to the docking community as we might expect. In short, because of the casual nature of the prevailing system of employment, occasional recourse to 'blacklegging' was probably an economic necessity. Indeed, as can be seen through the earlier writings of Charles Booth, many dockers may have been introduced to the work as strike-breakers and thereafter remained in that work. These men were thereafter grudgingly accepted

---

[54] *Glasgow Echo*, 7 Sep. 1893, p. 4.
[55] Ibid., 6 Jul. 1893.
[56] Ibid., 21 Sep. 1893; report of 'Special Meeting of Govan Trades Council' the previous day.
[57] Ibid., 4 Oct. 1894.
[58] Ibid., 18 Oct. 1894.

by those who worked in the dock industry, whereas men like McHugh and McGhee (see Chapter 9) could not accept this situation because neither had the practical knowledge of what committing themselves to the day-to-day trials and tribulations of dock work really meant. In other words, they did not fully understand the industry and their departure in 1893 perhaps helped towards the solution of a problem that did not require the GHLU to fully atone for their former misdeeds.

In the final analysis it was perhaps essential that the NUDL approached the matter pragmatically. Hence their desire to amalgamate with the old union, rather than seek its extermination. Had the latter been achieved, and the testimony of the Webbs show that this was part of the NUDL strategy for a time, they may have pushed a potential impulse for future division underground. In other words, a possible cause of disunity was removed and this enabled the NUDL to influence and control a difficult situation. General dock unionism, therefore, was not hampered to the same degree in Glasgow as it was in other ports, such as London, or Hull. Indeed, the NUDL seemed able to bridge the sectional differences in Glasgow (as the union did later, to a lesser degree, at Liverpool), whereas in London, and particularly Hull, Ben Tillett's Dock Wharve and Riverside General Labourers' Union (DWRGLU) could not. Thus, despite the differences that did exist in Glasgow, the NUDL could still exert a degree of control locally that did not exist at Hull. By the late 1890s it was argued that a local union should be set up in Hull 'in view of the manifest failure of the national organisation' to organise workers there.[59] The quasi-federal and semi-autonomous nature of the different NUDL branches, up to 1893 at least, did allow for a degree of localism in the running of the various branches which was evidently missing in the structure of Tillett's DWRGWU.

After 1890 the initial force of 'New Unionism' began to dissipate. From around the middle of the 1890s, however, the situation improved somewhat on Clydeside. While nationally the NUDL saw the number of branches fall from thirty-four in 1889 to fifteen by 1895, Glasgow saw an increase from one branch to two over the same period.[60] The NUDL in Glasgow thus maintained a presence and continued to exert some control over industrial relations within the port. When the NUDL amalgamated with the GHLU in 1899 they were active in the port and organised at least one significant dispute involving 1,200 dockers.[61] After the turn of the century the situation was to change significantly, and in this climate of change came the decline of the NUDL in the affairs of the docker in the port of Glasgow. However, the survival of the NUDL in Glasgow was to continue an organisational link with the period of New Unionism through to the first stirrings of unrest during the period 1910–1914. And while the union's presence at Glasgow was to dwindle to meaningless levels by 1910, it arguably left an adequate foundation upon which to build a new organisation in 1911.

---

[59] Brown, *Waterfront Organisations*, p. 92.
[60] Taplin, *Dockers' Union*, see *Appendix*, pp. 168–9.
[61] *Report on Strikes and Lockouts for 1899* (*PP*, 1900, lxviii, Cd. 316), p. xlii.

# CHAPTER NINE

# The National Union of Dock Labourers in Glasgow, 1889 to 1910: A Pioneering Organisation for New Unionism

In the aftermath of the Great London Dock Strike, in September 1889, Harry Quelch, of the South Side Protection League in London, wrote how the dispute had created 'the impetus and enthusiasm for combination, and resulted in the formation of trade unions among large numbers of workers who had hitherto been unorganised'.[1] This episode is viewed as one of great historical significance in labour history and became known as the period of the New Unionism. And the dockers of Glasgow were to the forefront of this movement when, some seven months earlier, the National Union of Dock Labourers (NUDL) came into existence. In the words of the NUDL's President and General Secretary, the NUDL was to go on and become a 'pioneering organisation' for what came to be called 'New Unionism', an organisation whose 'aims were lofty . . . its methods novel and daring'. More importantly, by October 1893, when these words were spoken, the NUDL was still in existence after a period of sustained counter-attack by the port employers in league with the Shipping Federation. The NUDL Executive proudly boasted they were still 'solvent, independent and full of vital energy'.[2] Indeed, the NUDL was to remain so for some time to come.

The developments leading to the formation of the NUDL in Glasgow have been referred to throughout this study. It has also been noted that the NUDL was in a terminal state of disintegration by 1910. What has been missing so far, however, is an explanation of the nature and importance of the NUDL's existence at the Port of Glasgow between 1889 and 1910. The chronological significance is of course obvious. The NUDL's tenure began with the New Unionist impulse of the late 1880s, and came to end just as we begin to detect the first stirrings of a new wave of workers' unrest and discontent with the advent of the labour unrest of 1910–14. These two events were very important episodes in the history of the British labour movement as a whole, but they were fundamental to the development and future direction of dock trade unionism too. This chapter will consider this period in relation to Clydeside and its dock labour force. It will investigate more fully the forces which aided the NUDL formation, the union's relationship with Glasgow Trades Council and the Seamen's Union, and will consider too the relationship with the GHLU (from the perspective of the NUDL and its membership). The

[1] H. Quelch, *Trade Unionism, Co-operation and Social Democracy* (1892), pp. 3–4.
[2] NUDL *Annual Report*, Fifth Annual Congress, Liverpool 1893, p. 16.

chapter will close by analysing the cause of the NUDL's collapse at Glasgow c.1908–10, while comparing the different experience of the Clydeside dock labour force between the two decades either side of 1900. The principal aim will be to show that the disintegration of the union on Clydeside was due to an array of factors. It will also be argued, however, that much of the blame for the collapse of the NUDL on Clydeside can be laid at the door of the executive of the NUDL in Liverpool, and James Sexton in particular. It will be further argued that the Clydeside dock labour force exhibited a stubborn streak of independence throughout this period, that they engendered a strong sense of their own history and that this strengthened their occupational solidarity and their commitment to a self-conscious Clydeside-centric dock unionism. It will be suggested that dockers' trade unionism at Glasgow did not so much fail, but rather that trade unionism failed the Glasgow dockers. But from the ashes, which were the remnants of the NUDL, was to rise a new organisation, the Scottish Union of Dock Labourers (SUDL). This new organisation would carefully guide Clydeside and other sections of the Scottish dock labour force through to the formation of the Transport and General Workers Union in 1922 and beyond, towards the next important phase of Clydeside dock unionism.

## Towards the Formation of the National Union of Dock Labourers

The link between Glasgow Trades Council and the dockers was without doubt a very important one. So too was the Seamen's Union, which together with Glasgow Council worked to encourage the formation of a general union among dockers at Glasgow. This productive partnership was indeed a profitable one in terms of the growth in new trade union membership among the quayworkers at Glasgow and elsewhere. In the *Annual Report* of the Glasgow Trades Council of 1888–89 particular mention was made of the success in organising parts of Glasgow's dock labour force, and that an attempt had first been made at the beginning of February 1889 to form a society among the dockers. This process was taking place in tandem with a dispute that involved the National Amalgamated Sailors' and Firemen's Union (NASFU), whose membership had swelled throughout the country by the early months of 1889.[3] According to Glasgow Trades Council the Seamen's Union had recruited a further 600 members in 1889 alone and that by 1890 they numbered 7,500. But while doing so their efforts had helped to create the impetus for the formation of a new dock union. Work amongst the dock labour force had continued apace and the Council felt that this warranted special mention:

> We think the notice of those who have set a good example during the year would be incomplete if no mention was made of the Dock Labourers, a body of men who have been looked upon very much as if it was impossible to make anything of them in the way of improving their position . . . They are now in a position, effectually and at once, to checkmate any attempt to deal unfairly with them either by the great companies they work for, or, what is more to be

[3] Hobsbawm, *Labouring Men*, p. 217.

dreaded, the great men of authority. It is good to be able to say so much for such a large and hitherto underestimated body of men.[4]

The Report ended by noting that membership of the new society had reached nearly 4,000 by the autumn of 1889 and that the NUDL were also by then affiliated to the Trades Council.

The link with the Seamen's Union is important, principally because seamen and dockers often came from the same cultural background, lived within the same community, and were intimately linked to a similar system of casual employment. Indeed, according to Frank Broeze, 'it is reasonable to accept that many dockers had served at sea before settling down ashore'.[5] If Broeze is correct, then the relationship between the seamen and the dockers was a particularly strong one. Charles Booth also noted a link between dock work and the seamen in his investigations. He suggested that the stevedores who operated within the port of London were 'largely made up of seamen settling down to shore work'. Booth claimed that around 50% of the estimated 3,000 membership of the United Stevedores' Society, formed in 1889, were men who had previously been at sea.[6] Moreover, and as Lovell pointed out, they were also largely composed of Irishmen. Kenneth Buckley notes a further example of the linkages between both docker and seaman in his considerations of the port of Aberdeen.[7]

An investigation of the birthplaces of dockers in Glasgow, taken from the 1891 Census of Scotland, shows that there were many men drawn from all over the world listed as dockers. It would seem probable that they made first contact with Glasgow in their capacity as seamen. Thus we find men from America, Norway, Sweden, France, Greece and the colonial areas such as Gibraltar, Australia and Canada. While this group of foreign-born dockers forms a tiny minority of the overall workforce, this does not mean that the many men born in England, Ireland, Wales, or the Colonies, did not also make their initial contact with Glasgow in a similar fashion.

A cursory examination of the Census enumerators' reports give some indication of numbers of ex-seamen employed as dockers at this time. The Census returns record the various locations around Britain, and further afield, where the children of dockers were born. Even if the docker was not an ex-seaman, members of his family often were. There are numerous examples of such connections to be seen in Census returns from in and around the dockland areas on the north and south side of the River Clyde.[8] Eric Hobsbawm noted that the sailor was a major factor in helping to unite the docker with other dockers throughout Britain at this time. This was in part due to the inter-

---

[4] Glasgow Trades Council, *Annual Report*, 1888–89, p. 8.
[5] Broeze, 'Militancy and Pragmatism', p. 169.
[6] Booth, *Life and Labour*, viii, p. 429.
[7] Buckley, *Trade Unionism in Aberdeen*, p. 101.
[8] Census of Scotland 1891, the father of dock labourer Angus McPherson (born in Ross-shire), of Blackburn Street on Glasgow's south side, was a seaman; see Enumerator Reports for the Anderston District [644–10–1 to 40]; Plantation District [646–1–1 to 43]; Broomielaw District [644–7–1 to 77].

changeability of function that occasionally took place between members of both occupational groups. Such information helps us clarify the linkages between the seaman and the docker, and further strengthens Broeze's argument that the waterside community had an extended occupational interactivity. At a basic level this helped engender a high degree of familiarity and solidarity and aided the formation of trade unionism along the waterfront in Britain. But it also helped to forge international linkages between waterside communities across many countries in the late nineteenth and early twentieth centuries.[9] The docker and the sailor operated within the same community and thus shared many common cultural and social values.[10] Such a symbiosis could help to explain the considerable sympathy and solidarity shown by the dock labour force and the seamen when it came to pressing their joint demands whilst in dispute. As the Census enumerators report implies, many of these workers lived in the same areas, and on some occasions came from the same households. In Glasgow these occupational groups lived close to the Clyde, mostly on the north of the river along the Broomielaw and surrounding streets. It may be suggested that, on occasion, each group sought employment within the sphere of other.

An earlier example of such a link between dockers and seamen at the port of Aberdeen helps to illustrate this bond. A Shore Workers' Union had been established in Aberdeen as early as July 1883,[11] and it was this union which, with the assistance of Aberdeen Trades Council, was instrumental in organising the seamen there in January 1889. Indeed, Aberdeen Trades Council made itself responsible for the expense of organising a meeting of the Aberdeen seamen, and Havelock Wilson, secretary of NASFU, was invited by the Trades Council to address the meeting. This meeting took place at the Shore Labourers' Society's hall, and there a branch of the NASFU was set up and a 100 men joined immediately.[12] Both of these unions went from strength to strength only to be irreparably damaged in the aftermath of the employer's counter-attack with the Shipping Federation in 1893. By then, noted Kenneth Buckley, 'no organisation of either seamen or dockers existed in Aberdeen'.[13] Nevertheless, the main point here is to note the interconnection between both the seamen and the dockers, and the role that the Scottish Trades Councils played in aiding the process of emergent trade unionism within the ranks of both. NASFU reformed as the National Seamen's and Firemen's Union (NSFU) in 1984.

While there was indeed much to bind both groups together, in so far as they shared a great degree of irregularity in employment, there were also other associated factors which, at face value, worked against combination. As Eric Hobsbawm suggests, when dockers and seamen were particularly hard-pressed they may have accepted employment as strike-breakers. He argued that 'the

[9] Broeze, 'Militancy and Pragmatism', p. 169.
[10] Ibid.
[11] SRO, FS 7/86, Aberdeen Shore Workers' Union, Registrar for the Friendly Societies in Scotland,
[12] Buckley, Trade Unionism in Aberdeen, pp. 36–7.
[13] Ibid., p. 43.

waterside was constantly haunted by the spectre of the blackleg, the spare seaman or docker drawn from the pool of casual labour that existed everywhere'.[14] Because of the problems associated with casualism, occasional blacklegging may have been an unpalatable but unavoidable occupational consideration from time to time: a course of action born out of simple necessity. The use of replacement labour by port and shipping employers in industrial disputes was a factor that constantly threatened waterside trade unionism.

If there was a significant degree of movement between the various occupational groupings around the waterfront, this may help to explain the high incidence of blacklegging which occurred within the transport industry as a whole, not least in the docks or on board ship. This tradition may have been built up over the preceding years when the Irish, and the Highlanders, were beginning to penetrate these areas of employment, particularly in times of depression, or during trade disputes. It would not seem to be a coincidence that the seamen attempted to organise the dock and quay labour force when they themselves were in dispute with their employers, the same employers who recruited dock workers. The seamen may have felt it necessary to organise the dockers in order to stem a possible source of replacement labour. (Dockers did, after all, have a considerable working knowledge of many different types of shipping, more so if they had been seamen prior to settling into dock work.)

As the NUDL was formed during the seamen's strike of January-February 1889, the link is therefore self-evident, at least in the context of the Glasgow waterfront. During this time the leaders of the NASFU worked hard to gain the support of Glasgow's quayworkers, while the Glasgow Trades Council vigorously supported the seamen's efforts. John Eddy, Vice President of the Council, argued that in this particular dispute 'the quay labourers were more dangerous than the ship owners'. He warned the assembled dockers that if they 'betrayed the seamen they would be false to their own best interests'.[15] Thereafter, the meeting unanimously agreed full support for the seamen. The process of organising Glasgow's general dock labour force, and the quayworkers in particular, was under way.

Over that weekend, another meeting was held where Hugh Johnson, who the *Glasgow Herald* reported as 'having a strong Irish accent', reiterated the dockers' support for the seamen and pledged that they would refuse to work until the seamen's demands were met. The *Herald* was also to report that the employers were finding the situation difficult. They had attempted to replace the striking workforce, but at that point this strategy had proved unsuccessful. They had requested the assistance of the employers of Dundee in their quest for replacement workers, but were told that the dockers there 'had just recently formed a union', and that they could not be expected to 'act in an hostile manner against their brethren in Glasgow'.[16] The employers also attempted to replace strikers with men from the Highlands, but to no avail. As Havelock Wilson and Keir Hardie observed, when

[14] Hobsbawm, *Labouring Men*, p. 204.
[15] Ibid.
[16] *Glasgow Herald*, 4 Feb. 1889.

speaking at a meeting in support of the seamen at Glasgow, these men would be 'some time in coming'.[17]

The extension of labour organisation around Scottish ports at this time was of fundamental importance to the short-term success of the seamen's dispute, as well as the long-term existence of the NASFU and the fledgling NUDL. The NASFU had been formed some time earlier in 1887 by Havelock Wilson, and had only formed a branch at Glasgow as recently as 1888.[18] Even at that point, despite their relative strength in numbers, the continued existence of the NASFU was far from guaranteed. In 1887 the Glasgow Harbour Mineral Workers' Union had been formed, but by 1888, just as the Glasgow NASFU was being established, the GHMWU union was 'broken up' after the employers introduced imported labour from Belfast in tandem with a lock-out at the mineral docks at Glasgow.[19] Had the impetus for organisation not spread further afield at this time to ports such as Dundee, for example, the same fate might have beset the NASFU in this early period. Moreover, it may be argued that the NASFU were aware of this potential weakness, hence the industriousness exhibited in eliciting the support of the quayworkers during their dispute with Glasgow's shipowners. Having blocked the supply of replacement labour from Dundee, and legislated for the problems associated with the supply of Highland labour, it would have been deemed imperative that the dockers of Glasgow did not become a potential source of blackleg labour.

The evidence strongly suggests that the quay labourers were considered an essential element of the seamen's dispute. It was Havelock Wilson who argued that the dock workers should form an organisation of their own, which would thereafter affiliate with the NASFU 'with a view to their mutual co-operation in all future disputes'. Indeed, Wilson seemed so determined to gain the support of as many quay labourers as possible, that he extended the parameters of the dispute to include the demand for a rise in wages for the dockers. This was agreed, and James Gray, representing the dock labourers, moved that their demands be placed jointly before the employers, with the promise 'that each group would support the other until [these] demands were met'.[20]

This was a significant and vigorous campaign on the part of various leading players in the Glasgow labour movement at this time, and provided the basis of the move towards the formation of the dockers' union at Glasgow. It would seem clear, however, that part of this strategy was geared towards ensuring that the dock and quay workers, with the direct and indirect knowledge of seagoing work, would not

[17] Ibid., 5 Feb. 1889.
[18] Taplin, Dockers' Union, p. 27.
[19] SRO, FS 7/73, details contained in a letter from James Conlan, GHMWU secretary, sent to Registrar of Friendly Societies 16 May 1889. It was noted that members of the Union had made no contribution since Sep. of 1888. Essentially, the Union was bankrupt after the 'Masters' at Glasgow had initiated a lock-out, with all the funds being distributed among the membership. In the year ending Dec. 1888 the accounts show a one-time balance of over £400, but after Sep. £350 was paid out to members who were caught up in the lock-out by the mineral firm Martins. The Registered Office of the Union was 10a Norfolk Street, which was situated in the Gorbals. It was in the Gorbals area in Jan. and Feb. of 1889 that meetings of the National Union of Dock Labourers were held.
[20] Glasgow Herald, 5 Feb. 1889.

be utilised by the employers as replacements for the seamen once they had committed themselves to the dispute with the Glasgow shipowners. In this respect, the seaman and the docker shared much in common and in particular the need to protect their industry from the encroachment of outsiders at times of trade dispute or trade depression. This common goal was to prove the essence of the solidarity each was to show for the other during significant periods of industrial discontent at Glasgow from 1889 onwards.

### 'A New Union for Glasgow'!

On 6 February 1889, the *Glasgow Herald* reported that there existed a 'newly formed union of dock labourers in Glasgow'. The report stated that the Glasgow men were now enthusiastic to learn how a 'new union' should operate, based on the simple premise that no model had hitherto existed in Glasgow which involved the ordinary quayworker. On that basis Irishman Hugh Johnson visited Greenock where he had been enquiring into the working of the union there. Subsequently he reported back to the membership at Glasgow. The Greenock Union, noted Johnston, operated with around 600 members, and they charged an entry fee of 16s followed by a weekly subscription of 3d. However, Johnston suggested that in Glasgow's case no entry fees should be charged for the present, but that in time a charge of 1s would be sufficient. Thus the entry fee into the new union would be small and would not act as a bar to membership. Johnston also urged caution, realising that the new union was still weak, and therefore vulnerable. But it would get stronger, if they took it slowly:

> He knew no one would be able to open their mouths just now, but when they been six or seven weeks connected with the union they would all be Dan O'Connells and Henry Grattans. (laughter)[21]

As we saw in Chapter 5, both O'Connell and Grattan were politically and historically of great significance for the great mass of Irish who lived in Britain at this time, and those who had settled around the docks of Glasgow were no different. It was an appeal to their sense of history.

Within a week of the NUDL's formation, writes Taplin, Edward McHugh was invited to become General Secretary and Richard McGhee the President. By the first Congress in November 1889, their positions were formally recognised. Both were Irish by birth, but McHugh since childhood had lived in Scotland and McGhee, aged thirty-eight, had lived in Scotland for the previous seventeen years. Both were strong supporters of Irish and Scottish Land Reform and colleagues of Henry George, said to have had a profound and considerable influence on British Socialism. George had endeared himself to many Irish and Highland people at this time because of his advocacy of taxing revenue raised by landlords, or the 'unearned increment' from land rental. This helped to form support for the campaign for Land Nationalisation. His book, *Progress and Poverty*, was read widely

[21] *Glasgow Herald*, 6 Feb. 1889.

by many who had an interest in Land Reform, such as McHugh and McGhee.[22] Both men were active in politics and McGhee was also an organiser for the American Knights of Labour in Glasgow. After the formation of the NUDL McGhee decided to devote his energies to the further development of the NUDL. But as an unpaid official he had at the same time to continue his 'work as a commercial traveller during his association with the union'.[23]

The underlying Irish nature of the NUDL as an organisation was, from the very beginning, of considerable importance, not simply in terms of the impetus towards the initial formation of the union, but also in terms of its struggle for existence in those early formative years. The roles of McHugh and McGhee were of fundamental importance to the NUDL's success at Glasgow, not only because of their deep commitment to Irish Home Rule, but also because of their commitment to the dockers' cause. From the outset, states Taplin, both McHugh and McGhee 'dominated the Union and the Executive'. Both were involved in local politics in Glasgow, and McHugh was one of four Labour representatives who stood for election to the Municipal Council in Glasgow in 1889. Although defeated, the votes polled for each candidate were not inconsiderable. This augured well for the future, it was noted by Glasgow Trades Council, in the fight against 'the interest of capital and the classes against the masses'.[24] McHugh was clearly playing his part towards this vision of the future. In the industrial sphere, both McHugh and McGhee were to become associated with militancy and were seen as particular irritants by the powerful Glasgow shipowners and numerous smaller employers, as well as the stevedores. The tactics that they were to advocate for the NUDL were to bring them into direct conflict with this body of employers and they in turn singled both men out for some harsh criticism.

### A First Challenge for NUDL – The Strike of June–July 1889

It is clear that both McHugh and McGhee were considered major troublemakers in Glasgow. Between the period of the NUDL's formation and both men's resignation in December 1893, they made a number of enemies, and, as noted above, these were not wholly confined to those within the ranks of the employing class. It was McHugh who introduced the strategy of 'Ca'canny' after the collapse of the strike between June-July 1889. The strike was ultimately broken with the help of imported labour, with whom the employers had declared themselves satisfied. McHugh and McGhee seized upon this, and advised returning NUDL members to 'work like the farm workers worked' (the strike-breakers). Soon afterwards McHugh was approached by the shipowners, who promised wage increases if the men would work normally. The go-slow had won concessions for the NUDL and both McHugh and McGhee's tactics were applauded. Thereafter, 'Ca'canny' became a major industruction

---

[22] T. May, *An Economic and Social History of Britain 1760–1970* (1987), pp. 74–5.

[23] Taplin, *Dockers' Union*, p. 28 for brief biography of Edward McHugh and Richard McGhee, see J. Bellamy and J. Saville (eds.) *Dictionary of Labour Biography*, Vol. II (1974).

[24] Glasgow Trades Council *Annual Report*, 1888–89, p. 8.

trial relations strategy of the NUDL, and McHugh and McGhee's reputations were considerably enhanced as a result.[25]

It is clear that other strategies pursued by the Union and its executive caused the employers further problems. George Monro, a Glasgow stevedore, felt that union officials were becoming 'the masters and not the stevedores'. He also noted the disruptive effect of sympathetic action, referring to the boycotting of iron-ore shipments from Barrow-in-Furness, where the NUDL was also in dispute. He noted too that NUDL also continued to black vessels from Belfast, which were not manned by members of the NASFU. They simply disallowed all work on any vessel manned by non-union labour. He concluded, 'things had almost come to a standstill at the time until the Federation came to the stevedores' assistance'.[26]

The representative of the Allan Shipping Line, Mr J. Smith Park, who was also representative of the Glasgow shipowners, was no less critical of the antagonistic tactics of the NUDL at this time. He noted that the employers' tactic of replacing striking labour, which had been relatively easy in the period before 1889 when men were scarce, was then difficult to pursue because of 'threats of bodily injury and boycotts' (although he failed to mention that finding replacement labour was difficult with the much improved state of trade after 1889). Men who did not strike, he reported, or those who replaced strikers, were now 'terrorised by strikers', and he furnished an example of how some 600 men berthed on labour ships 'were afraid to leave and were literally in a state of siege'.[27] Smith Park further outlined various examples of intimidation, one of which involved him personally. He was chased across Jamaica Bridge while a crowd of stone throwers followed his cab. One man who ran alongside the cab smashed a side window while attempting to open the door. The man was later arrested and fined. However, Smith Park noted that the Union had covered the fine as they did in all cases of violence. Unlike Mr Smith Park, the men who continued to work were afraid to bring any charges against any assailant.[28] It would seem that this was part of a concerted campaign, waged against the Allan Line in particular, and which was to last some ten months, between March and December 1890. The main aim of the boycott was to push the employers to recognise the NUDL and to enter into negotiations with the union on wages and conditions at the port. It was also stated that the NUDL wanted only their members to be employed by the firms affected by the boycott.[29]

Smith Park noted that both McGhee and McHugh had promised to do everything in their power to achieve their ends, including an unsuccessful attempt to gain sympathy action on the part of stevedores in America with a view to joining the boycott of the Allan ships at New York. He also noted that the NUDL were against the employment of weekly men because they felt they should get paid the full hourly rate.[30] It may have been more the case that weekly men were distrusted by

[25] Taplin, *Dockers' Union*, p. 30.
[26] *RC on Labour, 2nd Report*, 1892, evidence, Monro, Q. 12,696.
[27] Ibid., evidence, Smith Park, Q. 12,791, Q. 12,792.
[28] Ibid., Q.12,794 and Q.12796.
[29] Ibid., Q.12,801 and Q.12,802.
[30] Ibid., Q. 12,817.

the casual dockers as they would have been more susceptible to employer pressure, in as much as weekly employment amounted to a form of permanency. The weekly men, therefore, had more to lose, apart from functioning at a different level within the employment structure. Control over them would have proved difficult when they did not share the same value system as the great mass of casual dock labourers.

William Hannay Raeburn, chairman of the District Committee of the Shipping Federation in Glasgow, offered further testimony against both 'McHugh's Union' and the NASFU. The biggest problem, as he viewed it, was that neither organisation recognised 'the rights of the non-unionist'. He was also scathing about their use of sympathetic action, noting that if an employer displeased one union 'you have all of them on your top'. He also disliked the 'dictatorial' nature of the leadership and the intimidation that followed in the wake of any dispute.[31] All of this prompted the employers to turn to the Glasgow Harbour Labourers' Union to aid them in their fight against the 'unscrupulous agitators' of the NUDL and the NASFU, who, in the words of another shipowner, 'had nothing to lose and everything to gain by propagating evil council'.[32] The employers' strategy of using the GHLU ultimately proved a useful one. Not only was it to check the development of labour organisation along the Clyde, they even managed to disrupt the TUC in Glasgow in 1892.

It may have been the problems that were created through the strikes of June-July 1889 which prompted the employers to consider a renewed role for the Glasgow Harbour Labourers' Union. The *Glasgow Herald* reported the dispute extensively, as did the *North British Daily Mail*. The paper's first major article on the strike, on 13 June 1889, began as follows:

> Metaphorically speaking the atmosphere along the Glasgow docks smelt of powder yesterday. The telegrams which came to hand on the previous night intimating the departure of contingents of labourers to fill the places of strikers here had the effect of bringing all hands to deck. Although the same methods have been adopted elsewhere with the sailors, this was the first case heard of where it was proposed to oust the dockmen. [33]

It was not of course the first time that the employers had used such tactics with the dockers, as the case of the breaking of the Mineral Harbour Labourers in 1888 illustrates, and further inaccuracies of this sort were to follow. But the report correctly stressed the degree of solidarity that was being manifested by the dockers. It was also noted that the dockers had adopted the battle cry of 'No Surrender'. It was reported that 'they would sell their household furniture before deserting the cause of the seamen, or accept their old rate of wages'. The article noted too that the shipping companies had managed to secure the services of fifty men from Dundee, and sixty from Tilbury, as well as a number of others from Peterhead, Paisley, Barrhead and the surrounding districts, to replace the striking dockers.[34]

[31] Ibid., evidence, Reaburn, Q.13,417.
[32] Letter by John Burns *Glasgow Herald*, 18 Feb. 1889.
[33] *North British Daily Mail*, 13 Jun. 1889.
[34] Ibid.

Upon discovering they were breaking a strike, however, the Dundee men went back with members of the NUDL accompanying them. The NUDL representative then explained the reasons for the strike to the Dundee dockers. The following day it was reported that the men from Dundee were 'displaying great enthusiasm' by joining the NUDL in great numbers.(150 had joined in the last twenty-four hours alone).[35] Dundee then joined the Glasgow dockers in their strike action and it was reported that Derry, Greenock, Leith, Aberdeen and Liverpool were also on strike, and were later joined by Grangemouth and Burntisland. The NUDL went on to set up branches in all these ports.[36] Throughout the period of dispute other bodies of workers too took sympathetic action. McHugh singled out Glasgow carters for the assistance in 'bringing out the Dundee men' and making them aware that they were brought to Glasgow 'by false pretence and falsehood'.[37] A donation was sent by dockers at Derry to help 'board men on strike at Glasgow', despite the fact they themselves were on strike. The Seamen's Union also donated £500 to the NUDL strike fund, and later there was to be a donation of £450 from the dockers of Cardiff.[38]

With the continued support of Glasgow Trades Council, the degree of solidarity that was manifest at Glasgow at this time was significant. But it was also clear, as reported by the *North British Daily Mail*, that the shipowners from the start had shown 'little inclination to yield' and were making 'strenuous efforts to keep the docks operating'. It was reported in the press that the stevedores had in fact conceded the wage rise to the dockers, but it was the shipowners who were resisting the rise and they had persuaded the stevedores to stand with them.[39] At that point the strike was reported as being 'generally very orderly', despite the mass introduction of blacklegs. However, this was not to last for long. The attack on Smith Park, as noted above, was widely reported in the Glasgow press, as were several attacks on the police, not to mention the strike-breakers themselves, and the frequency and severity of such incidents increased as the dispute wore on.[40]

By the middle of June, Edward McHugh argued that activities surrounding the strike were now being misrepresented. He was principally targeting the newspapers 'who were disseminating propaganda around the city of Glasgow'. McHugh gave one example to illustrate this point. He noted that a woman had arrived at the NUDL offices looking for her husband who, she stated, 'left the house nearly a fortnight before'. She came to the NUDL because she had read reports in the press that imported labour had been mistreated and even kept against their will. This was typical, argued McHugh, of the way the reporting of the strike had 'enlightened the public mind'.[41] One case was said to have involved a man who was 'captured, taken to some dingy rooms and tied up with others' and then 'threatened, beaten and

---

[35] Ibid., 14 Jun. 1889.
[36] Ibid., various reports throughout Jun. and early Jul.
[37] Ibid., 13 Jun.
[38] Ibid., 27 Jun.
[39] Ibid., 14 Jun.
[40] Ibid., 18 Jun.
[41] Ibid., 17 Jun.

intimidated'. This self-publicised victim reported that he saw men from all over Britain during his incarceration, and that he had recognised the secretary of the NUDL, Edward McHugh, because 'he had seen him spouting in the square [George Square] of . . . Home Rule or Land Restoration'.[42]

As the strike progressed the case for the employers seemed to be gaining favour with the media, and their thoughts on the dispute were being regularly reported. The shipowners also sent letters to the Home Secretary complaining of the 'inflammatory speeches' made in support of the dockers by Keir Hardie, for example.[43] But by the end of June it was being predicted that the dockers would not last much longer and that the shipowners were pursuing every means available to them to keep the port working, although at that time it was still estimated that around 3,000 dockers were on strike. Despite the reports that suggested the Glasgow men were weakening, the strike was to continue for some time to come. By 1 July both the seamen and the dockers found renewed strength and it was asserted that as far as Glasgow was concerned the strike was 'the greatest of this generation', and that the cost to the shipowners had been unparalleled, estimated at around £250,000.[44]

The violence also continued to intensify, but it was not always the blacklegs who were the victims. One report noted that sixty blacklegs left their depot accommodation, armed with 'knives, pieces of iron and sticks' and attacked eight harbour labourers acting as pickets. The men reported that they would have been 'done for' had it not been for the actions of the police.[45] By 6 July, however, the strike was nearing an end and the employers were managing to bring in sufficient imported labour to satisfy their needs, despite McHugh's claim that it took thirty scabs to do the work of ten NUDL men (which was to create the logic behind the strategy of 'Ca'canny'). Men were beginning to return to work at Glasgow, but around 2,000 were still on strike.[46] But after 6 July the strike barely received more than a passing reference. To all intents and purposes the dispute was over. The employers had won this particular battle, in so far as the men returned to the old rate of pay, but the war was far from over. Indeed, in many respects this dispute can be seen as a dress rehearsal for what was to occur over the next two years or so.

*Dispute and Conflict, 1890 to 1892: The NUDL and the Old Society*

The strikes that took place between 1890 and 1892 and the role of the GHLU in those strikes have already been discussed in the preceding chapters and need not be repeated here. However, some points require further consideration. For example, it would seem that much of the information that the Webbs had on the actions of the GHLU was drawn from reports of the TUC Conference, which took place at Glasgow in 1892. On the face of it the GHLU were accused of

[42] Ibid., 21 Jun.
[43] Ibid., 19 Jun.
[44] Ibid., 1 Jul.
[45] Ibid., 2 Jul.
[46] Ibid., 4 Jul., 5 Jul. and 6 Jul.

blacklegging. Congress accepted this and their expulsion was thereafter a foregone conclusion. But this oversimplifies the case. Moreover, the decision to expel the GHLU did have other ramifications which the Webbs failed to recognise: mainly, that the GHLU was reconstituted, sometime earlier between the late 1880s and the early 1890s, from its previous disintegrated and moribund state. Indeed, it may well have been the case that the employers themselves were behind the moves to resuscitate the GHLU. In this manner the GHLU could be used as a bulwark against the growing and solidifying power of the NUDL, while also acting as a force which could help to undermine the leadership of the union at Glasgow.

The actions of the GHLU as strike-breakers have been well documented thus far, but their expulsion was not straightforward as it might seem. Indeed, the joint forces of the seamen and the NUDL mounted a formidable campaign in order to bring the matter to the attention of Congress in the first place. Despite several attempts by Havelock Wilson and Edward McHugh to raise the matter from the floor of Congress, and in spite of McHugh's withdrawal from the Congress over the issue, the GHLU delegation remained at the conference for several days.[47] Moreover, over those first days of conference there was a considerable amount of literature disseminated around Congress which stated unequivocally that the GHLU were, amongst other things, 'the shipowners' paid agents sitting and voting' at Congress. And worst still, that the Standing Orders Committee knew of the actions of this 'blackleg union', and that they were clearly guilty of 'prostituting the principles of trade unionism'.[48] It was only under some considerable duress that a resolution was eventually pushed through condemning the role of the GHLU as strike-breakers and their partnership with the Shipping Federation. It was stated that the problem first arose when the Federation introduced what became known as the 'blackleg ticket' sometime in 1891. For the privilege of securing this ticket workers were charged one shilling.[49] The NASFU objected to the introduction of the ticket, which meant that workers were in effect part of an employers union for without the ticket they would not be employed. Later the seamen secured the sympathy of the NUDL in attempting to fight the introduction of the ticket. It was stressed that the members of the GHLU then took the places of the NUDL members who had come out in sympathy with the seamen, and that the GHLU 'had been blacklegging ever since'. They also took the place of strikers at Dublin and were aided in this endeavour by Mr G. Hunter, 'the man who took the credit of being the champion union smasher of the world'.[50] McHugh then spoke on the matter stating that he had proof of the

---

[47] TUC *Annual Report*, Glasgow, 1892, 4th Day of Congress, 8 Sep., pp. 49–50.

[48] Ibid., 5th Day, 9 Sep., p. 64.

[49] L. H. Powell, *The Shipping Federation 1890–1950* (1950), p. 7; Powell makes no mention of any charge for the ticket, but states that it came out early in 1891 and pledged the holder to carry out his 'agreement . . . whether the remainder of the crew were union or non-union'. It was simply a safeguard, states Powell, 'against interference' and not an attempt to 'force wages down'.

[50] Collison, *Apostle of Free Labour*, pp. 267–7; for reference to a Mr Hunter, close friend and colleague of Collison, and a leading activist in the Free Labour Association; see also Kenefick, *Ardrossan*, pp. 10–14.

GHLU's role as strike-breakers. Once he had presented this evidence he argued that Congress would have no option but to:

> purge themselves of the abomination of a scab element in their midst [men] who had systematically engaged in the business of scabbing, not only in Glasgow, but wherever there was a struggle for the emancipation of labour.

He also noted the testimony confirming the GHLUs' strike-breaking role as presented to the Royal Commission which supported the facts as they had been presented to Congress.

The President then asked if a delegate of the GHLU wished to address Congress on the matter, to which the GHLU's leading spokesman, Captain Glen, responded, somewhat enigmatically, that this was neither the time nor the place and that he would make his reply 'as a practical dock labourer' when the time was right. After a vote it was finally decided by a large majority to expel the GHLU. Amidst the applause it was noted that Captain Glen 'took off his hat to Congress' and left the hall.[51] Ostensibly, the matter was over, but it is not clear why the GHLU sent a delegation that year, as they had not done so for some considerable time. It could be that their presence was only ever intended to cause disruption. However, they may have attended purely on the basis that the Congress was being held in Glasgow. Thereafter, they attended only one more Congress, in 1894, and there seems to have been little concern shown regarding their presence at the Norwich venue.[52]

At the TUC at Belfast in 1893 the question of expulsions was once again on the agenda, but this time it concerned McHugh himself when he was expelled on the fourth day of Congress. He was accused and found guilty of not being a *bona fide* delegate, in so far as he was not a docker. It had been brought to the attention of the Standing Orders Committee (although there is no indication who raised the matter) that McHugh was an indentured compositor and had only served for one month as a docker some thirty years before. Despite arguments to the effect that Congress had no power to determine the credentials of a delegate, particularly as a delegate owed his position to the votes of the dockers themselves, McHugh was expelled.

He was then allowed to address Congress, stating that he accepted the decision with the 'utmost respect for that body'. However, McHugh argued that had it not been for his part in the 'purging of a scab union at Glasgow' the previous year, these actions would never have been raised against him. Moreover, he noted that the decision would give considerable 'satisfaction to the shipowners and the sweating stevedores in the United Kingdom'.[53] The following day the decision was over-turned, after a resolution had been forced through by Havelock Wilson, and McHugh resumed his role as delegate.[54] But Belfast had proved a problematic Congress for McHugh. Not only had his credentials as an NUDL delegate to the TUC been questioned, but also the event acted to undermine his position as leader

---

[51] TUC *Annual Report*, Glasgow, 1892, pp. 65–6.
[52] TUC *Annual Report*, Bristol, 1894, lists 1 delegate representing 650 members.
[53] TUC *Annual Report*, Belfast 1893, 4th Day of Congress, 8 Sep., pp. 60–3.
[54] Ibid., 5th Day, 9 Sep., p. 7.

of the NUDL. Indeed, it may have been more by design than by accident that McHugh and McGhee were to resign from the NUDL some three months later (McGhee had no *locus standi* in that he too was not a 'docker proper').[55]

It has been suggested that the resignations were connected with McHugh and McGhee's 'lack of the finer technicalities of dock work'. The source also recognises that a degree of 'treacherous intrigue' was used against both men. Put simply, it was being argued that only 'a practical docker' could legitimately lead and represent a dockers' union. This was how the original complaint was phrased in the accusations levelled at McHugh at the Belfast Congress, that in relation to dockwork he was not 'a practical workman'.[56] Ironically, it would seem that Captain Glen's words, made during the previous year's Congress, had ultimately been fulfilled, when he stated he would reply to the accusations levelled against his union, by McHugh, as 'a practical dock labourer' when the time was right for him to do so. Whatever the merits or demerits of this line of argument, it is clear that McHugh's leadership of the NUDL had been brought into question. It would not be difficult to imagine that the Shipping Federation played some subterranean role in all this, although no evidence has been found to substantiate such an assumption. Whatever the explanation, Captain Glen's somewhat portentous remark was ultimately made good, and when he tipped his hat before leaving the Glasgow Congress the gesture was perhaps aimed at McHugh more than any other.

Whatever the reasons for the demise in the popularity of both McGhee and McHugh, there is no denying the important role they played in the early years of the NUDL's existence. Nor can it be overlooked that others also played a considerable part in the formation of the NUDL in the first instance. The NASFU and Glasgow Trades Council had a significant role to play, as had Irishmen Hugh Johnston and James Gray. The NUDL, in partnership with the NASFU, fought against the shipowners for both recognition and pay increases, and throughout the period 1889–93 they waged a formidable campaign against the employers at Glasgow. But it was a campaign that in the end produced more failures than victories. Yet despite this, significant levels of solidarity and militancy were shown by the rank and file. This attitude in turn prompted a campaign of counter-attack on the part of the Clydeside employers, often in league with the Shipping Federation, which resulted in periods of frustration and in turn severely weakened the NUDL membership base.

There was to be no official recognition of the NUDL's position in Glasgow, at least in terms of any formulated joint procedural agreement with the larger shipowners. This was not to occur to any extent until after the transport strike of 1911. However, from the mere fact that the NUDL survived in Glasgow it can be assumed that its continued existence needed the tacit recognition of at least some employers, most likely the smaller stevedore companies working on the coastal

---

[55] Taplin, *Dockers' Union*, p. 47. Taplin suggests the reasons behind the departure of both Edward McHugh and Richard McGhee still 'remain obscure', but he makes no reference to any of the events that were to unfold at the 1892 or 1893 TUC Conferences.
[56] TUC *Annual Report*, Belfast, 1893, 7 Sep., p. 60.

trades.[57] There is no doubt that with McHugh's resignation and James Sexton's elevation to the leadership by December 1893 there came a significant seachange in the strategy and the tactics of the NUDL. The strategy developed by Sexton acted to lessen tensions between the employers and the union. It was this strategy, argues Taplin, that helped to maintain the NUDL's presence in various British ports until the amalgamation with the Transport and General Workers' Union in 1922. Thus the change in direction initiated by Sexton during this period arguably aided the union's chances of survival. Ironically, however, while Sexton's role in maintaining the NUDL's presence cannot be denied, his attitude regarding the wishes of the rank-and-file on Clydeside was to prove one of the main reasons for the eventual extinction of the NUDL as the dockers' union at Glasgow and on Clydeside.

### Survival and Consolidation – 1893 to 1900

The 1890s were problematic years for the NUDL. When the decade began it had an estimated membership of 4,000, but by 1892 membership had fallen dramatically by over 50% to 1,885.[58] By 1895, according to the breakdown of individual NUDL branch membership to the TUC for that year (this was done only for this one year during the entire 1890s), the Glasgow branches had fallen further to around 1,400.[59] By the late 1890s numbers were on the rise again, and when the NUDL affiliated with the newly formed Scottish Trades Union Congress in 1897 they registered a membership of 2,850.[60] However, after 1897 the NUDL was only ever represented at the STUC by delegates from east-coast branches of the union, mainly Aberdeen and Bo'ness, and this continued to be the case up until 1912. Glasgow and Clydeside had no representation at all, and it is not clear why Glasgow's NUDL branches ceased to send representation to the STUC after the 1897 inaugural conference.[61] It may well be that members of these branches were more concerned with local Clydeside issues, hence their continued affiliation to Glasgow Trades Council, or perhaps were too involved in maintaining their own existence at Glasgow.

The NUDL's determination to amalgamate with the GHLU could have been an indication that they were locked in a struggle for survival at this time. The inclusion of the 670 members of the GHLU in 1899 would have significantly expanded their membership and their overall authority within the whole dock labour force at

[57] Wilson, The Dockers, p. 79.

[58] Glasgow Trades Council Annual Report, 1889–1890, p. 8; for 1892 figures see Taplin, Dockers' Unions, Appendix, p. 169.

[59] TUC Annual Report, 1895, calculated from TUC Affiliated Trade Unions membership list for the individual branch numbers pertaining to the NUDL in 1895. Glasgow No. 1 Branch had 1,000 members, while Glasgow No. 2 Branch had 400.

[60] Scottish Trades Union Congress Annual Report, 1897, see Affiliation Lists.

[61] After 1912 Glasgow was represented by the newly formed Scottish Union of Dock Labourers (1911). From 1912 onward the SUDL is responsible for the revival of docker unionism on the west coast, while on the east coast the NUDL's influence became confined to the ports of Methil, Burntisland, Grangemouth and Leith, under the Scottish leadership of James O'Connor Kessack. This information is gleaned from STUC Annual Reports, 1897 to 1913, from affiliation and membership lists.

Glasgow.[62] This would have resulted in a combined membership of around 3,500, and therefore by the end of the 1890s the NUDL in Glasgow had almost returned to the 1889 levels. There was certainly involvement on the part of the Glasgow membership in the British Trades Union Congress throughout the 1890s and delegates from Glasgow were represented at Congress on many occasions. At the TUC in Bristol 1898, for example, three out of the NUDLs delegation of six came from Glasgow. One of those delegates was Irishman Charles Kennedy – who was to move to Liverpool in 1900 according to the list of delegates' addresses to the TUC of that year. Indeed, Kennedy had been a leading activist for the NUDL from its formation and would have been a well-respected voice for the Glasgow dockers. After the 1903 Congress, however, most delegates were drawn from the Liverpool area, which could indicate that the Glasgow membership ceased to be interested in the affairs of the NUDL nationally, or perhaps they believed that the union's Liverpool executive was now operating against the interests of Glasgow. To all intents and purposes the NUDL was now seen as a Liverpool union.

It is true that the NUDL was never intended to remain a strictly Clyde-based union. As its title suggests, and as the Webbs argued, it was intended to be a truly 'national' union. According to Taplin, Hugh Johnston wished to attempt to organise the men of Dublin, Belfast, Derry, Cork and Waterford, and this determination towards the formation of a national union stemmed from the symbiosis that existed between the NUDL and the NASFU.[63] However, as the decade wore on and trade became more depressed, and as the struggles with the employers intensified, the NUDL at Glasgow may have become more concerned with the practical problems of survival in their own backyard (particularly in light of the departure of both McHugh and McGhee in 1893). Nevertheless, the pact with the NASFU was to remain an important one in the minds of dock unionists at Glasgow, and their early successes were never forgotten. Indeed, it was to become written into their folk lore that in September 1889, when NUDL officials met with a delegation of Glasgow port employers, the dockers were informed by the employers 'that had it not been for the pact [with the seamen] they would not have secured any advance on their wages' in the dispute of that year.[64] It is possible that memories such as these would later evoke similar responses towards a resurgence of trade unionism among the dock labour force in the following decade, as they had done in the preamble to the formation of the NUDL in February 1889 when once again the Glasgow's dockers would be Dan O'Connels and Henry Grattans.

The relationship between the NUDL and Glasgow Trades Council was also always important and contrasted significantly with that forged between the NUDL and the Liverpool Trades Council. The NUDL were only members of the Liverpool Trades Council for one year in 1893. Thereafter, they were to resign from the Council and did not rejoin again until 1906.[65] It would seem that the Trades Council in

[62] Membership figure for the GHLU is from the STUC affiliates and membership list in the *Annual Report*, 1899.
[63] Taplin, *Dockers' Union*, p. 29.
[64] Glasgow Trades Council Meeting, 11 Sep. 1889.
[65] Taplin, *Dockers' Union*, p. 54.

Liverpool did not appreciate the influence of those of the NUDL leadership who came from outside Liverpool. The Glasgow Trades Council was without doubt a very different organisation in that they were unequivocal in their support of the early efforts of both the Seamen and Dockers' Unions.[66] However, and as posited by Joan Smith and Tom Gallagher, this may have been due more to Glasgow's 'municipal socialist traditions' and to the fact that Liverpool was a more religiously divided city than Glasgow. Glasgow's dock labour force was not a 'distinct and competing' body based on Protestant and Catholic division, as was the case at Liverpool (religious discrimination against Catholics was a great cause for concern at Liverpool, and the root of many disputes). Therefore, as Hugh Paterson rightly argued, 'discrimination against Catholics was not a major complaint in Glasgow'.[67]

It may be this very factor which helps to explain why the two organisations of dockers at Glasgow finally came together. Both were made up mostly of Irish Catholics and could therefore find racial and ethnic ties, which helped unite them. Moreover, the other biggest group of workers within the Glasgow dock labour force was the Scottish Highlanders, and here too there were common bonds, not least the popular and political goal of Land Reform. Whatever the reason for the amalgamation of the NUDL and the GHLU it would seem that by the turn of the century the Glasgow dockers had regained some of the influence they had lost as a group in the early part of the 1890s. With a membership of around 3,500 the NUDL at Glasgow looked to be in reasonably good shape.

## Decline and Disintegration, 1900 to 1910

During the first decade of the twentieth century the fortunes of the NUDL in Glasgow changed considerably. Indeed, it would seem that in Scotland generally they were finding it difficult to maintain their position and more difficult still to form new branches. Aberdeen had halted an employer campaign to convert it to a 'free labour' port because of the action of Jim Larkin after 1906, but this had come too late for Dundee which had become a free labour port in 1904.[68] By 1910 Glasgow was lost and in 1911 the NUDL's influence in Scotland was to rest entirely with the east-coast ports of Aberdeen and Bo'ness (and even Bo'ness was to switch to the SUDL shortly after its formation in 1911). When James Sexton's correspondence to the Glasgow Trades Council was read in February of 1911, notifying Council of the closure of the Glasgow branch of the NUDL, he was merely rubber stamping a process which had already reached a climax in the closing months of the previous year.[69] By then it was finally recognised that the NUDL had no future in Glasgow. The dock labour force itself had decided so.

In November 1910, for example, it was widely reported in various quarters that the membership of the NUDL in Glasgow were leaving the union in large numbers

---

[66] Glasgow Trades Council, *Annual Report*, 1889–90, pp. 9–10.
[67] Paterson, 'Seamen on the Clyde', p. 173.
[68] *RC on Poor Laws*, 1910, evidence, John Malloch, Clerk to the Harbour Trustees of Dundee, pp. 64–7.
[69] Glasgow Trades Council Minutes, 15 Feb. 1911.

because they had been denied official sanction to strike by the union's executive body in Liverpool. The immediate result of this was the temporary resignation of the then Scottish organiser of the NUDL, James O'Connor Kessack.[70] After being persuaded to rescind his resignation O'Connor Kessack returned to Glasgow in order to persuade the Glasgow men to re-join the union. But within a month of his return he had 'retired' from the Trades Council even after having secured an agreement from them that the council would again assist in bringing the dockers back to trade unionism.[71] He remained the Scottish organiser for the NUDL until he joined the Armed Forces on the outbreak of war, but was to play no more part in the reorganising of Clydeside's dock labour force. However, he was to have some considerable success along the east coast.[72]

Why then did the NUDL fail at Glasgow? There is no denying that there were real problems between the Glasgow rank and file and the Liverpool executive of the NUDL by 1910. But did these troubles have a far longer history than the evidence relating to the period 1908–10 suggests? We know that Sexton's approach to industrial relations was essentially one of containment. Relations with the employers were to be based more on conciliation and joint negotiation and less on militancy and direct action. This was a major departure from the strategy adopted and followed religiously by the previous leadership. Between 1893 and 1905 Sexton's conciliatory approach was perhaps necessary in order to ensure the NUDLs continued presence along significant portions of the British waterfront. However, after 1905 Sexton himself seemed to detect a clear change in attitude, noting that the docker 'seemed to thrive on strikes and lock-outs'.[73] Jim Larkin went on to make some spectacular advances for the union between 1906 and 1908 and increased the membership of the NUDL by around six thousand, the great majority of whom were in Ireland. But while successful, Sexton disapproved of Larkin's methods and his advocacy of direct militant action, which more often than not was accompanied by a considerable degree of violence and lawlessness.[74] This brought the two men into conflict, even while it was clear that direct militant action was a strategy that carried the general approval of the rank and file.

Larkin's successes in Scotland were moderate by comparison to those achieved elsewhere, but he did single-handedly reorganise Aberdeen, despite considerable opposition from the Free Labour Association there, and in 1907 he succeeded in forming a new branch of the NUDL at Govan (although it did not remain in

---

[70] Ibid., 9 Nov. 1910.
[71] Ibid., 21 Dec. 1910, notification of James O'Connor Kessack's retirement, 25 Jan. 1911.
[72] STUC *Annual Reports*; see affiliation lists for 1909 to 1914. O'Connor Kessack brought the membership of the NUDL on the east coast to over 3,500 by May 1914, from a level of around 500 in 1909, and increased the number of branches from 3 (Glasgow, Aberdeen and Bo'ness) to 8, to include Methil, Burntisland, Grangemouth, Leith and Alloa.
[73] Taplin, *Dockers' Union*, p. 74.
[74] Ibid., pp. 71–4. Larkin was to form branches of dockers at Dublin, Cork and Belfast. By 1908 this new membership numbered around 6,000 in total. He also saw success elsewhere. In Preston the NUDL began to operate the port as a closed shop and in Belfast Larkin brought together Protestant and Catholic in 2 branches, which accounted for a membership of 3,000. While Sexton applauded such achievements, he condemned the methods Larkin advocated and the considerable violence which followed.

existence for long). Larkin also spent six months attempting to re-form the branch at Glasgow, where he overcame 'considerable employer opposition' in order to set up some dialogue between the employers and Sexton. However, according to Larkin's biographer, these initiatives achieved little and they failed to solve any of the long-term problems associated with dock work at Glasgow. It is argued that Larkin felt many of the problems he encountered at Glasgow, and elsewhere, were partly due to the attitude of Sexton himself. Put simply, Sexton would not back up talks with even the threat of strike action.[75]

Larkin also faced considerable employer hostility in Glasgow, mostly in the form of the Shipping Federation of which he was to report 'nearly every shipowner was a member'.[76] However, he was having some success with the smaller shipowners and stevedores at the port. This was a productive strategy in so far as the smaller employer was often more 'amenable to trade union pressure' and the first to break the employers' 'concerted line of defence' (it was a strategy he was to employ to great effect later in Ireland).[77] In Glasgow this group of employers may have felt the need, if only occasionally, to enter into negotiations with the NUDL, which would have given the union some credibility in the eyes of the ordinary docker. This clearly did not constitute full recognition, but it may in part explain the continued existence of the NUDL at the port. It was at least a starting point.

By the end of 1908, however, Larkin was suspended from the NUDL after refusing to return to Aberdeen. By August of the following year he was to be arrested, charged and jailed for conspiracy to defraud the NUDL. These charges were alleged to have been concocted by the authorities in Ireland, although Sexton himself gave evidence for the prosecution at the trial in June 1910.[78] For W. P. Ryan, 'it was a story that seemed scarcely credible'.[79] And a contemporary of Larkin, Frank Pearce, in 1911, put his thoughts on these events clearly and concisely in a pamphlet entitled, *James Larkin, a Labour Leader and an Honest Man*. Pearce argued that Sexton had 'conspired with the employers' to engineer the prosecution of Larkin in 1909. Indeed, Sexton seemed to become embroiled in litigation at this time and later brought libel charges against Pearce for the accusations he made in that publication. Larkin was to give evidence for the defence, but Sexton still won his case and was awarded damages of £200.[80] It may well be the case that Sexton was falsely accused, but it can equally be argued that others felt that Larkin had been falsely accused and convicted, and that Sexton had played a role in that process.[81]

The affair left a bitter legacy, which perhaps worked against the initiatives of James O'Connor Kessack, particularly at Glasgow, after he assumed the role of Scottish

---

[75] Emmet Larkin, *James Larkin*, pp. 18–19.

[76] Ibid., pp. 18–19.

[77] A. Boyd, *The Rise of the Irish Trade Unions* (Dublin, 1972), p. 79.

[78] Taplin, *Dockers' Union*, p. 85.

[79] Ryan, *The Irish Labor Movement*, pp. 209–15.

[80] Taplin, *Dockers' Union*, p. 75.

[81] The case against Larkin seems to have had some legitimacy, but many believed that Larkin had got himself into a 'muddle rather than anything illegal' over finances concerning the Cork Branch of the NUDL. Indeed, Sexton strenuously argued the Cork Branch had never come into existence; see Boyd, *Irish Trade Unions*, pp. 85–6.

Organiser of the NUDL in 1909, in the wake of Larkin's dismissal. Indeed, it must have been strange for O'Connor Kessack to attend Glasgow Trades Council meetings and hear his predecessor being defended and, by implication, the role of his union impugned, as the following resolution, passed unanimously in June 1910, indicates:

> That this Council denounces the methods which have taken place to attempt the crushing of Mr Jim Larkin, declares its belief in his honesty and integrity and pledges itself to use its influence to see the scandalous sentence passed on him revoked.[82]

It was a petition raised by Dublin Trades Council that succeeded in securing Larkin's release on 1 October 1910 – after serving only three months of a twelve-month sentence.[83] Nevertheless, it would seem that Glasgow Trades Council had taken Larkin to their hearts, and in his defence suggested that they did not approve of the man who had helped bring about the charges in the first instance – Sexton – regardless of any argument that would exonerate him from any complicity in 'engineering' them.

The differences between Sexton and Larkin may help to explain the deepening gulf that was developing between Sexton, the Liverpool executive and the needs and wants, indeed the desires, of the ordinary docker at Glasgow. By the latter half of 1910 there could have been a resolution to these problems, after a campaign by the Scottish executive of the NUDL to draft new regulations covering working conditions at the port of Glasgow. It was a campaign inspired by O'Connor Kessack and was wholeheartedly supported by the men. Indeed, they had already struck in support of the new proposals on 19 November 1910,[84] at a time when trade on Clydeside was beginning to improve considerably.[85] Many clearly felt that the time was right to reclaim some ground lost after almost a decade of virtual depression.[86] But proposals for follow-up strikes were not given approval by Sexton and the Liverpool executive. It was a decision which may ultimately have caused the final break between the Glasgow rank and file and Liverpool. It was after this period that the men began to leave the NUDL in great numbers, arguing that there was no point in remaining members.

Eric Taplin suggests that Glasgow may have been 'too large a port' and its labour force unwilling to be a 'mere branch of an English Union' (not an uncommon position in relation to Scottish branches of trade unions at this time).[87] But it would seem more

---

[82] Glasgow Trades Council Minutes, 29 Jun. 1910.

[83] Boyd, *Irish Trade Unions*, p. 79.

[84] Glasgow Trades Council Minutes, 21 Dec. 1910, as reported by O'Connor Kessack to the meeting.

[85] Board of Labour *Gazette* Monthly Reports, Feb. to Dec. 1910. The Feb. report stated that employment was 'quite good' (pp. 59–60), it remained 'moderate' until Jul. when it 'improved' (p. 242), but by Aug. 'employment was slack'(p. 279). From Sep. of that year until Jan. 1911 there was a general improvement and employment at the harbour thereafter was described as 'moderate' (see p. 315 for Sep., p. 351 for Oct., p. 387 for Nov., p. 422 for Dec. 1910, and p. 26 for Jan. 1911.).

[86] At the Glasgow Trades Council, Annual Meeting for 1910–11, it was argued similarly: 'If the improvement in trade is likely to continue it would offer the organised workers of the country time to recover what they had lost during the years of depression'.

[87] Taplin, *Dockers' Union*, p. 78.

likely that it was the attitude of Sexton that was the main stumbling block with the dockers at Glasgow and this was the main reason that they were leaving the NUDL *en masse*. Indeed, this seems to be borne out by later events at Glasgow at the time of the dockers' transference to the TGWU in 1923. The *Glasgow Herald* reported in that year that the dockers of Glasgow were as unhappy about joining the TGWU for reasons similar to their rejection of the NUDL in 1910. Mr Bernard Havilan, the last President of the then recently dissolved Scottish Union of Dock Labourers, summed up the dockers' feeling by offering a potted history of organised dock unionism at the port of Glasgow. Essentially, the Glasgow dockers believed that after the NUDL moved its headquarters to Liverpool in 1891, the wishes of the Glasgow members were being ignored, they were not allowed to manage their own affairs, and because of this the membership continued to drop to the point where numbers were so low that in 1910 the NUDL went out of existence. Havilan was wrong to suggest that the membership of the NUDL at Glasgow continued to fall after 1891. Numbers did fall at that time, but the real decline in only took place from around 1900 onwards. However, he would seem to be correct in arguing that Glasgow's dockers wanted to manage their own affairs, and this meant having their own headquarters in Scotland and more parti-cularly in Glasgow.[88] In this sense, Taplin's analysis has considerable validity, and it is a theme which again becomes important when the Glasgow dockers began to organise their campaign to secede from the TGWU by the early 1930s.

## Economics of Decline

It can be seen therefore that there had been rank-and-file dissatisfaction at Glasgow for some considerable time before the demise of the NUDL in 1910. However, could this have been exacerbated by the depressed economic conditions that prevailed during this time? It was arguably no accident that the main phase of New Unionism at the port of Glasgow, as elsewhere in Britain, coincided with a general prosperity in trade that was experienced at that time, and which helped to create the conditions which in turn saw the general advance in the cause of unskilled trade unionism. Could it be similarly argued that trade depression could therefore reverse this process? The correspondent of the Board of Trade in 1890 seems to suggest that this was a distinct possibility, because he was not entirely convinced 'that these unions now formed for fighting purposes only will be able to survive the ordeal of bad trade and an overcrowded labour market'. This, he concluded, 'remains to be seen'.[89]

The previous section has shown that some waterfront unions did not survive the depression which followed and those that did were severely weakened. Table 9.1 offers some indication as to why this may have been the case. With high levels of unemployment employers did not need to negotiate with trade unions, while at the same time unemployment kept in check the natural impulses of the docker to take direct industrial action. This was indicative of the problems caused by depression,

---

[88] *Glasgow Herald*, 18 Aug. 1923.
[89] *Report on Strikes and Lockouts for 1889* ( *PP*, 1891, lxxviii, C 6176), pp. 60–1.

and this may be further illustrated by investigating both the strike rates and the unemployment rates, for the transport industry as a whole, for the period before 1889 through to 1913. Clearly, during the period 1901–10 the total level of strike activity in the transport industry dropped to 177 strikes from a level of 409 recorded disputes in the previous decade, which was a fall in strike activity of 57%. Only in 1907, when twenty-seven disputes are recorded, does the level of strike activity exceed the lowest level of twenty-two strikes (recorded for 1898) during the previous decade.

Table 9.1: *Numbers of Strikes, Number on Strike in the Transport Industry and the Rate of Unemployment in Britain 1888 to 1913.*

| Year | Annual Number of Strikes | Annual Number of Strikers | Unemployment Rate |
|------|------|------|------|
| 1888 | 9 | 2,000 | 5.7 |
| 1889 | 184 | 144,000 | 2.4 |
| 1890 | 163 | 72,000 | 2.4 |
| 1891 | 61 | 33,000 | 4.1 |
| 1892 | 38 | 13,000 | 7.3 |
| 1893 | 43 | 15,000 | 8.7 |
| 1894 | 48 | 12,000 | 8.0 |
| 1895 | 27 | 2,000 | 6.7 |
| 1896 | 25 | 3,000 | 3.8 |
| 1897 | 48 | 12,000 | 3.8 |
| 1898 | 22 | 3,000 | 3.3 |
| 1899 | 47 | 12,000 | 2.3 |
| 1900 | 50 | 20,000 | 2.9 |
| 1901 | 20 | 3,000 | 3.8 |
| 1902 | 14 | 1,000 | 4.7 |
| 1903 | 15 | 2,000 | 5.5 |
| 1904 | 10 | 2,000 | 7.0 |
| 1905 | 11 | 2,000 | 5.8 |
| 1906 | 19 | 2,000 | 4.2 |
| 1907 | 29 | 8,000 | 4.3 |
| 1908 | 21 | 4,000 | 9.1 |
| 1909 | 19 | 4,000 | 9.0 |
| 1910 | 19 | 19,000 | 5.5 |
| 1911 | 99 | 439,000 | 3.5 |
| 1912 | 73 | 143,000 | 3.7 |
| 1913 | 123 | 77,000 | 3.6 |

**Source:** derived from J. E. Cronin, *Industrial Conflict in Modern Britain*, Appendix B, Tables B1, B2 and B8.

There is also a major difference between the numbers on strike between the two decades. The total number of workers on strike dropped from 125,000 to 47,000, a fall of around 62%. From this standpoint it can be argued that the period 1901–10 proved a difficult one for the labour force and for organised labour in particular. Indeed, when the levels of strike activity for these two decades are compared to the periods of unrest that occurred before and after, a much clearer picture of strike activity across the period as a whole begins to take shape, as summarised in the following table.

Table 9.2: *Total Number of Strikes and Number on Strike in the Transport Industry, and Average Rate of Unemployment, for 1888–90, 1891–1900, 1901–10, and 1911–13.*

| Period | No. of Strikes | No. of Strikers | Ave/unemployment* |
|---|---|---|---|
| 1888–90 | 356 | 236,000 | 3.43 |
| 1891–1900 | 409 | 125,000 | 5.09 |
| 1901–10 | 177 | 47,000 | 5.89 |
| 1911–13 | 295 | 659,000 | 3.50 |

*Average national unemployment levels are indicated here. The numbers for those unemployed on the docks were never known; only estimates were made before 1914. The national figures are offered to give some illustration of unemployment trends over this period.

**Source:** James Cronin. *Industrial Conflict in Modern Britain*, calculated from tables B1, B2 & B3, *Appendix B.*

It can be seen that in unemployment terms there are significant differences too. Overall, the general experience after 1900 was much worse than what went before. For example, despite the rising rate of unemployment between 1891 and 1895 strike activity still remained relatively high. Moreover, strikes at this time were not wholly without some success and this tendency continued through to the turn of the century. In 1896 two strikes in Dundee and one in Aberdeen were described as 'successful' by a correspondent of the Board of Trade.[90] In 1898 one of two strikes to take place in Aberdeen was reported as successful.[91] In Glasgow, in May 1899 some 1,200 dockers working for three firms struck for a period of twenty-one days for improved wages and conditions. Only the men of one firm, however, were successful in their demands. This example nevertheless illustrates that workers were strong enough to attempt to take strike action in sufficient numbers, and were also able to sustain such action over a considerable period of time.[92]

The slump of the early 1890s did not affect the dock labourers in Glasgow to the same degree as it did labourers in other industries.[93] But the slumps of 1904–5 and 1908–10 were a different matter. Unemployment nationally was to rise from 3.8% in

[90] *Report on Strikes and Lockouts for 1896* ( *PP*, 1897, lxxxiv, C 8643).
[91] *Report on Strikes and Lockouts for 1898* (*PP*, 1899, xcii, C 9437).
[92] *Report on Strikes and Lockouts for 1899* (*PP*, 1900, lxviii, Cd 316).
[93] *Report on Relief of the Able-bodied*, 1893–94, pp. 11–12.

1901 to reach 7% by 1904, but between 1908 and 1909 this increased to levels of 9% and more. Even by 1910, when the economy had made a significant recovery, the unemployment rate nationally was still at a level of 5.5%. According to Treble, however, the levels of unemployment on Clydeside were well above national rates. Moreover, and in terms of the severity of depression, the result was an increased and prolonged period of unemployment, and this was accompanied by a fall of around 10% in real wages for those lucky enough to find work. The problems on Clydeside, therefore, were particularly acute and touched every trade.[94]

How then did these cyclical downturns in economic activity affect the dock labour force on Clydeside? Treble argues that the period 1907–10 was a particularly difficult one, and, citing the *Glasgow Herald*, he argued that dock labour was experiencing worse conditions at this time than at any time during the previous thirty years. The *Glasgow Herald* also estimated that some 2,000 dockers were idle and that their wages were half their former levels,[95] suggesting increased levels of underemployment also. It was later reported that this situation was made many times worse by the influx 'of other men from other walks of life' into the docks because of 'the dullness in trade'. As a result, the *bona fide* docker, reported the *Glasgow Herald*, was being deprived of what he considered to be his regular work.[96] The employers exploited the situation.[97] Evidence presented to the Royal Commission on the Poor Laws and Relief of Distress, between 1905 and 1909, clearly shows that the employers welcomed new men onto the docks. Colonel Smith Park stated that 'a better selection of steady able bodied men' was to be found among the 'strangers'. The 'strangers', he noted, only usually took work from what he classified as the 'third class of docker' (a rather arbitrary division, which Smith Park himself admitted). The 'strangers' did not, however, take work from the first and second class dockers, and within their ranks 'there was little unemployment'. So while there was some unemployment within the third class, Smith Park felt that this problem largely 'lay in their own hands': because of their 'unsettled habits' and the fact that they rarely 'exerted themselves'. There was no unemployment problem among the other 'two classes of men', who according to the estimates of Gerald Walsh, in 1908, numbered around 5,000 in total.[98]

Evidence submitted by other employers at the port, to the same Royal Commission, however, suggested that about half of the total dock labour force were unemployed. Indeed, Glasgow stevedore McCulloch Graig was to suggest that the situation in the industry at that point was 'chronic'.[99] He also suggested that the number of dockers operating around the port at this time was somewhere between 6,000 and 7,000 (which would mean that the 'third class' group of dockers, noted by

---

[94] J. H. Treble. 'Unemployment in Glasgow 1903 to 1910: Anatomy of a Crisis', *SLHJ*, 25, 1990, p. 12.

[95] Ibid., p. 14: see also the *Glasgow Herald*, 2 Sep. 1908.

[96] *Glasgow Herald*, 10 Mar. 1908.

[97] Bean, 'Employers Associations', p. 366; Bean notes, from a report printed in the *Liverpool Courier* dated 23 Jan. 1891, that the employers considered 'widespread unemployment to be the best card in the pack for keeping labour in its place'.

[98] See Chap. 3 for analysis of Gerald Walsh's investigation of Glasgow, *Report on Dock Labour*, 1908.

[99] *RC on Poor Laws*, 1910, written evidence, Glasgow Stevedore, McCulloch Graig, p. 1,098.

Smith Park, had to number something in the region of 1,000 to 2,000). If this was the case, then the unemployment rate among the dock labour force of Glasgow was somewhere between one third and one half. This would mean that there was perhaps between 2,000 and 3,500 dockers unemployed in Glasgow, at a time when Smith Park denied that unemployment amongst dockers was a problem at all. Moreover, the term under-employment is never mentioned as a problem affecting the dockers at this time – it is merely hinted at.

**Table 9.3:** *Percentage of General or Casual Labour Applying for Relief Work in the Parishes of Govan, Partick and Glasgow Between 1907 and 1913 and the Total Numbers for Glasgow over the same Period.*

| Year | Govan | Partick | Glasgow | Total/Glasgow |
|------|-------|---------|---------|---------------|
| 1907 | 49.84 | 21.86 | 51.43 | 7,906 |
| 1908 | 49.70 | 20.86 | 39.17 | 14,001 |
| 1909 | 34.05 | 10.55 | 34.06 | 6,654 |
| 1910 | 13.75 | 11.92 | 31.92 | 2,423 |
| 1911 | 54.43 | 19.29 | 39.57 | 1,802 |
| 1912 | *n/a | *n/a | *14.98 | 653 |
| 1913 | n/a | n/a | **72.28 | 531 |

*Govan and Partick were incorporated into the City of Glasgow in the Boundary changes of 1912. **Because of the effects of the previous year's boundary changes on all three authorities, the figures for 1913 may be suspect. This would explain the rapid fall in the percentage rate in 1912 and its equally rapid increase in 1913. The total figures for Glasgow are however less problematic.

**Source:** *Reports by the Local Government Board of Scotland*, 1907-13 ( *PP*, 1907, Cd 3830; *PP*, 1908, Cd 4470; *PP*, 1909, Cd 4946; *PP*, 1910, Cd 5409; *PP*, 1911, Cd 5119; *PP*, 1912, Cd 6501, and *PP*, 1913, Cd 7127).

It should be stressed, of course, as Treble argues, that the port transport industry was 'grotesquely overstocked' in any case, and, because of the casual system, would generally experience high levels of underemployment. However, the levels of unemployment estimated above are still quite substantial. Add to this the influx of new men and the easing out of the less able, or less desirable, elements (possibly those who were known committed union members), and the level of distress increases considerably. Table 9.3. above gives some indication of the extent of the problem among the general and casual labouring population of Glasgow between 1907 and 1913. It shows that a great many unskilled men were applying for relief over the early period, which coincided with the depression of 1907–10. In addition of course there were a high numbers of skilled men also seeking work.

It should be recognised, however, that unemployment rates in this case are expressed, or defined, in terms of numbers on relief work. While these figures are as good as any for this period, they may simply reflect the availability of relief work, rather than real levels of unemployment. Finally, it must be borne in mind that it is underemployment, rather than unemployment, that most affects the docker. What was occurring within the dockers' ranks was a greater degree of under-employment, for the available evidence suggests that there was less work to be had around the docks during this period, and that levels of distress, as the *Glasgow Herald* reported at the time, were greater than anything experienced hitherto.

From the evidence presented in this chapter, it clear that it was a combination of factors that helped to weaken trade unionism within the port of Glasgow to the point where it finally collapsed completely by December 1910. Without doubt, Clydeside suffered considerably in the severe economic depressions of 1904–5 and 1908–10. To attempt to maintain a trade union foothold at this time would have been difficult. There would seem little doubt that this situation would have severely curtailed the activities of the NUDL in Glasgow and lessened their chances of maintaining, let alone promoting, trade unionism within the dock labour force. There had been an influx of 'strangers' into the docks during the height of the 1907–10 slump too, and these new men were considered by the employers to be more 'able-bodied'. By definition they would have no connection with dock unionism, and would arguably have expressed little desire to join a union, particularly when unemployment was high and real wages were low. It was in every sense a buyers' market. For those of the 'regular' dock labour force who were union members the whole situation may have forced them to rethink their position. If this was coupled with the general dissatisfaction manifested by Glasgow dockers with the NUDL leadership in Liverpool, then this could explain the rapid decline in the membership of the NUDL at Glasgow by 1910. Indeed, the NUDL had already collapsed along the other west-coast ports before then.

Other ports suffered high unemployment and under-employment levels also, particularly London and Liverpool. Yet the DWRGLU and the NUDL did not fall into decline at these ports. This may offer proof of the severity of the depression on Clydeside when compared to that generally experienced elsewhere. In the final analysis, however, if economic factors are not as important in this equation, other factors must assume greater significance. The tenacity of the Glasgow dockers and their commitment to trade unionism still remained strong, and this is best illustrated in the dockers' response to Glasgow Trades Council's campaign of trade union reorganisation in 1911. Within six short months of the failure of the NUDL in Glasgow, in December 1910, the Scottish Union of Dock Labourers was formed. The Glasgow dockers flocked into its ranks. This clearly manifested their desire for trade unionism, and in time the SUDL would prove that organised dock labour on Clydeside would once again become a real force to be reckoned with.

# CHAPTER TEN

# 'The Best Organised Little Trade Union in Britain': The Scottish Union of Dock Labourers and the Labour Unrest before the Great War

The Scottish Union of Dock Labourers came into existence in mid-July of 1911, just over six months after the dockers of Glasgow had finally left the ranks of the NUDL. The dockers flocked into the ranks of the new union and before the year was out the SUDL had extended its influence along the Clydeside waterfront as far as the ports of Ardrossan and Ayr on the Ayrshire coast. This event in itself would suggest that the dockers of Clydeside, and Glasgow in particular were seriously committed to trade unionism and recognised the need for combination, despite the fact that they had rejected trade unionism beforehand in the form of the NUDL.

This chapter considers the experience of dock unionism in the form of the SUDL in the important years before the outbreak of the First World War. The period from 1914 until the absorption of the SUDL into the Transport and General Workers' Union (TGWU) in January 1923 will be examined briefly in the following and final chapter of this study. So too will the experience of the Glasgow dock labour force in the 1920s and 1930s. Both this chapter, and the epilogue which follows, give a sense of the psychology of the Glasgow dock labour force, their ideas and attitudes, which helps us understand more fully why they abandoned the NUDL in 1910, or the manner in which they came to reject the Transport and General Workers' Union in 1932. For there is little doubt that the same forces were at work on both occasions and that was the determined desire on the part of the Glasgow dockers to shape their own independent organisation. With such an organisation in place, the Clydeside dock labour force would prove their continued commitment to dock trade unionism

Eric Taplin suggests the reason the Glasgow dockers left the NUDL in 1910 was that they were unwilling to be a 'mere branch of an English Union'.[1] But, as the preceding chapter has shown, this explanation does not adequately clarify the position at Glasgow; and even if Taplin is correct, why had it taken them almost twenty years to come to this decision? Reproduced below is a report published by the *Glasgow Herald* in August 1923, when Glasgow's dockers were attempting to leave the TGWU (which they reluctantly joined in January that same year). It was their first attempt to set up their own union on Clydeside. Long-time dock worker

[1] Taplin, *Dockers' Union*, p. 78.

and trade union activist, Bernard Havilan, offered this retrospective historical analysis (and on first reading it does seem to sustain Taplin's thesis):

It began with the formation of the National Union of Dock Labourers in Glasgow in 1889. Thereafter, the union went on to organise thirty-five other branches, including Liverpool and Birkenhead. The first conference was held in Glasgow in 1890, but the next went to Liverpool, because it had more individual branches. Many resolutions were passed thereafter, which went against the wishes of the Scottish members, particularly that the head office moved to Liverpool, which resulted in a drop of 1,200 members because of that move in 1891. The men felt that they did not get the same attention when the head office went to Liverpool. Year by year the membership dropped until the union went out of existence in 1910. Shortly afterwards the Scottish Union of Dock Labourers was formed and this union thereafter became the best organised little trade union in Britain.

All went well until the Miners' strike in 1921. At that time it was agreed that they (the NTWF) assist the miners but the resolution was rescinded by all the dockers in the United Kingdom with the exception of the Scottish Dockers' Union, who kept their members out for 5 weeks and spent the whole of their funds. The Federation did not advise them to go back to work until they had exhausted all their funds and had borrowed £4,000. They were thereafter advised that the only way to pay off this debt was to become part of the Transport and General Workers' Union.

Two votes had been taken on amalgamation and were defeated twice, as there had not been a [five-sixth] majority in favour. An effort was then made to get the men and officials to transfer – the officials going first. The men went over mainly because they didn't want two organisations within the city. Since then there had been a great deal of dissatisfaction at the docks and there was now a desire on the part of many men to have their headquarters in Scotland again. This was the reason they were resuscitating the old union. While they were quite willing to help others they wished to have management of their own affairs in their own hands.[2]

In many ways, this statement covers the most important part of the SUDL history: namely, that the SUDL was to be formed out of the disintegration of the NUDL. Indeed, Bernard Havilan himself was very much part of the NUDL from the early days of its formation onward, and was therefore delivering an analysis based on his

---

[2] 'Attempts to Resuscitate the Scottish Union of Dock Labourers by Glasgow Dockers', article printed in the *Glasgow Herald*, 18 Aug. 1923. Mr Bernard Havilan, 'acting temporary Honorary Secretary of the new Scottish Transport Workers Union', suggested that they had already enrolled around 800 enthusiastic young men at that point. The campaign was started by distributing handbills around the port, stating that the members would not be required to pay for 'exorbitant salaries' and that any permanent officer elected 'would receive the same wage as the man who worked on the docks during the week'.

own observations.[3] What Havilan illustrates is the deep sense of history which was
apparent at Glasgow, coupled with a profound sense of injustice and the dockers'
desire to handle their own affairs.

In terms of the constitution and rules there was little or no difference between
the NUDL and the SUDL. Indeed, the SUDL rules seem to have been almost
entirely based on the NUDL's, to the point where the entrance fee and contributions were exactly the same.[4] There is little doubt that the SUDL proved attractive
to the Glasgow dockers, but it was not because of the less expensive, or preferential,
union rates. Clearly, there were other forces at work, which had accounted for the
demise of the NUDL, and the Glasgow dockers' detestation of that organisation.
There were several critical moments in the history of dock unionism on Clydeside
which were to prove very influential in helping to shape the attitudes of the dock
labour force, and not far removed from those events as described by Bernard
Havilan in 1923. The eventual secession in 1932, however, cannot simply be
explained in terms of the Glasgow dockers' dislike of being a branch of an English
trade union, or blamed completely on the actions and attitude of the TGWU and its
executive in the 1920s. The impulse for secession ran deeper than this. It came
from the self-recognition that Glasgow was capable of running its own affairs, and
that Glasgow could, and did, function at the centre of a broader organisation. It was
felt that a Glasgow union could extend its influence throughout Clydeside, and
Scotland generally, without absorption into a British-wide organisation such as the
NUDL or the TGWU (organisations which, the Glasgow dockers believed, rode
roughshod over regional and local concerns). The roots of this independent
impulse stretched back to the period of New Unionism. But it was finally and
more forcefully accomplished with the formation of the Scottish Union of Dock
Labourers in 1911, which made its grand entrance at the time of the labour unrest
on Clydeside.

## The Formation of the SUDL and the Great Strike Wave of 1911–12

The historian, with his ampler opportunities of taking long views, may be
able to state the value and the significance of the labour movement of our
time. In the meantime with our more limited horizon, we may be forgiven
for tracing some of our troubles to the disintegrating effect of the Trades
Dispute Act and the rest to the fermentation of a socialist leaven in
untutored minds. The forces of revolt have not learned the meaning of

---

[3] Bernard Havilan was recorded as delegate for the NUDL to Glasgow Trades Council between
1889 and 1891. He does not appear again in this capacity until 1902, but thereafter remained in
this position until 1910. He also became a delegate to the Trades Council for the SUDL in the
years from 1918 through to 1922 (see Glasgow Trades Council *Annual Reports* 1889 to 1922, list
of delegates of affiliated trade unions). Bernard Havilan was also one of the first delegates of
the NUDL to the Scottish Trades Union Congress in 1897. He was a delegate to the STUC with
the SUDL after they affiliated in 1912 (see STUC *Annual Reports* of 1897 and 1913 to 1922, list of
delegates of affiliated trade unions).

[4] See *Constitution and Rules of NUDL* (1889) and *SUDL Constitutional Rules* (1914): over this period
as a whole membership fees did not rise and remained remarkably consistent.

discipline. Practically every outstanding upheaval of recent days has been an insurrection.[5]

This extract is from an editorial printed in the *Glasgow Herald*, 31 January 1912. It came at a time when the dockers once again mounted a serious challenge to the waterside employers on Clydeside. It was also noted in the Board of Trade *Gazette* that this situation had been threatening since December 1911 when the employers first began to enforce 'new working conditions' at the port of Glasgow. Despite the fact that both the employers and trade union leaders had accepted the new conditions, the reduction of gang sizes in the loading and unloading of all types of ships and goods, the dockers rejected the new proposals. As a result by 29 January 1912, over 7,000 dockers were on strike on Clydeside.[6] The dockers now had the confidence to take the port employers head-on.

The SUDL was officially formed on the evening of 19 July 1911, at St Mungo's Hall in Glasgow. It was at this meeting that the 2,000 dockers present unanimously elected Joseph Houghton, who was representing Glasgow Trades Council, as General Secretary of the union. The meeting agreed that the Executive Council of the union was to consist of dock labourers employed by the various shipping lines, coal trimmers, grain-weighing squads and other classes of workers at the port. It was decided to appoint Mr A. W. French, Secretary of the Seamen and Firemen's union, as Honorary President. The only condition that was imposed by the meeting was that the position of Treasurer 'should not be taken from the ranks of the dock labourers'.[7] This last point suggests that Eric Taplin was correct when he argued that one of the main problems with the Glasgow branch of the NUDL was that it suffered from 'fraudulent branch officers'.[8] Glasgow's dockers, too, perhaps recognised that embezzlement had been a problem and a weakness in the past and did not want it to happen again.

It is perhaps ironic that the Glasgow Trades Council's involvement with the dockers was due to the Scottish Organiser of the NUDL. James O'Connor Kessack had made the appeal to the Council to assist in 'getting the men back' into the union on 21 December 1910.[9] By 25 January 1911, however, O'Connor Kessack had 'retired' as delegate to the Council, and shortly afterwards the Glasgow branch of the NUDL was officially closed by James Sexton. The task of reorganising Glasgow's dockers now ostensibly lay with the ten-man committee which the Trades Council selected in January.[10] Indeed, this committee was at work within Glasgow docks almost immediately, and by 15 June 1911 the dockers were sufficiently reorganised to take part in a national strike of seamen and firemen and other transport workers. The national strike was to continue from June through to August, and by its conclusion 120,000 transport workers had been out at one stage or another

---

[5] *Glasgow Herald*, 31 Jan. 1912.
[6] Board of Trade *Gazette*, Feb. 1912, p. 68.
[7] *Glasgow Herald*, 20 Jul. 1911.
[8] Taplin, *Dockers' Union*, p. 71.
[9] Glasgow Trades Council Minutes, Dec. 21 1910.
[10] Ibid., Jan. 25 1911, James Sexton's notification of the official close of Glasgow Branch read out as correspondence 15 Feb. 1911.

(discounting the railway workers).[11] As in the period of New Unionist activity, the dockers struck with the seamen up and down the country. In a sense history was repeating itself, when once again we see seamen and the Glasgow Trades Council become involved in organising the dock labour force. Again, as in 1889, the dockers joined forces with the seamen to demand a wage rise for all operations in and around the port. In 1889, however, the dockers were ultimately unsuccessful in their demands, but in 1911 they were to secure a series of wage increases across large areas of the Clydeside waterfront, and particularly at Glasgow. As an organised trade union body, the dockers were much stronger in 1911 than at any other time in their existence, and the actions taken during that year were the first major disputes of any significance since the last years of the previous century.[12]

The strike wave of 1911 was in fact fairly sporadic, with different dockers striking in different parts of the port at different times. It is far from clear if this 'rolling strike-wave' was part of an SUDL strategy, but it most certainly proved to be very effective. For example, on 23 June dockers at Yorkhill and Finnieston struck for less than half an hour and received a wage increase.[13] Dock labourers who worked for the Allan and Donaldson Line were on strike for only twenty-four hours between 27 and 28 June before wage increases were conceded, and the SUDL was firmly established among the men regularly employed by this line.[14] A one-day strike among dockers of the Clan Line, which ended on 28 June, was particularly significant, not only because the men secured wage rises, but because they forced the employers to concede an increase in squad size from twelve to sixteen.[15] This concession was without doubt significant. As we shall see, the employers were determined to reverse it as soon as the time was right, and the general Clydeside strike of January and February the following year was to be specifically fought over the question of gang sizes. By that time the employers wanted to reduce them, while the dockers not only wished to maintain current manning levels but also demanded absolute control over gang sizes. It was to become the critical and central issue of the 1912 strike.

During July the rolling strike wave continued, and the SUDL began to influence an ever-increasing number of dockers. The employers operating the ultra-modern, purpose-built mineral port at Rothesay Dock yielded to the wage demands of 400 workers on 3 July, as well as conceding recognition of the SUDL (although it should be added that reports of men being victimised followed).[16] By 12 July the *Glasgow Herald* was reporting on the mixed successes of the dockers, but the general impression was that many gains had been made across Clydeside. Dockers at both Queen's and Princes' Docks had won wage increases of between 20 and 25%.

[11] B. Mogridge, 'Militancy and Inter-Union Rivalries in British Shipping, 1911–1929', *IRSH*, xi, 2, 1961, p. 382.

[12] *Report on Strikes and Lockouts 1899* (*PP*, 1900, lxviii, Cd 316): around 1,200 dockers took part in a 3–week strike during May 1899. (For reference to June 1911 Strike see Board of Trade *Gazette*, Jul. 1911, p. 268.

[13] *Glasgow Herald*, 24 June 1911.

[14] Ibid., 27 and 28 Jun. 1911.

[15] Ibid., 29 Jun. 1911.

[16] Ibid., 3 Jul. 1911.

Dockers were continually reported to be refusing to work with non-union labour, and this became an intrinsic element of the dockers' demands thereafter.[17] Indeed, this strike pattern was to continue through to August, and sometime later there was a general cessation of hostilities. However, by mid-July – because of the sympathetic action of the dockers in refusing to work on ships manned by non-union seamen – the Glasgow employers and shipowners were considering a lock-out. The *Glasgow Herald* had little doubt about the reason for the dispute:

> Dockers have no direct cause for complaint against the shipowners, who have already satisfied their demands, but out of sympathy with the Seamen's union the dockers refuse to load or discharge certain steamers because they allege that their owners employ non-union seamen and firemen.[18]

Despite the condemnation of the dockers' sympathetic action by the press, there seems little doubt that it was proving effective. On 31 July it was reported that the seamen's strike was over, and that every shipping line and shipping firm had granted recognition to the Seamen's Union.[19]

It was an historic industrial relations breakthough and the long-term significance of the strike was 'the measure of recognition' granted to the transport workers.[20] This may not have been instantly apparent by late July and early August of 1911, or even by 1912, particularly when it seemed that the Shipping Federation were still determined to 'get the better of Havelock Wilson and his Seamen's Union'.[21] But in retrospect, it was without doubt the main achievement of the 1911 transport workers' strike. On Clydeside the situation was little different and the dockers were to continue their campaign of sporadic strikes throughout August over demands for wage increases, improved conditions and the refusal to work alongside non-union labour. But the employers seemed equally determined – particularly in the grain trade – and stated that they would 'only employ dock labourers who indicated that they would work in harmony with non-union men'.[22] Nevertheless, the dockers had made some significant gains from June to August, and this had a knock-on effect on membership. On 16 August Emanuel Shinwell informed the Glasgow Trades Council that the SUDL had by then a membership of 5,000.[23]

Dock trade union membership in Glasgow had never been this high before. This was the first time that the levels achieved during 1890 and 1891 had been exceeded, and the trend was to continue upwards. By the end of September the SUDL were fully affiliated to the Trades Council. Joseph Houghton informed the council that the SUDL numbered 6,400 in Glasgow, and they had organised both Dundee and Ayr – who had a membership was 200 and 100 respectively.[24] On 1 November

---

[17] *Glasgow Herald*, 10 July 1911: refusal to work alongside non-union labour was referred to in press reports throughout the period, but became more vocal by Jul.

[18] Ibid., 19 Jul. 1911.

[19] Ibid., 29 Jul. and 31 Jul.

[20] Mogridge, 'Militancy and Inter-Union Rivalries', pp. 382–3.

[21] Ibid., p. 386.

[22] *Glasgow Herald*, 8 Aug. 1911.

[23] Glasgow Trades Council Minutes, 16 Aug. 1911.

[24] Ibid., 27 Sep. 1911.

Houghton was to report to the Glasgow Council that a transport workers' committee had been set up for Clydeside – comprising the SUDL, the Seamen's Union,
the cranemen, ships' riggers and cooks and stewards – and had met with the
coasting shipowners 'for the first time in their history'.[25] Before the year was out the
dockers were again in dispute along Clydeside, and in Dundee. In the interim
period the SUDL became affiliated to the National Transport Workers' Federation
(NTWF).[26] The ground was now being prepared for the extensive general strike
that was to take place during January and February of 1912.

## Employers' Attitudes to the Unrest

Many employers felt that the industrial problems they were encountering after 1910
were directly related to the Trades Disputes Act. They were suffering the repercus-
sions of those provisions of the Act, which ensured that a trade union could not be
sued for damages, and which made peaceful picketing legal. As a result, they argued
there was not only a significant increase in picketing, but this was now increasingly
accompanied by considerable coercion, intimidation and violence on the part of
strikers. As a result the trade unions were now in a much more powerful position, and
many employers felt that this created the impetus for the wave of strikes they were
having to deal with. It is clear, however, that the employers did not unanimously
agree on the reason for these disputes, or the best methods to combat them.[27]
William Raeburn – a leading and active supporter of the Shipping Federation's
'coercive approach' to industrial relations – was calling on the Clyde Trust to
demand that the government repeal the Trades Disputes Act. This was in response
to the seamen's strike of mid-1911 in particular, but it was not long before the same
worrying trend was to be manifested by the dockers. Not all were convinced of
Raeburn's argument, however, and the Treasurer of the Trust, Mr Graham,
disapproved of both his resolution and his explanation as to why the strike had
begun in the first instance. He viewed the existing industrial strategy of employers at
the port as one major factor in the heightening of industrial tensions at the port:

> If any individual was responsible for what occurred at Glasgow Harbour, then
> that man was Mr Raeburn . . . Had not he and his Federation declined talks
> . . . the outrages that had been complained about would not have happened.
> The shipping trade was in a very good position, and when the workmen who
> had miserable starvation wages asked for some increase, the Shipping Fed-
> eration, of which Mr Raeburn was a burning and shining light, would not meet
> with them . . . If ever there was a strike justified in Glasgow, it was the strike of
> seamen for better wages.

Another Trustee, Mr W. F. Anderson – a progressive councillor, very much
concerned with the bad living conditions of the working class – stressed the

[25] Ibid., 1 Nov. 1911.
[26] Ibid., 22 Nov., 10 and 20 Dec.
[27] *Glasgow Herald*, 8 Nov. 1911; report of Clyde Navigation Trust Meeting.
[28] Ibid., Mr Raeburn's concluding remarks on his resolution.

Shipping Federation's 'miserable handling' of trades disputes. He argued that Raeburn and his Federation never granted the men an opportunity to air their grievances and treated their employees with 'all sorts of contempt'. Anderson castigated Raeburn's attitude to labour affairs:

> When 50,000 men were walking the streets in Glasgow, Mr Raeburn did not bring forward a resolution to relieve them, but immediately the shipping people are appealed to for an increase in wages, he asks them [the trustees] to memorialise the Government in order that peaceful picketing should be stopped. The whole thing was a hollow fraud.

As another Trustee and port employer put it:

> It was his opinion that shipowners had made the biggest mistake of their lives when they failed to recognise trade unionism. From his own standpoint he would rather deal collectively than individually with his men.

Another employer added that if the Trust were to approach government and demand changes to the law, then they would only 'foment political feeling'. But Mr Raeburn could not accept that the blame lay with him, the shipowners, or their federation:

> There was no doubt that syndicalism, accompanied with rioting and anarchy, had swept over the land, and if they could not do anything as peaceful citizens to get some repeal of the Act . . . that was surely a straight forward piece of business which no man need be ashamed of.[28]

The central fact is that there was no single discernible employers' attitude at this time. On the one hand there were those who obviously felt that the time for joint negotiation had come, while the Raeburn camp remained stubbornly anti-union and draconian in their attitudes. However, despite what seemed to amount to a confused industrial policy on the part of the employers, the events of 1911 and 1912 did signal a decisive movement towards accepting joint procedural arrangements to discuss wages and conditions of employment along the Clydeside waterfront. There was another attitude, however, as demonstrated by both Mr Graham and Mr Anderson. Their analysis was that the causes of poverty were self-evident and could be blamed on the general attitude of the employers, and the discontent that was caused by this was therefore understandable.

### The Strike of 1912 and the 'Struggle for Control'[29]

The strike wave that swept over Clydeside in 1911, and was a prelude to the strikes of 1912, welded together the vast majority of dockers within one trade union body. During 1911 the SUDL strengthened its position on Clydeside by instituting a series of rolling strikes and by doing so perhaps recruited 'strategically vital' groups of

[29] Title of chap. by W. Kenefick, in Kenefick and McIvor, *Roots of Red Clydeside.*
[30] Hobsbawm, *Labouring Men,* pp. 209–10.

port workers – the dockers who handled the export cargo, the coaltrimmers, for example, or the mineral workers at Rothesay Docks. This strategy aimed to prevent the 'stronger' sections of the dock labour force from forming their own 'quasi-craft unions', while leaving the weaker elements to the 'mercies of the market', as exemplified at the port of Bristol.[30] This success was partly due to the political influence of the NTWF, constantly arguing the case for industrial unionism, who helped forge greater solidarity between dockers and other groups, such as the seamen and railwaymen, while at the same time drawing the dock labour force closer together.

The upturn in trade at this time was also of great importance, as was the long tradition of combination on Clydeside, but so too – it would seem – was the political agitation that was taking place between 1910 and 1914. On Clydeside the role of the Glasgow Trades Council, in conjunction with other leading political organisations, was central to the movement. The Seamen and Firemen's Union, close allies of the dockers and the leadership of the SUDL, arranged with the Glasgow Trades Council that Madame Sorgue, a leading spokesperson for the French Syndicalist union, the Confédération Générale du Travail (CGT), was to address the Council on the need to organise an International Federation of Trades Unions. She believed that this was the only way that the working classes could win against the massed International Employers' Organisations and the combined forces of capital.[31]

Before the strike wave of 1912 many familiar names in the British labour movement addressed Glasgow Trades Council, including such luminaries as Captain Edward Tupper of the Seamen's Union.[32] Indeed, Tupper made special note of the strike that was to follow his meeting in Glasgow, noting also that the seamen had to come out in sympathy in support of the dockers there. He observed that the strike that was to follow was to become 'a very bitter battle where there was serious rioting and grave disorders'[33], what Shinwell was to describe later as the 'great unrest at Glasgow Harbour'.[34] Tom Mann too was active in Glasgow at this time, speaking on the 'solidarity that was growing in the movement'.[35] By March the Trades Council was organising a protest demonstration on Glasgow Green against Mann's arrest on a charge of incitement to mutiny.[36] This referred to Mann's

---

[31] Madame Sorgue's address was reported in the 31 May minutes of Glasgow Trades Council. Joseph Houghton, prior to his election as General Secretary of the SUDL, moved that the Council would 'render all assistance possible' to help her and the International Federation to secure that end.

[32] Glasgow Trades Council Minutes, 14 Jan. 1912. It was noted that Captain Tupper was addressing a large meeting of seamen and dockers who had rejected the shipowners new conditions concerning manning levels on ships and gang size reductions for the loading and discharging of vessels. Emanuel Shinwell and Joe Houghton also addressed the meeting, stating that a strike was imminent due to the desire of the men to refuse to work alongside any non-union labour.

[33] Captain E. Tupper, *Seamen's Torch: The Life Story of Captain Edward Tupper, National Union of Seamen* (1938), p. 74.

[34] Glasgow Trades Council Minutes, 15 May 1912.

[35] Ibid., 17 Jan. 1912.

[36] Ibid., 27 Mar. 1912.

'Don't Shoot' pamphlet which demanded that they refuse any orders to shoot at strikers, as occurred at Liverpool in the dispute of 1911 when two dockers were killed.[37] After his release some six months later Mann was once more involved with the SUDL, actively campaigning on behalf of strikers at the Port of Ardrossan in Ayrshire.[38]

That there was a considerable degree of political activity at this time is not in doubt. But it is not clear to what extent the ordinary worker was influenced by such political campaigning. Could the dockers' involvement in the general strike with the seamen and firemen between June and August of 1911, for example, have been influenced by syndicalist tendencies – as the seamen's obvious patronage of Madame Sorgue perhaps suggests? It is clear from various reports by the right-wing press, in particular the *Glasgow Herald*, between 1911 and 1912, that syndic-alism and socialism were at least in part to blame for the unrest (it should be noted that they never really made any attempt to distinguish between syndicalism and socialism). According to Emanuel Shinwell, reported in *Forward*, the main and effective weapon was sympathetic action. He concluded that, in this type of action, 'the seeds of revolution had been sown on Clydeside'.[39]

The next major industrial dispute on Clydeside was the strike of January and February 1912. Although there were many issues involved in the dispute, the pivotal factor was the dockers' demands to control gang sizes. This issue served to engender a high degree of solidarity within the Clydeside dock labour force. The Board of Trade noted that some 7,000 workers became involved in the strike. In order of magnitude only the strike at Singers at Clydebank, during March and April 1911, involved more workers.[40]

The strike of 1912 began on 29 January after the employers initiated a lock-out around Glasgow harbour. The first phase of the dispute was brought officially to an end on 10 February, following an agreement between the employers and the trade union officials.[41] However, the dockers were to reject this agreement, and 6,400 dockers came out on strike again, against their leaders' advice, on 12 February.[42] This second and unofficial phase of the strike was short-lived. Within two days, after the intervention of George Askwith of the Board of Trade, at a meeting at the Central Hotel in Glasgow, the matter was referred to arbitration. Captain Tupper, in his autobiography, wrote of this particular meeting with Askwith, at which he, Shinwell, and Joseph Houghton were present, along with Glasgow shipowners. He also notes that Winston Churchill became involved in the talks on his arrival from

---

[37] Bellamy and Saville, *Dictionary of Labour Biography*, vii, p. 178: for copy of Mann's letter see R. and E. Frow and M. Katanka, *Strikes: A Documentary History* (1971), p. 148.

[38] For case study of this strike see Kenefick, *Ardrossan*.

[39] *Forward*, 12 Aug. 1911.

[40] Duncan and McIvor, *Militant Workers*, p. 83 (see Table 1 for list of principal disputes).

[41] The agreement referred to was noted in full in the Feb. edition of the Board of Trade *Gazette*, p. 43. The agreement covered the loading and discharging of all types of vessels and cargo at the port such as liners and ocean steamers and coasting vessels. The agreement also decided on gang sizes on all vessels dependent on tonnage and type of cargo handled, such as mineral ores and coal, etc.

[42] Ibid., Mar. 1912, p. 86.

Belfast. Tupper argued that Churchill's involvement showed the concern of the government with this particular dispute. 'It was strange to relate', wrote Tupper, 'but that night, the owners gave way to some of the demands of the union negotiators.' He could only conclude that, 'the Glasgow owners were up against something new – and it was too much for them'.[43]

The unofficial nature of the second part of the strike, and the rank-and-file rebellion against the recommendations of the leadership, do point to a strong syndicalist impulse. This would also conform with John Lovell's definition of syndicalism, which, in the trade union sense, can be taken to mean the use of 'direct industrial action intended to wrest control of industry through workers' own organisations'.[44] It may have been the fear of an active 'syndicalist factor' to the dispute that brought the Glasgow shipowners to the conference table in the first instance. Indeed, as Captain Tupper argued, syndicalism may have been that 'something new' that the employers were up against.

There are other elements of the strike action manifesting syndicalist traits. The strike was first and foremost a general strike of dockers in the Clydeside region, and this was accompanied by a significant degree of sympathetic action on behalf of the dockers. The seamen's union refused to work alongside any non-union docker or any blacklegs, where they had managed to gain entry. The carters declared that they would help the dockers 'gain a glorious victory', and in the name of brotherhood, trade unionism and solidarity, they would stand by the dockers. Jim Larkin sent similar messages of support from Dublin. Indeed, it was reported early in the dispute that arrangements were 'in place to hold up ships of the Anchor Line at New York'.[45] It was also clear that it was the dockers' intention to have a greater say over who controlled the process of work and recruitment, and, fundamentally, who had the right to decide on gang sizes and determine local working conditions.

The dockers did, in the words of Joseph Houghton, throw down the gauntlet to the employers.[46] Certainly the employers on Clydeside were fearful that political influences were acting on the minds of their workers. This is perhaps best illustrated in the dockers' rejection of their trade union leadership's recommendations. In order to fully assess the nature, or the extent, of syndicalism in relation to this dispute, it is necessary to examine in greater detail major elements of the dispute, including the political mood of the period, from the standpoint of both the employer and the employed.

The *Glasgow Herald* was later to report that the dockers' actions were 'a slightly varied form of the old question of shop management'. The dispute had taken on the same character as the engineers' lock-out in 1897–98, noted the report. As then, the employers refused to recognise the bargaining rights of trade unions. Even if recognition were to be achieved, employers would not budge on the right to manage:

[43] Tupper, *Seamen's Torch*, pp. 75–6.
[44] Lovell, *British Trade Union History*, pp. 46–7.
[45] *Daily Record and Mail*, 1 and 3 Feb. 1912.
[46] *Daily Record and Mail*, 29 Jan. 1912: part of a statement made by Joseph Houghton, General Secretary of the SUDL, in response to the employers' lock-out notices around Glasgow Harbour, Jan. 1912.

So long as they [the employers] are responsible for financing and conducting their works . . . they must retain in their own hands the management of their establishments . . . The right of combination may be freely granted to all workmen, but the right of dominion must be refused. The Glasgow dockers, in their newly found enthusiasm for trade unionism, have adopted one and usurped the other . . . The Dockers had an organisation stronger and better managed than anything of the kind which has ever existed at the port. If it had not got out of hand it may have been a power for good. But it has got out of hand. Its great weakness has been proved to lie in its strength. [47]

It was argued that the 'shipowners could hardly call their boats their own' and the SUDL was now suffering from an 'exaggerated idea of its own importance'. The *Daily Record and Mail* also reported extensively on the dispute, and noted Joseph Houghton's analysis of the dockers' determined stance. 'All the men understood what they were doing', Houghton stressed, 'and they knew full well the serious consequences that might ensue.'[48] The battle lines were now drawn in what the *Glasgow Herald* was to describe as 'the labour war' at Glasgow'. The phraseology itself suggests something much more political in content, particularly as the dockers were challenging the employers over who had the right to manage the industry.

One further example of this was the dockers' insistence that foremen be forced to join the SUDL, and *Forward* offered the example of the Anchor Line paying £1 per head to the SUDL for each of its eighteen foremen. The report went on to say that the employers at Glasgow were inclined to 'rebel against such impositions'.[49] The reason for forcing the foremen into the union seemed to be to place some curb on their power and aid the fight against any reductions in gang sizes, which was principally an attempt to control the level of work intensification. As noted in *Forward*, 'the dockers had been brutally overworked, badly paid and sworn at sometimes in a most disgusting manner'. A common phrase was 'you lazy Irish bastard!'[50] Such 'brutality' was inevitably laid at the doorstep of the foremen, thus providing one reason that the dockers sought to control them.

The dockers' attitude to the foremen may also serve to further illustrate points made earlier in this study. Chapter 1 noted the words of Henry Mayhew, writing in the mid-nineteenth century, describing the power of the foreman with the phrase 'the one whose voice could give the docker work'. Beveridge went further and, as we saw in Chapter 2, wrote at some length about 'grave abuses of power, and the corruption, which were associated with the patronage of the foreman'. In Chapter 4 it was noted that Jim Larkin, too, stressed the extent of malpractice associated with foremen who 'expected and accepted favours from men driven to pay for the privilege of being employed'. Chapter 7, considering the issue of occupational health and safety, noted that the foreman often 'pestered injured dockers not to

---

[47] *Glasgow Herald*, 29 Jan. 1912.
[48] *Daily Record and Mail*, 29 Jan. 1912.
[49] *Forward*, 27 Jan. 1912.
[50] Ibid., 3 Feb. 1912.

report accidents', while Eric Taplin intimated that if an accident was reported, dockers would not be taken back on after they recovered. As Beatrice Potter argued, 'the foreman was distinctly the official'.[51] Therefore, the foreman was the person who could ensure that a docker was prevented from being employed or not. Dockers had long memories, and when a dispute arose they took the opportunity to settle old scores. The foreman was very often the first in the line of fire. In the final analysis, it was the foreman who held sway over this system and, as executor of the employers' business, personified its worst excesses. If the dockers could bring the foremen under their control, then they would, in effect, control the hiring system – a critical element of the casual system.

A considerable level of propaganda had been circulated around Glasgow at this time about the dockers and their habits, and this focussed principally on their hard-drinking reputation. One employer, reported in *Forward*, made his views on the matter very clear: 'the employers think the dockers are more fond of liquor than they are of work and if the men drank less whisky, things would go more smoothly'.[52] This attitude was well illustrated in an open letter published in *Forward* on 3 February 1912. Entitled 'The Dock Strike: Questions by an Employer'. Its writer claimed to be 'in sympathy with the ideals of *Forward*', but felt it necessary to raise certain questions regarding the dockers' general attitude to work. Among other things he accused the dockers of being not only well paid but lazy, seen in the recent 20% increase in the cost of unloading a ship. Some men also got 'helplessly drunk' and were protected by their gang mates, who threatened to strike should the offending docker not be paid for being there. He also stated that a union official, on seeing a man sweating, insisted that the dockers were being overworked and demanded that gang sizes be increased. The employers had the right to manage their own business, he concluded. He signed himself 'Fair Do'.

The employers refused to budge on the matter of who had the right to reduce gang sizes and were determined to push this point. On Saturday, 27 January, they stepped up their campaign and initiated a lockout. Notices to that effect were posted around the port and undersigned by 132 shipowners with business interests at Glasgow harbour. It was generally believed that the dockers had been spoiling for a strike for some time (although *Forward* suggested that this was not the case). The report also noted that the employers were 'anxious for a lockout'. Thus it was the lockout notice which signalled the beginnings of the dispute.[53]

It is a strange paradox, indeed, that at this point the employers, like the press, had observed that agreements about working conditions had been accepted in Dundee and at Liverpool, but that in Glasgow they refused to accept the agreement thrashed out by the leadership of the SUDL. According to the *Glasgow Herald*, however, 'the employers had now learned their lesson' and had finally, even if reluctantly, come into line with other port employers around the country. They now accepted the principal of joint collective bargaining and accepted the need for

---

[51] Beatrice Potter cited in Booth, *Life and Labour*; Potter offers a full analysis of what she believes were the main differences between the docker and the foreman, pp. 22–3.
[52] *Forward*, 27 Jan. 1912.
[53] Ibid.

procedural agreement within the dock industry. All the shipowners wanted now was for the dockers to accept the conditions of the joint agreement, but what was occurring within the ranks of the SUDL was 'the tyranny of the majority'. 'Mob rule was now in effect', they reported, 'and when the dockers rejected the recommendations of the leaders they merely became an uncontrollable mass.' The report saw this as evidence of syndicalism, and this was reiterated in almost every report between 29 January and 15 February 1912.[54] The employers in 1911, however, were still not convinced that they needed to consider new industrial strategies, and many felt that political intervention of another sort was needed to control the massed ranks of labour during times of industrial discontent.

By the time the strike was coming to an end, the *Glasgow Herald* was advising the dockers 'that they had gained the machinery of conciliation and that it was up to them to see that it was a success'.[55] The *Daily Record and Mail* underlined this when it reported on part of a speech by William Raeburn given at a function sponsored by the Glasgow Shipowners and Shipbrokers' Benevolent Association Dinner on the evening of 2 February 1912: 'The great cry had been recognition of the union, and the great demand, collective bargaining, the Shipowners had conceded both'. He stressed, however, that they would not give over to the docker 'the management and control of their businesses'. Despite the fact that the port had come to a complete standstill, the employers held out on this issue of the 'right to manage'. The resistance they faced was not insubstantial and, when coupled with the actions of other port workers in sympathy with the dockers, was a formidable force indeed.

## Resolution and Aftermath of the 1912 Dispute

The conflict finally came to an end when the case over who had the right to control gang sizes went before a court of arbitration. The arbiter was Lord Mersey and he found in favour of the employers. He stated clearly that the employers had the absolute right to decide on gang sizes. With this decision the shipowners brought the lockout to an end and while there were still some pockets of resistance around the port, the dispute was effectively over. The decision of Lord Mersey effectively meant that the employers had won.

But the SUDL leadership was not entirely unhappy with the final outcome.[56] Joe Houghton reported to the Glasgow Trades Council that while they had some difficulty in getting the men back to work, the negotiations with the shipowners had been positive, and that the men had achieved an advance on wages. He also argued that the reduction in gang sizes had little effect on the men either.[57] In the long-term, however, the most significant achievement for the SUDL was the creation of joint-negotiation machinery within the port transport industry on Clydeside and at the port of Glasgow. This had a critical impact on the future of industrial relations along the Glasgow and Clydeside waterfront. The formulation of Lord Mersey's

---

[54] Ibid., 3 and 8 Feb. 1912.
[55] Ibid., 12 Feb. 1912.
[56] *Glasgow Herald*, 21 Jan. 1912.
[57] Glasgow Trades Council Minutes, 21 and 28 Feb. 1912.

decision also illustrates that the dockers themselves had won considerable concessions at Glasgow, despite losing the point regarding gang sizes. Mersey had allowed that if 'any hardship resulted from the practice of the shipowners in relation to gang size, then the dockers had the right to appeal to the joint committee, by virtue of paragraph four of the conditions of employment'. Similar to the arrangements between employers and dockers at Liverpool, the recognition by employers at Glasgow was to prove the 'start of a continuing relationship with the union and brought about a new era of collective bargaining and joint negotiation'.[58]

Can the actions of the Glasgow dockers, or the attitude of their leadership, be described as characteristic of a syndicalist position? It could be argued that the dockers did attempt to exert greater control over their industry than they had ever attempted before. There is little evidence to suggest, however, that their actions were intended to undermine the capitalist system, that they actively rejected parliamentary politics, or that they manifested strict adherence to any other radical political philosophy. This is further confirmed by the fact that the leadership of the SUDL was happy to accept joint regulation of the port transport industry on Clydeside. There is little doubt that Joseph Houghton, like his close associate Emanuel Shinwell, was a convinced socialist, and although he and Shinwell consorted with well-known syndicalists such as Tom Mann or Madame Sorgue, it was never claimed that they were themselves syndicalists.

The actions of the dockers during this period could perhaps be best described as a type of 'proto syndicalist behaviour', one that fell between 'vague revolt and clear cut revolutionary action'.[59] The unofficial nature of some of the disputes at Glasgow, for example, could be construed as 'ideology in action', as was rank-and-file defiance of the recommendations of their own trade union's leadership. But, apart from this short-lived period of rank-and-file rejection of the leadership of the SUDL's recommendations, and the dockers' use of direct action (a traditional characteristic of their industrial strategy in any case), their actions do not seem to conform to specifically syndicalist principles. In the final analysis, neither the dockers nor the leadership of the SUDL exhibited any rigid set of political goals, and, despite evidence of a very resolute industrial stance, there is little to suggest a determined syndicalist impulse.

The industrial strategies of the dockers were, perhaps, more clearly industrial unionist, in so far as they would back the use of the general strike as an industrial weapon. This can be seen by the dockers' involvement in the general strikes of 1911 and 1912. After the strikes of early 1912 there are only sporadic reports of labour disputes on the docks at Glasgow, and on Clydeside generally, normally over wages, and usually settled quickly. The only exception to the industrial peace thereafter was the ten-week strike which took place at the Ayrshire port of Ardrossan between October 1912 and January 1913. This dispute was in many ways a re-run of the early strikes experienced at Glasgow, and the same political content was to be identified.

---

[58] Bean, 'Employers Associations', p. 382.
[59] Holton, British Syndicalism, p. 76.

Ardrossan was perhaps somewhat different, however, in so far as the Ardrossan Harbour Company, who owned and controlled the port, attempted one of the few concerted counter-attacks to be seen along the British waterfront during the period of labour unrest. Despite a considerable degree of violence and the importation of labour into Ardrossan, the strike ended when the employers and the SUDL reverted to joint negotiation.[60] On Clydeside generally, industrial relations along the waterfront settled down and more or less remained that way through to the war and beyond. Thus the employers, and the SUDL leadership, had achieved stability along the waterfront in the long term, something that the employers clearly thought impossible before and during the disputes of 1911 and 1912.

Despite the relative peace that was to descend upon the Clydeside waterfront after 1912, it should not be forgotten that, for a time at least, there was a considerable degree of discontent, and that some of this was perhaps politically motivated. When the dockers and the seamen of Glasgow openly challenged the might of the Clydeside employers and, more importantly, the shipowners, it forced a major rethink on how best to regulate industrial relations. This was perhaps even more necessary when the employers could see that almost every meeting of dockers and seamen around the Clydeside docks and wharves was accompanied by speeches from well-known leaders of the labour movement.[61]

Given the political activity that was apparent at this time, the conciliatory nature of the employers may indeed have been intended to 'placate the labour force and prevent them from being taken *en masse* by growing socialist and syndicalist ideologies'.[62] Many employers believed that syndicalism and socialism were a major cause of the unrest. They also felt that if recognition was not granted to the trade unions 'further political feeling would be fomented'. Perhaps fear of the political

---

[60] Kenefick, *Ardrossan.* There were also serious disturbances at Leith in 1912 and in 1913. According to Sue Mowat, the Shipping Federation did become involved in the 1913 strike at the invitation of the employers at Leith. The strike was to involve the NUDL and 3,000 men were on strike (see *The Port of Leith: Its History and its People* (Edinburgh, 1994), chap. 16). It would seem to be the case, however, that while the dockers stood firm during the strike, there was not the same level solidarity shown at Leith among other transport workers as there had been in similar disputes at Glasgow, or Ardrossan. There were 2,800 dockers on strike and 200 coal trimmers, and because of their actions 600 seamen were made idle, and many railwaymen and around 200 carters were similarly effected. But while the seamen supported the dockers the railwaymen and the carters did not, and in the last weeks of the strike were reported to working freely around the port handling all cargoes. The strike ended in defeat for the dockers, and the men were asked to return to work by O'Connor Kessack of the NUDL because the Shipping Federation and the employers were stepping-up their actions. Hitherto he was in absolute support of the dockers and promised further support from the NTWF, but within a matter days changed this position. The evidence would seem to suggest that James Sexton and the NUDL, Liverpool executive forced O'Connor Kessack's hand. See the *Leith Observer* 26 Jun. to 14 Aug. 1911.

[61] See *Glasgow Herald* and *Forward,* Jan. to Feb. 1912, for illustrations of the extent of political activity at this time; see also *Ardrossan and Saltcoats Herald,* for later examples of political speeches and appearances of both Tillett and Mann during dispute at Ardrossan between Oct. 1912 and Jan. 1913; also Kenefick, 'The Dock Strike: The Labour Unrest of 1910–1914, with particular reference to the Ardrossan Dock Strike, 1912 to 1913', chap. one, section 3 (University of Strathclyde, Honours dissertation, 1991), and Kenefick, *Ardrossan.*

[62] Arthur McIvor, 'Employers Organisations and Strike Breaking in Britain, 1911–1914', *IRSH*, xxix, 1, 1894, p. 12.

consequences led to recognition of the SUDL, and with this came the formalisation of joint procedural agreements. In the long-term, this was the most significant effect of the disputes of 1912.

In the short-term, however, the strikes of 1911 and 1912 did cause great alarm, and while they may not have led to further discontent, there was a genuine fear that the 'labour war' at Glasgow could have acted as a prelude to widespread political unrest, revolt, and insurrection on Clydeside. This is clearly articulated in the reported remarks of various employers at the port of Glasgow at this time as well as in the wider social context beyond the confines of Clydeside and Glasgow. For G. D. H. Cole the labour unrest was real, possessing both direction and determination, and without doubt was syndicalist in form.[63] H. G. Wells was to write of the times:

> The discontent of the labouring mass of the community is deep and increasing. It may be that we are in the opening phase of a real and irreparable class war . . . New and strange urgencies are at work in our midst, forces for which the word 'revolutionary' is only too faithfully appropriate.[64]

Even if the prospect of Clydeside's dockers going over to syndicalism *en masse* was more apparent than real – at least from today's viewpoint – the fear was nevertheless genuine enough in the eyes of the employers, the press, and society in general, between 1911 and 1912. After these disputes however, relations along the waterfront on Clydeside, as along the entire British waterfront, were placed on 'a more orderly and stable basis'.[65] And this was to remain the case from then until the widespread and general industrial action undertaken by the dockers and the SUDL in their lone sympathetic action with the miners during 1921.

However, if anyone did have doubts as to the Clydeside dockers' ability to sustain their new union, these would have been quickly dispelled. By the time war was declared in August 1914 the SUDL had become firmly established along the entire west coast of Scotland, and had organised several west-coast English ports, including Workington and Whitehaven, and two ports on Scotland's east coast, Dundee and Bo'ness. For the first time they were in joint-negotiation with port employers regarding wages and condition of labour. This last factor alone proved a watershed in the history of dock unionism along Clydeside and in Glasgow in particular – given the Glasgow port employers' stern resistance to any type of joint negotiation – and the war years only served to broaden and enhance the profile of the union. By the end of the war the SUDL had a membership of 10,000, and represented other groups of workers such as female munitions workers at Nobel's Ardeer factory in Ayrshire, and chemical and distillery workers in various locations in the Clydeside area.

The SUDL was indeed a very well organised trade union, and was of significant benefit to its members throughout most of its short existence. It is also true that the fortunes of the SUDL were to turn dramatically because of the union's ill-fated

---

[63] G. G. H. Cole, *The World of Labour* (1913), p. 33.

[64] H. G. Wells, 'The Labour Unrest', in W. Warren Wager (ed.) *Journalism and Prophecy 1893–1946* (1965), p. 43.

[65] Bean, 'Employers Associations', p. 382.

sympathy action with the miners, in the aftermath of the failure of the 'Triple Alliance' and 'Black Friday'. This much is true of Bernard Havilan's short history of the union. However, Havilan's account gives no indication of the struggle that went on during the early years of the SUDL's existence, or the importance of this struggle in relation to the Clydeside dock labour force, who flocked in ever greater numbers to join the ranks of the SUDL. But his analysis offers an illustration of the central philosophy of Glasgow dock unionism and how it began to take on a determined and tangible form before 1914. These roots were firmly based in precedents set in the past, but were ultimately expressed in increased demands for self-regulation, organisational democracy, and political independence within a small and unified trade union framework. Thus came into existence the Scottish Union of Dock Labourers, which, in the eyes of its membership was 'the best organised little trade union in Britain': a description assured by events after 1914.

# Epilogue

# A Survey of Glasgow Docks, 1914 to the 1930s

*The First World War*

The impact of war had two main effects on the dock labour force at Glasgow. The first was the intervention of the state in port affairs. The second – leading on from the advances made during the labour unrest – was to enhance the status of the dockers, and incorporate their trade union organisations within the wider labour movement. The dockers were to affiliate to the NTWF, and through the NTWF they were incorporated into the Triple Industrial Alliance. They therefore held an influential position in labour affairs, more than at any other time in the history of dock trade unionism. As they also played such an important role within the wartime economy, it was vital that the state controlled this group of workers principally through courts of arbitration and conciliation. Jonathan Schneer argued that 'war was very beneficial for the dockers'; uncertainty in employment 'practically disappeared', and 'temporarily halted the spread of new mechanical appliances into the docklands of Britain'. Because of such initiatives, the docklands became pacified during the war.[1] As Ben Tillett was to put it in 1919:

> Our own union has been able to command such improvements in the conditions of labour, such advantages in real wealth as to make me kick myself now and again to ascertain whether I am awake.[2]

The docker was now a respected member of both the labour movement and society at large. This was a decisive break with a past in which the dockers were generally viewed with a degree of suspicion. After the period of unrest before the war the dockers took a more prominent role in labour affairs. On Clydeside they strengthened their links with the Seamen's Union and the Glasgow Trades Council. Despite their affiliation to bodies such as the Glasgow Trades Council, the STUC, the NTWF and the Triple Alliance, they still tended to concern themselves principally with matters relating to port work and dock life. SUDL Executive Minutes do testify to wider considerations in the political arena: concerns over housing, education, and food prices. However, these minutes do not give the

---

[1] Jonathan Schneer, 'British Dockers During 1914–1918', p. 103.
[2] Ibid., p. 99: Tillet made this statement at the Dock, Wharf, Riverside and General Labourers' Union Triennial Conference, 1919.

impression that such issues led to the formation of a more radical political philosophy. Perhaps this is why the dockers were not to figure in any prominent way in the events that came to characterise Red Clydeside. By contrast, when the state made any overtures suggesting the introduction of 'Tally Schemes', the militarisation of dock labour, or any scheme intended to register the dockers at Glasgow, the whole tenor of the minutes changes.[3] This suggests that the dockers were concerned with defining and defending their own territory, which perhaps militated against them becoming involved in the political developments associated with Red Clydeside. But as the SUDL minutes for the period 1911–15 are lost, it cannot be stated categorically that they were not more concerned with the events of Red Clydeside, such as the Rent Strikes, for example. In newspaper reports of the period, however, the dockers are conspicuous by their absence, although there is a mention of dockers' involvement in a peace demonstration on Glasgow Green on 13 August 1914 – nine days after war was declared. The meeting had been organised by the Glasgow Independent Labour Party (ILP) and John Maclean's British Socialist Party. The ILP newspaper *Forward* reported:

> The gathering was cosmopolitan in character and included doctors and dock workers and rebels of every possible brand from the mild peace advocates to the wildest of revolutionaries. [4]

The dockers do seem to have been well controlled by the state: by a direct appeal to their patriotism on the one hand, and through the successful set-up of arbitration and conciliation boards to handle labour affairs on the other. A similar incorporation occurred when the dockers affiliated with the NTWF. All national wage matters and industrial and inter-union disputes were dealt with through the arbitration and conciliation services provided by the state, and overseen on the dockers' behalf by the NTWF. The role of the NTWF during the war years, however, was very different from that assumed before the war, when they were characterised more or less as a pseudo-syndicalist organisation, led by such confirmed syndicalists as Tom Mann. But, whereas before 1914, it may have been suggested that the NTWF illustrated the dockers' attachment to syndicalist ideas, by the war years it came to represent the dockers' more conciliatory tone. The NTWF now played a pivotal role in stabilising industrial relations in the transport sector, and the dockers rarely strayed far from the recommendations that it made concerning wartime social, political, or economic matters.

There was also a constant dialogue with the NTWF over the question of congestion on the docks, and the threat of intervention by the military at Glasgow and Ardrossan. When analysing the SUDL correspondence over the war years, it is instantly apparent that this small union had been elevated in a way that its relatively small membership base would not have achieved during peacetime. But this was perhaps inevitable, given that many governmental organisations now had influence

---

[3] SUDL Executive Minutes, Feb. 1916 to Mar. 1917.
[4] W. Kenefick, 'War Resisters and Anti-Conscription', in C. M. M. MacDonald and Elaine McFarland (eds.) *Scotland and the Great War* (Edinburgh, 1999), p. 63.

in labour affairs. The Board of Trade, the Ministry of Labour, the Committee on Production and the Admiralty, 'all developed industrial relations functions' during the war.[5] Joseph Houghton and other delegates for the SUDL were dispatched south on numerous occasions either to attend special conferences such as the Food Conference in London in November 1916[6] or a conference on National Defence, organised by Neville Chamberlain, in March 1917.[7] Indeed, this was often seen in reverse, too, with Neville Chamberlain addressing the 1917 STUC Conference at Falkirk, the same year as Joseph Houghton was elected to the Parliamentary Committee of the STUC.[8]

It would seem, however, that 1917 was to mark a turning point for the SUDL and the dockers' union generally. At the SUDL Congress of 17 April 1917 it was noted that the union had experienced some troubles in connection with the Compulsory Service Bill, the Military Service Bill, and the threatened Proclamations of both Glasgow and Ardrossan (the authorities complained about congestion at these and other ports), which would have placed both under military control. But they had come through all this 'without putting the union into serious problems with the government'.[9]

However, a short time later, it was being noted that the Munitions of War Act was 'being increasingly employed for the purposes of industrial coercion and subjection', and that the military had put their own men into four of the west-coast ports.[10] The strike rate around 1917 was on an upward trend.[11] By 1918, unemployment was once again a problem at Glasgow. It was reported that somewhere between 1,000 and 2,000 men were regularly idle at the port.[12] Rising unemployment, resulting in greater underemployment, was again a major concern, and this fact, more than any other, was responsible for the rise in the level of industrial disputes on Clydeside. The dockers may not have been intimately involved in the campaigns and disputes associated with Red Clydeside, but, in April 1921, they once again illustrated their militant credentials when they struck in sympathy with the miners and in response to the expected general strike of the Triple Industrial Alliance. It was an episode in the SUDL's history that was to have significant implications for Clydeside dock unionism thereafter.

## Failure of the Triple Industrial Alliance and the Miners' Strike in 1921

The miners' strike of 1921 was essentially fought over the issue of de-control of the industry on the part of the government. According to James Hinton, the miners

[5] Coates and Topham, *The Making of the Transport and General Workers' Union*, p. 613.
[6] SUDL Executive Minutes, 4 Nov. 1916.
[7] Ibid., Mar. 16 1917.
[8] STUC Annual Report, Falkirk, Apr. 1917.
[9] Report of the first day of the proceedings of 4th Annual Congress of the SUDL to the Executive Council Meeting of 17 Apr. 1917.
[10] SUDL Executive Minutes, 6 Feb. 1918, and 11 May 1918.
[11] Ibid., 9 Jun. 1918; see also minutes of Jan. to Jun. 1919, and also Glasgow Trades Council Minutes for same period for report of Joseph Houghton on the extent of wage rises on the docks (as obtained by the NTWF).
[12] SUDL Executive Minutes, 7 Aug. 1918.

had secured from the government a guarantee that they would negotiate with the mine-owners to establish a national wages board by the end of March 1921, as a reward for calling off their strike action during October 1920. By the time March came round it was obvious that the government had no intention of honouring its previous guarantees. The miners struck on 1 April 1921. They requested the support of the Triple Industrial Alliance and they agreed to strike on 15 April. The sympathetic action on the part of the Triple Alliance never materialised and the 'General Strike' was called off. It was this episode that became known as 'Black Friday'.

According to Hinton, 'Black Friday' marked the end of the Triple Alliance as an effective industrial weapon, and the 'beginning of a major attack on wages'. Key sections of the trade union movement were to be defeated in the confrontations that followed.[13] This is what undoubtedly happened to the SUDL, who did strike, but returned defeated, demoralised and dejected. This strike action was to financially ruin the SUDL and bring it to the point of disintegration. It also left a bitter legacy on Clydeside, one that the dockers never forgot. It is clear from the minutes of the Executive Council of the SUDL that they were in full support of the proposed strike action by the Triple Alliance and had made detailed strike plans. The SUDL first set up an Emergency Committee to oversee the strike. Thereafter, a meeting was organised with the Scottish Co-operative Wholesale Society to arrange for food supplies in lieu of cash – in the 'event of cash being commandeered by the Government'.[14] Meetings were organised all around the port of Glasgow to inform all members of the arrangements for the strike.[15] By 17 April, however, Houghton was informed that the strike had been called off. The NTWF had agreed that certain sympathetic action could be taken, in particular that no foreign coal brought into the country should be handled, but it was stressed that no further action would be taken unless they sanctioned it.

At the STUC Conference of 20–23 April 1921, the delegates of the SUDL demonstrated their commitment to the miners. The SUDL delegates identified those whom they blamed for the failure of the Triple Alliance. The proceedings were brought to a close when a resolution was passed 'calling upon workers in Scotland to support the miners'.[16] It is not clear whether this resolution encouraged the SUDL to enter into this particular dispute, but by 6 May it was reported that the whole Rothesay Dock 'had knocked off'. Shortly after the rest of the Glasgow dockers downed tools, Ardrossan and Dundee came out, then Ayr, and other branches followed later. Around forty blacklegs were brought in to work with coal imports, and the military and the navy were mobilised to guard them.[17] However, there was to be little support for the industrial action of the Clydeside

---

[13] James Hinton, *Labour and Socialism*, pp. 113–15.

[14] SUDL Executive Council (E.C.), Emergency Committee, 11 Apr. 1921.

[15] Ibid.

[16] Scottish Trades Union Congress, Aberdeen 1921, debate on 'The Call-Off of the Triple Industrial Alliance General Strike', Apr.15 1921.

[17] SUDL E.C. Emergency Committee 6, 9 and 12 May, and Special Executive Committee Meeting, 14 and 18 May.

dockers in 1921, with the exception of some railwaymen who had refused to transport 'blackleg' coal from Glasgow harbour.[18] The NTWF embargo on all incoming foreign coal, while considered inadequate by the SUDL, was not even being adhered to in certain ports – notably on the east coast. Indeed, SUDL Executive Council minutes note that James Sexton, leader of the NUDL, 'ordered striking dockers at Leith to go back to work on Belgian coal'. Sexton clearly did not support the miners' actions and by refusing to allow NUDL members to go on strike, the only other workers in dispute in support of the miners in Scotland were the members of the SUDL.

The SUDL and the dockers felt they had been 'deserted', particularly by the NTWF, who would not endorse a national stoppage. The SUDL were now on their own, and on 23 May the Executive recommended that the men went back to work.[19] Somewhat reluctantly the dockers did so, but not, it would seem, until June.[20] The Clydeside dockers' strike was over, but it would be some time before the recriminations would end. The strike was to mark the prelude to the slow disintegration of the SUDL.

A resolution, passed by Glasgow Trades Council during September 1921, offers an illustration of the changing fortunes of the SUDL. The Council promised 'every possible assistance to the Scottish Dockers in order to bring about the solidarity they had known at the Port of Glasgow prior to the strike'.[21] There was little chance of this occurring. The dockers were already drawing back from their previous close involvement with the wider labour movement, and they came to distrust the type of 'corporate' trade unionism symbolised by the NTWF. In Glasgow, the dockers were now similarly distrustful of the actions of the SUDL leadership. The dockers' honeymoon was over. Before the strike began the SUDL's financial balance was £20,330 8s 2d. After the strike it was £1,894 1s 9d.[22] Over and above this the SUDL owed £4,000 to the NUR, repayment of which was demanded by January 1922.[23] The overall cost of the strike was estimated to have been £24,262 13s 6d.[24] The SUDL's financial position was disastrous. Drastic cuts were therefore enforced on individual branches in order to prevent their imminent financial collapse.[25]

This was the situation when the SUDL was again asked to amalgamate with the proposed Transport and General Workers' Union towards the end of 1921. The membership had rejected amalgamation in two earlier ballots. Although there was a large majority in favour, in neither case did the ballot produce the five-sixths majority of the total membership, which, according to the constitutional rules, was the number needed to officially wind up the union.[26] By November Ernest Bevin

---

[18] Glasgow Trades Council Minutes, 14 May 1921.
[19] E.C. Emergency meeting, 23 May 1921.
[20] SUDL Executive Minutes, 6 Jun. 1921.
[21] Glasgow Trades and Labour Council Industrial Committee Minutes, 5 Sep. 1921.
[22] SUDL Executive Minutes, 25 Dec. 1920, and 2 Nov. 1921.
[23] SUDL E.C. Emergency Committee Meeting, 19 Jan. 1922.
[24] Ibid., 16 Feb. 1921; see also SRO, FS 10/3, calculation as presented to the Registrar of Friendly Societies for year ending Dec. 1921.
[25] SUDL Executive Minutes, 4 Nov. 1921.
[26] Ibid., 4 Jan. 1922; see *SUDL Constitutional Rules*, Rule xix, Clause 1

informed the Executive Council of the SUDL that the membership would have to transfer to the TGWU, as the cost of balloting the 300,000 TGWU members would be exorbitant. It was stressed, however, that the TGWU would clear all the SUDL's debts and accept all legal liabilities, and that Joseph Houghton was to become Scottish organiser for the TGWU. Bevin also agreed that no more affiliation fees should be paid to the NTWF.[27] The SUDL was all but finished by the end of December 1922 and finally laid to rest when the Certificate of Registration was cancelled by request on 9 November 1923.[28]

During the amalgamation discussion it was stressed to TGWU officials that there was a strong minority in Glasgow who might legally challenge the transfer procedure over the five-sixths majority clause. It was also known at this time that a committee from Glasgow docks branch had independently approached the employers to draw up a 'new agreement', the first clear indication that Glasgow's dockers were intent on deciding affairs for themselves at the port.[29] However, John Veitch, the Area Secretary of the TGWU, dismissed such reports. He felt sure that this minority would come over to the TGWU and in doing so 'bring unity where unity was so much desired'.[30] Unity, however, was the last thing that this strong and influential minority wanted, and unity was something that the TGWU would ultimately fail to achieve at Glasgow.

## From Dock Branch to Independent Trade Union, 1923 to 1939

Many of the problems that were to beset the TGWU in their dealings with the dock workers of Clydeside were already well in evidence before 1923. First, there was a hard core of Glasgow dockers unhappy with the transfer of their membership to the TGWU in December 1922. Secondly, a faction representing the dockers of Glasgow had already approached employers there to draw up their own agreement as to wages and working conditions. Thirdly, the Glasgow branch members of the SUDL had shown on numerous occasions that they had an independent streak and questioned the rulings of the SUDL's Executive Council. A fourth factor was that the dockers of Glasgow exhibited a great sense of their own history, and their place in the development of dock unionism nationally. They always felt that the base for such an organisation should be in Glasgow – the antecedents of which stretched back to the New Unionist period of the late 1880s and early 1890s. Fifthly, their own traditions had shown that they would not function well as a 'mere branch of an English trade union', as illustrated by the disintegration of the NUDL at Glasgow in 1910. In short, they would always want to have control of their own affairs and maintain their headquarters in Scotland.

When considering the 'breakaway' that was to take place at Glasgow in January

---

[27] SUDL Executive Minutes, 18 and 25 Nov. 1922.
[28] SRO, FS 8/18, Registrar of Friendly Societies in Scotland
[29] SUDL Executive Minutes, May 24 1923.
[30] Executive Meeting of the Scottish Union of Dock Labourers and Transport Workers Dec. 19 1922. Typed Minute signed by John Veitch, Area Secretary of the Transport and General Workers' Union, on accepting the transference of the liabilities and membership of the SUDL.

1932 the above factors need continually to be borne in mind. There are, however, other considerations. It was shown through Joseph Houghton's evidence before the Shaw Inquiry that the Glasgow dockers would not accept the principle of decasualisation and the necessary prerequisite of registration. It was reported widely in the press that Glasgow would have 'divided the Federation' (the NTWF) in 1920, rather than accept registration. Ernest Bevin noted at that juncture that 'Glasgow had opposed a great many reforms until they were shown to be good'. He concluded 'this was perhaps part of the Scottish temperament'.[31] This clearly illustrates Bevin's thoughts on trade union democracy – evident in the use of the phrase 'shown to be good'. This could quite easily translate into 'forced to accept what is perceived to be good', as he saw it. Indeed, this was exactly what he, and the TGWU, attempted to do in Glasgow.

It was perhaps inevitable that during the first years of the TGWU's existence it would experience some teething troubles. The all-powerful figure of Ernest Bevin, however, was also part of the problem. According to David Wilson, it was Bevin's association with authoritarianism and the climb-down of the Triple Alliance in 1921, which led to the first docks revolt at London and saw the London officials resign *en masse* for a period (shortly after the TGWU's formation in 1922). Bevin's acceptance of wage cuts was another factor that further exacerbated the matter.[32] By 1923 the pressure was mounting on the TGWU, and in August of that year the *Glasgow Herald* reported on some of the problems that dogged the fledgling TGWU at that juncture. The first major report concerned attempts at Glasgow to 'resuscitate the SUDL', while another noted that some London dockers had already seceded from the union and formed the National Amalgamated Stevedores and Dockers (NASD).[33]

There was also an earlier report of protest by Greenock dockers because preference of employment was being offered to members of the TGWU. These dockers did not wish to join the TGWU, preferring to stay in their own local union. As a result they could not work within Greenock docks and staged an elaborate protest to bring attention to their plight and the actions of the TGWU in the matter. According to the *Glasgow Herald*, the protest involved thirty-five dockers, who, with their wives and families, marched in a procession to the Greenock Poor House and gained entry there on 31 March.[34] This incident is an illustration that many ordinary dockers were unhappy with the TGWU and disliked the loss of their local autonomy. The incident also shows, however, that the TGWU was determined to force dock workers into their ranks. Such methods were simply viewed as further examples of the authoritarian nature of the TGWU. It was this very point that was to create problems at many ports around Britain, not least at the port of Glasgow.

It was the subject of registration, however, that was to bring together the various strands of discontent evident among dockers at this time. Perhaps the biggest problem with registration was that it carried the support of the leadership of the TGWU, and Ernest Bevin in particular. It seemed evident to the rank-and-file that

---

[31] *Glasgow Herald*, 'The Case For Glasgow', 19 Feb. 1920.
[32] Wilson, *The Dockers*, p. 80.
[33] *Glasgow Herald*, 18 and 21 Aug. 1923.
[34] Ibid., 2 Apr. 1922.

registration was a pact entered into between union officials and the employers in order to control the workforce.[35] By 1925 Glasgow's dockers were arranging meetings around the docks and voted strongly 'against the adoption of registration at Glasgow'.[36] There seems to have been a genuine fear that registration was potentially 'destructive of union power'.[37] This could be seen at Ardrossan, where the men had accepted the register in 1919 then demanded its suspension later because they wished to 'de-register non-unionists'.[38] In this instance the register allowed non-unionists to participate in dock work.

Determining who was to be admitted onto the register was one of the main difficulties highlighted by the Port of London Registration Committee, which had been set up in 1920 to oversee the re-introduction of registration at London, following the recommendations of the earlier Roche Committee of 1919. The main problem lay in properly identifying the credentials of each applicant to see whether they had a legitimate right to register, although the report did not highlight any problem in relation to the registration of 'non-unionists' as occured at Ardrossan the year before. During the war registration schemes had been set up in forty-five ports around Britain, but by November 1922, however, only twelve ports still operated a register. No port in Scotland by that time operated a register.[39] The TGWU had always backed proposals for registration, as had Ernest Bevin (repre-senting the NTWF), in line with the Shaw Inquiry conclusions planning for the future of the port transport industry in 1920. In partnership with the Port Labour Employers (who together with the TGWU made up the National Joint Council), and with the backing of the Ministry of Labour (responsible for establishing the Maclean Committee of 1924, which further forced the issue of registration on the industry), they set about promoting Joint Registration Schemes across the country, and by 1927 had successfully established schemes in twenty-eight ports.[40] The pressure to impose registration on the dockers was clearly mounting.

It was during 1928 in Glasgow that the movement against registration finally began to gather momentum. TGWU minutes clearly state that it was Glasgow Docks Branch that set up the Anti-Registration League, and that the committee of the league was 'practically made up of the Glasgow branch'. Later the branch was suspended by the TGWU and Bevin personally endorsed the actions of the area committee in this matter.[41] It would seem that the 'strong minority' which the Area Secretary, John Veitch, had been warned about as early as December 1922 was

[35] This was most definitely stated through the minutes of Area 7 Committee of the TGWU (which covered Clydeside as well as the central belt of Scotland) when it was noted that the National Joint Industrial Council for the Port Industry adopted the principle of decasualisation of the industry in 1924. Noted in Area 7 Committee of the Transport and General Workers' Union Quarterly Minutes, 14/7/24, p. 3.

[36] Ibid., 19 Jun. 1925, p. 9.

[37] Phillips and Whiteside, Casual Labour, p. 225.

[38] Ibid., p. 222.

[39] PRO, LAB 101/18, Port Transport Memorandum, section iii, paras. 13–16, pp. 4–5.

[40] Ibid., Port Transport Memorandum, section iv, para. 28, p. 8.

[41] Minutes illustrate that Glasgow branch refused to carry out the orders of the Docks Group, the Area Committee, or the National Executive of the TGWU, including those of Bevin, TGWU, Area 7 Committee Minutes, 17 Apr. 1928, p. 18.

much stronger than some had thought. For some time this 'minority' had been working in the background, using any means possible to undermine the TGWU as it existed along the waterfront at Glasgow. There seems little doubt that it was members of this group who attempted to set up the Scottish Transport Workers' Union in the later months of 1923, a 'new union', it was noted, that was not only active in Glasgow, but also in Greenock.[42]

However, as one problem was solved between Glasgow and London, another issue would quickly appear, or one would be quickly seized upon. It was also clear that a determined minority was creating many of these difficulties, and any decision made by London would always be questioned. By December 1927, the main issue was the decision to carry out the TGWU Biennial Conference resolution to issue Glasgow Clyde Trust men a union badge, which Glasgow Docks Branch absolutely refused to accept.[43] The main reason behind the move to keep the Clyde Trust men out of the dockers' branch was that they were considered 'permanent men', and if they were made unemployed, as members of the Docks Branch they could legitimately take up casual employment on the docks.[44] It would seem clear that the underlying fear was that the casual docker would lose out to these men who had hitherto no commitment to casual employment. The key factor in this instance was the fear of losing control over union membership and, therefore, entry into dock work, which could mean displacement from regular work. Joseph Houghton was in fact severely censured for his actions by a mass meeting of dockers on 7 February 1928. Houghton had no doubt where the blame lay for the problems they were experiencing at Glasgow at that time: it lay firmly with the 'old die-hards still doing their best to reform the old Scottish Dockers' Union'.[45] Glasgow branch would not budge, however, and neither would the executive of the union; and by April 1928 the big question once more centred on the issue of registration.

### 'An Unusual Awareness of History and Tradition': Glasgow Dockers and Anti-Registration

It was the question of registration that was to prove of major significance at Glasgow. It helped to galvanise the dock labour force there, and from 1928 onwards formed the basis for the mass defection from the ranks of the TGWU, which followed sometime later. Glasgow dockers had for some considerable time held out against registration and the distribution of tallies. They had rejected schemes devised by the SUDL in 1912 and 1917, and it was stated categorically at the Shaw Inquiry that the Glasgow men would never accept such a system.[46] They had constantly refused to accept any system of decasualisation or any interference with their traditional

---

[42] Ibid., references made to the Scottish Transport Workers' Union in Minutes of 16 Oct. 1923, p. 10 and 16 Jan. 1924, p. 3.

[43] Letter from Ernest Bevin to Joseph Houghton, 23 Dec. 1927, and letter from Francis McCabe, Secretary of the Clyde Trust Branch, 30 Jan. 1928.

[44] SUDL Executive Minutes, 7 Dec. 1917.

[45] Letter to Ernest Bevin from Joseph Houghton, regarding Glasgow Docks' entrance fee and the Clyde Trust victimised members, 14 Feb. 1928.

[46] Shaw Inquiry, i, testimony, Joseph Houghton, General Secretary of the SUDL, p. 158.

sphere of control in trade union or in industrial matters. It was in this manner that
the dockers of Glasgow 'revealed the characteristic desire of dockers generally to
protect right and status from any outside interference'.[47]

Registration, in the minds of the dockers of Glasgow, was seen as a principal
method of imposing control over them and their work. In this perceived struggle
for control the dockers of Glasgow formed the Anti-Registration League, along with
dockers at the port of Aberdeen.[48] The Scottish Area Minutes of the TGWU show
that the League was up and running in Glasgow by April 1928.[49] Two months later
Joseph Houghton informed Ernest Bevin that the Anti-Registration League
claimed 2,000 members, and that they would not simply confine themselves to
Registration questions. He also stated that a meeting was to be arranged and that if
Bevin himself could attend this gathering they could 'endeavour to surmount
[their] present difficulties'.[50] Houghton's tone, however, gave the impression that
the situation was not a serious one. In any event Bevin stated that he would not be
able to attend such a meeting, but was disturbed to read of Houghton's claim that
the League had 2,000 members. He wrote to the Area Secretary, John Veitch, to ask
whether he should intervene in the matter, but stated that he was under the
impression that the League was just a small clique.[51]

John Veitch informed Bevin that he felt Houghton's estimates were too high and
that the League actually had only around 1,000 members, 'the greatest proportion of
which had joined through intimidation'. Once again, it would seem, Veitch underestimated the true extent of the feeling at Glasgow (not dissimilar to his disregard of
David Marshall's warnings of the influence of a 'strong minority' in December 1922).
Houghton clearly did not underestimate the influence of the Anti-Registration
Movement at Glasgow, but Veitch simply refused to accept this. The saga was to
continue for many years to come, and it is also clear that Glasgow Docks Branch were
in the habit of moving the goal posts when it suited them. Whenever any attempt was
made to placate the Glasgow branch over one issue, another would be put up in its
place. The question of distributing the union badge, for example, became enmeshed
with the question of constitutionality, and in turn this became interwoven with the
question of registration, which was also later linked to the question of whether
Glasgow had the right to elect its branch officials annually.[52]

The *Glasgow Herald* followed events at this time in some considerable detail,
noting that the situation was 'causing much interest in trade union circles', and by
December 1931, reported on the increasing 'rebelliousness and contrariness' of the
Glasgow dockers. The paper then attempted to trace the roots of the problem:

> The origins lay in the years before amalgamation and the formation of the
> TGWU. The SUDL was one participating union, an organisation that was
> comparatively local in its scope, and within its narrow limits, the officials and

[47] Phillips and Whiteside, *Casual Labour*, p. 226.
[48] Ibid., p. 225.
[49] Area 7 Committee Minutes, 17 Apr. 1928, p. 18.
[50] Letter to Bevin from Houghton, 25 Jun. 1928.
[51] Letter to Veitch from Bevin, 28 Jun. 1928.
[52] Resolution by Glasgow Docks Branch to Docks Group Secretary, 29 Aug. 1928.

the leaders were conscious of independence and direct responsibility. The rank and file was also in closer touch with authority and were more readily able to make their desires known. It was presumably the consciousness of the possession of these privileges, which caused the stubborn resistance of the Scottish dockers to amalgamation and has been responsible for the existence of a continuous feeling of dissatisfaction ever since.[53]

There is much to be said for this particular analysis. Subsequent reports, however, illustrated an inability on the part of the reporter to grasp the mood of the dockers at Glasgow, or their dogged determination to gain greater autonomy in branch affairs. It would be foolish, argued one report, to take antagonistic resolutions enthusiastically passed at branch meetings too seriously.[54] One week later, on 28 December, it was stressed that, 'despite the Glasgow members' threat to form an independent union, there was a strong possibility that negotiations would avert such a situation'.[55] The following week it was reported that the dockers had carried out their threat. They had finally seceded from the TGWU and had formed a new union – the Scottish Transport and General Workers' Union.

## *The Scottish Transport and General Workers Union*

There is perhaps no better evidence of the commitment of the dockers of Glasgow to their own style and type of trade unionism than the fact that the STGWU existed independently for over forty years. There is little doubt that the STGWU caused something of a stir when it broke away from the TGWU in January 1932. The *Glasgow Herald* noted that the STGWU issued its manifesto under the title 'Scotland Forever'. One spokesman stressed that the STGWU members were not a 'break-away'. Rather they provided a manifestation that the Glasgow dockers 'were loyal to the principles of trade unionism.' At least now, they added, they had the satisfaction of 'appointing their own officials'.[56] The most enthusiastic response by the media at this time was seen in the columns of the Nationalist publication the *Scots Independent*. It noted that the Glasgow men had rejected the 'tyranny of English trade unionism', but more importantly, as they saw it, the formation of the STGWU was:

A significant sign of the inevitability of Nationalism in the practical, economic sphere, and is commended to the consideration of Trade Unionists in other industries. It is becoming clear that Scottish interests are sacrificed through centralised London Trade Unionism just as much as through centralised London government.[57]

It is not entirely clear that what was occurring at this time was nationalistic-inspired, but nor can this be ruled out. By the time of the STGWU's Third Annual

[53] *Glasgow Herald*, leading article, 19 Dec. 1931, p. 8.
[54] Ibid.
[55] Ibid., 28 Dec. 1931.
[56] *Glasgow Herald*, 12 Jan. 1932; see also *Forward*, 2, 16, 23 Jan. 1932, and 6 Feb. 1932, where it was stated that the 'cardinal issue in Glasgow was the appointment of officials' and that the breakaway had secured this overriding principle.
[57] *The Scots Independent*, Feb. 1932, p. 54.

Report in June 1934, the political direction of the Glasgow dockers seemed to be changing somewhat, and the following resolution was suggested for consideration:

> The General Executive Council are meantime considering the Union's position from the political side with the object of striking out a new line. We are convinced that the allegiance to the orthodox Labour Party is not a real and definite challenge to the present policy of the powers that be.[58]

Three other reports still survive as documentary evidence for the 1930s, but no further mention is made of any distinctive political break with orthodox labour politics, at least before 1939.[59]

The STGWU did not become the power in Scottish trade union terms that the initial euphoria of formation promised. It had set up a branch at Grangemouth, but quickly lost it back to the TGWU, although it did create a more permanent foothold at Campbeltown.[60] Despite their earnest desire to organise all Scottish transport workers, however, Campbeltown was as far as their organisation was to take them geographically; along with galvanisers at Lochaber, and agricultural workers at Campbeltown. STGWU reports of the 1930s testify to the great efforts made by the TGWU to exclude the STGWU from the National Joint Council for the Port Transport Industry. But by this time the STGWU was already negotiating directly with the Glasgow shipping employers on working conditions and wages – an arrangement that the TGWU was also attempting to break up.[61] By 1935, however, the Glasgow dockers had agreed favourable conditions with the employers, but the final agreement, it was argued, was being held up because of the National Joint Councils' procrastination in London. Despite further attempts by the TGWU to exclude the STGWU from joining the National Joint Council, by 1945 the STGWU were co-signatories to the National Agreement alongside the TGWU, the National Union of General and Municipal Workers, and the National Amalgamated Stevedores and Dockers.[62]

It can be seen that, when attempting to re-create the events that led to the secession of the Glasgow dockers from the TGWU and the formation of the STGWU, there is no one simple answer as to why this should occur at Glasgow. It is also clear that, when considering the experience of Glasgow during this period, it is necessary to place the analysis in a firm historical context. The events leading to

---

[58] Mitchell Library, TUS 331 880941 SCO C. 372406, *Scottish Transport and General Workers' Union, General Executive Report and Financial Statement*, year ending Jun. 1934, p. 2.

[59] Ibid., see report for Jan. 1932 to Jun. 1933, C. 372405; Report for Jun. 1934, C. 372406; *Annual Report* for Jun. 1935, C. 372407, and *Annual Report* Dec. 1938, C. 372408. Oral evidence does suggest that the final break with the Labour Party came in the 1950s and 1960s, when the STGWU affiliated to the Scottish National Party, with the full and active support of the STGWU leadership. It was also suggested, however, that the rank and file, on an individual basis, still leaned to the Labour Party in Scotland. The oral evidence is drawn from the testimony of Tom O'Connor, Executive Member of the STGWU in the 1970s, during various conversations during 1992.

[60] Ibid., Campbeltown is noted in all the accounts registering income in all the above reports.

[61] Ibid., p. 3, *Executive Report*, 1932–33.

[62] National Joint Council Agreement, amended 21 Dec. 1945, p. 54: edition of Agreement between the co-signatories and the National Association of Port Employers, which included the STGWU for the first time.

secession in 1932 cannot be understood without some appreciation of the historical developments of dock unionism at Glasgow from the time of the SUDL, or the early days of the National Union of Dock Labourers which preceded it.

What seems certain is that what was occurring at Glasgow during this period was something more than mere parochialism. The impact of Glasgow dock unionism before 1914 extended well beyond the geographical confines of the port of Glasgow to cover the entire Clydeside waterfront. It is from Glasgow that dock unionism spread from the early months of 1889, and again later, after 1911, following the formation of the SUDL at Glasgow. The SUDL not only assumed the central role of re-organising Clydeside ports, but also two Scottish east-coast ports, as well as two in England. It was in this manner that Glasgow led the way, while others followed, not least in its heartland, Clydeside.

Indeed, before the spread of national unionism among dockers in Scotland, Glasgow had been one of only a few ports, which could trace the early roots of dock trade unionism to the mid-1850s. Glasgow's dockers were well aware of the historic significance of these developments, and, rightly or wrongly, perceived that they had played a pivotal role in drawing up the blueprint for what came to be known as New Unionism, the NUDL being hailed as a 'pioneering organisation' of that movement. The dockers of Glasgow therefore clearly conform to Phillips and Whiteside's definition in that they showed 'an unusual awareness of history and tradition' that had been evident for a generation or more at the time of the STGWU's formation in 1932.

It would also seem clear that the executive officers of the TGWU in Scotland – with the possible exception of Joseph Houghton – never fully understood the dockers of Glasgow. Ernest Bevin believed that strict central control over TGWU affairs was the best way forward for dock unionism and the dock industry in general, and thus strongly influenced trade union affairs at local level. It is equally evident that he was not made fully aware of the extent of the problem that existed at Glasgow, although he was given some prior warning of the dockers' attitudes to registration during the Shaw Inquiry of 1920. John Veitch, on the other hand, consistently underestimated the strength of feeling at Glasgow, and understood neither the dockers nor the dock industry. He thus disregarded all the warnings about the dockers' general level of dissatisfaction, and the lengths that they would go to achieve the trade union autonomy that they had formerly known.

Glasgow's dockers were castigated for their 'rebelliousness and contrariness' – a phrase first used and reported in the *Glasgow Herald* on 19 December 1931. This was evident in the formation of the STGWU, and while Bevin vowed that the Glasgow dockers would 'eat grass', instead they defended and maintained their independent Scottish union for over forty years.[63]

---

[63] The term 'eat grass' is noted in David Wilson, *Dockers: The Impact of Industrial Change* (1972) and was referred to on many occasions in the oral testimonies of those Glasgow dockers consulted for this book. The phrase had become a proud part of the Glasgow dockers' history, and that Bevin never made good his threat was to prove an abiding source of pride and achievement. Discussion with Charles Ward, 25 Jun. 1992; Gordon Banders, 16 Jun. 1992, and Tom O'Connor (all from Glasgow), Mar. 1993.

# Conclusion

By 1914 Glasgow was one of Britain's leading ports and Scotland's largest single port. It came to handle many different types of goods: principally fine goods, iron and steel, grain, timber, coal, ores, provisions, oils, and fruit, and a great variety of other miscellaneous products. Glasgow was a relatively compact port, with the great bulk of its trade being conducted within an area extended along a short stretch of river from Kingston Bridge to Queen's Dock on the north and Princes Dock on the south side. While other ports had an equal record of economic activity, the concentration of labour was much less widely dispersed.

Within this relatively small area of trading activity was a highly concentrated labour force, which numbered somewhere between 5,000 and 7,000 by the late nineteenth and early twentieth centuries. Almost 50% of the Scottish dock labour force was located on Clydeside, and around 40% of the Scottish totals worked along the relatively compact Glasgow waterfront. Moreover, with little or no shed or warehouse space, the great bulk of the work was executed along the dockside. Cargo was instantly dispatched onto carts, and other vehicles, or prepared for loading the moment the cargo touched the quayside. In other words, there was considerable activity along the quaysides of Glasgow.

The dockers lived around their place of work, in areas such as Anderston and the Broomielaw on the north side, and the Gorbals and Tradeston on the south side of the Clyde. They therefore worked and lived within a relatively confined area. They were largely Irish and they brought with them values of community and kinship, which in time stabilised conditions along the waterfront. The Irish constituted over 60% of the dock labour force at Glasgow by the late nineteenth century. Glasgow, therefore, provides an exaggerated example of Lovell's thesis, with the added dimension, unknown at London, or any other English port, of the Scottish Highlanders.

The Irish and the Highlanders shared memories of a rural past, evident, for example, in their dock union's commitment to Land Reform. Both groups shared a strong attachment to the concept of the sub-division of land, where survival depended on access to land, however limited. In the industrial context, dock work and casualism functioned in a similar manner. If casualism can be seen as the 'sub-division' of employment, where survival depended on access to work, however limited, then it is no surprise that the dockers of Glasgow staunchly defended that system.

Perhaps it was to be expected that this fiery combination of the Irish and Highland Scots – fuelled by a unique set of industrial traditions particular to Glasgow – would make it inevitable that strong trade unionism would develop at the port. As was noted in a Parliamentary report in the early nineteenth century:

It is unhappily too well known, that in both Ireland and Scotland, combinations amongst workmen have existed . . . and being highly organised and formidable . . . that as they have become more numerous, their proceedings have acquired a greater degree of openness and audacity . . . with numerous reports of warnings, threats, assaults and the infliction of the most cruel injuries.[1]

It is clear, of course, that what is being considered here is a very different age. But perhaps the remarks still hold good for the later nineteenth century. The dockers of Glasgow were often accused of employing the same tactics, and this study has shown that they manifested the same formidable sense of strength and solidarity during the period of New Unionism when the volatile mix of Irish and Scot came together to great effect.

John Burns, speaking in London in 1890, stated that the dockers had 'more pluck, energy, and enthusiasm than the older unions, and . . . the Dockers' Union had done more to better the conditions of its members in twelve months, than half the old unions did in as many years.'[2] Indeed, at the time of Burns' speech, the dockers of Glasgow were already engaged in an industrial war with the Glasgow shipowners and other employers of dock labour. By the mid-1890s, however, many of the gains of the New Unionist period had been lost. Some felt that this was inevitable, given the nature of new union organisations. In his Presidential address to the Trades Union Congress, at Cardiff in 1895, John Jenkins stressed this very point:

The fire of combination which suddenly possessed these classes in '89, '90 and '91 had burnt itself out and they had lapsed into the disorganisation of former times. Constant excitement and frequent conflict did not in his opinion foster permanency in union.[3]

Without doubt Jenkins, an 'Old Unionist', had a point. Like many an outside observer, however, he failed to fully understand the nature of the industry of which he was speaking. The type of industrial strategy so despaired of by Jenkins was based on the concept of conflict through direct action. While this strategy did prove problematic at times, it was nevertheless appropriate within the framework of the port transport industry. Ships came and went, and the docker only had industrial power when ships were in port. It made sense. Jenkins was also incorrect to suggest that union formation could never be permanent in an environment of continual industrial dispute. Conflict at times seems to have been the lifeblood of the Glasgow dockers – a tendency that James Sexton felt was characteristic of dockers generally. Conflict helped to bring about a greater degree of solidarity at the port of Glasgow. This was particularly evident in the period of the 'Labour Unrest', when the newly

---

[1] Report on the Select Committee on Combination Laws and Industrial Relations, ii, session 1825, *Irish University Press Series of British Parliamentary Papers* p. 8.
[2] *Minutes of the First Annual Conference of the DWRGLU*, held in the Great Assembly Hall, London, 30 Sep. to 4 Oct. 1890; introductory remarks by John Burns on the first day of Conference.
[3] TUC *Annual Report*, Cardiff, 3 Sep. 1895.

formed Scottish Union of Dock Labourers adopted the tactic of direct action to re-organise the dockers.

In the mid-nineteenth century John Ruskin wrote that to get the best out of any man one had to make a direct appeal to his affections. In this manner, he argued, the will or spirit of the creature is brought to its greatest strength. Perhaps the same psychology was used to develop the dockers' affection for trade unionism at Glasgow, through successful appeals to their affection for Irish Home Rule, or Land Reform. This helped to amalgamate political considerations and substantial industrial discontent into a cohesive and united force. It was an appeal that brought out the best in the dockers in relation to the development of dock unionism.

When the established forms of work were being threatened by outside inter-ference, whether by the employers, the trade unions, or the state, the dockers would rise to the defence of that system. This can be seen through the mass rejection of any form of decasualisation, or registration, at Glasgow. By fusing Glasgow's desire for greater autonomy and democracy, and the determination of the dockers to elect their own branch officials, a direct appeal was being made to the affections of the Glasgow dockers. This helped create the best conditions for a united front.

Other ports rejected schemes for registration; most notably Aberdeen which, with Glasgow, was one of only two principal ports noted by the Standing Advisory Committee for the Port Transport Industry, in December 1936, not to be regis-tered.[4] Indeed, by the eve of the Second World War both Aberdeen and Glasgow were still not operating registration schemes, despite the recommendations of the Standing Advisory Committee that the NJC made representation to the Ministry of Labour to 'arrange for inquiries to be held at these ports'.[5] The main difference between Aberdeen and Glasgow, however, is that the former stayed to fight within the TGWU, and showed no inclination to follow Glasgow's example and secede from the union. Indeed, there were secessions at other ports. At London the NASD, formed in 1923, refused to have any dealings with the TGWU and remained a separate union. Their numbers, however, were not as great as at Glasgow, and the NASD did not involve the entire casual dock labour force of the port of London.

What occurred at Glasgow therefore was unparalleled elsewhere along the British waterfront. This is what makes Glasgow unique. While the dock labour force shared much with other dockers, it was sufficiently different in composition and attitude to fuel a fierce and stubborn streak of independence, which was not evident in anywhere near the same degree outwith the port of Glasgow. This determination and self-assurance were to serve and sustain Glasgow's dockers well in their conflict with the TGWU during the 1920s and 1930s.

When in January 1932 the *Scots Independent* predicted that the STGWU would become an example to all Scottish trade unionists in signalling a new nationalistic direction for Scottish labour, the newspaper failed both to properly gauge the true political feelings of the wider movement. It failed to understand the real concerns

[4] PRO, LAB 101/18, *Port Transport Memorandum*, section vi, para. 38, p. 11.
[5] Ibid, *Port Transport Memorandum*, para. 41, p. 13.

of the Glasgow dockers. The STGWU was above all an organisation that was formed to protect the interests of the Glasgow dockers. If the STGWU came to organise other Scottish dockers, this was an added bonus, and some in the leadership certainly believed that this was to be their ultimate goal. However, the initials STGWU could easily have been altered to GTGWU – Glasgow Transport and General Workers' Union.

The dockers of Glasgow had a well-deserved reputation for 'rebelliousness and contrariness', and they were proud of it. They had an abiding memory of the tyranny of English-based trade unionism, dating back to the relocation of NUDL headquarters from its birthplace in Glasgow to Liverpool in 1891. This was cited as one reason why the Glasgow dock labour force eventually left the NUDL in 1910. The incident might have occurred some twenty years before, but the memory of that betrayal remained fresh in the minds of many at Glasgow even through to the 1920s. (The secession from the TGWU in 1932 was building on the same apprehension.) Dockers in general had long memories, and the indignities that were frequently heaped upon them were never forgotten.[6] The dockers of Glasgow were simply an exaggerated example of this condition.

In the final analysis, it is perhaps this factor that sets them apart.[7] The Glasgow dockers had more bitter memories than most and more scores to settle. 'Rebellious and contrary', perhaps, but the dockers of Glasgow always seemed to know the direction in which their trade union organisation should take them. When assessing the actions of the Glasgow dockers over the previous twenty-odd years, and with due recognition of their history, cultures and traditions, their rejection of the NUDL in 1910 or the secession of 1932 should not be seen as the action of hot-headed men. Rather, it was a considered solution to the vexed problem of who had the right to control and influence trade unionism at Glasgow.

The question of trade union democracy was one the dockers of Glasgow had been addressing since the early period of New Unionism. Twenty years had elapsed before the Glasgow dockers decided to reject the NUDL. It took them just ten years to decide to leave the TGWU. In total it had taken the Glasgow dock labour force over forty years to find a solution to their problems. The Glasgow men 'were out and they were staying out', stated the *Glasgow Herald*, when it reported the dockers' secession in 1932. They were to remain out for forty years, until the STGWU was officially closed down in 1972. That the Scottish Transport and General Workers' Union came into existence at all is an illustration of the patience and determination of Glasgow's dock labour force: that the organisation survived independently for four decades is proof of this.

The STGWU was already finished as a positive force by the early 1970s when it amalgamated with the TGWU. The port of Glasgow was also in a terminal state of decline by that time. The Glasgow dock labour force was broken up and transferred to other ports, such as Hunterston on the Ayrshire coast. The deep sense of community and occupational solidarity that existed at Glasgow, however, was not

---

[6] Taplin, 'When is a ship a factory?', p. 8.
[7] Phillips and Whiteside, *Casual Labour*, p. 226.

entirely forgotten. Even to this day, the surviving members of Glasgow's long-redundant dock labour force meet annually for the traditional June outing (a tradition that dated back to that first visit 'doon the water', to Saltcoats on the Ayrshire coast in June 1932). As an illustration of the dockers' stubborn defence of traditions it has been said that the annual trip will continue until the last Glasgow docker is gone.[8]

Many of Glasgow's dock labour force never worked at any other trade, and even those younger dockers who crossed over to other occupations still saw themselves for a time as dockers first and foremost. This tradition dated back to the time when their fathers and grandfathers worked only in the dock industry, and the history of this occupational community stretches back even further to a different land and a different culture. Their experiences left an indelible memory that will not readily be forgotten. It is to be hoped that some real sense of that history has filtered through and become a part of this study.

[8] STGWU *Annual Reports*, 1932, the first Annual Outing was to Saltcoats. I personally attended one outing with the ex-dockers of Glasgow on Tuesday 16 Jun. 1992. I was made most welcome. Much of the oral testimony used so infrequently in this study was gathered on this outing, or on subsequent visits to a selected group of dockers over the following months. With following outings already at the planning stage the remnants of Glasgow's dock labour force will again shortly be on the move, for it has been said that this tradition will continue until the last docker is gone and the memory finally fades away.

# Appendices

## Table I: *Berth Occupation in Glasgow Harbour, 1911.*

| Quay | Berth number | Owner/Agent Allocated Berth | Trade |
|---|---|---|---|
| | | *NORTHSIDE* | |
| RIVERSIDE QUAYS | | | |
| Custom House Quay | No numbers | West Highland Carrying Co | West Highlands |
| (Upper Harbour) | – | John Nisbet & Co | General |
| | | Steel & Bennie Ltd | General |
| Broomielaw | 2 | D MacBrayne Ltd | Inveraray etc |
| Broomielaw | 4 6 | – | River Passenger teamer |
| Broomielaw | 8–22 | G & J Burns | Liverpool/Belfast |
| Broomielaw | 24,26,28 | M Langland & Son | Liverpool/Manchester |
| Anderson Quay | 30,32,34 | Laird Line | Londonderry etc |
| Hydepark Quay | 36 | G & J Burns | Dublin |
| Hydepark Quay | 38 | Rennie & Watson | Isle of Man |
| Lancefield Quay | 40,42 | D MacBrayne Ltd | West Highlands |
| Lancefield Quay | 44 | M Orme & J McCallum | West Highlands |
| Lancefield Quay | 46 | M Langlands | Manchester |
| Finnieston Quay | 48,50 | – | Crane Berths |
| Stobcross Quay | 52,54 | – | Crane Berths |
| Stobcross Quay | 56–64 | – | General |
| Stobcross Quay | 66,68,70 | Anchor Line | India |
| Yorkhill Quay | 1,2 | " | General |
| Yorkhill Quay | 3,4,5 | " | United States |
| Yorkhill Quay | 6,8 | A Holt & Co | China, Austrialia |
| Yorkhill Quay | 7,9 | – | General |
| Meadowside Quay | – | – | General |
| Merklands Quay | – | – | Timber & General |
| | | | |
| QUEEN'S DOCK | | | |
| South Quay | 1,3 | I & P Hutcheson | Spain, France |
| South Quay | 5–17 | – | General |
| East End of South Basin | 19 | – | General |
| Central Pier,South Basin | 21–29 | G Smith & Sons | India, SouthAfrica, etc. |
| Central Pier,West End | 31 | – | General |
| Central Pier,North Basin | 32 | P Henderson & Co | Burma & South Africa |
| Central Pier,North Basin | 22–30 | Cayzer, Irvine & Co | India & South Africa |
| East End of North Basin | 20 | – | General |
| North Quay | 2–18 | – | Mineral Trades. |
| | | | |
| ROTHESAY DOCK | – | – | Mineral Trades |

**Table I** *contd*

| Quay | Berth number | Owner/Agent Allocated Berth | Trade |
|---|---|---|---|
| | | *SOUTH SIDE* | |
| RIVERSIDE QUAYS | | | |
| Clyde Place Quay | 1,3 | Henry Lamont & Co | Liverpool |
| Clyde Place Quay | 5 | Hill & Co | Arran |
| Clyde Place Quay | 7,9 | James Little & Co | Stranraer, Preston, etc |
| Clyde Place Quay | 11,13 | R Gilchrist & Co | Liverpool |
| Windmillcroft Quay | 15–21 | William Sloan & Co | Bristol, SouthWales, etc |
| Windmillcroft Quay | 23,25 | Clyde Shipping Co | London, etc |
| Windmillcroft Quay | 27 | – | General |
| Springfield Quay | 29–35 | – | General |
| General Terminus Quay | 37–53 | – | Coal Trade |
| Mavisbank | 55–63 | – | Mineral Trades |
| Plantation Quay | 65 | – | Antwerp |
| Plantation Quay | 67–75 | Allan Line | United States/Canada, |
| Plantation Quay | 77 | – | General |
| Plantation Quay | 79 | Prentice, Service, Henderson | West Indies |
| Plantation Quay | 81 | – | 60 ton Crane |
| Plantation Quay | 83 | – | General |
| Shieldhall Wharves | – | – | Timber |
| | | | |
| KINGSTON DOCK | | | |
| North Quay | 2 | Lock Fyne & Glasgow S.P.Co | Inveraray, etc |
| North Quay | 4 | J Hay & Sons | Portrush, etc |
| North Quay | 6 | – | General |
| North Quay | 8 | Campbelltown S.P.Co | Campbelltown |
| North Quay | 10 | – | General |
| South Quay | 1,11 | – | General |
| East Quay | A | – | General |
| West Quay | B | William Robertson & Co | London etc |
| | | | |
| PRINCE'S DOCK | | | |
| North Quay, North Basin | 1–4 | Allan Line | United States/Canada |
| East End of North Basic | 5 | – | General |
| South Quay, North Basin | 6–8 | – | United States/Canada |
| West End of North Pier | 9 | – | General |
| North Quay,Centre Basin | 10–12 | – | General |
| East End of Centre Basin | 13 | – | General |
| South Quay,Centre Basin | 14–17 | Donaldson Bros | United States/Canada |
| West End of South Pier | 18 | – | General |
| North Quay, South Baisin | 19–22 | – | United States/Canada |
| East End Of South Basin | 23 | – | General |
| South Quay | 24–28 | – | Mineral/Timber Trades |
| West Quay | 29–31 | – | General & Crane Berth |

**Source:** John F. Riddel. Clyde Navigation: A History of the Development and Deepening of the River Clyde (Edinburgh, 1979).

**Table II:** *Progress of Trade and Total Revenue from 1882 to 1920 (Rounded down to the nearest Pound)*

| Year | Tonnage of Vessels | Tonnage of Goods | Total Revenue |
|------|------|------|------|
| 1882 | 6,098,414 | 3,366,866 | 264,549 |
| 1883 | 6,352,630 | 3,724,678 | 283,998 |
| 1884 | 6,629,662 | 3,708,672 | 291,182 |
| 1885 | 6,314,671 | 3,732,220 | 291,658 |
| 1886 | 6,110,660 | 3,732,282 | 282,912 |
| 1887 | 6,208,188 | 3,723,058 | 287,933 |
| 1888 | 6,638,376 | 4,084,309 | 311,495 |
| 1889 | 6,793,366 | 4,383,345 | 331,492 |
| 1890 | 6,979,815 | 4,794,562 | 356,202 |
| 1891 | 6,728,990 | 4,477,506 | 354,580 |
| 1892 | 7,191,041 | 4,896,817 | 369,226 |
| 1893 | 7,020,566 | 4,879,312 | 368,497 |
| 1894 | 7,559,521 | 5,070,392 | 371,976 |
| 1895 | 7,318,773 | 4,504,962 | 353,813 |
| 1897 | 8,086,151 | 5,673,152 | 410,190 |
| 1898 | 8,563,764 | 7,102,199 | 430,327 |
| 1899 | 8,583,479 | 6,959,845 | 427,943 |
| 1900 | 8,761,193 | 7,215,368 | 441,419 |
| 1901 | 8,761,363 | 7,273,533 | 444,077 |
| 1902 | 9,293,650 | 7,471,821 | 458,845 |
| 1903 | 10,427,136 | 8,567,443 | 497,868 |
| 1904 | 10,833,490 | 9,138,029 | 517,491 |
| 1905 | 11,121,336 | 9,025,806 | 513,547 |
| 1906 | 11,294,885 | 9,256,218 | 528,569 |
| 1907 | 11,799,613 | 9,795,093 | 547,861 |
| 1908 | 11,993,591 | 9,530,693 | 556,965 |
| 1909 | 11,975,558 | 9,618,563 | 537,667 |
| 1910 | 12,354,788 | 10,097,283 | 555,403 |
| 1911 | 12,498,468 | 10,359,202 | 577,322 |
| 1912 | 12,220,538 | 9,524,662 | 582,554 |
| 1913 | 13,469,191 | 10,418,324 | 624,826 |
| 1914 | 13,821,425 | 10,067,302 | 633,758 |
| 1915 | 13,123,333 | 9,579,961 | 647,673 |
| 1916 | 12,117,920 | 9,710,969 | 705,976 |
| 1917 | 11,074,647 | 8,433,437 | 683,375 |
| 1918 | 8,520,865 | 7,973,613 | 752,719 |
| 1919 | 7,930,879 | 6,941,997 | 887,246 |
| 1920 | 10,180,608 | 7,028,020 | 1,077,998 |

**Table II** *contd*

| Year | Tonnage of Vessels | Tonnage of Goods | Total Revenue |
|------|-------------------|------------------|---------------|
| 1921 | 9,785,893  | 5,821,839 | 1,058,134 |
| 1922 | 11,807,274 | 6,021,375 | 1,015,728 |
| 1923 | 12,823,195 | 8,042,053 | 1,067,061 |
| 1924 | 12,738,772 | 7,667,162 | 985,867 |
| 1925 | 13,890,393 | 7,446,960 | 1,082,712 |
| 1926 | 13,367,601 | 6,745,538 | 1,017,617 |
| 1927 | 13,246,553 | 6,765,036 | 1,014,677 |
| 1928 | 14,007,053 | 7,377,908 | 1,083,528 |
| 1929 | 13,793,006 | 6,960,876 | 1,059,497 |
| 1930 | 14,429,199 | 7,446,696 | 1,012,784 |
| 1931 | 13,759,193 | 6,262,583 | 865,475 |
| 1932 | 12,584,687 | 5,669,505 | 768,319 |
| 1933 | 12,061,225 | 5,317,065 | 733,721 |
| 1934 | 13,017,968 | 6,116,452 | 796,935 |
| 1935 | 13,699,071 | 6,480,970 | 869,277 |
| 1936 | 14,309,455 | 6,437,441 | 918,137 |
| 1937 | 15,132,553 | 6,742,977 | 949,935 |
| 1938 | 15,721,920 | 7,264,775 | 1,012,470 |
| 1939 | 15,758,478 | 6,189,184 | 955,931 |
| 1940 | 16,321,741 | 7,975,141 | 1,027,353 |
| 1941 | 15,201,002 | 8,744,364 | 1,153,775 |
| 1942 | 14,331,716 | 7,989,315 | 1,255,216 |
| 1943 | 16,051,714 | 8,797,694 | 1,335,064 |
| 1944 | 18,140,522 | 9,219,580 | 1,386,774 |
| 1945 | 16,233,116 | 8,949,343 | 1,339,799 |
| 1946 | 11,353,516 | 6,226,630 | 1,180,123 |
| 1947 | 10,942,751 | 5,259,419 | 1,104,114 |
| 1948 | 11,851,832 | 5,595,956 | 1,501,637 |
| 1949 | 12,664,010 | 5,753,853 | 1,577,463 |
| 1950 | 12,825,271 | 5,539,425 | 1,646,805 |
| 1951 | 13,538,645 | 5,655,428 | 1,676,033 |
| 1952 | 13,680,519 | 6,010,369 | 1,824,374 |
| 1953 | 14,225,005 | 5,633,750 | 1,898,934 |
| 1954 | 14,554,375 | 5,919,739 | 2,075,078 |
| 1955 | 14,635,546 | 6,719,308 | 2,186,706 |
| 1956 | 14,478,175 | 7,089,404 | 2,359,248 |
| 1957 | 14,113,220 | 7,023,008 | 2,588,525 |

Source: Glasgow City Archives, T-CN Coll, Clyde Navigation Trust Papers.

**Table III (i):** *Net Registered Tonnage, Inwards and Outwards, Imported and Exported for Coal, cargo and bunker; Iron and steel, and Iron Ore between 1905 and 1935.*

| Year | Coal | Iron/Steel | Iron Ore |
|------|------|------------|----------|
| 1905 | 3,442,056 | 928,048 | 1,170,958 |
| 1906 | 3,364,987 | 1,024,227 | 1,231,429 |
| 1907 | 3,617,415 | 1,187,303 | 1,280,293 |
| 1908 | 3,649,441 | 1,137,899 | 1,033,263 |
| 1909 | 3,961,405 | 1,055,039 | 1,200,130 |
| 1910 | 4,014,532 | 1,037,685 | 1,379,867 |
| | | | |
| 1911* | 4,176,630 | 1,142,319 | 1,406,915 |
| 1912 | 3,747,106 | 1,111,991 | 1,054,995 |
| 1913* | 4,016,070 | 1,286,621 | 1,279,455 |
| 1914 | 4,024,360 | 1,192,326 | 1,111,825 |
| 1915 | 4,131,648 | 852,365 | 1,163,595 |
| 1916 | 3,794,857 | 1,040,967 | 1,198,676 |
| 1917 | 3,182,522 | 672,572 | 1,306,709 |
| 1918 | 3,425,961 | 84,775 | 1,211,667 |
| 1919 | 2,467,385 | 474,229 | 1,238,611 |
| 1920 | 1,903,283 | 751,299 | 1,002,470 |
| | | | |
| 1921 | 1,445,508 | 900,625 | 512,385 |
| 1922 | 2,644,081 | 532,404 | 159,685 |
| 1923 | 3,523,666 | 886,557 | 592,497 |
| 1924 | 3,149,513 | 845,452 | 617,316 |
| 1925 | 2,949,301 | 842,804 | 405,817 |
| 1926 | 2,704,216 | 813,766 | 268,334 |
| 1927 | 2,183,203 | 820,775 | 284,040 |
| 1928 | 2,657,186 | 971,816 | 540,166 |
| 1929 | 2,433,658 | 1,094,390 | 387,665 |
| 1930 | 2,786,443 | 1,145,769 | 557,624 |
| | | | |
| 1931 | 2,464,575 | 806,279 | 180,170 |
| 1932 | 2,372,096 | 515,241 | 77,056 |
| 1933 | 2,221,309 | 497,224 | 33,085 |
| 1934 | 2,321,883 | 605,268 | 209,834 |
| 1935 | 2,398593 | 696,916 | 218,657 |

*These years recorded the highest levels for these products.

**Source:** Glasgow City Archives, T-CN Coll, Clyde Navigation Trust Papers.

**Table III (ii):** *Net Registered Tonnage, Inwards and Outwards, Imported and Exported for Selected Goods: Grain; Flour; Fruits and Preserved Fruit; and Oils and Petrol, between 1905 and 1935.*

| Year | Grain | Flour | Fruit/Preserved | Oils/Petrols |
|------|-------|-------|-----------------|--------------|
| 1905 | 427,756 | 272,851 | 91,409 | 92,327 |
| 1906 | 512,593 | 305,082 | 81,675 | 93,761 |
| 1907 | 422,064 | 296,378 | 84,035 | 101,117 |
| 1908 | 469,013 | 311,194 | 94,742 | 108,519 |
| 1909 | 389,283 | 273,109 | 83,973 | 102,270 |
| 1910 | 454,742 | 272,049 | 87,034 | 112,427 |
| 1911 | 393,696 | 281,949 | 91,698 | 121,086 |
| 1912 | 452,551 | 285,185 | 100,628 | 130,189 |
| 1913 | 491,094 | 272,653 | 94,920 | 131,110 |
| 1914 | 487,314 | 273,104 | 77,254 | 111,581 |
| 1915 | 439,750 | 266,457 | 97,918 | 99,908 |
| 1916 | 477,817 | 282,640 | 89,414 | 128,476 |
| 1917 | 510,100 | 282,406 | 73,839 | 103,778 |
| 1918 | 500,341 | 342,286 | 30,145 | 110,522 |
| 1919 | 379,376 | 268,244 | 54,548 | 396,491 |
| 1920 | 506,484 | 294,635 | 79,773 | 427,047 |
| 1921 | 453,400 | 268,271 | 98,605 | 409,990 |
| 1922 | 402,194 | 318,028 | 108,188 | 345,810 |
| 1923 | 410,667 | 270,130 | .122,759 | 353,867 |
| 1924 | 464,641 | 269,530 | 123,563 | 191,210 |
| 1925 | 446,515 | 283,794 | 139,392 | 352,563 |
| 1926 | 366,856 | 262,117 | 129,949 | 298,911 |
| 1927 | 322,543 | 267,154 | 136,175 | 295,750 |
| 1928 | 376,335 | 265,253 | 126,995 | 299,673 |
| 1929 | 397,502 | 238,085 | 125,032 | 292,408 |
| 1930 | 326,997 | 257,758 | 120,699 | 313,833 |
| 1931 | 372,881 | 247,745 | 122,722 | 364,743 |
| 1932 | 414,360 | 264,896 | 125,477 | 282,029 |
| 1933 | 381,110 | 247,309 | 130,942 | 317,600 |
| 1934 | 342,745 | 233,469 | 136,299 | 477,867 |
| 1935 | 336,824 | 283,489 | 146,388 | 544,633 |

**Source:** Glasgow City Archives, T-CN Coll, Clyde Navigation Trust Papers.

**Table IV:** *Showing the Number and Tonnage of Sail and Steam Ships Arriving at the Port of Glasgow between 1856 and 1908*

| YEAR | Sailing Ships | | Steam Ships | | Totals | |
|---|---|---|---|---|---|---|
| | Nos. | Tons. | Nos. | Tons. | Nos. | Tons. |
| 1856 | 5,779 | 445,976 | 11,804 | 1,227,120 | 17,583 | 1,673,096 |
| 1857 | 5,762 | 439,409 | 12,808 | 1,173,182 | 17,960 | 1,612,681 |
| 1858 | 5,506 | 451,364 | 12,640 | 1,113,527 | 18,146 | 1,564,891 |
| 1859 | 5,414 | 440,607 | 12,403 | 1,104,182 | 17,817 | 1,544,789 |
| 1860 | 4,502 | 415,715 | 11,476 | 1,033,154 | 15,978 | 1,448,869 |
| 1861 | 4,804 | 474,740 | 11,281 | 1,029,480 | 16,085 | 1,504,220 |
| 1862 | 4,573 | 478,189 | 11,291 | 1,052,453 | 15,864 | 1,530,642 |
| 1863 | 4,620 | 491,797 | 10,555 | 1,035,982 | 15,175 | 1,527,779 |
| 1864 | 4,569 | 483,305 | 9,962 | 1,044,934 | 14,531 | 1,528,239 |
| 1865 | 4,499 | 457,774 | 11,856 | 1,261,284 | 16,355 | 1,719,058 |
| 1866 | 4,113 | 463,736 | 12,612 | 1,400,464 | 16,725 | 1,864,200 |
| 1867 | 3,732 | 448,419 | 11,433 | 1,334,453 | 15,165 | 1,782,872 |
| 1868 | 3,711 | 482,168 | 11,710 | 1,336,970 | 15,421 | 1,849,138 |
| 1869 | 3,452 | 475,653 | 12,255 | 1,440,804 | 15,707 | 1,916,507 |
| 1870 | 3,372 | 502,517 | 12,712 | 1,489,593 | 16,084 | 1,992,110 |
| 1871 | 3,087 | 461,009 | 12,713 | 1,558,699 | 15,800 | 2,049,708 |
| 1872 | 3,337 | 462,972 | 12,125 | 1,665,407 | 15,462 | 2,128,379 |
| 1873 | 3,116 | 395,800 | 11,517 | 1,800,401 | 14,633 | 2,196,201 |
| 1874 | 2,870 | 369,267 | 11,176 | 1,832,154 | 14,046 | 2,201,421 |
| 1875 | 2,768 | 423,553 | 11,213 | 1,826,304 | 13,981 | 2,249,857 |
| 1876 | 2,816 | 431,522 | 11,770 | 1,866,554 | 14,586 | 2,298,076 |
| 1877 | 2,866 | 471,873 | 11,997 | 1,956,743 | 14,863 | 2,428,616 |
| 1878 | 2,727 | 457,290 | 13,210 | 2,154,733 | 15,937 | 2,612,023 |
| 1879 | 2,213 | 393,681 | 14,052 | 2,286,876 | 16,265 | 2,680,557 |
| 1880 | 1,862 | 321,721 | 14,948 | 2,350,478 | 16,810 | 2,672,199 |
| 1881 | 1,948 | 369,563 | 15,815 | 2,687,970 | 17,763 | 3,057,533 |
| 1882 | 1,825 | 288,859 | 15,468 | 2,760,378 | 17,293 | 3,049,237 |
| 1883 | 1,794 | 327,686 | 15,858 | 2,972,014 | 17,651 | 3,299,700 |
| 1884 | 1,567 | 292,825 | 16,298 | 3,068,362 | 17,874 | 3,361,187 |
| 1885 | 1,385 | 259,296 | 15,454 | 2,941,362 | 16,839 | 3,200,658 |
| 1886 | 1,302 | 259,354 | 14,576 | 2,822,118 | 15,878 | 3,081,472 |
| 1887 | 1,279 | 234,954 | 15,047 | 2,883,561 | 16,326 | 3,118,515 |
| 1888 | 1,340 | 221,440 | 15,466 | 3,116,230 | 16,806 | 3,337,670 |
| 1889 | 1,268 | 223,850 | 15,632 | 3,186,741 | 16,900 | 3,410,591 |
| 1890 | 1,244 | 240,405 | 15,401 | 3,256,443 | 16,645 | 3,496,848 |

**Table IV** *contd*

| YEAR | Sailing Ships | | Steam Ships | | Totals | |
|---|---|---|---|---|---|---|
| | Nos. | Tons. | Nos. | Tons. | Nos. | Tons. |
| 1891 | 1,280 | 239,334 | 14,855 | 3,135,775 | 16,135 | 3,375,109 |
| 1892 | 1,193 | 249,272 | 14,736 | 3,376,626 | 15,929 | 3,625,898 |
| 1893 | 1,137 | 178,780 | 14,374 | 3,363,487 | 15,511 | 3,515,267 |
| 1894 | 993 | 178,535 | 15,083 | 3,600,006 | 16,076 | 3,778,541 |
| 1895 | 913 | 143,642 | 14,479 | 3,523,422 | 15,392 | 3,667,064 |
| 1896 | 960 | 158,572 | 15,430 | 3,789,910 | 16,390 | 3,948,482 |
| 1897 | 712 | 128,731 | 15,728 | 3,953,321 | 16,440 | 4,082,052 |
| 1898 | 653 | 150,750 | 16,333 | 4,165,558 | 16,986 | 4,316,308 |
| 1899 | 567 | 124,446 | 15,558 | 4,234,292 | 16,125 | 4,358,738 |
| 1900 | 547 | 125,765 | 15,352 | 4,235,832 | 15,899 | 4,361,598 |
| 1901 | 585 | 108,641 | 14,696 | 4,276,782 | 15,281 | 4,385,423 |
| 1902 | 552 | 133,877 | 14,934 | 4,555,711 | 15,486 | 4,689,588 |
| 1903 | 520 | 133,060 | 15,147 | 4,969,223 | 15,667 | 5,102,283 |
| 1904 | 484 | 118,924 | 15,020 | 5,220,831 | 15,504 | 5,339,755 |
| 1905 | 533 | 127,206 | 15,554 | 5,343,800 | 16,087 | 5,471,006 |
| 1906 | 509 | 113,473 | 15,492 | 5,447,254 | 16,001 | 5,560,727 |
| 1907 | 458 | 96,521 | 15,939 | 5,703,770 | 16,397 | 5,800,291 |
| 1908 | 436 | 125,808 | 15,856 | 5,882,958 | 16,292 | 6,008,766 |

**Source:** J. D. Marwick, The River Clyde and the Clyde Burghs, 1909 (Glasgow, 1909).

**Table V:** *Particulars of Accidents Caused by Defective Gear and Machinery.*

| Cause of Accident | Nature of Injury |
|---|---|
| Breaking of Rope Sling – used for discharging sugar – rope was old and Worn | Both legs broken, and internal injuries resulting in death. |
| Unguarded wheel cogs of ship's winch. | Loss of two forefingers and thumb, half of hand, and part of wrist. |
| Breaking axle pin – not examined for some time before accident, and not sufficiently oiled. | Fractures skull, resulting in death. |
| Falling of iron ball comprising upper portion of chain used to hoist, bolt supporting it gave way. | The palm of right hand was torn away, the whole hand severely crushed and injured. |
| A bale falling through being hoisted on hooks. | Crushed to death. |
| Explosion of Gas – bad ventilation. | Injuries to face, hands and arms. |
| Collapsed staging – badly erected. | Concussion of the brain. |
| Collapse of platform across hatch – badly erected and causing man to be thrown down onto ballast tanks, the lids of which had been left off. | Both legs broken. |
| Breaking shackle pin – old and worn. | Injured shoulder and muscle sprain to spine. |
| Falling bale through hatchway – left open. | Injury to spine causing paralysis and death. |
| Unguarded winch wheel. | Shock – hand crushed and one finger lost. |
| Breaking chain in hold – old and worn. | Two broken ribs and injured right shoulder. |
| Breaking plank – defective and rotten. | Shock – fractured knee and bruised ankle. |
| Left open hatches after discharge – no guard. | Back broken and concussion, died later. |
| Falling moveable mast – improperly secured. | Severe scalp wound. |
| Defective hatch giving way – fell into hold. | Concussion of the spine |
| Chain sling used instead of rope sling on greasy iron tubes – tubes consequently slid out. | Injury to nose causing abscess to lower brain and eventual death. |
| Giving way of hatches on which man was ordered to stand by foreman. | Internal injuries and two severe outward injuries. |
| Hit by load of iron, due to incompetence. | Collar bone broken. |
| Badly stowed tin on dockside – toppled over and erected by order of foreman. | Compound fracture of the legs and sprained ankle. |

**Table V** *contd*

| Cause of Accident | Nature of Injury |
| --- | --- |
| Falling gear due to shackle pin giving way. | Fractured skull. |
| Fell into coal bunker in darkness – foreman's fault. | Serious injuries to head and body. |
| Fall on board ship. | Injuries to body. |
| Struck by coal while minding coal tip. | Injuries to head. |
| Crushed by basket of ballast. | Killed. |
| Defective gear falling into hold – fault of foreman. | Killed. |
| Hurt while drawing out piece of timber. | Severely bruised. |
| Knocked over by ballast tub. | Severely bruised. |
| Barrel falling out of sling. | Severely bruised. |
| Falling bucket due to chain breaking. | Foot badly injured. |
| Fell into hold with improperly fastened hatch. | Injuries to back and head. |
| Defective rope – struck by bag of salt. | Injuries to head. |
| Fell into hold – faulty staging. | Injuries to head and body. |
| Fell into hold – faulty staging. | Injuries to head and body. |
| Fell into hold – faulty staging. | Injuries to head and body. |
| Struck by rope and carried away. | Injuries to spine. |
| Fell into dock – faulty staging. | Shock. |
| Breaking of crane chain link. | Injuries resulting in death. |
| Rope breaking. | Permanently injured – unable to work. |
| Fall into hold through unprotected hatch. | Killed. |
| Unsecured plank tilting. | Drowned. |
| Hit by falling gear – defective. | Killed. |

*Note – there were also two accidents reported but extent of injuries were not noted.

**Source:** Report of the Executive of the National Union of Dock Labourers, half year ending December 1892 (adopted, Annual Congress October 1893)

**Table VI (i):** *Number of Disablements and Fatalities and Percentages of Total Numbers employed in seven selected industries for the year 1909.*

|  | Disablement | (%) | Fatalities | (%) | Total Numbers Employed |
|---|---|---|---|---|---|
| Shipping | 6,486 | 2.70 | 334 | 0.13 | 240,080 |
| Factories | 123,134 | 2.86 | 650 | 0.01 | 4,302,217 |
| Docks | 6,486 | 4.98 | 118 | 0.09 | 130,000 |
| Mines | 141,106 | 13.62 | 1,493 | 0.14 | 1,035,694 |
| Quarries | 5,536 | 6.22 | 83 | 0.09 | 88,880 |
| Construction | 7,221 | 7.82 | 129 | 0.13 | 92,298 |
| Railways | 20,245 | 5.51 | 358 | 0.09 | 366,844 |

**Source:** Home Office Workmen's Compensation Statistics 1909 [Cd 5386, 1910]

**Table VI (ii):** *Number of Disablements and Fatalities and percentages of Total Numbers employed in seven selected industries for the year 1910.*

|  | Disablement | (%) | Fatalities | (%) | Total Numbers Employed |
|---|---|---|---|---|---|
| Shipping | 6,410 | 2.55 | 456 | 0.18 | 250,583 |
| Factories | 139,825 | 2.97 | 650 | 0.01 | 4,692,313 |
| Docks | 11,950 | 9.27 | 174 | 0.13 | 128,878 |
| Mines | 151,332 | 14.19 | 1,347 | 0.12 | 1,066,239 |
| Quarries | 5,220 | 5.78 | 91 | 0.10 | 90,212 |
| Construction | 5,790 | 5.92 | 110 | 0.11 | 97,719 |
| Railways | 19,292 | 5.15 | 410 | 0.10 | 374,240 |

**Source:** Home Office Workmen's Compensation Statistics 1910 [Cd 5896, 1911]

**Table VI (iii):** *Number of Disablements and Fatalities and percentages of Total Numbers employed in seven selected industries for the year 1911.*

|  | Disablement | (%) | Fatalities | (%) | Total Numbers Employed |
|---|---|---|---|---|---|
| Shipping | 6,848 | 2.74 | 501 | 0.20 | 249,758 |
| Factories | 161,361 | 3.26 | 999 | 0.02 | 4,943,732 |
| Docks | 13,853 | 10.47 | 196 | 0.14 | 132,246 |
| Mines | 161,959 | 5.57 | 1,711 | 0.16 | 1,039,642 |
| Quarries | 5,192 | 5.64 | 83 | 0.09 | 91,957 |
| Construction | 6,026 | 6.03 | 102 | 0.10 | 99,889 |
| Railways | 20,736 | 5.46 | 393 | 0.10 | 379,226 |

**Source:** Home Office Workmen's Compensation Statistics 1911 [Cd 6493, 1912]

**Table VI (iv):** *Number of Disablements and Fatalities and percentages of Total Numbers employed in seven selected industries for the year 1912.*

|  | Disablement | (%) | Fatalities | (%) | Total Numbers Employed |
|---|---|---|---|---|---|
| Shipping | 8,301 | 2.74 | 515 | 0.20 | 254,398 |
| Factories | 88,480 | 3.26 | 1,037 | 0.02 | 5,250,431 |
| Docks | 16,937 | 10.47 | 225 | 0.14 | 154,398 |
| Mines | 167,959 | 15.57 | 1,246 | 0.16 | 1,086,113 |
| Quarries | 5,440 | 5.64 | 64 | 0.09 | 84,703 |
| Construction | 6,111 | 6.03 | 85 | 0.10 | 115,218 |
| Railways | 24,368 | 5.46 | 369 | 0.10 | 461,544 |

**Source:** Home Office Workmen's Compensation Statistics 1912 [Cd 7088, 1913]

**Table VI (v):** *Number of Disablements and Fatalities and percentages of Total Numbers employed in seven selected industries for the year 1913.*

|  | Disablement | (%) | Fatalities | (%) | Total Numbers Employed |
|---|---|---|---|---|---|
| Shipping | 8,191 | 3.17 | 497 | 0.19 | 258,272 |
| Factories | 208,949 | 3.91 | 1,091 | 0.02 | 5,342,625 |
| Docks | 17,147 | 12.17 | 207 | 0.14 | 140,820 |
| Mines | 195,387 | 17.53 | 1,312 | 0.11 | 1,114,210 |
| Quarries | 6,001 | 6.85 | 66 | 0.07 | 87,541 |
| Construction | 6,568 | 6.70 | 96 | 0.09 | 97,954 |
| Railways | 26,444 | 5.65 | 450 | 0.09 | 467,931 |

**Source:** Home Office Workmen's Compensation Statistics 1913 [Cd 7669, 1914]

**Table VI (vi):** *Number of Disablements and Fatalities and percentages of Total Numbers employed in seven selected industries for the year 1914.*

|  | Disablement | (%) | Fatalities | (%) | Total Numbers Employed |
|---|---|---|---|---|---|
| Shipping | 7,377 | 2.92 | 515 | 0.20 | 251,880 |
| Factories | 190,130 | 3.80 | 1,061 | 0.02 | 4,995,668 |
| Docks | 14,602 | 11.70 | 196 | 0.15 | 124,708 |
| Mines | 179,899 | 17.19 | 1,768 | 0.16 | 1,046,357 |
| Quarries | 5,674 | 6.86 | 83 | 0.10 | 82,709 |
| Construction | 6,248 | 6.93 | 104 | 0.11 | 90,061 |
| Railways | 24,309 | 5.21 | 441 | 0.09 | 465,728 |

**Source:** Home Office Workmen's Compensation Statistics 1914 [Cd 8079, 1915]

**Table VI (vii):** *Number of Disablements and Fatalities and percentages of Total Numbers employed in seven selected industries for the year 1919.*

|  | Disablement | (%) | Fatalities | (%) | Total Numbers Employed |
|---|---|---|---|---|---|
| Shipping | 3,867 | 1.82 | 309 | 0.14 | 211,422 |
| Factorics | 183,358 | 2.99 | 1,165 | 0.01 | 6,127,706 |
| Docks | 10,196 | 6.31 | 135 | 0.08 | 161,371 |
| Mines | 134,991 | 11.40 | 1,248 | 0.10 | 1,184,038 |
| Quarries | 2,973 | 6.38 | 34 | 0.06 | 49,235 |
| Construction | 3,107 | 3.12 | 52 | 0.05 | 99,547 |
| Railways | 16,536 | 3.14 | 324 | 0.06 | 525,864 |

**Source:** Home Office Workmen's Compensation Statistics 1919 [Cmd 1185, 1920]

**Table VI (viii):** *Number of Disablements and Fatalities and percentages of Total Numbers employed in seven selected industries for the year 1922.*

|  | Disablement | (%) | Fatalities | (%) | Total Numbers Employed |
|---|---|---|---|---|---|
| Shipping | 4,707 | 2.17 | 287 | 0.13 | 216,181 |
| Factories | 138,478 | 2.70 | 708 | 0.01 | 5,119,388 |
| Docks | 9,843 | 8.06 | 92 | 0.07 | 122,030 |
| Mines | 201,370 | 17.93 | 1,067 | 0.09 | 1,122,511 |
| Quarries | 3,897 | 6.20 | 35 | 0.05 | 62,781 |
| Construction | 4,805 | 5.15 | 40 | 0.04 | 93,183 |
| Railways | 13,982 | 2.97 | 232 | 0.04 | 469,535 |

**Source:** Home Office Workmen's Compensation Statistics 1922 [Cmd 2007, 1923]

**Table VI (ix):** *Number of Disablements and Fatalities and percentages of Total Numbers employed in seven selected industries for the year 1925.*

|  | Disablement | (%) | Fatalities | (%) | Total Numbers Employed |
|---|---|---|---|---|---|
| Shipping | 6,923 | 1.82 | 303 | 0.14 | 207,194 |
| Factories | 201,413 | 2.99 | 860 | 0.01 | 5,318,658 |
| Docks | 9,843 | 6.31 | 92 | 0.08 | 142,550 |
| Mines | 197,388 | 11.40 | 1,235 | 0.10 | 1,157,085 |
| Quarries | 6,742 | 6.38 | 89 | 0.06 | 76,274 |
| Construction | 8,813 | 3.12 | 67 | 0.05 | 108,813 |
| Railways | 122,022 | 3.14 | 313 | 0.06 | 446,479 |

**Source:** Home Office Workmen's Compensation Statistics 1925 [Cmd 2785, 1927]

**Table VI (x):** *Number of Disablements and Fatalities and percentages of Total Numbers employed in seven selected industries for the year 1928.*

|  | Disablement | (%) | Fatalities | (%) | Total Numbers Employed |
|---|---|---|---|---|---|
| Shipping | 7,905 | 4.08 | 313 | 0.16 | 193,568 |
| Factories | 201,779 | 3.69 | 848 | 0.01 | 5,455,652 |
| Docks | 13,779 | 9.64 | 87 | 0.06 | 142,835 |
| Mines | 185,823 | 19.67 | 1,067 | 0.11 | 944,666 |
| Quarries | 6,638 | 9.00 | 52 | 0.07 | 73,691 |
| Construction | 8,898 | 7.06 | 58 | 0.04 | 125,898 |
| Railways | 19,939 | 4.81 | 247 | 0.05 | 414,374 |

**Source:** Home Office Workmen's Compensation Statistics 1928 [Cmd 3481, 1930]

**Table VI (xi):** *Number of Disablements and Fatalities and percentages of Total Numbers employed in seven selected industries for the year 1931.*

|  | Disablement | (%) | Fatalities | (%) | Total Numbers Employed |
|---|---|---|---|---|---|
| Shipping | 7,525 | 4.19 | 189 | 1.05 | 179,241 |
| Factories | 152,186 | 3.04 | 702 | 0.01 | 4,993,641 |
| Docks | 10,616 | 10.02 | 83 | 0.07 | 105,875 |
| Mines | 170,887 | 19.81 | 996 | 0.11 | 862,314 |
| Quarries | 6,530 | 8.98 | 51 | 0.05 | 72,639 |
| Construction | 11,589 | 5.15 | 84 | 0.07 | 236,777 |
| Railways | 17,870 | 4.62 | 190 | 0.04 | 386,056 |

**Source:** Home Office Workmen's Compensation Statistics 1931 [Cmd 4244, 1933]

**Table VI (xii):** *Number of Disablements and Fatalities and percentages of Total Numbers employed in seven selected industries for the year 1934.*

|  | Disablement | (%) | Fatalities | (%) | Total Numbers Employed |
|---|---|---|---|---|---|
| Shipping | 7,680 | 5.01 | 222 | 0.14 | 153,200 |
| Factories | 174,853 | 3.27 | 650 | 0.01 | 5,342,697 |
| Docks | 10,362 | 10.44 | 76 | 0.07 | 99,161 |
| Mines | 158,852 | 20.24 | 906 | 0.11 | 784,643 |
| Quarries | 5,910 | 6.38 | 46 | 0.06 | 65,597 |
| Construction | 8,273 | 9.00 | 64 | 0.03 | 166,476 |
| Railways | 16,976 | 4.64 | 238 | 0.06 | 365,422 |

**Source:** Home Office Workmen's Compensation Statistics 1934 [Cmd 5077, 1936]

**Table VI (xiii):** *Number of Disablements and Fatalities and percentages of Total Numbers employed in seven selected industries for the year 1937.*

| | Disablement | (%) | Fatalities | (%) | Total Numbers Employed |
|---|---|---|---|---|---|
| Shipping | 8,851 | 5.77 | 236 | 0.15 | 153,377 |
| Factories | 238,946 | 3.69 | 751 | 0.01 | 6,133,802 |
| Docks | 11,866 | 11.14 | 84 | 0.07 | 106,428 |
| Mines | 169,250 | 21.34 | 914 | 0.11 | 792,744 |
| Quarries | 7,751 | 10.33 | 55 | 0.07 | 74,989 |
| Construction | 10,822 | 4.42 | 69 | 0.02 | 244,497 |
| Railways | 20,661 | 5.47 | 234 | 0.06 | 377,486 |

**Source:** Home Office Workmen's Compensation Statistics 1937 [Cmd 5955, 1939]

**Table VI (xiv):** *Number of Disablements and Fatalities and percentages of Total Numbers employed in seven selected industries for the year 1938.*

| | Disablement | (%) | Fatalities | (%) | Total Numbers Employed |
|---|---|---|---|---|---|
| Shipping | 8,654 | 5.52 | 285 | 0.18 | 156,706 |
| Factories | 217,599 | 3.04 | 718 | 3.63 | 5,985,493 |
| Docks | 10,672 | 9.55 | 74 | 0.06 | 111,655 |
| Mines | 162,094 | 20.35 | 983 | 0.12 | 796,382 |
| Quarries | 7,974 | 10.14 | 73 | 0.09 | 78,573 |
| Construction | 12,945 | 4.69 | 84 | 0.03 | 275,743 |
| Railways | 19,856 | 5.22 | 246 | 0.06 | 379,694 |

**Source:** Home Office Workmen's Compensation Statistics 1938 [Cmd 6203, 1940]

# Bibliography

## MANUSCRIPT SOURCES

Ardrossan, Library and Archives
  Local History Collection
    Ardossan Harbour Company Annual Reports, 1910 to 1914
    Census Enumerators Returns, Parishes of Ardrossan and Stevenston, 1891.

Edinburgh, Scottish Records Office, West Register House
  Registrar for Friendly Societies in Scotland
    Aberdeen Shore Workers Union, Annual Returns, SRO, FS 7/86
    Glasgow Harbour Labourers Friendly and Protective Society, 1886, SRO, FS 7/10
    Glasgow Harbour Labourers Union, New Constitution and Rules, May 1980, SRO, FS 7/81
    Glasgow Harbour Mineral Workers Union, letter from secretary to Registrar of Friendly Societies, 16 May, 1889, SRO, FS 7/73
    Greenock Dock Labourers Union, Rules and Regulations, October 1887, SRO, FS 7/106
    Scottish Union of Dock Labourers, Annual Returns, 1911 to 1923, SRO, FS 10/3
    Scottish Union of Dock Labourers, Cancellation of Certificate of Registration, 1911 to 1923, SRO, FS 8/18

Glasgow, Mitchell Library, Glasgow City Archives
  Clyde Navigation Trust Papers, T-CN Files
    Ardrossan Harbour Company Director's Minutes, Volumes 3 to 5, T-CN-45
    'Progress of Trade' Reports, 1840 to 1960, T-CN 6/5/7
    'Statement of the Number of Accidents to Employees and Amounts of Compensation paid under the Workmen's Compensation Act, 1906, 1909 to 1912', T-CN 6/7

Glasgow, Mitchell Library, Glasgow Room
  Census Enumerators Returns for Glasgow, 1891, List of Returns
    North Side (River Clyde)
      Anderston District 644(10) 1–24
      Anderston District 644(10) 25–40
      Blythswood District 644(7) 1–24
    South Side (River Clyde)
      Gorbals 644 (12) 1–24
      Gorbals 644 (12) 49 to 72.
      Plantation District 646(1)17–43

Glasgow, Mitchell Library, Medical Records Archive
  Register of Deaths, Glasgow 1936, HB 6/5/63
    Register of Patients at the City of Glasgow Fever Hospital, Shieldhall, June 1913,
    HB 17 2/144


Glasgow, Mitchell Library, Social Sciences
  Glasgow Trades Council Annual Reports, 1889 to 1920
    Scottish Trades Union Congress, *Annual Report*(s), 1897 to 1922
    Trades Unions Congress, *Annual Report*(s), 1889 to 1914
  Scottish Transport and General Workers Union (TU.f. 331 88 TRA)
    General Agreement with Glasgow Docks No 1 Branch, January 1932, (based on a
    modification of the National Agreement, May 1920), C372312
  Scottish Transport and General Workers Union (S.F. 331.8811 3871 SCO)
    Annual Report of the General Executive Council, December 1938, C 372408
  Scottish Union of Dock Labourers (S.F. 331.8811 3871 SCO)
    Report of Executive of the National Union of Dock Labourers, Liverpool 1893,
    By Richard McGhee and Edward McHugh, President and General Secretary,
      C 317714–II
    Executive Council Minutes, 1916 to 1919, C 372146
    Executive Committee Minutes, 1919 to 1922, C 372146–8
    Executive Committee Minutes for year ending December 1920, C 372148
  Scottish Union of Dock Labourers Rules, 1914 (S.F. 332.8811 3575) C 440941
    Transport and General Workers Union (TU.f. 331 88 TRA)
    Area 7, Management Committee Minutes – Quarterly Reports, C 372170–2
    Correspondence, September 1927 to September 1928, C 372254
      David Marshall, Secretary of Glasgow Docks Branch
        to Ernest Bevin, General Secretary of the TGWU, 5/9/1927
      Ernest Bevin to John Veitch, Scottish TGWU Area Secretary,
        'Re: Glasgow Docks Branch', 29/91927
      John Veitch to Ernest Bevin, 18/10/1927
      Ernest Bevin to John Veitch and Joseph Houghton, 21/11/1927
      John Veitch to Ernest Bevin, 15/11 and 21/12/1927
      Ernest Bevin to Joeseph Houghton, 23/12/1927
      Francis McCabe, Secretary of the Clyde Trust Branch, to
        J. Houghton, 30/1/1928
      J. Houghton to F. McCabe and Ernest Bevin, 7/2/1928.
      J. Houghton to Ernest Bevin, 'Re: Glasgow Docks entrance fee
        and the Clyde Trust victimised members', 14/2/1928
      David Marshall to J. Houghton, 'Re: resolution from Glasgow
        Docks Branch', 25/3/1928
      J. Houghton to Ernest Bevin, 29/3/1928
      J. Houghton to Ernest Bevin, 3/4/1928
      Reply from Bevin to Houghton, 4/4/1928
      Ernest Bevin to J. Houghton, 13/4/1928.
      J. Houghton to Ernest Bevin, 25/6/1928
      Ernest Bevin to J. Veitch, 28/6/1928
      Reply, Veitch to Bevin, 29/6/1928
      Letter to the TGWU National Executive, 'Re: meeting with Glasgow
        dockers, 8 July, regarding the problems at Glasgow, 9/7/1928

Memorandum issued by Bevin to a specially convened TGWU Area 7
Sub-Committtee, 'Re: how to deal with the problem at Glasgow
and Glasgow Docks branch, 28/8/1928.

London, Public Records Office
Ministry of Labour (LAB2)

# PRINTED PRIMARY SOURCES

A. OFFICIAL PUBLICATIONS

British Parliamentary Papers Relating to Irish Emigration, 'Destination of Emigrants –
Native to Ireland', and 'Destination of Migrant Labourers from the Provinces of
Leinster, Munster, Ulster and Connaught', *Irish University Press* , 27, 1891.
Census of Scotland, 1861 to 1951.
Census of Scotland, 'Movement within the City of Glasgow between 1901 and 1911',
*Special report,* 1911.

B. PARLIAMENTARY PAPERS

(Note: Parliamentary Papers are presented as related volumes
not in strict chronological order)

1888, xxi (448): *Select Committee of the House of Lords on the Sweating System, 2nd Report
Minutes of Evidence.*
1890, xxi (169): *Select Committee of the House of Lords on the Sweating System, 5th Report
Minutes of Evidence.*
1892, xxiv (C 6708–II): *Report of Royal Commission on Labour, 1st Report, Group B, Precis of
Evidence, ii.*
1892, xxxv (C 6708–V): *Report of Royal Commission on Labour, 1st Report, Group B, Minutes of
Evidence, v.*
1892, xxxvi, pt. III (C 6795–II): *Report of Royal Commission on Labour, 2nd Report, Group B,
Minutes of Evidence, ii.*
1902, xliii (Cd 1151): *Report of Royal Commission on the Port of London, Minutes of Evidence,*
1901.
1909, xxxvii (Cd 4499): *Report of Royal Commission on the Poor Law and Relief of Distress*
1910, xlix (Cd 5068): *Royal Commission on Poor Law Relating to Unemployment, Minutes of
Evidence*

BofS, *Report on Relief of the Ablebodied Unemployed During the Winter of 1893–94* (Scotland)
Board of Supervision (*PP*, 1894, lxx, C 7413).
BofT, *Report on Strikes and Lockouts,* 1889 (*PP*, 1891, lxxviii, C 6176).
BofT, *Report on Strikes and Lockouts,* 1890 (PP, 1890–91, lxviii, C 6476).
BofT, *Report on Strikes and Lockouts,* 1891 (PP, 1893–94, lxxxiii, C 6890).
BofT, *Report on Strikes and Lockouts,* 1896 (PP, 1897, lxxxiv, C 8643).
BofT, *Report on Strikes and Lockouts,* 1898 (PP, 1898, xcii, C 9437).
BofT, *Report on Strikes and Lockouts,* 1899 (*PP*, 1900, lxviii, Cd 316).
BofT, *Board of Trade Report on Trade Unions* (*PP*, 1899, Cd 422).
BofT, *Report of an Enquiry into the Earnings and Hours of Labour of Working People in the*

*United Kingdom*, 'Harbour and Dock Services, 1906' (*PP*, 1912–13, cviii, pt. VIII, Cd 6556).

BofT, *Report on the State of Employment in the United Kingdom, October 1914* (*PP*, 1914, Cd 7703).

BofT, *Report of Trade Statistics of Imports and Exports Through British Ports, 1913* (*PP*, 1918, Cmd 7585).

BofT, *Report of Statistics of Imports and Exports Through British Ports, 1918* (*PP*, 1918 Cmd 366).


Sixth *Annual Abstract of Labour Statistics of the United Kingdom* (*PP*, 1900, lxxxiii, Cd 119).

Seventh *Annual Abstract of Labour Statistics of the United Kingdom* (*PP*, 1901, lxxiii, Cd 495).

Eighth *Annual Abstract of Labour Statistics of the United Kingdom* (*PP*, 1902, xcvii, Cd 1124).

Ninth *Annual Abstract of Labour Statistics of the United Kingdom* (*PP*, 1903, lxvii, Cd 1755).

Tenth *Annual Abstract of Labour Statistics of the United Kingdom* (*PP*, 1905, lxxvi, Cd 2491).

Eleventh *Annual Abstract of Labour Statistics of the United Kingdom* (*PP*, 1907, lxxx, Cd 3690).

Twelfth *Annual Abstract of Labour Statistics of the United Kingdom* (*PP*, 1908, xcviii, Cd 4413)


1900 (Cd 142): *Statistics of the Proceedings of Workmen's Compensation Courts in England, Wales, Scotland, and in Ireland, 1899.*

1900 (Cd 223): *Report Upon the Causation and Prevention of Accidents at Docks, Wharves and Quays.*

1902, x (Cd 998): *Home Office Report of the Committee Appointed to Inquire into the Notification of Industrial Accidents.*

1904, lxxxviii (Cd 2208): *Report of the Committee into the Law Relating to Compensation for Injuries to Workmen, i, Report and Appendices, Appendix VIII,* 'Comparative Mortality Rates of Males 25–65, 1890–1892'.

1905, lxxv (Cd 2334): *Report of the Committee into the Law Relating to Compensation for Injuries to Workmen, ii, Minutes of Evidence and Index.*

1905, lxxv (Cd 2458): *Report of the Committee into the Law Relating to Compensation for Injuries to Workmen, iii, Supplementary Appendix.*

1908, xcii (Cd 4391): *Report on Dock Labour in Relation to Poor Law Relief,* by the Hon. Gerald Walsh.


1907 (Cd 3830): *Report by the Local Government Board of Scotland,*

1908 (Cd 4470): *Report by the Local Government Board of Scotland,*

1909 (Cd 4946): *Report by the Local Government Board of Scotland,*

1910 (Cd 5119): *Report by the Local Government Board of Scotland,*

1911 (Cd 5409): *Report by the Local Government Board of Scotland,*

1912 (Cd 6501): *Report by the Local Government Board of Scotland,*

1913 (Cd 7127): *Report by the Local Government Board of Scotland,*


1920, xxiv (Cmd 936): *Enquiry into the Wages and Conditions of Employment of Dock and Waterside Labour, i, Report and Evidence.*

1920, xxiv (Cmd 937): *Enquiry into the Wages and Conditions of Employment of Dock and Waterside Labour, ii, Appendices, Documents, and Indexes;*

   Appendix No 75 (Clause 43): Agreement between J. S. Spencer, Stevedore, and the Scottish Union of Dock Labourers, for the Port of Glasgow, April 1919, for estimates involving Stevedoring gang.

Appendix No 77, estimated size of Glasgow dock labour force 1919.

Appendix No 78, Table H/16 – (Glasgow 3/Glasgow 4): 'Comparison of Wages Paid to Dock Labourers, between August 1914 and November 1919'.

Appendix No 80, 'Proposed Scheme for Registration of Dock Labour at the Port of Glasgow'.

Appendix No 81, Table H/16 – (Glasgow 7): 'Comparison of Wages of Various Classes of Labourer in Glasgow District, between August 1914 and December 1919'

Appendix No 85 Table H/17 – (1b), 'Progressive Statement, 1825 to 1914'.

Appendix No 87 Table H/17 – (Statement 2): 'Men Employed by Clyde Navigation Trust'.

Appendix No 91, Statement by Mr D. Hopkins, Mineral Traffic Superintendent of the Clyde Navigation Trust, 'Mineral Gang Sizes, 1913'.

Appendix No 129 – (IX), 'Figures from Board of Trade Summaries, 1913'.

Appendix No 129 – (X), 'Imports through individual Ports'.

Appendix No 130, Table H/40, 'Rates of Wages at Principal Ports 1914 and 1918'.

1910, lxxxii (Cd 5386): *Home Office Statistics of Compensation under the Workmen's Compensation Act* (1906) *and Employers Liability Act* (1880), 1909.

1911, lxxv (Cd 5896): *Home Office Statistics of Compensation under the Workmen's Compensation Act* (1906) *and Employers Liability Act* (1880), 1910.

1912, lxxv (Cd 6493): *Home Office Statistics of Compensation under the Workmen's Compensation Act* (1906) *and Employers Liability Act* (1880), 1911.

1913, lxxx (Cd 7088): *Home Office Statistics of Compensation under the Workmen's Compensation Act* (1906) *and Employers Liability Act* (1880), 1912.

1914, lxl (Cd 7669): *Home Office Statistics of Compensation under the Workmen's Compensation Act* (1906) *and Employers Liability Act* (1880), 1913.

1915, lxl (Cd 8079): *Home Office Statistics of Compensation under the Workmen's Compensation Act* (1906) *and Employers Liability Act* (1880), 1914.

1920, xi (Cmd 1185): *Home Office Statistics of Compensation under the Workmen's Compensation Act* (1906) *and Employers Liability Act* (1880), 1919.

1921, xi (Cmd 1545): *Home Office Statistics of Compensation under the Workmen's Compensation Act* (1906) *and Employers Liability Act* (1880), 1920.

1923, xxiv (Cmd 1793): *Home Office Statistics of Compensation under the Workmen's Compensation Act* (1906) *and Employers Liability Act* (1880), 1921.

1923, xxv (Cmd 2007): *Home Office Statistics of Compensation under the Workmen's Compensation Act* (1906) *and Employers Liability Act* (1880), 1922.

1924/5, xxiv (Cmd 2567): *Home Office Statistics of Compensation under the Workmen's Compensation Act* (1923), 1924.

1927, xxiv (Cmd 2785): *Home Office Statistics of Compensation under the Workmen's Compensation Act* (1923), 1925.

1928, xxv (Cmd 3005): *Home Office Statistics of Compensation under the Workmen's Compensation Act* (1923), 1926.

1928/29, xxii (Cmd 3249): *Home Office Statistics of Compensation under the Workmen's Compensation Act* (1923), 1927.

1929/30, xxix (Cmd 3481): *Home Office Statistics of Compensation under the Workmen's Compensation Act* (1923), 1928.

1930/31, xxix (Cmd 3781): *Home Office Statistics of Compensation under the Workmen's Compensation Act* (1923), 1929.

1931/32, xxvi (Cmd 4000): *Home Office Statistics of Compensation under the Workmen's Compensation Act* (1923), 1930.

1933, xxvi (Cmd 4244): *Home Office Statistics of Compensation under the Workmen's Compensation Act* (1923), 1931.

1933/34, xxvi (Cmd 4484): *Home Office Statistics of Compensation under the Workmen's Compensation Act* (1923), 1932.

1934/35, xxiii (Cmd 4784): *Home Office Statistics of Compensation under the Workmen's Compensation Act* (1923), 1933.

1936, xxv (Cmd 5077): *Home Office Statistics of Compensation under the Workmen's Compensation Act* (1923), 1934.

1936/37, xxvi (Cmd 5557): *Home Office Statistics of Compensation under the Workmen's Compensation Act* (1923), 1935.

1937/38, xxviii (Cmd 5722): *Home Office Statistics of Compensation under the Workmen's Compensation Act* (1936), 1936.

1939, xxvi (Cmd 5955): *Home Office Statistics of Compensation under the Workmen's Compensation Act* (1923), 1937.

1940, xi (Cmd 6203): *Home Office Statistics of Compensation under the Workmen's Compensation Act* (1923), 1938.

## C. NEWSPAPERS

*Ardrossan and Saltcoats Herald*
*Daily Record*
*Evening Times*
*Forward*
*Glasgow Echo*
*Glasgow Herald*
*Glasgow Sentinel*
*Leith Observer*
*North British Daily Mail*
*Glasgow Herald Trade Review*
*Glasgow Herald Mid-Year Review*
*Scots Independent*

## D. CONTEMPORARY COMMENTARIES

*New Statistical Account of Scotland*, 1845

*Abridged Statistical History of Scotland* (Edinburgh, 1855).

BEVERIDGE, W. H., *Unemployment: A Problem of Industry* (1930 edn.).

BAXTER, G., (Engineer to the Clyde Navigation Trust) 'Dock Equipment: Appliances at Glasgow Harbour', in the *Glasgow Herald*, March 8 1910.

BOOTH, C, *Life and Labour of the People in London* (First Series, Vol. iv, 1902).

BOOTH, C, *Life and Labour of the People of London* (Second Series, Vol. vii, 1903).

CAMPBELL, R., 'Report as manager of foreign animals wharf at Merklands', *Municipal Glasgow: Its Evolution and Enterprises, 1911 to 1914* (Glasgow, 1914).

COLLISON, W., *The Apostle of Free Labour* (1913).

HOBSON, J. A., *The Problem of the Unemployed* (1906 edn.)

MARWICK, Sir J. D., *The River Clyde and the Clyde Burghs* (Glasgow, 1909).

MARWICK, W.H., 'Early Trade Unionism in Scotland', *EHR*, v, 2, 1935

QUELCH, HARRY., *Trade Unionism, Cooperation and Social Democracy* (1892).

RYAN, W. P., *The Irish Labour Movement: From the Twenties To Our Own Day* (New York, 1920).

SAUNDERS, C, *Seasonal Variations in Unemployment* (Oxford, 1936).

TUPPER, CAPTAIN EDWARD., *Seamen's Torch: The Life Story of Captain Edward Tupper, National Union of Seamen* (1938).

WEBB, S., and B. (eds.), *The Public Organisation of the Labour Market: Being Part of the Two Minority Reports of the Poor Law Commission* (1909).

WEBB, S., and B., *Industrial Democracy* (1913).


E.   NON DOCUMENTARY SOURCES.

Recorded Testimony:
WILLIAM CRAWFORD, Ardrossan, interviewed July 1990.
Non-Recorded Oral Testimony:
WILLIAM BRANNEN, ex-docker, Ardrossan, July 1990.
GORDON BANDERS, ex-docker (began working at Glasgow Docks in 1924); discussion, Kirkcaldy, Tuesday, 16 June 1992.
CHARLES WARD, ex-docker (began work at Glasgow Docks in 1942); discussion, Partick, Glasgow, Thursday, 25 June 1992.
TOM O'CONNOR, ex-docker (began work at Glasgow Docks in late 1950s); discussion, Glasgow, Thursday, 4 March 1993.


F.   OTHER MATERIALS

SLOANE, W., 'Assimilation of the Highland and Irish Migrants in Glasgow, 1830 to 1870', University of Strathclyde, unpublished M. Phil. thesis, 1987.

PATERSON, H., 'Seamen on the Clyde, 1887–1914: Work and Industrial Relations in the Clyde Shipping Industry', University of Strathclyde, unpublished M. Phil. thesis, 1992.

BELCHEM, J., 'Sectarianism, ethnicity and welfare: collective mutuality among the Liverpool Irish', unpublished pre-circulated paper presented to the Ninth British-Dutch Labour History Conference, Netherlands, 1994.

TAPLIN, E., 'When is a Ship a Factory? Working conditions, accidents and compensation at the waterfront from the 1880s', unpublished pre-circulated paper presented to the Ninth British-Dutch Labour History Conference, Netherlands, 1994).

DICK, D. B., 'Dundee: A Case Study in the Decline of the Liberal Party', unpublished pre-circulated paper presented to 'Scottish Dimensions' Conference, History Workshop, *Ruskin College, Oxford, March 1995*.

Board of Labour *Gazette* (Published monthly) for 1910 to 1914.

*National Agreement, 5 May 1920* (and subsequent Agreements in modification thereof) between the National Association of Port Employers and the Transport and General Workers Union and other Signatory Unions (1969 ed).


G.   SECONDARY SOURCES

(Note: place of publication is London unless otherwise stated)
ALDCROFT, D., and FEARON, P., *Economic Growth in Twentieth Century Britain* (1969).

ALDCROFT, D., *The British Economy Between the Wars* (Oxford, 1893).

ALDERMAN, G., 'The National Free Labour Association: A Case Study of Strikebreakers in the Late Nineteenth and Early Twentieth Century', *IRSH* xxi, 3, 1976.

ALLEN, M., 'Post War Dock Strikes 1945–1955', *North West Labour History Bulletin*, 15, 1990/91.

BAGWELL, P.S., 'The Triple Industrial Alliance, 1913–1922', in A. Briggs and J. Saville (eds.) *Essays in Labour History* (1971).

BAGWELL, P.S., and ARMSTRONG, J., 'Coastal Shipping', in M. J. Freeman and D. A. Aldcroft (eds.) *Transport in Victorian Britain* (Manchester 1988).

BARTRIP, P., 'The Rise and Decline of Workmen's Compensation', in Paul Weindling (ed.) *The Social History of Occupational Health* (1983).

——, and Burman, S. (eds.), *The Wounded Soldiers of Industry* (1985).

BEAN, R., ''The Liverpool Dock Strike of 1890', *IRSH*, xviii, 1, 1973.

——, 'Employers' Associations in the Port of Liverpool, 1890–1914', *IRSH*, xxi, 3, 1976.

——, 'Custom, Job Regulation and Dock Labour in Liverpool 1911–1939', *IRSH*, xxxvii, 3, 1982.

BELLAMY, J., and SAVILLE, J., (eds.), *Dictionary of Labour Biography*, Vol VII (1974).

BENSON, J. (ed.), *The Working Class in England, 1875–1914* (New York, 1985).

BILTON, T. (et al.), *Introductory Sociology* (1984 edn.).

BRIGGS, A., and SAVILLE, J. (eds.), *Essays in Labour History* (1971).

BROEZE, F., 'Militancy and Pragmatism: An International Perspective on Maritime Labour, 1870–1914', *IRSH*, xxxvi, 1, 1991.

BROWN, R., *Waterfront Organisation in Hull 1870–1900* (Hull, 1972)

BUCKLEY, K. D., *Trade Unionism in Aberdeen 1887 to 1900* (Aberdeen, 1955)

BULLOCK, A., *The Life and Times of Ernest Bevin* (1960).

BUXTON, N., and Aldcroft, D. (eds.), *British Industry Between the Wars*, 1970.

CAMPBELL, A., 'Essays in Labour History', *Society for the Study of Labour History* (*SSLH*), Bulletin, 39, 1979.

CLEGG, H., *History of British Trade Unionsm*, Vol II (Oxford, 1985).

COATES, K., and TOPHAM, T., *The Making of the Transport and General Workers Union*, Volume 1, pts. 1 and II (Oxford, 1991).

COLE, G. D. H., and POSTGATE, R., *The Common People 1746–1946* (1961)

COLLISON, W., *The Apostle of Free Labour* (1913).

CRONIN, J. E., *Industrial Conflict in Modern Britain* (1979).

——, J. E., and SCHNEER, J. (eds.), *Social Conflict Political Order in Modern Britain* (1982).

CUNNISON, J., and GILFILLAN, J. B. S. (eds.), *The Third Statistical Account of Scotland: Glasgow* (Edinburgh, 1958).

DAUNTON, M. J., 'Inter-Union relations on the Waterfront in Cardiff, 1888–1914', *IRSH*, xxii, 3, 1977.

DEANE, P., *The First Industrial Revolution* (Cambridge, 1986, 2nd edn.).

DEVINE, T.M., and MITCHISON, R. (eds.), *People and Society in Scotland*, Vol I, 1760–1830 (Edinburgh, 1988).

——, 'Urbanisation', in T. M. Devine and R. Mitchison (eds.) *People and Society in Scotland*, Vol I, 1760–1830 (Edinburgh, 1988).

DICKSON, T. (ed.), *Capital and Class in Scotland* (Edinburgh, 1982).

DUNCAN, R., and McIVOR, A. (eds.), *Militant Workers: Labour and Class relations on the Clyde, 1900–1950* (Edinburgh, 1992).

FREEMAN, M. J., and ALDCROFT, D. (eds.), *Transport in Victorian Britain* (Manchester, 1988).

FELDING, S., 'Irish Politics in Manchester 1890–1914', *IRSH*, xxxiii, 3, 1988.

FISCHER, C, and KNOX, W., 'Shedding the Blinkers: German and Scottish Labour Historiography from C1960 to Present', *SLHS*, 26, 1991.

FRASER, W. H., and MORRIS, R. J. (eds.), *People and Society* Vol II, 1830–1914 (Edinburgh, 1990).

FRENCH, W. M., *The Scottish Ports: Including Docks and Harbour's* (Glasgow, 1938).

FROW, R., FROW, E., and KATANKA, M., *Strikes: A Documentary History* (1971).

GALLAGHER, T., 'A tale of Two Cities: Communal Strife in Glasgow and Liverpool before 1914', in R. Swift and S. Gilley (eds.) *The Irish in the Victorian City* (1985).

GERTH, H., and HILLS, C W. (eds.), *From Max Weber: Essays in Sociology* (1948).

GILLESPIE, R., *Glasgow and the Clyde* (Glasgow, 1976).

BUTT, J., and GORDON, G. (eds.), *Strathclyde: Changing Horizons* (Edinburgh, 1985).

GRAY, R. Q., *The Labour Aristocracy in Victorian Edinburgh* (Edinburgh, 1976).

CROSSICK, G., *An Artisan Elite in Victorian England* (1978).

HILL, S., *The Dockers: Class and Tradition in London* (1976).

HILTON, J. (et al.), *Are Trade Unions Obstructive: An Impartial Enquiry* (1935).

——, J., *Labour and Socialism: A History of the British Labour Movement, 1867–1974* (1983).

HOBSBAWM, E., *Labouring Men* (1964).

——, 'Trade Union History', *EHR*, xx, 2, 1967

——, E. Hobsbawm, *Worlds of Labour* (1984).

——, *Industry and Empire* (1986, edn.)

HOLTON, B., '*British Syndicalism 1900–1914* (1976).

HUME, R. J., 'The Visible Heritage', in Butt, J., and Gordon, G. (eds.), *Strathclyde: Changing Horizons* (Edinburgh, 1985).

HUNT, E. J., *British Labour History* (1981).

JACKSON, G., *The History and Archaeology of Ports* (Kingswood, 1983).

JACKSON, M. P., *Labour relations at the Docks* (Westmead, 1973).

JONES, A. C 'Decasualisation of the Dock', *The Socialist Review*, 128, 1924.

KEELING, F., 'Towards the Solution of the Casual Labour Problem', *The Economic Journal* March 1913.

KENEFICK, W., *The Key To the Clyde: With Particular Reference to the Ardrossan Dock Strike, 1912–1913* (Irvine, 1993).

——, and McIVOR, J. (eds.), *The Roots of Red Clydeside 1910–1914: Labour Unrest and Industrial Relations in West Scotland* (Edinburgh, 1996).

——, 'The Struggle for Control: The Importance of the Great Unrest at Glasgow Harbour, 1911–1912', W. Kenefick and A. McIvor (eds.), *The Roots of Red Clydeside 1910–1914: Labour Unrest and Industrial Relations in West Scotland* (Edinburgh, 1996).

——, 'An Historiographical and Comparative Survey of Dock Labour c.1889–1920 and the Neglect of the Port of Glasgow', *SLHS*, 31, 1996.

——, 'Irish Dockers and Trade Unionism on Clydeside', *Irish Studies Review*, 19, 1997.

——, ' "Quixotically Generous . . . Economically Worthless": Two views of the dockers and the dockland community in Britain in the 19th and early 20th centuries', *The Historian*, 56, 1997.

——, 'War Resisters and Anti-Conscription in Scotland: an ILP Perspective', in C. M. M. Macdonald and E. McFarland (eds.), *Scotland and the Great War* (Edinburgh, 1999).

——, 'A Struggle for Recognition and Independence: The Growth and development of Dock Unionism at the Port of Glasgow', in Sam Davies (et al.), *Dock Workers: International Explorations in Comparative Labour History, 1790–1970* (Two Volumes), (Ashworth, 2000).

KIRKALDY, A. W., *British Shipping: Its History and Importance* (1914).

LARKIN, E., *James Larkin: Irish Labour Leader 1876–1947* (1965).

LASCELLES, E. C P., and BULLOCK, S. S., *Dock Labour and Decasualisation* (1924).

LENG, P. J., *The Welsh Dockers* (Ormskirk,1981).

LINDROP, F., 'Seamen and Dockers Unofficial Trade Union Militancy in the 1920s', *SSLH,* Bulletin, 38, 1979.

——, F., 'Oral Interviews with Dockers', *SSLH,* Bulletin, 39, 1979.

LONGMATE, N., 'Class War on the Clyde', in *Milestones in Working Class History* (1975).

LOVELL, J., *Stevedores and Dockers* (1969).

——, 'The Irish and the London Docker', *SSLH,* Bulletin, 35, 1977.

——, *British Trade Unions 1875–1933*(1977).

——, 'Sail, Steam and Emergent Dockers' Unionism in Britain, 1850–1914', *IRSH*, xxxii, 3, 1987.

McIVOR, A., 'Employers Organisations and Strike Breaking in Britain, 1911 to 1914', *IRSH* xxix, 1, 1984.

——, 'Manual Work, Technology, And Industrial Health, 1918–39', *Medical History*, 31, 1987.

MacDOUGALL, I., *Labour Records in Scotland* (Edinburgh, 1978).

MAY, T., *An Economic and Social History of Britain 1760–1970* (1987).

MANN, TOM, *Memoirs* (1923).

MARWICK, SIR J. D., *The River Clyde and the Clyde Burghs* (Glasgow, 1909).

MARWICK, W.H., 'Early Trade Unionism in Scotland', *EHR*, v, 2, 1935

MATTHEWS, D., '1889 and All That: New Views of the New Unionism', *IRSH*, xxxvi, 1, 1991.

MELLING, J., 'Scottish Industrialists and the Changing Character of Class Relations in the Clyde Region C1880–1918', in T. Dickson (ed.) *Capital and Class in Scotland* (Edinburgh, 1982).

MITCHELL, M. J., *The Irish in the West of Scotland 1797–1848* (Edinburgh, 1998).

MOGRIDGE, B., 'Militancy and Inter-Union Rivalries in British Shipping, 1911–1929', *IRSH* , xi, 2, 1961.

MORRIS, R. J. 'Urbanisation and Scotland', in W. H. Fraser and R. J. Morris (eds.) *People and Society Vol II* 1830–1914 (Edinburgh,1990).

MORE, C., *Skill and the English Working Class, 1870–1914* (1980).

MORT, F., *Lanarkshire* (Cambridge, 1910).

MOREWEDGE, H., *The Economics of Casual Labour: A Study of the Longshore Industry* (Berne, Switzerland, 1970).

MUSSON, A. E., *British Trade Unions, 1800–1875* (1972).

O'TUATHAIGH, GEAROID., *Ireland Before the Famine, 1798–1848* (Dublin, 1972).

PELLING, H., *A History of British Trade Unionism* (1992, edn.).

PHILLIPS, G., and WHITESIDE, N., *Casual Labour: The Underemployment Question in the Port Transport Industry 1880–1970* (Oxford, 1985).

POWELL, L. H., *The Shipping Federation 1890–1950* (1950).

PRICE, R., *Labour in British Society* (1986)

PRYDE, G. S., *Scotland From 1603 to the Present Day* (1963).

QUELCH, HARRY., *Trade Unionism, Cooperation and Social Democracy* (1892).

QUENNELL, P. (edn.) *Mayhew's London: Being a Selection from 'London Labour and the London Poor'* (Date unknown)

RIDDELL, J. F., *Clyde Navigation: A History of the Development and Deepening of the River Clyde* (Glasgow, 1979).

RYAN, W. P.,*The Irish Labour Movement: From the Twenties To Our Own Day* (New York, 1920).

SAUNDERS, C., *Seasonal Variations in Unemployment* (Oxford, 1936).

SCHNEER, J., 'The War, the State, and the Workplace: The British Docker During 1914–1918', J. E. Cronin and Jonathan Schneer (ed.) *Social Conflict and the Political Order in Modern Britian* (1982).

SEXTON, SIR JAMES., *Sir James Sexton, Agitator. The Life Story of the Dockers' M.P.* (1936).

SIMEY, T.S. (ed.), *The Dock Worker: An Analysis of Conditions of Employment in the Port of Manchester* (Liverpool, 1956).

SLAVEN, A., and CHECKLAND, S., *Dictionary of Scottish Business Biography Vol II* (Aberdeen, 1990).

SMITH, J. and McSHANE, Harry., *Harry McShane: No Mean Fighter* (1978).

——, 'Labour Traditions in Glasgow and Liverpool', *History Workshop Journal*, 1984.

SWIFT, R., and GILLEY, S. (eds.), *The Irish in the Victorian City* (1985).

——, *The Irish in Britain* (1990).

TAPLIN, E., *Liverpool Docker and Seamen* (Hull, 1974).

——, *The Dockers' Union: A Study of the National Union of Dock Labourers, 1889–1922* (Leicester, 1986).

TREBLE, J., *Urban Poverty in Britain 1830–1914* (1979).

——, 'Unemployment in Glasgow 1903 to 1910: Anatomy of a Crisis', *SLHS*, 25, 1990.

TUPPER, CAPTAIN EDWARD., *Seamen's Torch: The Life Story of Captain Edward Tupper, National Union of Seamen* (1938).

WALKER, W. M., *Juteopolis: Dundee and its Textile Workers 1885–1923* (Edinburgh, 1979).

WEBB, S., and B., *Industrial Democracy* (1913).

WEINDLING, P. (ed.) *Social History of Occupational Health* (1983).

WILLIAMS, F., *Ernest Bevin, Portrait of a great Englishman* (1952).

WILSON, D.F., *Dockers: The Impact of Industrial Change* (1972).

WOHL, A., *Endangered Lives: Public Health in Victorian Britain* (1983).

WOODS, D., 'Community Violence', in John Benson (ed.) *The Working Class in England, 1875–1914* (New York, 1985).

ZEITLIN, J., 'From Labour History to the History of Industrial Relations', *EHR*, xl, 1987.

# Index

Aberdeen (port) 28, 59, 63, 202; Seamen's Union at 28, and close links with dockers 185; anti-registration 54, 158, 246; Larkin halts employer Free Labour campaign, 200, 201; Shore Workers Union/Trades Council 119, 185; sympathy action with NUDL (Glasgow, 1889 strike) 193; strikes at 206

Alderman, G. 28

American Knights of Labour 190

Anderson, William Fleming (CNT Trustee) 135, 216–217

Antwerp (port) 36, 178

Ardrossan (port) 29, 70, 88, 109, 121, 232, 238; comparison with other ports 88; ethnic and racial composition 115; SUDL organised (1911) 210, Tom Mann at (1921–113) 219, 224–225

*Ardrossan and Saltcoats Herald* 88, 225

Ardrossan Harbour Company 70

Armstrong, J. 67, 68

Askwith, George (BoT) 219–220

Aspinwall, B. 122, 162

Ayr (harbour) 88, 109; SUDL organised (1911) 210

Ayrshire (Irish dockers in, 1911) 115

Bagwell, P.S. 67, 68,

Baltic trade 38

Barnes, George 117

Bartrip, P. 141, 144, 151, 161, 163; Bartrip, P. and Burman, S. 141, 142, 144, 153, 160, 162

Baxter, George (CNT engineer) 89–90, 135–138

Bean, R. 26, 27, 29, 33, 39, 48, 53, 104, 133, 168, 207, 224, 226

Belchem, J. 162–163

Belfast (port) 93, 152, 178, 179; TUC (1893) 196; Larkin forms dock branch 201

Benson, J. 22

Beveridge, William 17, 28, 48, 49, 51, 149, 221

Bevin, Ernest 5, 100, 163; backing proposals for Registration 238–241; critique of casualism 47, 52, 53; DWRGLU Executive member

representing NTWF at Shaw Inquiry 33 – on Glasgow 46, on poverty 46; Glasgow Docks Branch TGWU, Bevin's relationship with 237–241; relationship with STGWU and Glasgow dockers 243; Shaw Inquiry, enhanced reputation 31; viewed as dictatorial 34, 235–237

Birt, Colonel G.R. 83, 84, 128, 133

Black Friday 32, 227, 234

Board of Trade (BoT) 16, 30, 44, 143, 171, 204, 233; *Gazette* 203, 212, 213, 219

Bo'ness (port) 31, 117

Booth, Charles 15–16, 42, 44, 52, 84, 148, 185 (noting close cultural and racial links with the seamen)

Bowling (harbour) 65

Boyd, A. 202, 203

Bristol (port) 18, 100, 152, 218; TUC (1898) 151, 196; fatal accidents at 153

Broeze, F. 27, 180, 185, 186

Brown, R. 27, 28, 29, 177

Buckley, K. 28, 185

Bullock, A. 156

Bullock, S.S. 17, 31, 47, 53

Burns, John (on New Unionism) 245

Butt, J. 57

Canadian sea passages 38

Cardiff (port) 27, 29; sympathy donation to NUDL (1889 strike) 193

Chamberlain, Neville 233

Checkland, S. 58, 60, 66, 111

Churchill, Winston (involvement in 1912 strike, Glasgow) 219–220

Clegg, H. 29

Clyde District Committee of the Shipping Federation 173 (*see also* W. Raeburn)

Clyde Navigation Trust (CNT, *also* Clyde Trust) 2, 65–66, 67, 73–74, 78–79, 84, 89, 90, 169, 179, 216–217, 250, 252, 254; as employers of labour, 100–105; health and safety issues 153, mechanisation/modernisation 102–103, 130, 135–138

Clyde Trust Branch (TGWU) 239

Clydebank (*see* Rothesay Docks) 115, 130, 137

Coates, K. and Topham, T. 31, 33, 233

Kopik.

26 critique of historians / Labour
　　　　　　　　　　　　unrest
　　　　　　　　　　not m.l.
　　　　　　　　　　or Irvi

28 scale of employers
　　　contract work 50/1905.

30 Labourism syndicalism 1910/14

40 Casualism + eng & Scot.

42 Structure in London & 61,

53/5 Dockers refuse of casual lin